Anthony Ham

Madrid

The Top Five

1 Chueca
Feel the best nightlife buzz in this pulsating barrio (p136 & p141)

2 Parque del Buen Retiro
Take a colourful Sunday stroll in the green heart of Madrid (p87)

3 Plaza Mayor
Bask in the grandeur of the capital's emblematic square (p65)

4 Museo del Prado
Marvel at the masterpieces of the Spanish Old Masters (p83)

5 Salamanca
Shop for Spanish designer fashions around Calle de Serrano (p161)

The Authors

Anthony Ham

On his first night in Madrid in 2001, Anthony watched spellbound as the Plaza de la Puerta del Sol thronged with energy and people, and the Plaza Mayor came alive with street musicians and the languages of the world. In that moment, he fell irretrievably in love with the city. Less than a year later, Anthony arrived in Madrid on a one-way ticket, with not a word of Spanish and not knowing a single person in the city. After only a few years, Anthony speaks Spanish, is married to a Madrileña and has just finished renovating an apartment overlooking his favourite plaza in Madrid. When he's not writing for Lonely Planet, Anthony is the Madrid stringer for Melbourne's *Age* newspaper.

Anthony's Top Madrid Day

Madrid is not a city that gets up early, which suits me fine. For breakfast it has to be *chocolate y churros* at El Brillante, before sampling one of Europe's finest café cultures – for this I escape the crowds for a cake or early *mojito* at Delic on Plaza de la Paja in La Latina. Then I'm off to Calle de la Cava Baja for some fine tapas at Taberna Algorta or the nearby Casa Revuelta. If it's a cold winter's day, I'll make a beeline for one of Madrid's world-class galleries – the Museo Thyssen-Bornemisza is a personal favourite. I start my long Madrid night in the bars of Lavapiés, probably La Inquilina and, if I can tear myself away, I'll take the metro to the Glorieta de Bilbao and have a meal somewhere along Calle de Manuela Malasaña. The night is still young, so I head for one of my two favourite bars, El Jardin Secreto in Conde Duque or Café Belén in Chueca, before diving headlong into the perpetual high of the bars and clubs of Malasaña or Chueca with not a single thought for tomorrow.

PHOTOGRAPHER
Krzysztof Dydyński

Born and raised in Warsaw, Krzysztof discovered a passion for travelling, which took him on various trips across Europe, Asia, South America, and finally to Australia where he now lives. He first visited Spain in 1974 and has returned regularly ever since. Madrid is one of his favourite cities, where he has been back time and again, revisiting his old secret corners and looking for new inspirations.

Contents

Published by Lonely Planet Publications Pty Ltd
ABN 36 005 607 983

Australia Head Office, Locked Bag 1, Footscray,
Victoria 3011, ☎ 03 8379 8000, fax 03 8379 8111,
talk2us@lonelyplanet.com.au

USA 150 Linden St, Oakland, CA 94607,
☎ 510 893 8555, toll free 800 275 8555,
fax 510 893 8572, info@lonelyplanet.com

UK 72–82 Rosebery Ave, Clerkenwell, London,
EC1R 4RW, ☎ 020 7841 9000, fax 020 7841 9001,
go@lonelyplanet.co.uk

© Lonely Planet Publications Pty Ltd 2006
Photographs © Krzysztof Dydyński and as listed
(p227) 2006

Introducing Madrid

There will come a moment while you're in Madrid when you will fall irreversibly in love with this beguiling city and wonder how you can bear to live elsewhere. It might strike you at 3am when you spill onto impossibly crowded streets from a bar in Chueca. Or it could happen as you wander amid the masterpieces of the Museo del Prado. But it will happen because this is a city that creeps up on you, weaves its way into your soul and then sings happily into your ear.

Madrid may have few signature, world-famous monuments, but it makes up for it with astonishingly diverse attractions for, in truth, there are many Madrids.

There is the Madrid that never sleeps, a city inhabited by people who work hard by day and party long into the night. Madrid has more bars than any city in the world and your entry point into nightly celebration couldn't be easier – just head to Malasaña, Chueca, Lavapiés or Huertas and follow the crowds.

In case you're wondering whether you're too old for Madrid's night-time energy, think again. Among the many reasons to leave your hotel room after the sun goes down are world-class flamenco which stirs the soul; the most glamorous football team on the planet; and a vibrant live music scene, from classy jazz to Malasaña rock, all of which can be enjoyed while you sip your cocktails and plan to sleep in the following day.

Madrid is as deservedly famous for its range of outstanding restaurants as it is renowned as a place to have a good time. This is a city where eating is a convivial pleasure treated with the utmost seriousness. Madrileños have discerning palates and poor restaurants last about as long here as it takes to decipher a Metro map. Just about anything is possible, ranging from tasty tapas and the latest innovations sweeping Spanish kitchens to hearty local cuisine and regional specialities from all

over Spain. These excellent home-grown offerings share the Madrid table with international flavours of the highest quality.

Then there is the Madrid of high culture, a sophisticated European city with an exceptionally rich artistic heritage. Most of it is on show in the Museo del Prado, the Museo Thyssen-Bornemisza or the Centro de Arte Reina Sofía – each of which is reason enough to come to Madrid – but galleries, museums and palaces are scattered all across the city and contain priceless treasures, whether they be the latest in contemporary art or hoary old masters. Sitting at an outdoor table in one of the city's beautiful plazas after a day of fine art will feel as civilised as any experience on earth.

Behind this fast-living metropolis of the night and refined home of culture is a confident, often sassy city which is riding a wave of optimism and prosperity. The March 2004 train bombings and Madrid's third-placing in the bid to host the 2012 Olympics have done nothing to shake either that confidence or the unmistakeable air of a city on the upswing.

Sometimes this is manifested in the curiously Madrileño obsession with shopping. Nowhere is this pastime more stylish than in the designer boutiques of Salamanca, where the world's top brand names of the catwalk cannot, try as they might, upstage the stunning works of art turned out by Spanish designers who are taking the world by storm. This is not shopping for its own sake – it serves the purpose of making Madrileños look the part for the serious business of eating and the live-for-the-moment good time that the Madrid night promises. This is the Madrid that you'll see when you arrive.

But we would be doing only half our job if we didn't let you into a Madrid secret that is essential to getting the most out of your stay here. Madrid is a city of barrios (districts), each with its own identity, and the key to shedding your tourist skin and starting to feel like a local is getting inside the life of each barrio. This could be exclusive Salamanca, gay Chueca, alternative Malasaña, quirky La Latina or gritty Lavapiés, each of which is its own distinctively Madrileño world. In writing this book, we work on the assumption that you don't just want to visit the Prado, buy the frilly flamenco dress or bullfighting poster emblazoned with your

LOWDOWN

Population 3.29 million

Time zone (GMT + one hour)

Average three-star double room €100 to €130

Tapas of cocido a la Madrileña (Madrid's hearty chickpea stew) at Malacatín €5

Top Tip Unless you want to walk, take the metro wherever you go because it's one of the best subway systems in the world

Coffee At the bar, around €1

Paseo del Arte ticket to enter the Prado, Thyssen and Reina Sofía €12

Metrobús 10-ride ticket €6.15

Don't...assume that everyone in Madrid supports Real Madrid – at least half shun the glamour and support Atlético

Do...keep to the right side on escalators – Madrileños are sticklers for keeping the left side free for those in a hurry

name, and eat or drink surrounded by other tourists. By using this guide, you'll stop feeling like a tourist and start to feel like a Madrileño, you'll eat where Madrileños eat and experience Madrid as if you've lived in this intoxicating city all of your life.

We've saved perhaps the best secret for last. Madrid has always been a city of immigrants, from the rest of Spain and, more recently, from the rest of the world. This polyglot past, built around a core of true-blue Madrileños, has fostered a tolerance and openness to outsiders that few cities in the world can match. The most eloquent symbol of this welcome-mat to the world is the oft-heard Madrid phrase: *Si estas en Madrid, eres de Madrid* (If you're in Madrid, you're from Madrid). Sound like an exaggeration? Come and see for yourself.

City Life ■

City Life

MADRID TODAY

Madrid is buzzing; it's a feel-good city that won't let even the most terrible tragedy knock it off its stride.

When terrorists attacked three commuter trains on 11 March 2004, killing 191 people, many wondered whether it would spell the end of that special feeling of being in one of the world's most open cities. Scarred as it is, Madrid is back, hard at work and joyful at play. While the rest of Europe struggles with sluggish economies and crises of confidence, Madrid is in the midst of an unprecedented economic boom and, in the process, riding a wave of hard-to-shake optimism. Even the city's failure to win the 2012 Olympic Games (Madrid came third behind London and Paris) was greeted with a sense that the world didn't know what it was missing – Madrileños don't need the Games to feel good about themselves.

Olympics or not, Madrid's authorities have turned the city into a building site on an Olympic scale. Madrid's metro system, already the envy of the world, just keeps on growing; new ring roads and massive housing developments are expanding the city limits, and, coupled with the regeneration of its river frontage, highlight the fact that this city possesses a limitless capacity for re-inventing itself. It may all drive Madrileños crazy as traffic becomes a study in gridlock and noise levels surpass even the usual Spanish disregard for silence. But deep down, they're inordinately proud of their city, one of Europe's most modern.

This may be a city that's going places, but there are plenty of uncertainties. The social lives of Spaniards have been transformed by the Socialist government of José Luis Rodríguez Zapatero, which was elected in the tumultuous days following the March 2004 train bombings. Gay marriage has been legalised, divorce has never been easier, smoking has been banned in many public places, almost a million formerly illegal immigrants have been granted residence and proposals for greater autonomy for Catalonia and the Basque Country have divided the country. How Madrid – which has always been a window on the soul of the Spanish heartland – reacts to these changes will most likely decide Spain's future.

A booming housing market in which prices seem to rise inexorably with every passing year is another concern at the forefront of Madrileños' minds, keeping poorly paid Spaniards awake at night.

As with any modern city, crime is an issue. Although statistics consistently show crime falling across the city, the growing phenomenon of the high-profile *bandas latinas* (Latin gangs) has many Madrileños worried. Still it's as much about perception as experience and, as with the mafia elsewhere in the world, it rarely touches the lives of ordinary citizens.

HOT CONVERSATION TOPICS

- It's great living in a city that's constantly being improved, but the day when there are no more roadworks can't come soon enough.
- So Mr Ruiz-Gallardón (Madrid's mayor), we think you could be our next prime minister, but we're just not sure for which party.
- What has happened to Real Madrid? More money than sense, most locals say.
- Why don't the Basques and Catalans like us? Fine, we'll boycott Catalan champagne then.
- Madrid is changing – less siesta and longer working hours – but we're determined not to lose our soul.
- We're not sure what we think of immigrants (we're still new to the idea), but without them, the social security system (and our pensions) would collapse.
- Just how do Madrileños manage to afford these spiralling house prices on Spanish salaries? We're all mortgaged to the hilt, that's how.
- The 2020 Olympics? Now there's an idea. If only our politicians would learn to lobby like the British.
- Madrid's nightlife just ain't what it used to be – time to reclaim the city.

The issue does, however, lay bare the touchy subject of immigration. It was not until 1992 that more people came to live in Spain than left it. Madrid's immigrant population doubled in the five years to 2004 and the country as a whole has received almost as many immigrants in five years as France did in the last four decades. This significant demographic shift is proving unsettling for some. But the fact remains that Madrid can still be defined by its tolerance. After all, in the aftermath of the 2004 train bombings, there was not even the merest hint of a backlash against the rapidly growing Moroccan community in Madrid.

Such weighty matters notwithstanding, Madrid is characterised, above all, by excess. To wander Malasaña, La Latina and Huertas is to enter an all-night jungle of bars and clubs. True, it's not as wild and hedonistic as it once was and there's now a semblance of order to the chaos, but that's because the city has grown up. Along the way, it hasn't for one moment forgotten how to live.

CITY CALENDAR

Just in case you hadn't already guessed, Madrileños love to party. Most often that means an impromptu night out. However, there are times when there's method in the madness, whether it's Carnaval in February or the local fiestas in central Madrid's barrios (districts) in the stifling heat of August.

Given that there's always something going on, the weather can be an important factor when planning your visit. In winter, Madrid most often enjoys cool but crystal-clear days, although cold winds blow in off the Sierra del Guadarrama and cold snaps can be bitterly cold (snowfalls are rare but do happen). In July and August, expect unrelenting heat with occasional, apocalyptic storms. In August, Madrid's frenetic energy takes a break and the city is uncharacteristically quiet. City streets empty, restaurants close and offices run in neutral as locals head for the coast in search of a sea breeze or the hills in pursuit of high-altitude respite.

For a full list of official public holidays in Madrid, turn to the Directory (p212); also, visit es.madrid.com for more details on the city's festivals.

JANUARY
AÑO NUEVO
Noche vieja (New Year's Eve) is often celebrated at home with family, before people head out after midnight to paint the town red. Nonetheless, many Madrileños gather in Puerta del Sol to wait for the 12 *campanadas* (bell chimes) that signal Año Nuevo (New Year's Day) whereupon they try to stuff 12 grapes (one for each chime) into their mouths and make a wish for the new year.

REYES
Epifanía (the Epiphany) on 6 January is also known as the *Día de los Reyes Magos* (Three Kings' Day), or simply *Reyes,* perhaps the most important day on a Madrileño kid's calendar. Although a December visit from Santa Claus has caught on, traditionally young Spaniards wait until *Epifanía.* Three local politicians dress up as the three kings (three wise men) and lead a sweet-distributing frenzy of *Cabalgata de Reyes* (horse-drawn carriages and floats) from the Parque del Buen Retiro to Plaza Mayor at 6pm on 5 January.

FEBRUARY
CARNAVAL
Carnaval spells several days of fancy-dress parades and merrymaking in many barrios across the Comunidad de Madrid, usually ending on the Tuesday, 47 days before Easter Sunday. Depending on the dates, it can spill over into March.

FESTIVAL FLAMENCO
A combination of big names and rising talent come together for five days of fine flamenco music in one of the city's theatres (often the Teatro Albéniz, but check). The dates are moveable.

ARCO
www.arco.ifema.es
One of Europe's biggest celebrations of contemporary art, the Feria Internacional de Arte Contemporánea draws gallery reps

and exhibitors from all over the world. It's staged around mid-February in the Parque Ferial Juan Carlos I exhibition centre and lasts for five days.

MARCH & APRIL

JUEVES SANTO

Jueves Santo (Good Thursday) kicks off the official holiday period known in Spain as Semana Santa (Holy Week). Local *cofradías* (lay fraternities) organise colourful and often solemn religious processions where hooded men (looking scarily like the Ku Klux Klan) and barefoot women dragging chains around their ankles and bearing crosses are among the parading figures. For many Madrileños it also marks the start of a much-needed *puente* (bridge, or long weekend) and they take the chance to escape the city.

VIERNES SANTO

Viernes Santo (Good Friday) and Easter in general are celebrated with greater enthusiasm in some of the surrounding towns. Chinchón, in particular, is known for its lavish Easter processions.

ARTEMANÍA

www.pcm.tourspain.es
The Feria de Arte y Antigüedades sees antique dealers from all over Spain converge on the Palacio de Congresos y Exposiciones on Paseo de la Castellana. You can admire anything from Picasso lithographs to ancient pottery. The fair usually lasts for a week and takes place towards the end of April.

JAZZ ES PRIMAVERA

Three weeks of jazz across the city.

MAY

FIESTA DE LA COMUNIDAD DE MADRID

On El Dos de Mayo (2 May) in 1808, Napoleon's troops put down an uprising in Madrid, and commemorating this day has become an opportunity for much festivity. The day is celebrated with particular energy in the bars of Malasaña.

FIESTAS DE SAN ISIDRO LABRADOR

The merry month of May is nowhere merrier than in Madrid. In the wake of the

Dos de Mayo festivities comes the city's big holiday on 15 May, when it celebrates the feast day of its patron saint, San Isidro (the 'peasant'). On this day the townsfolk gather in central Madrid to watch the colourful procession which kicks off a week of cultural events across the city. Locals also traipse across the Puente de San Isidro to the saint's chapel and spend the day there picnicking; many are in traditional dress, and sip holy water and munch on *barquillos* (sweet pastries). The country's most prestigious *feria* (bullfighting season) also commences and continues for a month at the bullring Plaza de Toros Monumental de Las Ventas.

FESTIMAD

www.festimad.es
This is the biggest of Spain's year-round circuit of major music festivals. Bands from all over the country and beyond converge on Móstoles (on the MetroSur train network), just outside Madrid, for two days of indie music indulgence.

JUNE

DÍA DE SAN JUAN

Celebrated in other parts of Spain with fireworks and considerable gusto, the eve of this holiday (24 June) is a minor affair in Madrid. The action, such as it is, takes place in the Parque del Buen Retiro.

DÍA DEL ORGULLO DE GAYS, LESBIANAS Y TRANSEXUALES

www.orgullogay.org
The city's gay and lesbian Pride festival and parade take place on the last Saturday of the month. It's an international gig, with simultaneous parades taking place in cities across Europe, from Berlin to Paris. The inner-city barrio of Chueca is the place to be.

JULY

VERANOS DE LA VILLA

As if the traditional local fiestas weren't enough to amuse those Madrileños who stay behind in the broiling city summer heat, the town authorities stage a series of cultural events, shows and exhibitions, known as 'Summers in the City'. Concerts, opera, dance and theatre are performed in the Centro Cultural de la Villa, in the Palacio del Conde Duque and other venues around town. The programme starts in July and runs to the end of August.

AUGUST
FIESTAS DE SAN LORENZO, SAN CAYETANO & LA VIRGEN DE LA PALOMA
These three local patron saints' festivities (which revolve around La Latina and Plaza de Lavapiés) keep the otherwise quiet central districts of Madrid busy during the first fortnight of August. An almighty din fills the hot night air as locals eat, drink, dance and generally let their hair down. Why not? It's too hot for sleep anyway.

LA ASUNCIÓN
Also known as the Fiesta de la Virgen de la Paloma, 15 August is a solemn date in the city's religious calendar, celebrating the Assumption of the Virgin Mary.

SEPTEMBER
LOCAL FIESTAS
Several local councils organise fiestas in the first and second weeks of September. They include Fuencarral-El Pardo, Vallecas, Arganzuela, Barajas, Moncloa-Aravaca and Usera. In the last week of the month you can check out the Fiesta de Otoño (Autumn Festival) in Chamartín. These are very local affairs and provide a rare insight into the barrio life of the average Madrileño.

FIESTA DEL PCE
www.pce.es (in Spanish)
In mid-September the Partido Comunista de España (PCE; Spanish Communist Party) holds its annual fundraiser in the Casa de Campo. This mixed bag of regional-food pavilions, rock concerts and political soap-boxing lasts all weekend.

NOVEMBER
DÍA DE LA VIRGEN DE LA ALMUDENA
Castizos (true-blue Madrileños) gather in Plaza Mayor to hear Mass on the feast day (9 November) of the city's female patron saint.

EMOCIONA JAZZ
Groups from far and wide converge on the capital for a series of concerts in venues across town.

DECEMBER
FESTIVAL DE GOSPEL & NEGRO SPIRITUALS
In the week running up to Christmas, Madrid is treated to a feast of jazz, blues and gospel, usually in the Centro Cultural de la Villa.

NAVIDAD
Navidad, meaning Christmas, is a fairly quiet family time, with the main meal being served on *Nochebuena* (Christmas Eve). Elaborate nativity scenes are set up in churches around the city and an exhibition of them is held in Plaza Mayor.

TOP UNUSUAL EVENTS
- Fiesta de San Antón – The blessing of the pets takes place at the Iglesia de San Antón, home church of the patron saint of animals, on 17 January.
- Jesús de Medinaceli – Up to 100,000 people crowd the Iglesia de Jesús de Medinaceli on the first Friday of Lent to kiss the right foot of a wooden sculpture of Christ (*besapié*, kissing of the foot). Pilgrims make three wishes to Jesus, of which he is said to grant one.
- Fiestas de San Isidro Labrador – This is Madrid's biggest party, when *chulapos* (born-and-bred Madrileños) dress in short jackets and berets, and *manolas* (the female version of a once-common Lavapiés first name) don their finest *mantón de Manila* (embroidered silk shawl). If you're lucky, they'll even dance the *choti* (a traditional working-class dance not unlike the polka).
- Fiesta de San Antonio – Young Madrileños flock to the Ermita de San Antonio de la Florida (p96) on 13 June to petition for a partner. Whether spiritually inclined or not, the attitude seems to be 'why take a chance?'.
- Fiesta de Vallecas – The mischievous Brotherhood of Sailors in the working-class barrio of Vallecas stages a 'naval battle', in other words a massive water fight, in July to demand that the government provide Madrid with a seaport.

CULTURE

IDENTITY

The young, laid-back and sassy Madrid of the 21st century is a radically different world to that of the parents and grandparents of today's younger generation. Old Madrid was a world of strictures and strong social codes, of dour Francoist limits on freedom and conservative Catholic mores. Madrileños – primarily the older generation – developed a reputation for a certain reserve and for conservatism, forced to look inward by bleak Castilian winters and by spending too long living in close proximity to the powers-that-be.

Younger Madrileños could not be more different. Liberated from the shackles that bound their parents, those who grew up in the post-Franco years did so believing that theirs was a world without limits. One manifestation was a fervent adherence to the great maxim of Spanish legend that 'every Spaniard carries in his or her pocket a letter from the king which reads: This Spaniard is entitled to do whatever he or she feels like doing.' As such, they rebelled against everything and Madrileños don't take kindly to being told what to do.

Madrid's symbol: the bear and strawberry tree (below)

But the new breed of Madrileño is not simply the latest exemplar of the me-generation phenomenon. For young Madrileños, freedom is not just something to be enjoyed but is something to be defended and extended to all. Gay marriage? Not a problem. The mass legalisation of illegal immigrants? All in a good cause. Wage war in our name in Iraq? Take to the streets and say no to the government.

The now generation of Madrileños also rebels against the closed-world mentality of their parents. Madrileños are fascinated with the outside world and are leaving Spanish shores in ever-greater numbers to experience it for themselves. They're not entirely sure about the

THERE'S A BEAR IN THERE

Where most European cities have suitably serious emblems to reflect their historical stature, Madrid's is decidedly whimsical, if somewhat complicated – a she-bear nuzzling a *madroño*, or strawberry tree (so named because its fruit looks a little like strawberries), bordered by a frame bearing seven five-point stars and topped by a crown.

The process of constructing this patchwork symbol began when Alfonso VI took Madrid from the Muslims in 1085. At the time, the Christian forces hoped (correctly as it turned out) that Mayrit (Madrid) would be the first of a long line of conquests (starting from the north) that would propel the Christians south. Thus Madrid became an example of things to come, or a north point.

Taking the theme further, a group of seven stars that lies close to the North Star in the northern hemisphere forms a shape known as the Ursa Minor, or small she-bear. Thus the bear (once a common sight in the El Pardo area north of the city) and seven stars came to symbolise Madrid. The five points of the stars later came to represent the five provinces that surround Madrid (Segovia, Ávila, Toledo, Cuenca and Guadalajara).

The crown above the frame dates from the 16th century when Carlos I allowed Madrid to use the symbol of the imperial crown in its coat of arms after he cured a fever using *madroño* leaves (a popular medicinal herb).

This coat of arms appears on a deep-violet background to form the city's flag and adorns such important Madrid icons as the shirts of Atlético de Madrid football club (but not Real Madrid's).

When the Comunidad de Madrid was created as a region under the Autonomies Statute in the early 1980s, the town fathers had to come up with another flag. They chose to put the seven stars on to a red background, which symbolises the territories of Castile from which the new province was carved.

Confused? You're not alone. Madrileños love their symbol and routinely take visitors to the see the bear nuzzling a strawberry tree (*el oso y madroño*) in the Plaza de la Puerta del Sol (p64), but their eyes usually glaze over when you ask them to explain what it all means.

changing face of their city as a result of immigration – almost one-in-five Madrid residents is a foreigner – but by-and-large these newcomers are made to feel welcome.

One freedom that many Madrileños struggle to accept is the right of Spanish regions – principally the Basque Country and Catalonia – to self-determination. Partly it's a reaction to decades of Euskadi Ta Askatasuna (ETA; Basque Homeland and Liberty) terrorism, but it also stems from a passionate belief in the idea of Spain that makes them wonder why somebody wouldn't want to belong. Perhaps because of this, many Madrileños can't stand parochialism (except when it comes to football), provincialism (which they see as the manifestation of a small-world mentality) being made to feel guilty for speaking their own language when in Barcelona – this could never happen in Madrid, they say (the Franco years aside).

How Madrileños see themselves also depends on which barrio they're from. If you're from Chamberí, you're committed to the best of authentic Madrid. If you hail from Lavapiés, you love gritty, multicultural, melting-pot Madrid. If you live in Salamanca, you enjoy the sound of old money. If you've spent all your life in Vallecas or support Atlético Madrid, you belong to a community and wouldn't live anywhere else.

Spend any time in Spain and you'll soon discover that Spaniards love to recount stereotypes about other Spaniards. In this, Madrileños are no different. But how does the rest of the country view Madrileños? It sees them as *chulos*. Now this is a word to be wary of. It generally implies a degree of bravado and even arrogance. As an adjective it can simply mean 'cool' (usually in reference to an object). But to many people beyond Madrid, the word has quite negative characteristics – brash, showy – which are, in the eyes of Madrileños, no bad thing.

LIFESTYLE

Madrileños manage that rare city combination – leading generally frenetic lives but giving the impression of being quite relaxed about it all. People dash about all over the city and stay out till all hours, but they religiously stop for long, liquid lunches, think nothing of spending an entire afternoon with friends in a *terraza* (outdoor bar) and love to *pasear* (stroll).

People who live in central Madrid generally do so cheek by jowl and just about everyone lives in an apartment. Those who can afford it live in a *piso exterior* (an apartment that looks onto the street), but many have to make do with an *interior* (which can overlook anything from a grand internal courtyard to a shaft in the middle of a building).

Spain may be hurtling towards parity with the rest of Western Europe, but Spanish pay packets lag far behind. Apartment and rental prices have more than doubled in the last five years – a decent flat of 100 sq metres in an average part of central Madrid will start at €500,000 and is impossible to rent for less than €1200 a month. At the same time, the minimum wage, at €490 a month, is among the lowest in Western Europe and many people in modest jobs (secretarial, teaching and so on) don't gross much more than €1000 a month.

So how do Madrileños get by? The simple answer is that they struggle to do so. Spaniards are rare among Europeans in that they cannot imagine being anything other than home owners, so in pursuit of their dream they live with their parents until well into their thirties, take on enormous amounts of debt (some banks now offer 50-year mortgages) and scan the windows of real estate agents for apartments that can be as small as 30 sq metre. The difficulty of making ends meet may also be one reason why Madrid, like the rest of Spain, has one of the lowest birth rates (1.2%) in the world.

As a consequence, Madrid is home to hugely divergent standards of living. Groups of students from the provinces crowd into large, often run-down flats in numbers far out of proportion to the apartments' floorspace. Unluckier ones may wind up with a *habitación ciega* (a 'blind room', ie without a window). Your average middle-class inhabitant of central Madrid, if they managed to purchase before the housing market went nuts in the mid-1990s, may well have a splendidly spacious apartment rambling over 150 sq metre, with balconies and wooden shutters, hardwood floors, high ceilings and interior bedrooms giving onto quiet courtyards. Luxury apartments of several hundred square metres with all the latest designer fittings, and occasionally even rooftop pools, also exist. Looking at buildings from the street, you simply have no idea what might lurk inside.

Increasingly, many Madrileños prefer the new to the old. New *chalets* (detached or semidetached houses) in *urbanizaciones* (housing estates) outside Madrid, luxury villas to

LAST CALL FOR THE SIESTA

As foreigners crawl red-eyed back to their hotel after a long night on the tiles, they are invariably puzzled by one question: how on earth do the locals stay out all night and then turn up for work the next day?

Apart from the fact that most nocturnal frolics don't generally start until Thursday – one day of suffering is perfectly tolerable – the answer used to be the siesta, that long and decidedly civilised practice of taking an afternoon nap. Working hours traditionally ran from 9am to 7pm or 8pm with a two- or three-hour break for lunch and a siesta in the afternoon. In summer (usually from 15 June to 15 September), many Madrileños work to an *horario intensivo* (intensive timetable), starting as early as 7am and finishing up by 2pm before the heat takes hold. In theory, this enables many to have a full 'night's' sleep in the afternoon.

But the days of the weekday siesta may be numbered. In 2005, a Europe-wide study revealed that Spaniards sleep 40 minutes fewer per day than other Europeans, work more hours per week and are significantly less productive while at work as a result. All of which has led to a campaign to bring Spanish working hours into line with the rest of Europe as a means of increasing efficiency, reducing workplace accidents (which cost the Spanish economy €13 billion in 2003) and enabling Spaniards to conduct business more easily with the rest of Europe.

There was an outcry at the mere thought of tampering with a tradition as Spanish as paella. Medical studies were released showing that a brief afternoon nap can help reduce stress and make workers less susceptible to heart disease. Even the Spanish prime minister, José Luis Rodríguez Zapatero, openly expressed doubts that it would be possible to change the national habits of a lifetime, claiming that the siesta 'is what distinguishes Spaniards, but it is also what defines us'.

Even so, hard-working Madrileños are finding it increasingly difficult to balance work and play, and now spend much of the week dreaming of the weekend when they can catch up on all the siestas they've missed during the week.

the north of the city in places such as La Moraleja or just plain new apartment blocks have a big market in Madrid. In no other culture are people so prepared to buy sight unseen or *sobre plano* (on the plan).

All sorts of people live in the heart of Madrid, filling it with human soul: the elderly who have never moved and still pay a peppercorn rent; families with children, cats and dogs; young, hip couples; executives who prefer city-centre living to commuting; student groups; and migrants in search of work. Every possible social class and type is present.

On summer evenings, people remain outside, eating and drinking at terraces amid a joyful chattering din until deep into the night. While the old money gets spent along the Paseo de la Castellana, a more mixed crowd frequents La Latina, where you're as likely to stumble over football-playing ankle biters (children) at 11pm as to run into drinking buddies. It is one of the endearing qualities of Madrid that children are so easily melded into their parents' nocturnal diversions and the elderly are as welcome (and often sighted) in bars at all hours.

One final thing: Madrileños can seem gruff and be economical with etiquette. In short, they're not too fussed with please and thank you. But this rarely signifies unfriendliness. One way in which you may notice people expressing their fellow feeling is the general *'buenos días'* (good day) they utter to all and sundry when they enter a shop, bar or even an elevator, and the *'adiós'* (goodbye) or *'hasta luego'* (see you later) when they leave.

FASHION

In the 18th century, Madrileños rioted when told by the king that they could no longer wear the sweeping capes that so distinguished them. Those days may be long gone, but they still take their fashion seriously in Madrid.

Madrid may not rival Milan or Paris as fashion capitals of Europe, but the Pasarela Cibeles (www.cibeles.ifema.es, in Spanish) runway fashion shows, staged in the Parque Ferial Juan Carlos I and running since the late 1990s, are becoming an essential stop on the European threads circuit, especially for spring and autumn collections.

Spanish fashion exploded out of the blocks after the fascist austerity of the Franco years. The psychedelic colours of *la movida Madrileña* (the sociocultural movement set off by the explosion of liberties after the death of Franco) in the 1980s have never really gone away and the candy-bright colours of Agatha Ruiz de la Prada (Andy Warhol was a fan) have now acquired

Designer fashions at Alma Aguilar (p163)

something of a middle-class respectability. Her work, widely available, encompasses everything from children's clothes to outrageous evening wear for adults.

This stylish-but-anything-goes approach has morphed into a fashion scene dominated by colour. Classic and more conservative lines are the preserve of Loewe, Sybilla, Ángel Schlesser and the Madrileña Alma Aguilar. A more formal/casual mix is favoured by designers such as Amaya Arzuaga, Purificación García, Roberto Torretta and Roberto Verino. Others to watch out for on the catwalk include the Madrileño, Javier Larraínzar (one of the city's top *haute couture* icons); Pedro del Hierro; Kina Fernández; Nacho Ruiz; and Montesinos Alama.

Less pricey and hence more mainstream is Adolfo Domínguez. More clean-lined and casual is Armand Basi, while the clothes of David Elfin span the divide between edgy and exclusive.

Spain is also famous for the quality of its shoes and the designers once known only to Spaniards and Madrileños are fast becoming fixtures on the international scene. Manolo Blahnik is perhaps the best known, and his shoes have become more a fixture at the Oscars than George Clooney. Other important names include Sara Navarro and Farrutx. Many of these designers also do great lines in handbags and other accessories (they wouldn't maintain the loyalty of Madrileñas if they didn't) and there's no finer exponent of the art than the hand-painted sophisticated-but-fun masterpieces of Iñaki Sampedro. For designer shoes and accessories at discounted prices, Calle de Agusto Figueroa (Map pp250–1) is the stuff of shopping legend.

Madrid's home of sophisticated designers are the boutiques of Calle de Serrano and the adjacent streets in chichi Salamanca. Combined with Calle de José Ortega y Gasset, Spain's *milla del oro* (golden mile) for showrooms by the most famous international designers, these are some of the most exclusive shopping streets in Europe. One other area to look out for is Calle de Piamonte (p165), where exceptional accessories fill almost every shop.

Contrast this with the inner-city barrio of Chueca where you'll find quirky, imaginative shops where the line between designer fashions and urban streetwear is decidedly blurred. On Calle de Fuencarral, the 60 shops of the Mercado Fuencarral is Madrid's spiritual home of alternative urban fashion, especially hip and edgy club wear.

The shopping explosion that began in the 1990s in Madrid shows no sign of abating and with it has come a host of *prêt-a-porter* fashion shops that are eminently affordable. Of the Spanish designers, the biggest of these success stories is Zara, with more than 800 stores throughout the world. And where would we be without the cool and casual shoes of Camper?

SPORT
Football

Depending on your perspective, Real Madrid (www.realmadrid.com) is either the best football club in the world (in 1998, FIFA declared it the greatest club of all time) or the symbol of a game gone mad with money.

When it comes to history, no-one can match Real Madrid's record at home or abroad – 29 Spanish *liga* (league) titles, the last in 2003; 17 Copas del Rey (Spanish Cups); nine European Cups (now known as the Champions League Trophy), including 1998, 2000 and 2002; two Uefa Cups; and the Spanish Supercopa a mere seven times.

Even against the backdrop of such a history, however, the recent headlines surrounding the club have been extraordinary. Since construction magnate Florentino Perez became club president in 2000, the club has spent hundreds of millions of euros buying the best players in the world, in the process building a team known as *los galacticos*. There's just one problem: while these superstars of the world game have shone as individuals, they've never really gelled as a team. In the three seasons following its Spanish league title in 2003, Real Madrid won

RIGHT ROYAL FOOTBALLERS

Few football teams arouse such contradictory passions as Real Madrid – *los blancos* (whites), *merengues* (meringues), *los galacticos* or simply *El Madrid,* as the team is variously known – and a quick look at its history shows why.

In 1920, King Alfonso XIII bestowed the *real* (royal) title upon the club. Fans of arch rival FC Barcelona will tell you that in the years of Primo de Rivera's dictatorship (1920s), and later under Franco, their team was frequently the victim of dodgy decisions. It's certainly true that Real Madrid dominated Spanish and European football throughout the Franco period and the little dictator frequently basked in Real Madrid's successes as if they were his own. Most famously, Barcelona won the first leg of their 1943 Spanish Cup semifinal against Real Madrid 3-0. Legend has it that before the return leg in Madrid, Franco's Director of State Security visited the Barcelona changing room and issued thinly veiled threats and berated the Catalans for their lack of patriotism. Madrid defeated a clearly frightened Barcelona 11-1 in the second leg.

It's a long time since Madrid had ties to royal power, but Real Madrid's opponents love to remind Madridistas (Real Madrid supporters) of their shadowy past and the club has never really lost its tag as the club of power.

nothing as the team went through four coaches and reports began to emerge of a changing room divided into various camps of over-swelled egos. In March 2006, Florentino Perez resigned, blaming the prima-donnas whom he himself had brought to the club.

It comes as a surprise to many visitors that a significant proportion of the population can't stand Real Madrid and actually support the capital's other team, Atlético Madrid (www.clubatleticodemadrid.com). Atlético have won nine *liga* titles (a feat bettered only by Real Madrid and FC Barcelona), the latest in 1996, and nine Copas del Rey. Atlético, which has something of a cult following, attracts passionate support – supporters of the *rojiblancos* (red-and-whites) declare theirs to be the *real* Madrid team, unlike the reviled and aristocratic 'Madridistas' up the road.

For details on how to see a Real Madrid or Atlético game, turn to p151.

Madrid's other team, Rayo Vallecano (www.rayovallecano.es), from the working-class barrio of Vallecas, has a history distinguished more by the passion of its fans than any success on the football field. They were last seen languishing in the Spanish third division.

Bullfighting

An epic drama of blood and sand or a cruel blood 'sport' which has no place in modern Europe? This most enduring and controversial of Spanish traditions is all this and more; at once picturesque, compelling theatre and an ancient ritual that sees 40,000 bulls killed every year in Spain. Perhaps it was best summed up by Ernest Hemingway – a bullfighting aficionado – who described it as 'a wonderful nightmare'.

Whatever your viewpoint, an afternoon of *la corrida* (bullfighting) is an essential part of Madrid life, particularly during the month-long season beginning with the Fiestas de San Isidro Labrador (p10) on 15 May at Las Ventas bullfighting ring. This is Spain's premier bullfighting season and it's most prestigious venue – when toreros (bullfighters) put in a starring performance at Las Ventas, their career is made.

On an afternoon ticket there are generally six bulls and three star toreros dressed in the dazzling *traje de luces* (suit of lights). The torero leads a *cuadrilla* (team) of fighters who make up the rest of the colourful band in the ring. It's a complex business but in essence the toreros aim to impress the crowd and jury with daring and graceful moves as close to an aggressive bull as possible. It's a one-sided event – the death of the bull is close to inevitable – but it's still a dangerous business. Despite the spectre of death that pervades *la corrida,* a day out at the bullring is a festive occasion with aficionados dressed to the nines and wine flowing freely.

While few modern fighters match the courage and skill of former greats such as Juan Belmonte (1892–1962), Manuel 'Manolete' Rodríguez Sánchez (1917–47), Antonio Ordoñez (1932–98) or Luis Miguel Dominguín (1926–96), there are some stars to look out for. Juan Antonio Ruiz ('Espartaco') was unbeatable in the early 1990s, while current stars include Jesulín de Ulbrique, Julián 'El Juli' López, José Miguel Arroyo (Joselito), Enrique Ponce and Manuel Díaz (El Cordobés).

For more details on how to see a bullfight in Madrid, see p152.

Basketball

Although they don't get the same publicity, Real Madrid's basketball players are as much champions as their footballing counterparts and their rivalry with Barcelona is equally fierce. The team has won 28 Spanish league titles, 22 Copas del Rey and eight European championships. Also popular is the less successful Adecco Estudiantes side. For match information see p152.

Marathons

In late April, the Maraton de Madrid (www.maratonmadrid.org) cuts a swathe through the city and attracts athletes from all over the world.

The less serious athletes among you may find the wonderfully festive San Silvestre Vallecana (www.sansilvestrevallecana.com) more to your liking. Staged on 31 December at 6pm, the 10km-course leads from Plaza de Castilla, all the way down Paseo de la Castellana and out to Vallecas, south of the centre. It is one of the more unusual races in Europe, and most athletes are fun-runners in fancy dress (although there are some serious competitors); musicians line the route and runners – who must pass through streets warming up for New Year's Eve – are pelted with eggs and tomatoes.

LANGUAGE

Español (Spanish), often referred to as Castellano (Castilian) to distinguish it from other regional languages spoken in Spain, is the language of Madrid. The conservative Real Academia Española, located near the Prado, watches over Cervantes' tongue with deadly solemnity and issues the country's version of the *Oxford English Dictionary*, the weighty *Diccionario de la Lengua Española*.

While you'll find an increasing number of Madrileños, especially younger people and hotel and restaurant employees, who speak some English, don't count on it. Those of you who learn a little Spanish will be amply rewarded as Spaniards always appreciate the effort, no matter how basic your mastery of the language. Madrileños tend to talk at high volume and high velocity. Although the Spanish you learned at school will be fine for most situations, you may start to flounder once the locals revert to local *cheli* (slang).

See the Language chapter (p222) for the basics.

ECONOMY & COSTS

Until recently, the regions of Catalonia and the Basque Country were the economic engines of Spain and they tended to look on Madrid as the country's capital in name only; but not any more.

Now Spain's undisputed financial capital (banks seem to occupy every Madrid street corner) and prime economic mover, Madrid attracts, according to one estimate, around 75% of all foreign investment destined for Spain. The Banco de España (central bank)

MADRID'S KEY ECONOMIC STATS

- National minimum wage – The second-lowest among the 15 'older' members of the European Union at €490 a month; the government has promised to raise this to €600 by 2008.
- Spanish pretax earnings – Some 49% of Spaniards earn less than €12,000 a year before tax, while 75% earn less than €21,000.
- Madrid incomes – Madrid's workers earn, on average, €2600 a month before tax, 18% higher than the national average.
- Regional GDP – Catalonia has the highest GDP in Spain, followed by Madrid.
- Unemployment – The national unemployment rate has dipped below 10% (it now stands at 8.7%) for the first time in living memory; the jobless rate in Madrid is 6.1%.

and the Ibex stock exchange are based here and, increasingly, international corporations with interests in Spain are establishing their main headquarters in Madrid. The construction sector and services sector (principally tourism) are key economic engines. Barcelona and Bilbao may have busy commercial ports, but Madrid has compensated for its landlocked location by diversifying its economy into the services and financial sectors to the point where the city's lack of a port distresses Madrileños only because they have to drive further to get to the beach.

For the European visitor, Madrid remains affordable, although it's fast catching up to the rest of Europe, especially when it comes to eating out and accommodation.

HOW MUCH?
El País newspaper €1
Souvenir T-shirt €10 to €22
Entrance to the Prado €6
One litre of mineral water in supermarket €0.40
One litre of petrol €0.95
A caña (small glass of beer) of Mahou €1.20
A tapa €1.50 to €4
Admission to dance clubs €10 to €20
Normal letter (up to 20g) within Europe €0.52
A cocktail €6 to €8

The exception is the *menú del día,* a fixed-price, all-in set lunch that can cost under €10. Public transport and taxis are cheap compared with most other European cities and it's possible to visit some museums for free (see boxed text, p57, for more information).

GOVERNMENT & POLITICS

Madrileños are presided over by three layers of government.

At the national level, the Partido Socialista Obrero Español, or Socialist Party, of José Luis Rodríguez Zapatero has held power since March 2004. The national Cortes (parliament) is divided into two houses, the Congreso de los Diputados (lower house) on Carrera de San Jerónimo, and the Senado (senate), off Plaza de España.

The Comunidad de Madrid, one of 17 Spanish autonomous regions, is led by Esperanza Aguirre of the conservative Partido Popular (PP; Popular Party), who is the country's first woman president of a Spanish region. Her mandate is, however, less than secure following her narrow win in an election re-run in October 2003 after two Socialist deputies defected.

The city government has been the preserve of the PP since 1991 and is led by the *alcalde* (mayor), currently Alberto Ruiz-Gallardón. Ruiz-Gallardón easily won the May 2003 election, winning 30 out of the 55 seats, and is one of Madrid's most popular politicians of recent times. That has, however, begun to unravel thanks to the disruptions caused by the seemingly endless infrastructure projects that are a semipermanent feature of Madrid life. Among his councillors (and a right-wing politician to watch) is Ana Botella, wife of José María Aznar, the former PP Spanish president. The city council operates out of the Ayuntamiento (town hall) on Plaza de la Villa in the heart of the old city.

The next city and regional elections are set for 2007, with national elections a year later.

ENVIRONMENT
THE LAND

At 650m above sea level on a high continental plateau, Madrid is the highest capital city in Europe. The Comunidad de Madrid – in the centre of which lies Madrid in a rough triangle – covers 7995 sq km, less than 2% of Spain's territory.

Madrid's northwest boundary consists of a series of mountain ranges which run from the northeast to the southwest for 140km as part of the longer chain known as the Cordillera Central. Known by Madrileños simply as the Sierra, they encompass the Somosierra, Sierra de Guadarrama and Sierra de Gredos. However, as the foothills of the Sierra lie a considerable distance from the city centre, little stands in the way of Madrid's relentless sprawl.

Within Madrid itself, there are plenty of gentle rises and falls to test weary legs, the most significant of which surrounds the ridge along which the original Islamic fortress town (the *alcázar*) was raised. From the Palacio Real, the Catedral de Nuestra Señora de la Almudena and Vistillas, the land falls away into parks towards the Manzanares.

To the east, the heart of old Madrid rises almost imperceptibly, drops down again to the great north–south boulevard, the Paseo de la Castellana, before climbing again towards Salamanca and the Parque del Buen Retiro.

GREEN MADRID

Madrid has an abundance of parks and gardens. The most central and attractive is the Parque del Buen Retiro, an expansive manicured stretch of greenery which once constituted the eastern boundary of the city and was also the preserve of royalty and nobles. With its sculpted gardens, artificial lakes and roaming paths, it's a wonderful escape from the din of central Madrid. Just down the hill from the Retiro is the charming little Real Jardín Botánico, a botanical garden packed with all sorts of exotic species.

Equally green and enticing for the romantic stroller is the Campo del Moro, which slopes away west of the Palacio Real, while the nearby Parque del Oeste is similarly hilly and delightfully green.

Altogether wilder is the Casa de Campo, west of the Manzanares.

ENVIRONMENTAL ISSUES

Spain's environmental problems are legion. At the time of writing, the country was suffering from its worst drought in 60 years and between 1990 and 2004, Spain's greenhouse gas emissions increased by 45%: more than any other developed country and three times the level it agreed to under the Kyoto Protocol.

The consequences for Madrid are potentially devastating. In the last 30 years, Madrid has seen a rise of 2.2°C in its average temperature, a greater increase than for any other European capital. At the start of 2006, Madrid's water reserves stood at just 36.4%, less than half the reserves from a year earlier and insufficient to last the year. The Madrid authorities have begun campaigns to encourage sensible water use among the city's residents (including brightly painted manhole covers in the streets encouraging residents to use water wisely) but water restrictions are not yet in place and the government's strategy seems to rely more on hoping for rain than on serious water conservation. (In late 2005, the 5200 inhabitants of Miraflores de la Sierra, a village 50km north of the capital in the Sierra, woke up to find that the village had simply run out of water.) The rains may have stayed away but there is also a man-made dimension to the problem – Madrid's 29 golf courses use as much water as a city of 100,000 inhabitants and half are under investigation for not using recycled water.

Noise pollution is another big problem throughout the city. Rowdy traffic, late-night rubbish collection, all-night road-

Banner protesting against Madrid's noise pollution (left)

works, the incessant sirens of emergency vehicles and horn-happy drivers all help to keep Madrileños' nerves well jangled. Long live double glazing.

Rubbish is collected every night, but recycling is optional and widely ignored.

URBAN PLANNING & DEVELOPMENT

Surrounded by concentric ring roads, Madrid just can't stop growing. Whole new suburbs are under construction and will swallow up pretty much all that remains of the available land in the Madrid municipal area by around 2020. Such an approach (with its inevitably speculative side) is fairly typical of the PP, and opposition parties and environmentalists alike have slammed the programme. Whoever's to blame, it's already too late to stop Madrid's transformation from a compact, manageable and high-density city into one that sprawls endlessly to the horizon.

Urban development in Madrid is not, however, all bad news. The modern metro system is constantly being redeveloped and expanded at a rate which other cities can only dream of.

And in the rush to push Madrid outwards, the downtown area is not being neglected. There is talk of building skyscrapers to the north of Plaza Castilla (near the top end of Paseo de la Castellana) as a partial solution to the critical shortage of space in central Madrid. Of far greater potential for urban renewal, the redevelopment of the ugly banks of the Río Manzanares – the M-30 motorway is being driven underground to be replaced by tree-lined and traffic-free riverside promenades – promises to transform one of Madrid's least attractive corners.

Arts & Architecture ∎

Arts & Architecture

Madrid has a buzzing artistic life. Soulful flamenco, vibrant contemporary music and Spain's acclaimed films are some of the more lively artistic forms you'll encounter, but there are also plenty of more 'static' attractions, among them splendid architecture, hidden literary treasures and fine arts – Madrid has one of the best collections of fine art on the planet – most of which you'll find only in Madrid. So much of what you'll see and hear will be new to many visitors, but that's only because, until recently, few contemporary Spanish artists and performers have been given much air time in the Anglocentric international arts scene. Not all of what you'll find will come from Madrid, but if it's happening in Spain, it will be happening here, where anyone who's anyone must come to make it on the Spanish scene. Whether you're new to Spanish culture or an old hand, you're in for a treat.

PAINTING & SCULPTURE

Few cities in the world can match Madrid's pantheon of master painters who all passed through and made the city their own: from Velázquez, El Greco and Goya to Picasso, Juan Gris and many others. Each left behind an astonishing collection of art that sits alongside many of the other great names of world painting. Throw in a vibrant contemporary art scene and it's not hard to see why art lovers fall in love with Madrid.

THE EARLY DAYS

The Spanish kings of the 16th century were the first to show an interest in the arts, beginning a long tradition of patronage that would turn Spain into one of the richest producers and storehouses of paintings anywhere in the world. The first Spaniard to find royal favour was Logroño-born Juan Navarrete (1526–79), also known as El Mudo (the Mute), one of Spain's first practitioners of Tenebrism, a style that largely aped Caravaggio's chiaroscuro style.

But Spain's monarchs had cultural cringe, and Felipe II – the monarch who made Madrid the permanent seat of the royal court – preferred the work of Italian artists such as Titian ahead of home-grown talent. Even some foreign artists who would later become masters were given short shrift, suggesting that the king's eye for quality was far from perfect. One of these was the Cretan-born Domenikos Theotokopoulos (1541–1614), known as El Greco (the Greek; see boxed text, p183), who was perhaps the most extraordinary and temperamental 'Spanish' artist of the 16th century but whom Felipe II rejected as a court artist.

VELÁZQUEZ & THE GOLDEN AGE

As Spain's monarchs sought refuge from the creeping national malaise of the 17th century by promoting fine arts, they fostered an artist who would rise above all others: Diego Rodríguez de Silva Velázquez (1599–1660). Born in Seville, Velázquez later moved to Madrid as court painter and stayed to make the city his own. He composed scenes (landscapes, religious subjects, snapshots of everyday life) that owe their vitality not only to his photographic eye for light and contrast but also to a compulsive interest in the humanity of his subjects so that they seem to breathe on the canvas. His masterpieces include *Las Meninas* and *La Rendición de Breda* (The Surrender of Breda), both on view in the Prado.

Francisco de Zurbarán (1598–1664), a friend and contemporary of Velázquez, ended his life in poverty in Madrid and it was only after his death that he received the acclaim that his masterpieces deserved. He is best remembered for the startling clarity and light in his portraits of monks, a series of which hangs in the Real Academia de Bellas Artes de San Fernando.

Other masters of the era whose works hang in the Prado, though their connection to Madrid was limited, include José (Jusepe) de Ribera (1591–1652), who was influenced by Caravaggio and produced fine chiaroscuro works, and Bartolomé Esteban Murillo (1618–82).

GOYA – A CLASS OF HIS OWN

There was nothing in the provincial upbringing of Francisco José de Goya y Lucientes (1746–1828), who was born in the village of Fuendetodos in Aragón, to suggest that he would become one of the towering figures of European art.

Goya started his career as a cartoonist in the Real Fábrica de Tapices (Royal Tapestry Workshop) in Madrid. In 1776 Goya began designing for the tapestry factory, but illness in 1792 left him deaf; many critics speculate that his condition was largely responsible for his wild, often merciless style that would become increasingly unshackled from convention. By 1799, Goya was appointed Carlos IV's court painter.

Several distinct series and individual paintings mark his progress. In the last years of the 18th century he painted enigmatic masterpieces such as *La Maja Vestida* (The Young Lady Dressed) and *La Maja Desnuda* (The Young Lady Undressed), identical portraits but for the lack of clothes in the latter. The rumour mill suggests the subject was none other than the Duchess of Alba, with whom he allegedly had an affair. Whatever the truth of Goya's sex life, the Inquisition was not amused by the artworks, which it covered up. Nowadays all is bared in the Prado.

At about the same time as his enigmatic *Majas,* the prolific Goya executed the playful frescoes in Madrid's Ermita de San Antonio de la Florida, which have recently been restored to stunning effect. He also produced *Los Caprichos* (The Caprices), a biting series of 80 etchings lambasting the follies of court life and ignorant clergy.

The arrival of the French and war in 1808 had a profound impact on Goya. Unforgiving portrayals of the brutality of war are *El Dos de Mayo* (The Second of May) and, more dramatically, *El Tres de Mayo* (The Third of May). The latter depicts the execution of Madrid rebels by French troops.

After he retired to the Quinta del Sordo (Deaf Man's House) west of the Manzanares in Madrid, he created his nightmarish *Pinturas Negras* (Black Paintings). Executed on the walls of the house, they were later removed and now hang in the Prado. A scandal erupted recently when it was claimed that these chilling works were painted by the artist's son, Javier, and sold as genuine Goyas by his grandson. The Prado strenuously denies the claims.

Goya spent the last years of his life in voluntary exile in France, where he continued to paint until his death.

THE MADRID SCHOOL, GOYA & BEYOND

While the stars were at work, a second tier of busy baroque artists beavered away in the capital and came to be known collectively as the Madrid School.

Fray Juan Rizi (1600–81) did most of his work for Benedictine monasteries across Castile; some hang in the Real Academia de Bellas Artes de San Fernando. Claudio Coello (1642–93) specialised in the big picture and some of his huge canvases adorn the complex at San Lorenzo de El Escorial, including his magnum opus, *La Sagrada Forma* (The Holy Form).

But these were mere window dressing compared to Goya (see boxed text, above), who cast such a long shadow that all other artists of the period have been obscured.

Although no-one of the stature of Goya followed in his wake, new trends were noticeable by the latter decades of the 19th century. Joaquín Sorolla (1863–1923) flew in the face of the French Impressionist style, preferring the blinding sunlight of the Valencian coast to the muted tones favoured in Paris. His work can be studied in Madrid's Museo Sorolla.

Leading the way into the 20th century was Madrid-born José Gutiérrez Solana (1886–1945) whose disturbing, avant-garde approach to painting revels in low lighting, sombre colours and deathly pale figures. His work is emblematic of what historians now refer to as *España negra* (black Spain). A selection of his canvases is on display in the Centro de Arte Reina Sofía.

PICASSO, DALÍ & JUAN GRIS

The 17th century may have been Spain's golden age, but the 20th century was easily its rival.

The Málaga-born Pablo Ruiz Picasso (1881–1973) lays claim to the title of the greatest and most original Spanish painter of all time. Although he spent much of his working life in Paris, he arrived in Madrid from Barcelona in 1897 at the behest of his father for a year's study at the Escuela de Bellas Artes de San Fernando. Never one to allow himself to be confined within formal structures, the precocious Picasso instead took himself to the Prado to learn from the masters, and to the streets to depict life as he saw it. Picasso went on to become the master of Cubism which was inspired by his fascination with primitivism, primarily African masks and early Iberian sculpture. This highly complex form reached its high point in *Guernica* (see boxed text, p82), which hangs in the Centro de Arte Reina Sofía.

Picasso was not the only artist who found the Escuela de Bellas Artes de San Fernando to be too traditional for his liking. In 1922, Salvador Dalí (1904–89) arrived in Madrid from Catalonia, but he decided that the eminent professors of the renowned fine-arts school were not fit to judge him. He spent four years living in the 'Resi', the renowned students' residence (which still functions today) where he met poet Federico García Lorca and future film director Luis Buñuel. The three self-styled anarchists and bohemians romped through the cafés and music halls of 1920s Madrid, frequenting brothels, engaging in pranks, immersing themselves in jazz and taking part in endless *tertulias* (literary discussions). Dalí, a true original, and master of the surrealist form, was finally expelled from art school and left Madrid, never to return. The only remaining link with Madrid is a handful of his hallucinatory works in the Centro de Arte Reina Sofía.

A Picasso masterpiece at Centro de Arte Reina Sofía (p80)

In the same gallery is a fine selection of the Cubist creations of Madrid's Juan Gris (1887–1927), who was turning out his best work in Paris while Dalí and Co were up to no good in Madrid. Along with Picasso and Georges Braque, he was a principal exponent of the Cubist style.

During the Franco years in Madrid, Antonio Saura (1930–98) was a shining light of surrealism and the dramatic brushstrokes of his portraits are sometimes seen as a reaction to the conventionality of public life under the dictator. In 1956 he publicly burned books of his paintings as a protest against Franco and the following year set up the El Paso group of artists whose aim was to provide a forum for contemporary art. Check out www.antonisaura.org for more info.

CONTEMPORARY ART

The death of Franco in 1975 unleashed a frenzy of activity and artistic creativity was central to *la movida Madrileña* (the sociocultural movement set off by the explosion of liberties after the death of Franco; see boxed text, p54). The Moriarty Gallery (Map pp250–1; ☎ 91 531 43 65; www.galeriamoriarty.com; Calle del Almirante 5, 1st fl; Ⓜ Chueca) became a focal point of exuberantly artistic reference and is still going strong. A parade of artists marched through the gallery, including leading *movida* lights such as Ceesepe (b 1958), whose real name is Carlos Sánchez Pérez, and whose busy paintings full of people and activity (but recently veering towards surrealism), and eight short films capture the spirit of 1980s Madrid. Another Moriarty protégé was Ouka Lele (b 1957), a self-taught photographer whose sometimes weird works stand out for her tangy treatment of colour. Her photos can be seen at the Centro de Arte Reina Sofía, Museo Municipal and the Museo de Arte Contemporáneo. Another *movida* photographer who still exhibits with Moriarty is Alberto García-Alix (b 1956).

The explosion of rebellious, effervescent activity in the 1980s tends to cloud the fact that the visual arts in the Franco years were far from dead. Many artists spent years in exile. One of Spain's greatest 20th-century sculptors, Toledo-born Alberto Sánchez (1895–1962) lived his last years in Moscow. He and Benjamín Palencia (1894–1980), an artist whose paintings occasionally show striking similarities with some of Sánchez' sculptures, were part of the so-called *Escuela de Vallecas* (Vallecas is now a working-class barrio in southern Madrid). The inheritors of their legacy, which is now more often called the *Escuela de Madrid,* include Francisco Arias, Gregorio del Olmo, Álvaro Delgado, Andrés Conejo and Agustín Redondela; all are on display at the Museo de Arte Contemporáneo.

The art of Eduardo Arroyo (b 1937) is steeped in the radical spirit that kept him in exile for 15 years from 1962. His paintings tend in part to pop art, brimming with ironic socio-political comment. Carlos Franco (b 1951) did the frescoes on the Casa de la Panadería on Playa Mayor.

Antonio López García (b 1936) takes a photographer's eye to his hyperrealistic paintings. Settings as simple as *Lavabo y Espejo* (Wash Basin and Mirror, 1967) convert the most banal everyday objects into scenes of extraordinary depth and the same applies to his Madrid street scenes which are equally loaded with detail, light play and subtle colour, especially *La Granvía* (1981) and *Vallecas* (1980). He won the coveted Premio Príncipe de Asturias for art in 1985. His contemporary, Alfredo Alcain (b 1936), whose textured paintings could at times be mistaken for aerial shots of patchwork fields, also won the Premio Príncipe de Asturias in 2004.

Many of the most prominent new abstract painters have a relatively small body of work, but Alejandro Corujeira, Alberto Reguera, Xavier Grau and Amaya Bozal are all names to watch. In the figurative tradition, the same could be said of Juan Carlos Savater, Sigfrido Martín Begué, Abraham La Calle and Fernando Bellver. All can be seen at the Museo de Arte Contemporáneo.

The big event for contemporary art in Madrid is the annual midwinter Arco contemporary art fair (p9; www.arco.ifema.es), which goes from strength to strength as a showcase for both emerging and established Spanish talent, although as it gains in prestige, it's taking on a more international flavour.

ARCHITECTURE

Compared with other European cities of culture, the Spanish capital is not distinguished by its architecture. This is largely attributable to Madrid's delayed emergence as a European capital and much of the Madrid you see today was built from the late 19th century on. Perhaps because of this fact, Madrid pleasantly surprises many first-time visitors with its architectural beauty and variety, and walking its grand boulevards, especially the north–south Paseo de la Castellana (under all its various names), is where you can best experience the grandeur and greenery that is modern Madrid. The whole effect, resplendent with swirling roundabouts and fountains, is the unmistakable feel of a capital that other Spanish cities, however replete with history, could never exude.

MADRID TO THE 16TH CENTURY

Madrid's origins as a Muslim garrison town yielded few architectural treasures, or at least few that remain. The only reminder of the Muslim presence in Madrid is a modest stretch of the town wall, known as the Muralla Árabe (Arab Wall) below the Catedral de Nuestra Señora de la Almudena. All that remains of the rich *mudéjar* style (developed by the Moors who remained behind in re-conquered Christian territory) in Madrid are the bell towers of the Iglesia de San Pedro El Viejo and Iglesia de San Nicolás de los Servitas. Visitors to Madrid with a yen for Muslim architecture should get the high-speed AVE train down to Córdoba to see the magnificent Mezquita mosque.

When Felipe II took the surprising decision in 1561 to establish Madrid as the capital of Imperial Spain, the 'city' was little more than a squalid ensemble of timber housing interspersed with the odd grand church or palace and laced with fetid lanes; thus it was that the elaborate edifices of Gothic architecture, a style that sprang from the humbler Romanesque style in France and saw the erection of great soaring churches across medieval Europe, largely passed Madrid by. Unless you're content with the much-interfered-with, late-Gothic Casa de los Lujanes (p65) or the beautiful, hidden-away Capilla del Obispo (p77), you'll need to head for Toledo, Segovia or Ávila for a greater appreciation of the genre.

RENAISSANCE & BAROQUE

After making Madrid his capital, Felipe II became preoccupied with building his monumental mausoleum/palace/summer getaway at El Escorial and did little to make his capital architecture worthy of the city's new stature. In spite of his neglect, architectural influences from elsewhere began to take hold in Spain.

The Italian-influenced special flavour of Plateresque is best appreciated in the city of Salamanca (see Lonely Planet's *Spain*), west of Madrid, while one of its main exponents, Alonso de Covarrubias (1488–1570), left his mark in his home city of Toledo, where he designed the *alcázar* (fortress). Juan de Herrera (1530–97) was perhaps the greatest figure of the Spanish Renaissance. Herrera developed a style unlike anything else being used during the period. His austere masterpiece was the palace-monastery complex of San Lorenzo de El Escorial (p195).

Even after his death, Herrera's style lived on in Madrid. The sternness of his Renaissance style fused with a timid approach to its successor, the more voluptuous, ornamental baroque. Together they formed a characteristic style known as *barroco Madrileño* (Madrid baroque). The façades of the Real Casa de la Panadería, the Palacio del Duque de Uceda (now the Capitanía General), the Ayuntamiento, and the Convento de la Encarnación all loosely fall into this category. The last two were designed by Juan Gómez de Mora (1586–1648), whereas his uncle, Francisco de Mora (1560–1610), had a hand in the Palacio del Duque de Uceda. Gómez de Mora was also behind the royal prisons facing Plaza de Santa Cruz, now the Ministry of Foreign Affairs. In Madrid one of the few other striking tastes of the style is the main entrance of what is now the Museo Municipal.

Ventura Rodríguez (1717–85) dominated the architectural scene in 18th-century Madrid much as Goya lorded it over the world of art. He redesigned the interior of the Convento de la Encarnación and did the Palacio de Liria. His style was controlled and clearly heading towards neo-Classicism.

Juan de Villanueva (1739–1811) designed the neo-Classical pile that would bear his name and eventually house the Museo del Prado, as well as numerous outbuildings of the royal residences such as San Lorenzo de El Escorial.

BELLE ÉPOQUE

As Madrid emerged from the chaos of the first half of the 19th century, a building boom began. The use of iron and glass, a revolution in building aesthetics that symbolised the embracing of modernity, became the fashion. The Palacio de Cristal in the Parque del Buen Retiro was built at this time.

By the dawn of the 20th century, known to many as the *belle époque* (beautiful time), Madrid was abuzz with construction. Headed by the prolific Antonio Palacios (1874–1945), architects from all over Spain began to transform Madrid into the airy city you see today.

Many looked to the past for their inspiration. Neo-*mudéjar* was especially favoured for bullrings. The ring at Las Ventas, finished in 1934, is a classic example. The most obvious of the neo-Gothic creations is the Catedral de Nuestra Señora de la Almudena, completed in 1992. A more bombastic interpretation of the style is Palacios' Palacio de Comunicaciones with its plethora of pinnacles and prancing ornaments, which was finished in 1917.

By the early 20th century, architecture in Madrid had come to be known as the 'eclectic' style, a hybrid form of competing influences as architects mixed and matched. Among the joyous and eye-catching examples – Gran Vía is jammed with them – are the 1916 Edificio Grassy and the 1905 Edificio Metrópolis.

Edificio Metrópolis (p62), architecture that lights up Madrid

CONTEMPORARY ARCHITECTURE

International experts are buzzing with the unprecedented energy surrounding Spanish architecture. At one level, Spanish architects such as Santiago Calatrava (who transformed Valencia and built the Olympic stadium in Athens among other signature projects) are taking the world by storm. At the same time, architects from all over the world are clamouring for Spanish contracts, in part because the projects for urban renewal currently underway in Spain are some of the most innovative in Europe and municipal governments are funding this extraordinary explosion of creativity. In early 2006, New York's Museum of Modern Art recognised the growing importance of Spanish architecture by launching an exhibition called 'On Site: New Architecture in Spain'. The catalogue of the same name can be found at **Naos Libros** (Map pp246–7; ☎ 91 547 39 16; www.naoslibros.es; Calle de Quintana 12).

For all that, Madrid has not been at the forefront of the trend, but that's not to say that contemporary architecture isn't weaving its way into Madrid's urban fabric; it is, and the best-known works are largely the preserve of world-class international architects. Henry Cobb is planning a tower of glass, the Torre Espacio, for the northern end of the Paseo de la Castellana; at least three other 45-storey skyscrapers, including ones designed by Sir Norman Foster and César Pelli, will join it to transform northern Madrid with apartment blocks, offices and shopping centres. Richard Rogers' new terminal four (T4) for Madrid's Barajas airport opened in 2006 and is a stunning, curvaceous work of art; Spanish architect Carlos Lamela also worked with Rogers on the project. The other major project for urban renewal in Madrid is the transformation of the M-30 beltway along the Río Manzanares in southwestern Madrid into 500,000 sq metres of landscaped greenery; 6km of the motorway is going underground. Some of the most prestigious international firms have tendered for the project.

Another transformational project in recent years has been the extension of the Centro de Arte de Reina Sofía by the French architect Jean Nouvel. It's a stunning red glass-and-steel complement to the old-world Antigua Estación de Atocha across the Plaza del Emperador Carlos V. Other urban renewal projects are regenerating some of Madrid's satellite suburbs such as Carabanchel to the south and Sanchinarro to the north with innovative approaches to the city's urban sprawl.

One truly Madrileño architectural team is the couple Ignacio García Pedrosa and Ángela García de Paredes, whose modern re-design of the Teatro Valle-Inclán (formerly the Teatro Olímpico) in Lavapiés has won huge plaudits. Emilio Tuñón and Luis Mansilla have joined forces to undertake the delicate task of building the Museum of Royal Collections, close to the Palacio Real.

Another important local name (perhaps *the* most important) is the Madrid-based Rafael Moneo who has bravely undertaken to modernise and extend the Museo del Prado. Moneo is no stranger to urban challenges. One of his first major tasks was the construction of the Bankinter building in Madrid in 1976. After the mania of the 1960s for destroying 19th-century mansions and replacing them with bland blocks, Moneo demonstrated another way and thus may have saved old Madrid from disappearing under the crushing weight of a lack of imagination. Apart from international works such as Barcelona's Auditori (1999) and the bizarre, bulging cathedral of Los Angeles (2000), Moneo met another major Madrid challenge with his remodelling of the Antigua Estación de Atocha in 1992. His Prado project involves modernising the main gallery and linking it with the Casón del Buen Retiro and what little remains of the cloisters of the Iglesia de San Jerónimo el Real.

To find out more about the changes underway and those planned for Madrid, the June–July 2005, issue No 478, of *Techniques & Architecture* is entitled 'Madrid: A Challenge' and devoted solely to the Spanish capital. It's available from Naos Libros.

Arts & Architecture

ARCHITECTURE

MADRID'S MOST NOTABLE BUILDINGS

- Palacio Real (p63)
- Centro de Arte Reina Sofía (p80)
- Plaza de la Villa (p64)
- Real Casa de la Panadería (p65)
- Antigua Estación de Atocha (p80)
- Teatro Valle-Inclán (p78)
- Palacio de Comunicaciones (p88)
- Sociedad General de Autores y Editores (p95)
- Plaza de Toros Monumental de las Ventas (p92)
- Edificio Metrópolis (p62)

Other important local and Spanish architects to watch out for include Enric Ruiz-Geli, Francisco Leiva Ivorra, Marta García and José Ignacio de Linazasoro.

And one final thing for those who love architecture: while in Madrid you really must stay at the Hotel Puerta América (p178), where each floor has been custom-designed by a world-renowned architect; the list includes Sir Norman Foster, David Chipperfield, Ron Arad, Zaha Hadid, Jean Nouvel and Arata Isozaki.

LITERATURE

FROM THE SIGLO DE ORO TO PÉREZ GALDÓS

In the late 16th century, Spanish literature took off and writers began to gravitate to the capital. The *Siglo de Oro* (Golden Century) of Spanish writing was very much Madrid's century.

With the exception perhaps of the greatest of all Spanish poets, Seville-born Luis de Góngora (1561–1627), the greatest writers of the age were either born or spent much of their time in the young capital (for playwrights, see p33). Francisco de Quevedo (1580–1645) spent much of his time in Madrid taverns scribbling some of the most biting, nasty and entertaining prose to come out of 17th-century Spain. His *La Historia de la Vida del Buscón Llamado Don Pablos,* tracing the none-too-uplifting life of antihero El Buscón, is laced with venom and is his most lasting work.

Miguel de Cervantes Saavedra (1547–1616), thought of as the father of the novel, was born in Alcalá de Henares and ended his turbulent days in Madrid. He started writing *El Ingenioso Hidalgo Don Quijote de la Mancha* (Don Quixote) as a short story to earn a quick peseta. It turned instead into an epic tale in 1605 and is now widely considered the first and greatest novel of all time, charting the journey of the errant knight and his equally quixotic companion, Sancho Panza, through the foibles of his era.

Benito Pérez Galdós (1843–1920), Spain's Balzac, spent virtually all his adult life in Madrid. His *Fortunata y Jacinta* recounts much more than a tormented love triangle, throwing light on the mores of late 19th-century Madrid.

TOP MADRID NOVELS

- *Fortunata y Jacinta,* Benito Pérez Galdós (1887)
- *La Colmena,* Camilo José Cela (1957)
- *Capital de la Gloria,* Juan Eduardo Zúñiga (2003)
- *Un Corazon tan Blanco (A Heart So White),* Javier Marías (2002)
- *Historias del Kronen,* José Ángel Mañas (1994)

CONTEMPORARY LITERATURE

The censors of Francoist Spain kept a leaking lid on literary development in Spain. Much of what was good in Spanish writing was penned by writers in exile. Since then, there has been a flowering of Spanish letters, and Madrid is at the heart of it.

Although not a Madrileño by birth, Camilo José Cela (1916–2002) wrote one of the most talked about novels on the city in the 1950s, *La Colmena* (The Beehive). This classic takes the reader into the heart of Madrid, the beehive of the title, in what is like a photo album filled with portraits of every kind of Madrid punter in those grey days. Cela took the Nobel Prize in Literature in 1989 and the most important Spanish literature prize, the Premio Cervantes, six years later.

Francisco Umbral (b 1935), a prestigious journalist and winner in 2000 of the Premio Cervantes, is yet another chronicler of the city. *Trilogía de Madrid,* which explores a whole range of different circles of Madrid life in the Franco years, is just one of several Madrid-centric novels to his credit. Some have praised Umbral as the greatest prose writer in Spanish of the 20th century (Cela would no doubt snort in disagreement, as was his wont).

In *Capital de la Gloria,* Juan Eduardo Zúñiga (born 1929) presents a moving portrayal of Madrid and its people in 10 stories set during the last months of Republican resistance against Franco's forces in the Civil War.

Murcia's Arturo Pérez-Reverte (b 1951), long-time war correspondent and general man's man, has become one of the most internationally read Spanish novelists. In *El Capitán Alatriste* (Captain Alatriste) we are taken into the decadent hurly-burly of 18th-century Madrid. The captain in question has become the protagonist of several novels.

The author of *the* cult urban tribal novel in Madrid is without doubt José Ángel Mañas (b 1971). In *Historias del Kronen* a band of young disaffected Madrileños hangs out in the Kronen bar and throws itself into a whirlwind of sex, drugs, violence and rock 'n' roll.

Madrileño Javier Marías (born 1951; www.javiermarias.es in Spanish) is a prolific and critically acclaimed novelist and essayist whose exceptional breadth and quality of work has led many to tip him as a future Nobel Prize winner. His *A Heart So White* (2002), set in Madrid and centring on a tale of subtle family intrigue, shows a miniaturist's eye for detail throughout this outstanding work of digressive and intimate storytelling.

Another emerging talent is José Machado (b 1974), whose *Grillo* is a heavily autobiographical look at a young Madrileño lad of good family determined to be a writer. It's a little like looking into a mirror that looks into a mirror…

Bibliophiles will love being in Madrid around the last week of May and first two weeks of June for the Feria del Libro when hundreds of booksellers from all over Spain set up stalls in the Parque del Buen Retiro.

MUSIC

CLASSICAL & OPERA

Madrid has never been at the forefront of great classical music and opera, and the Spanish composers of note (Isaac Albéniz, Enrique Granados, Joaquín Rodrigo and Manuel de Falla) all came from elsewhere in Spain.

The single obvious exception to the rule is Plácido Domingo (b 1934), the country's leading opera tenor and born *gato* (slang for Madrileño, literally 'cat'). Early childhood was where the charming singer's relationship with Madrid more or less ended, as his parents, *zarzuela* (satirical dance and music) performers, moved to Mexico, where he made his singing debut years later. Along with the Catalan José Carreras, Spain contributed two of the Three Tenors. Other notable opera singers include Montserrat Caballe.

Although not much of what you'll hear in Madrid originates here, you can still find a year-round programme of fine performances to choose from (see p147).

CONTEMPORARY MUSIC

Since the days of *la movida* in the 1980s, Madrid's home-grown rock scene has been vibrant. Seguridad Social is a good old-fashioned hard-rock group that has remained a surprisingly constant force since it first started in 1982. Another legend is rock poet Rosendo Mercado, who started off with the group Leño in the late 1970s, later went solo and hasn't stopped since.

After the delirious 1980s, in which such iconic groups as Radio Futura, El Último de la Fila and Nacha Pop (and punkier ensembles such as Alaska and Kaka de Luxe) came and went, the Madrid pop scene went a little quiet. One enduring group from *la movida*, Mecano, is now the subject of a blockbuster musical, and another to continue in popularity is Dover, a Madrid quartet that belts out energetic indie rock in English.

TOP MUSIC CDS

- *Otros Mares,* Seguridad Social – Good clean rock 'n' roll from Madrid's never-say-die band
- *La Movida de los 80* – All the biggies of *la movida,* including Alaska y Los Pegamoides, Radio Futura and Nacha Pop.
- *Pafuera Telearañas,* Bebe – You can hear the smoky Madrid bar scene in every chord.
- *Canciones Hondas,* Ketama – One of Ketama's best-ever CDs of rocky flamenco fusion; they're miles better than the Gypsy Kings!
- *Pokito a Poko,* Chambao – New flamenco fusion from Spain's hottest group of the moment.

Recently emerged from the rock bar scene in Malasaña is the pop quartet Balboa. Led by guitarist Carlos del Amo and his singer girlfriend Lua Ríos, they've combined the energy of rock with a strong guitar lead and a soft poppy touch in Lua's voice and lyrics.

Not everyone in Madrid is a head-banger. Three years after his band Nacha Pop split, Madrid-born Antonio Vega put out his first solo disc in 1991. Vega was one of the sensations of the mid-1990s with his soft pop-rock.

Another big star to recently emerge from the Madrid bar scene is Nieves Rebolledo, who goes by the stage name of Bebe. Her 2004 *Pafuera Telarañas* became one of the biggest albums of recent years and the signature track 'Malo' (Bad) managed that rare combination of becoming a dance-floor anthem while making serious social commentary (the song is an impassioned denunciation of domestic violence).

Other names enjoying huge popularity on the Spanish music scene include Estopa, La de Van Gogh, Amaral and the enduring Alejandro Sanz.

FLAMENCO

The musical and dance form most readily identified with Spain is rooted in the *cante jondo* (deep song) of the *gitanos* (Roma people) of Andalucía, and probably influenced by North African rhythms.

The melancholy *cante jondo* is performed by a singer, who may be *cantaor* (male) or *cantaora* (female), to the accompaniment of a blood-rush of guitar from the *tocaor* (guitar player). The accompanying dance (not always present) is performed by one or more *bailaores* (flamenco dancers).

Although flamenco emerged in southern Spain, since the mid-19th century, the best performers of flamenco have turned up at one time or another in Madrid. At first, the *gitanos* and Andalucians were concentrated in the area around Calle de Toledo. The novelist Benito Pérez Galdós found no fewer than 88 Andalucian taverns along that street towards the end of the 19th century. The scene shifted in the early 20th century to the streets around Plaza de Santa Ana.

The genre flourished in the 1920s but with the Civil War things went downhill. Not until the 1950s did flamenco come to life again. In those dark years of austere dictatorship, even fun was considered suspect and so the hidden world of smoky cabarets and *tablaos* (flamenco shows) was born. These shows, now often geared to tourists, often lack the genuine, raw emotion of real flamenco, but they're worth seeing. For more information on catching the best spine-tingling live flamenco performances in Madrid, see p145, while a good website

Feel the flamenco on Plaza Mayor (p65)

(in Spanish) for all things flamenco is www.deflamenco.com. To learn more you could also pass by El Flamenco Vive (p158) or Flamenco World (p160), both of which have a wide range of flamenco books and CDs. For flamenco courses, see p210.

FLAMENCO STARS

Paco de Lucía (b 1947) is the world's most famous flamenco guitarist. He has a virtuosity few can match and is the personification of *duende,* that indefinable capacity to transmit the power and passion of flamenco. Following in Paco de Lucía's footsteps are some fine flamenco guitarists, among them members of the Montoya family (some of whom are better known by the sobriquet of Los Habichuela), especially Juan (b 1933) and Pepe (b 1944).

Paco de Lucía's friend, El Camarón de la Isla (1950–92), was, until his death, the leading light of contemporary *cante jondo;* plenty of flamenco singers today try to emulate him.

The story of his life has been made into an excellent movie (*Camarón,* 2005), directed by Jaime Chávarri. Another artist who has reached the level of cult figure is Enrique Morente (b 1942), referred to by a Madrid paper as 'the last bohemian'. A venerable *cantaora* is Carmen Linares (b 1951).

Of Spain's countless flamenco dancers and choreographers, one of the greatest names is with little doubt Antonio Ruiz Soler (1921–96). One of the great all-time *bailaoras* was the fiery Barcelona-born Carmen Amaya (1913–63). Leading contemporary figures include the flighty, adventurous Joaquín Cortés (b 1969), and Antonio Canales (b 1962), who is more of a flamenco purist.

NUEVO FLAMENCO & FUSION

Possibly the most exciting recent developments in flamenco have occurred in its fusion with other musical forms. The purists loathe these changes – in the proud *gitano* world, innovation has often met with abrasive scorn – but a wider Spanish audience has had little hesitation in embracing this innovative musical experimentation.

Two of the earliest groups to fuse flamenco with rock back in the 1980s were Ketama and Pata Negra, whose music is labelled by some as Gypsy rock. Ketama, in particular, have been wide-ranging in their search for complementary sounds and rhythms, and their collaborations with Malian kora (harp) player, Toumani Diabaté *(Songhai I* and *Songhai II)* are underrated works of rare beauty. In the early 1990s, Radio Tarifa emerged with a mesmerising mix of flamenco, North African and medieval sounds. A more traditional flamenco performer, Juan Peña Lebrijano, better known as El Lebrijano, has created some equally appealing combinations with classical Moroccan music. Diego Cigala, one of modern flamenco's finest voices, relaunched his career with an exceptional collaboration with Cuban virtuoso Bebe Valdes (*Lagrimas Negras,* 2004).

More to the liking of flamenco purists willing to countenance a little modernising is Chambao, the most popular of the *nuevo flamenco* bands doing the rounds at the moment. They first captured attention with their 2002 *Flamenco Chill,* and they have just kept getting better with *Endorfinas a la Menta* (2003) and the sublime *Pokito a Poko* (2005). Also popular is Diego Amador (b 1973), a self-taught pianist. The piano is not a classic instrument of flamenco but Amador makes it work.

DANCE

Nacho Duato, head and principal dancer of the Madrid-based Compañía Nacional de Baile (http://cndanza.mcu.es/) since 1990, has transformed it from a low-profile classical company into one of the world's most dazzling and technically accomplished contemporary dance groups. Founded in 1978, the Ballet Nacional de España mixes classical ballet with Spanish dance. Both perform regularly in Madrid and around the country.

One performer that you absolutely must see if your visit coincides with her arrival in town is Sara Baras (www.sarabaras.com), a Cádiz-born performer whose flamenco ballet is unique and soul-stirring. Last time she was in Madrid she played at the Teatro Calderón.

CINEMA & TELEVISION

After the censorship of the Franco years, Spanish cinema emerged with great vitality with Madrid becoming the national film industry's uncontested capital. The annual Goya awards (Spain's Oscars) are held in Madrid in February and are the perfect stage for taking the pulse of the industry.

As elsewhere in Europe, the overwhelming preoccupation in Spain is the crushing predominance of Hollywood blockbusters. Spanish film-making is generally done on modest budgets and manages some great hits, but public funding has been falling for the last decade. Audience numbers remain quite steady, but only between 15% and 20% of box office takings are for Spanish films.

Madrid's senior cinematic bard is Juan Antonio Bardem (1922–2002). He wrote the script for Luis García Berlanga's 1952 classic, *Bienvenido Mr Marshall* (Welcome Mr Marshall), and followed in 1955 with *Muerte de un Ciclista* (Death of a Cyclist). His son, the Oscar-nominated heart-throb Javier, has become one of the best-known faces in Spanish cinema, starring in many local and several foreign flicks, including *Jamón Jamón* and *Before Night Falls*. Although from Spain's Canary Islands, the Bardems are Madrid identities and run a trendy tapas bar, Bardemcilla (Calle de Agusto Figueroa 47), in the inner-city barrio of Chueca.

Luis Buñuel (1900–83) was another film identity obliquely associated with Madrid. He spent part of his formative professional years in Madrid, raising hell with his fellow surrealist Salvador Dalí, although he later spent much of his life in Paris and Mexico. Buñuel became something of a surrealist icon with his 1929 classic *Un Chien Andalou*, on which he collaborated with Dalí. His often-shocking films included *Los Olvidados* (1950) and *Viridiana* (1961) – both won prizes at the Cannes Film Festival, although the latter was banned in Francoist Spain on the grounds of blasphemy.

Fernando Trueba (b 1955) has created some fine Spanish films, the best of which was his 1992 *Belle Epoque*. It portrays gentle romps and bed-hopping on a country estate in Spain in 1931 as four sisters pursue a slightly ingenuous young chap against a background of growing political turbulence. Behind the scenes on this and many Spanish movies is the publicity-shy, Madrid-based Rafael Azcona, surely one of the cinema's most prolific screenplay writers. *Belle Epoque* took an Oscar for Best Foreign Language Film in 1993.

The still-young Alejandro Amenábar (b 1973) was born in Chile but his family moved to Madrid when he was a child and he has since gone on to become one of Spain's most respected directors. He announced his arrival with *Tesis*, but it was with *Abre Los Ojos* (Open Your Eyes, which was later adapted for Hollywood as *Vanilla Sky*) that his name became known internationally. His first English-language film was *The Others* which received critical acclaim, but nothing like the clamour that surrounded *Mar Adentro* (The Sea Inside), his stunning portrayal of a Galician fisherman's desire to die with dignity which starred Javier Bardem. Not content with directing, Amenábar also writes his own films.

Further evidence that Madrid stands at the centre of the Spanish film industry can be found in the fact that Málaga-born Antonio Banderas moved to Madrid to launch his career.

A DIRECTOR LIKE NO OTHER

When Pedro Almodóvar (born 1951) won an Oscar in 2000 for his 1999 hit, *Todo Sobre Mi Madre* (All About My Mother), the world suddenly discovered what Spaniards had known for decades – that Almodóvar was one of world cinema's most creative directors.

Born into a small, impoverished village in Castilla La Mancha, Almodóvar once remarked that in such conservative rural surrounds, 'I felt as if I'd fallen from another planet'. After he moved to Madrid in 1969, he found his spiritual home and began his career making underground Super-8 movies and making a living by selling second-hand goods in El Rastro flea market. He soon became a symbol of Madrid's counter-culture, but it was after Franco's death in 1975 that Almodóvar became a nationally renowned cult figure. His early films *Pepi, Luci, Bom, y Las Otras Chicas del Montón* (Pepi, Luci, Bom and All Those Other Girls; 1980) and *Laberinto de Pasiones* (Labyrinth of Passions; 1982) – the film that brought a young Antonio Banderas to attention – announced him as the icon of *la movida Madrileña* (p54), the explosion of hedonism and creativity in equal measure in the early years of post-Franco Spain. Almodóvar had both in bucketloads; he peppered his films with candy-bright colours and characters leading lives where sex and drugs are the norm. By night Almodóvar performed in Madrid's most famous *movida* bars as part of a drag act called 'Almodóvar & McNamara'. He even appears in this latter role in *Laberinto de Pasiones*.

By the mid-1980s, Madrileños had adopted him as one of the city's most famous sons and he went on to broaden his fan base with such quirkily comic looks at modern Spain, generally set in the capital, as *Mujeres al Borde de un Ataque de Nervios* (Women on the Verge of a Nervous Breakdown; 1988) and *Átame* (Tie Me Up, Tie Me Down; 1990). *All About My Mother* was also notable for the coming of age of the Madrid-born actress Penélope Cruz, who had starred in a number of Almodóvar films and was considered part of a select group of the director's leading ladies long before she became a Hollywood star. Other outstanding movies in a formidable portfolio include *Hable Con Ella* (Talk to Her; 2002), for which he won a Best Original Screenplay Oscar, and *La Mala Educacioñ* (Bad Education; 2004), a twisted story of a drag queen, his brother, an abusive priest and a school–friend–turned–filmmaker, cemented his growing international following.

TOP FILMS SET IN MADRID

Many famous movies have been filmed at least partly in Madrid, among them *Doctor Zhivago, El Cid* and *The Fall of the Roman Empire*. But the following are where Madrid really plays a starring role:

- *La Colmena* (The Beehive; 1982) – Based on the classic novel by Camilo José Cela, this is a faithful rendition of Cela's portrait of a Madrid during the grey years of the 1950s.
- *Historias del Kronen* (1994) – In Montxo Armendariz's film, a slightly depressing story of alienated urban youth emerges from the heart of Madrid.
- *Carne Trémula* (Live Flesh; 1997) – This typically kaleidoscopic love thriller by Pedro Almodóvar contains the usual tortured themes of sex, violence and love, and stars Javier Bardem.
- *La Comunidad* (The Community; 2000) – Directed by the generally wacky Alex de la Iglesia, this cheerfully off-the-wall tale of greed in a Madrid apartment block stars Carmen Maura.
- *Los Fantasmas de Goya* (Goya's Ghosts; 2006) – Set in 1792 Madrid, this recent offering by Milos Forman tells the story of Goya, the Spanish Inquisition and the painter's many scandals; Javier Bardem and Natalie Portman play the lead roles.

More recent comic films that are of the highest quality but which you'll generally only find in Spain include *El Otro Lado de la Cama* (The Other Side of the Bed), *Los Días de Futbol* (Days of Football) and *Crimen Ferpecto* (Perfect Crime), all of which involve the outstanding Guillermo Toledo.

An eminent line-up of some of Spain's best actresses comes from Madrid. They include: Victoria Abril (b 1959), Ana Belén (b 1950), Penélope Cruz (b 1974), Carmen Maura (b 1945) and Maribel Verdú (b 1970). In the late 1990s Penélope Cruz took a leap of faith and headed for Hollywood where she has had success in such films as *Captain Corelli's Mandolin* (2001) and *Vanilla Sky* (2001).

At first glance, Spanish TV may seem to be dominated by clones of international reality TV – especially *Gran Hermano* (Big Brother) and *Operación Triunfo* (which propels singing unknowns to stardom) – or endless gossip programmes dissecting the lives of current celebrities. That's true to a certain extent, but there are some outstanding TV series to look out for. Telecinco's *Los Serrano* (www.losserrano.telecinco.es) is a mostly-comic, sometimes-serious family drama set in a Madrid chalet and featuring some of Spain's best-known movie actors, among them Verónica Sánchez, Antonio Resines and Belén Rueda. Anyone who has spent any time living in a Madrid apartment building will groan with recognition at *Aquí No Hay Quien Viva* (www.antena3.com/aquinohayquienviva/), a funny, fast-paced story of neighbours who know everyone else's business. Another excellent series is *Cuentame Cómo Pasó* (www.cuentamecomopaso.net) which is set in 1970s' Madrid.

THEATRE

The literary *Siglo de Oro* that characterised 17th-century Madrid also filled the sails of theatrical creation with the winds of genius. Some of the country's all-time greatest playwrights were at work in much the same period. One of Madrid's towering literary figures, Lope de Vega (1562–1635), also an exceptional lyric poet, was perhaps the most prolific: more than 300 of the 800 plays and poems attributed to him remain. He explored the falseness of court life and canvassed political subjects with his imaginary historical plays. You can visit his house (p80) even today. In the work of Tirso de Molina (1581–1648), in whose *El Burlador de Sevilla* (The Seducer of Seville) we encounter the immortal Don Juan, a likeable seducer who meets an unhappy end.

Waiting for (a) Madrileño outside Teatro Español (p147)

33

The works of Pedro Calderón de la Barca (1600–81) were laced with agile language and inventive dramatic techniques. His storylines were, however, comparatively run-of-the-mill. His most powerful are *La Vida es Sueño* (Life's a Dream) and *El Alcalde de Zalamea* (The Mayor of Zalamea).

A particularly Spanish genre that originated in Madrid is the *zarzuela*, light-hearted musical comedy in which the actors occasionally burst into song. Although it spread throughout the country in the 19th century it remains a very Madrid phenomenon. The Teatro de la Zarzuela keeps busy with a year-round programme of these melodic social dramas. For more information on this uniquely Spanish drama form, see boxed text, p146; for advice on where to see the best in Spanish theatre, turn to p146.

Food & Drink ∎

Food & Drink

Madrileños love their food. It's not that their own cuisine is anything special – traditionally Madrid's food was simple and hearty, more devoted to fortification against poverty and the extremes of a harsh climate than any gastronomic excitement. Madrileños, however, may disagree and will surely mount a passionate defence of the honour of their cuisine which they love above all others.

But this is a city which grew and became great because of the immigrants from all over Spain who made Madrid their home. On their journey to the capital, these immigrants carried with them recipes and ingredients from their villages, thereby bequeathing to the city an astonishing variety of regional flavours that you just don't find anywhere else. Travel from one Spanish village to the next and you'll quickly learn that each has its own speciality. Travel to Madrid and you'll find them all.

The laws of traditional Spanish cooking are deceptively simple: take the freshest ingredients and interfere with them as little as possible. While the rest of the world were developing sophisticated sauces, Spaniards were experimenting with subtlety, developing a combination of tastes in which the flavour of the food itself was paramount. Nowhere is this more evident than in the art of the humble tapas (bite-sized morsels) where carefully selected meats, seafood or vegetables are given centre stage and allowed to speak for themselves. Such are the foundations on which Spanish cooking is built.

What has happened in recent years is that Spanish chefs have begun to take the world by storm with their own special version of *nouvelle cuisine* which could just be Europe's most exciting culinary innovation. Chefs such as Ferran Adría and Mari Arzak have developed their own culinary laboratories, experimenting with all that is new while holding fast to the ideas of simplicity that defined traditional Spanish cooking. Suddenly the world knows about the mainstays of the Spanish table – paella, tapas, wine from La Rioja, sherry from Jeréz – and, thanks to this new age of culinary innovation, the world is suddenly discovering what it has been missing.

Food may be the centrepiece of Spanish life, but eating in Spain is a major social event, always taken seriously enough to allocate hours for the purpose of eating; and the conviviality of the surroundings and the company are almost as important as the food itself. It's something to share, a reason to get together with friends and family. Combined with the great food, that's why Spaniards spend more on food per capita than anyone else in Europe.

HISTORY & CULTURE

Medieval Madrid was a simple place. On the bleak plains of inland Spain, food was a necessity, good food was a luxury and the dishes which developed were functional and well-suited to a climate dominated by interminable, bitterly cold winters. Most Madrileños scraped by on a limited diet, the staple of which was cereals (often barley). Bread was a rarity, as was meat. Fruit and vegetables, typically grown along the Manzanares, were by no means available to all. Olive oil, a standard element of much Mediterranean cooking and an integral part of the Muslim diet, was an expensive luxury to Madrileños. In such a calorie-poor diet, wine played an important nutritional role, but even that was in chronically short supply.

Elsewhere in Spain, climate also played an important role and food was what would later become known as typically Mediterranean, liberal in its use of olive oil, garlic, onions, tomatoes and peppers. The country's long history of Muslim occupation was reflected in the use of spices such as saffron and cumin and, in desserts, the predominance of honeyed sweets. The high place accorded to almonds and fruit also betrays a lasting Muslim influence. Spain was also the centre of an empire and from its South American colonies came potatoes and tomatoes (not to mention coffee and chocolate).

As traders, pilgrims and journeymen headed to the capital or elsewhere, they holed up in inns where innkeepers, concerned about drunken men on horseback setting out from their village developed a tradition of putting a *tapa* (lid) atop a glass of wine or beer, partly to keep the bugs out, but primarily to encourage people not to drink on an empty stomach. Thus it was that tapas became an essential part of the Spanish eating experience.

As Spain grew in wealth, meat (especially roasts) became an integral ingredient of the Spanish table, particularly inland where game became common. Roast lamb or suckling pig still dominate the cuisine of Castile, especially in winter. The obsession with *jamón* (ham), not to mention chorizo, *lomo* (loin, usually pork) and *salchichón* (salami-like sausage), came from the south (as did olives) and was, like most things, embraced with enthusiasm by Madrileños.

Thus it is that the Spanish table has come to encompass such variety. From the Basque Country come *bacalao pil pil* (salted cod in garlic and oil), *pimientos rellenos* (capsicums stuffed with all manner of seafood), *chipirones en su tinta* (squid in its own ink) and *chuletas de buey* (enormous steaks). In recent years, *nouvelle cuisine Vasca* (Basque) has moved Spanish cooking into previously uncharted territory, although the Catalans are equally cutting edge and seriously inventive.

From Valencia came the paella, at its best a huge pan of saffron-coloured rice dripping with morsels of seafood. From the rainy north came cheeses, pungent or subtle, of extraordinary variety. Along Spain's Atlantic Coast in north-eastern Galicia (and from the south in Andalucía), *pescado* (fish) and *marisco* (seafood) became staples, especially tuna, squid, octopus, shellfish and a whole host of sea creatures you never imagined in your wildest dreams.

It all meets in Madrid, one of the biggest fish- and seafood-consuming cities in the world (although it is landlocked). Indeed, it is often said that Madrid is the best 'port' in Spain because the best seafood arrives fresh daily from both the Atlantic and Mediterranean fishing fleets. In the early days, this meant *bacalao* (salted cod) was carried by horse-drawn cart from the coast. Nowadays, tonnes of fish and seafood are trucked in daily from Mediterranean and Atlantic ports to satisfy the Madrileño taste for the sea. *Bacalao* remains king, but other favoured fish in Madrid are *merluza* (hake) and *besugo* (sea bream).

Vegetarians, and especially vegans, can have a hard time in Spain, but as the eating habits of Spaniards change, Madrid becomes home to an ever-growing selection of vegetarian restaurants.

ETIQUETTE

Before we talk about eating Spanish-style, it's necessary to first talk briefly about Spanish waiters. In smarter places, waiters are often young, attentive and switched on to the needs of patrons. In more traditional places, waiting is a career, often a poorly paid one, which is the preserve of old men (sometimes one old man) in white jackets and bow ties and for whom service with a smile is not part of the job description. In such places, they shuffle amid the tables, the weight of the world upon their shoulders, struggling with what seems a Sisyphean task. Getting their attention can be a challenge. Somewhere in between are the old barmen of Madrid who are as informal as they are informed and who love to shout their orders to the kitchen and generally create a breezy, infectiously casual atmosphere.

If you're eating just tapas – which Spaniards generally eat between meals, as an accompaniment to a drink or as a prelude to the main event – in many bars you can either take a small plate and help yourself or point to the morsel you want. If you do this, it is customary to keep track of what you eat (by holding on to the toothpicks for example) and then tell the barman when it comes time to pay. If you particularly like something you

Al-fresco dining on a terraza in Sol (p114)

can have a *media ración* (half ration) or even a full *ración* – most bars have menus listing what's available. In some bars you'll also get a small (free) *tapa* when you buy a drink.

A full meal generally comprises an *entrante* (starter), *plato principal* (main course) and *postre* (dessert). You can skip the starter and/or dessert without causing offence. Bread is routinely served with meals, but you pay extra for it (usually around €1.20) so let the waiter know if you don't want it.

Once your order is taken and the first course arrives, you may find service accelerates disconcertingly. This especially becomes the case as you reach the end of any given course. Hovering waiters (where were they when you wanted to see the menu?) swoop like lean eagles to swipe your unfinished dish or lift your glass of wine, still tinged with that last sip you wanted to savour. *'Todavía no he terminado'* ('I haven't finished yet') you may point out, but you'll be flashed a cheerful smile and your waiter will be off.

In simpler restaurants you may keep the same knife and fork throughout the meal. As each course is finished you set the cutlery aside and the waiter whisks away the plates.

Dessert depends on where you're eating. In your average simple Madrid eatery, you might get an apple or banana and a knife. If there's ice cream, it's probably of the sort you'd grab at the beach. In more sophisticated restaurants, desserts are pretty similar to what you'd find back home. Sadly, the delicious pastries that Madrileños love so much rarely appear on restaurant menus – they're for buying in *pastelerías* and savouring at home.

Don't jump out of your seats if people passing your table address you with a hearty *'buen provecho!'* They're just saying 'Enjoy your meal!'

And if you're in a bar, don't be surprised to see people throwing their serviettes and olive stones on the floor – you might as well join them because a waiter will come around from time to time to sweep them all up.

HOW MADRILEÑOS EAT

Most visitors complain not about the quality of Spanish food but its timing. *Comida/almuerzo* (lunch) rarely begins before 2pm (restaurant kitchens usually stay open until 4pm) and for *cena* (dinner), few Madrileños would dream of turning up before 9.30pm. On weekends some restaurants take reservations for two sittings, one starting at 9pm, the other at 11pm! Stay in Madrid long enough and you'll get used to it, and wonder how you lived any other way.

In the meantime, many bars serve tapas and *raciones* throughout the day. *Bocadillos* (filled rolls, usually without butter) are another option.

Desayuno (breakfast) is generally a no-nonsense affair taken at a bar on the way to work. A *café con leche* (half coffee and half warm milk) with a *bollo* (pastry) is the typical breakfast. Croissants or a cream-filled pastry are also common. Some people prefer a savoury start – try a *sandwich mixto,* a toasted ham and cheese; a Spanish *tostada* is simply buttered toast. Others, especially party animals heading home at dawn after a night out, go for an all-Spanish favourite, *churros y chocolate,* a deep-fried stick of plain pastry immersed in thick hot chocolate.

For those of you accustomed to grabbing a quick sandwich at lunchtime, Spanish lunches – the main meal of the day – may come as a shock. As modern work and living habits change for Madrileños, many no longer linger for hours over their afternoon meal during the week, but they're still likely to eat a three-course meal. On weekends, they revert to type and can spend a whole afternoon around the lunch table.

The traveller's friend is the *menú del día,* a set-price meal which comprises three courses, with bread, a drink (usually wine and water but coffee is extra) thrown in and generally only available at lunchtime Monday to Friday. You can often find them for around €10. You'll be given a menu with five or six starters, the same number of mains and a handful of desserts – choose one from each category and don't even think of mixing and matching.

Believe it or not, these cut-price lunches are not designed primarily for tourists. During the working week, few Madrileños have time to go home for lunch. Taking a packed lunch is just not the done thing, so most people end up eating in restaurants and all-inclusive three-course meals are as close as they can come to eating home-style food without breaking the bank. That's why across Madrid you'll find what are known as *casas de comida* – busy little restaurants that look like an expanded version of your grandmother's dining room and are rarely signposted as restaurants (they often just have a menu at the door). The meals are simple but hearty, the sort of thing that Madrileños might cook for themselves at home, and prices for the *menú del día* can be as low as €6.

If you can't face a full menu, a simpler option is the *plato combinado,* basically a meat-and-three-veg dish that will hardly excite taste buds but will have little fiscal impact. Prices vary, but are usually between €8 and €12.

If Spaniards have eaten a big meal at lunchtime, they may choose to *tapear* or *ir de tapeo* (go on a tapas crawl) in the evening. The situation changes somewhat on weekends when Madrid's restaurants are filled to bursting by Madrileños in the evening (many eat lunch at home with their family), either for its own sake or as a prelude to a night of revelry.

STAPLES & SPECIALITIES

Despite the innovations and outside influences sweeping Spain's kitchens, Madrileños are still proud of their cuisine and indeed eat it whenever they can.

When the weather turns chilly, that means *legumbres* (legumes) such as *garbanzos* (chickpeas), *judias* (beans) and *lentejas* (lentils). Hearty stews are the order of the day and there are none more hearty than *cocido a la Madrileña;* it's a kind of hotpot or stew which starts with a noodle broth and is followed by, or combined with – there are as many ways of eating *cocido* as there are Madrileños – carrots, chickpeas, chicken, *morcilla* (blood sausage) beef, lard and possibly other sausage meats too. *Repollo* (cabbage) sometimes makes an appearance. Madrileños love *cocido.* They dream of it while they're away from home and they wonder why it hasn't caught on elsewhere. There was even a hit song written about it in the 1950s. However, we'll put this as gently as we can: you have to be a Madrileño to understand what all the fuss is about because it may be filling but it's not Spain's most exciting dish.

Other popular staples in Madrid include *cordero asado* (roast lamb), *patatas con huevos fritos* (baked potatoes with eggs), *tortilla de patatas* (a thick potato omelette) and endless variations on *bacalao.*

Otherwise, the basics in Spanish cooking are simple enough: bread, olive oil and lots of garlic. Spices, on the other hand, are generally noticeable by their absence. If you're told something is *picante* (spicy, hot) it's likely to be little more than mild.

The typical *carta* (menu) begins with starters such as *ensaladas* (salads), *sopas* (soups) and *entremeses* (hors d'oeuvres). The latter can range from a mound of potato salad with olives, asparagus, anchovies and a selection of cold meats – almost a meal in itself – to simpler cold meats, slices of cheese and olives.

The basic ingredients of later courses can be summarised under the general headings of *pollo* (chicken), *carne* (meat), *mariscos, pescado* and *arroz* (rice). Meat may be subdivided into *cerdo* (pork), *ternera* (beef) and *cordero* (lamb). If you want a side order *(guarnición),* such as vegetables *(verduras)* you may have to order separately.

If you opt for tapas, it's handy to identify some of the common items: *boquerones* (white anchovies in vinegar which are delicious and tangy); *albóndigas* (good old meat balls); *pimientos de Padrón* (little green peppers from Galicia – some are hot and some not); *patatas bravas* (potato chunks bathed in a slightly hot red sauce); *gambas* (prawns, either done *al ajillo,* with garlic, or *a la plancha,* grilled); *chipirones* (baby squid, served in various ways); *calamares a la Romana* (deep-fried calamari rings)…the list goes on.

DRINKS

NONALCOHOLIC

For tap water (which is safe to drink) in restaurants, ask for *agua de grifo. Agua mineral* (bottled water) comes in innumerable brands, either *con gas* (fizzy) or *sin gas* (still).

Coffee, Tea & Hot Chocolate

The coffee in Spain is strong and slightly bitter. A *café con leche* (generally drunk at breakfast only) is about half coffee and half hot or *templada* (tepid) milk. Ask for *grande* or *doble* if you want a large cup, *en vaso* if you want a smaller shot in a glass, or a *sombra* if you want lots of milk. A *café solo* (usually just *un solo*) is a short black; *un (café) cortado* is a short black with a little milk (*macchiato* in Italy). For iced coffee, ask for *café con hielo;* you'll get a glass of ice and a hot cup of black coffee, to be poured over the ice.

Madrileños prefer coffee, but you can get hold of many different styles of *té* (tea) and *infusiones* (herbal teas such as camomile). Locals tend to drink tea black. If you want milk, ask for it to come separately *(a parte).*

A cup of *chocolate caliente* (hot chocolate) is an invitation to sticky fingers – it's dark and sweet and so thick you could stand your spoon up in it.

Fruit & Soft Drinks

Zumo de naranja (orange juice) is the main freshly squeezed juice available, often served with sugar. To make sure you're getting the real thing, ask for the juice to be *natural.*

Refrescos (cool drinks) include the usual international brands of soft drinks, local brands such as Kas, and, in summer, *granizado* (iced fruit crush).

A *batido* is a flavoured milk drink or milk shake. *Horchata* is a Valencian drink of Islamic origin. Made from the juice of *chufa* (tiger nuts), sugar and water, it's sweet and tastes like soya milk with a hint of cinnamon. A naughtier version is a *cubanito* and involves adding a fat dollop of chocolate ice cream.

ALCOHOLIC
Wine

Although beer drinking now outstrips wine, Spain remains a wine-drinking country and *vino* (wine) accompanies almost every meal. They even have a saying to convince the sceptics: *comer sin vino, comer mosquino* (a meal without wine is a stingy one).

ONE FOR THE ROAD

Spaniards can be a superstitious lot so there's one rule of drinking etiquette to be mindful of: never suggest having just one last drink. Madrileños almost always order the *penúltima* (next but last), even if it's really the last of the evening. To mention the *última* (last) is bad luck; it sounds like one's last drink on earth. Of course, the problem with ordering a *penúltima* is that it frequently leads to ordering another.

Buzzing bar-nightlife (p133) in central Madrid

Most of the best Spanish wine, whether *blanco* (white), *tinto* (red), or *rosado* (rosé), is produced in the north of the country, especially in La Rioja whose wines (mostly reds) are acquiring a reputation as some of the best in Europe. Not far behind are the wine-producing regions of Ribera del Duero and Navarra while the Valdepeñas area of southern Castilla-La Mancha has less variety but is generally well-priced and remains popular. For white wines, the Ribeiro wines of Galicia are well regarded, and have traditionally been popular, while the Penedès area in Catalonia produces whites and sparkling wine such as *cava,* the traditional champagnelike toasting drink of choice for Spaniards at Christmas. Jeréz sherry is the most famous alcoholic drink to emerge from Andalucía, while *sidra* (cider) is a Basque staple that has caught on elsewhere. All are widely available in Madrid.

Spanish wine is subject to a complicated system of wine classification, ranging from the straightforward *vino de mesa* (table wine) to *vino de la tierra,* which is a wine from an officially recognised wine-making area. If they meet certain strict standards for a given period, they receive DO (Denominación de Origen) status. An outstanding

THE SECRET LANGUAGE OF BEER

To slake your thirst at the bar you can just ask for a *cerveza* (beer) but it's better to give the bartender an idea of exactly what you're after.

The most common order is a *caña*, a *vaso* (small glass) of *cerveza de barril* (draught beer). In the heat of the summer, this is the best way to make sure they keep coming cold. A larger beer (about 300mL), more common in the hipper bars and clubs, usually comes in a *tubo* (a long, straight glass).

The equivalent of a pint is a *jarra,* unless of course you're in a pseudo-Irish pub, in which case you can also ask for a *pinta*.

If you just ask for a *cerveza* you may get bottled beer, which is more expensive. A small bottle of beer is called a *botellín* or *quinto* because it contains a fifth of a litre. A larger one (330mL) is often referred to as a *tercio* (as in a third of a litre).

A *clara* is a shandy, a beer cut with *gaseosa,* which is virtually the same as Sprite (pronounced in Spain e-sprite) or 7-Up.

Some bars also provide extremely large plastic beakers of beer (usually for the younger crowd); with no little irony, these huge containers are called *minis*. The beer is not always great (and often watered down), but it's cheap and abundant.

wine region gets the DOC (Denominación de Origen Calificada) while *reserva* and *gran reserva* are other indications of quality. The only DOC wines come from the Rioja region in northern Spain, which was demarcated in 1926, and the small Priorat area in Catalonia.

The young, light *vinos de Madrid* from the surrounding region have DO standing and some aren't bad at all, although the Comunidad de Madrid is not renowned for its quality wine production.

A drinkable bottle of table wine can easily be found for around €3 to €4 in supermarkets and wine merchants (especially the old kind, where they'll fill your bottle for you). In restaurants, apart from *vino de la casa* (house wine), you'll be looking at an average of €10 for a reasonable bottle and considerably more for something classy. You can also order wine by the *copa* (glass) in bars and restaurants.

Perhaps because their own wine is so good, Spaniards are not the most adventurous when it comes to foreign wines. A small selection is sold in some wine shops and the supermarket section of El Corte Inglés, but they rarely appear on restaurant menus.

Beer

If Madrid could be said to have a flagship drink, it would be lager-style beer. The most widespread local draught and bottled brand is Mahou, first produced in Madrid by a French entrepreneur in 1890. Cruzcampo is a lighter beer.

Otherwise, two Catalan companies, Damm and San Miguel, each produce about 15% of all Spain's beer. San Miguel is common; Damm's main brand, Estrella, is a little harder to come by. Plenty of foreign beers are also available.

Other Drinks

Sangria is a red wine–and-fruit punch (usually with lemon, orange and cinnamon), sometimes laced with brandy. It's refreshing going down but too many on a summer's afternoon can have a soporific effect and leave you with a sore head. The origins of sangria date back to the days when wine quality was not always the best and the vinegary taste needed a sweetener to make it palatable. Another version you might come across is *tinto de verano,* a mix of wine and Casera, a brand of *gaseosa* (lemonade).

There's no shortage of imported and Spanish-produced top-shelf stuff – *coñac* (brandy) is popular. Larios is a common brand of gin although it gets mixed reviews from resident Brits.

If you've ordered a *whisky con Coca-Cola* (whisky with Coke), you'll be expected to watch while the bartender pours your whisky…and continues pouring until you tell them to stop. You pay no extra regardless of the amount! Foreign whiskies are widely available, but Dyc (known locally as El Segoviano) is cheaper and fine if you're mixing it with coke.

Madrileños have also fallen in love with the *mojito,* a Cuban, rum-based drink with lashings of mint.

You will on occasion be asked if you'd like a *chupito* to round off a meal (usually it's on the house). This is a little shot of liqueur or liquor and the idea is to help digestion. Popular and refreshing Spanish ones are *licor de manzana verde* (green apple liqueur), *licor de melocotón* (peach) or *pacharán* (made from the sloe berry).

Madrid's emblematic drink, but one few locals actually bother with, is *licor de madroño* (strawberry-tree liqueur), a light-brown, high-octane drop extracted from the fruit of Madrid's symbolic strawberry tree.

Anisado de Chinchón is a very popular *anis* (aniseed-based drink) produced in the town of the same name south of Madrid. If you wander into a Galician restaurant you might come across their version of grappa, a clear firewater made with crushed grapes called *orujo.*

History

History

Madrid may be one of the great European cities of the 21st century but its glory days were a long time coming. Unlike Paris or Rome, Madrid was transformed gradually from an obscure backwater when it became capital in 1561 into a centre of empire, the focal point of one of modern Europe's most tumultuous historical tales and a magnet for immigrants who would make this the most Spanish of Spain's cities. The end result is a tolerant, sophisticated city that could just be Europe's most exciting.

THE RECENT PAST

On 11 March 2004, just three days before the country was due to vote in national elections, Madrid was rocked by 10 bombs on three rush-hour commuter trains heading into the capital's Atocha station. When the dust cleared, 191 people had died and 1400 were wounded, many of them seriously. It was the biggest such terror attack in the nation's history and it left the city deeply traumatised.

Some 36 hours after the attacks, more than three million Madrileños streamed onto the streets to protest against the bombings, making it the largest demonstration in Madrid's history. A further eight million marched in solidarity in cities across Spain.

Given the history of ETA violence, it came as no surprise that the ruling right-wing Partido Popular (PP; Popular Party) government insisted that Euskadi Ta Askatasuna (ETA; Basque Homeland and Liberty) was responsible. But as evidence mounted that the attack might have come from a radical Islamic group in reprisal for the government's unswerving support for the deeply unpopular invasion of Iraq, angry Spaniards turned against the government.

11 MARCH 2004 – A SPECIAL SILENCE Anthony Ham

There has never been a day quite like it in Madrid. Throughout Thursday 11 March 2004, an eerie silence reigned over a city long renowned as the most raucous and vibrant in Europe; the quietness of this day was profoundly unsettling, in part because of the devastating bombings which had caused it, but also because this is a city with a joyous disregard for noise.

The silence was broken only by the sirens of emergency vehicles and the sound of circling helicopters. As they laid out the bodies alongside the tracks at Madrid's Atocha station, many emergency workers stood in anguish, trying to decide whether to answer the ringing mobile phones of the victims. At the makeshift morgue on the outskirts of the city, an emotion-filled voice read out over a loudspeaker to the waiting families the names of those who had died.

And then there was the sound of a million mobile phones, as Madrileños overloaded mobile networks trying frantically to track down family and friends. After a desperate two hours spent trying to reach my wife's family – we knew that they had been close-by when the bombings took place – I finally got through. Suddenly, I found myself unable to speak.

Yet even these sounds could not drown out the silence of the empty bars, of normally clamorous streets filled with people standing in silence.

On Friday night, we joined the massive crowds on the streets of Madrid and together we marched past the wrought-iron balconies draped with Spanish flags – each tied with a black ribbon – or simply stood silently in the rain. Chants rose up, among them the defiant 'Se nota, se siente, Madrid esta presente' (You can see it, you can feel it, Madrid is here).

It took almost three hours to travel the 3km from Plaza de Colon to Atocha station. When this angry, grieving crowd, whose march had taken on the quality of a pilgrimage, reached its destination close to where the bombs had exploded, we all broke into spontaneous rounds of applause. And before the haunting silence of the Madrileños again took hold, there was one last resounding cry: 'ibamos todos en ese tren' (we were all on that train).

TIMELINE 854

854	1309
Muhammad I, emir of Córdoba, establishes fortress of Magerit (Mayrit)	The Cortes (royal court and parliament) sits for the first time in Madrid

44

In a stunning reversal of prepoll predictions, the PP was defeated by the Partido Socialista Obrero Español (PSOE; Spanish Socialist Workers' Party), whose leader José Luis Rodríguez Zapatero led the Socialists back to power after eight years in the wilderness.

For all the tragedy of March 2004, visit today and you'll find a city that has resolutely returned to normal. Bars and restaurants overflow with happy crowds and people throng the streets as they always have. Yes, security is a little tighter than before, but it's no more than in most other European cities.

The only reminder of the bombings is the poignant Bosque de los Ausentes (Forest of the Absent; p88) in the Parque del Buen Retiro, which was planted as a memorial to the victims.

The other ongoing fall-out from the events of March 2004 is the presence of a Socialist government at a national level. In addition to withdrawing Spanish troops from Iraq, the new government introduced a raft of liberalising social reforms. Gay marriage was legalised, Spain's arcane divorce laws overhauled and, in 2005, almost a million illegal immigrants were granted residence. Although Spain's powerful Catholic Church has cried foul over many of the reforms (especially the legalisation of gay marriage, the introduction of fast-track divorce and changes to teaching religion in schools), the changes played well with most Spaniards, ensuring the government remained one of the most popular of recent times.

The national government's negotiations with the Basque Country and Catalonia over the emotive issue of greater autonomy was, however, less popular, suggesting that future national political contests could go either way.

At a city level, it comes as a surprise to many visitors that free-swinging Madrid is ruled by a conservative right-wing government. The PP's Alberto Ruiz-Gallardón won the mayoral elections with an absolute majority in May 2003. His colleague, Esperanza Aguirre, became the country's first ever woman regional president in close-run elections for the Comunidad de Madrid in October 2003. But despite belonging to the same party, their political marriage has not always been a happy one and Aguirre makes little attempt to mask her dislike of Ruiz-Gallardón.

Aguirre is a tough right-wing PP member who served as a senator – at the 1996 general elections she won 1.6 million votes, more than any other woman senator in Spanish history – and as national education and culture minister in José María Aznar's first PP government.

Ruiz-Gallardón, on the other hand, comes unmistakeably from the liberal wing of the party. Although his popularity plummeted in 2005 due to the disruption caused by a staggering 67 major infrastructure projects underway at the same time, Ruiz-Gallardón is being touted as a politician to watch. Undaunted by Madrid's failure to win the 2012 Olympic Games, he has promised that Madrid will bid for the 2020 Games.

FROM THE BEGINNING

Amid the bustle of modern Madrid, it can be difficult to imagine the scene that must have greeted the nomads who gathered along the banks of the Río Manzanares in Mesolithic and Neolithic times. If they came from the desolate plains that lie to the south or east, even Madrid's less-than-mighty river must have seemed like paradise and the rocky bluff where Madrid would later be founded, and where the Palacio Real now stands, must have offered welcome shelter amid a landscape of unrelenting monotony. If they came from the mountains in the north or west, this combination of river and rocky perch must have felt like the last place of safety before crossing the vast plateau of central Iberia. They weren't tempted to stay, however, and Madrid was nothing more than a way-station en route elsewhere.

Later, when Madrid would become the capital of an empire on which the sun never set, imperial hagiographers would argue that Madrid was the site of a Roman city called

1479	1520
Isabel, Queen of Castile, marries Fernando, king of Aragón; the two become the Catholic monarchs of Spain	Madrid and Toledo rebel against Carlos I

TOP BOOKS ON THE HISTORY OF MADRID

- *Madrid,* Elizabeth Nash (2001) – An informative, entertaining and joyfully written account of various aspects of the city's past and present.
- *A Travellers Companion to Madrid,* Hugh Thomas (2005) – A fascinating compendium of extracts about Madrid from the great and the good.
- *The New Spaniards,* John Hooper (1995) – A highly readable account of the Franco years and the country's transition to democracy with Madrid taking centre stage.
- *Franco,* Paul Preston (1995) – The definitive English-language biography of the man who dominated 20th-century Spain.
- *Atlas Ilustrado de la Historia de Madrid,* Pedro López Carcelén (2004) – Charts Madrid's growth into a modern metropolis using historical maps and clear, Spanish text.

Mantua Carpetana. It's true that the Romans saw Iberia as part of their plans for world domination, sent armies onto the peninsula to subdue the Celtiberian tribes who roamed the interior and even founded cities such as Toletum (Toledo) and Complutum (near present-day Alcalá de Henares). But the truth is that the Romans never really bothered with Madrid.

Such historical revisionism was considered necessary to mask the fact that the capital of all things Spanish actually began life as a Muslim garrison settlement.

CAUGHT IN THE MIDDLE

The Muslim invasion in the 8th century, which displaced the Visigoths, gave rise to one of the greatest of all medieval empires but it would also convulse the Iberian Peninsula for more than 700 years.

In 756 the emirate of Córdoba was established in the south of what the Muslims called Al-Andalus. Córdoba, which was a beacon of religious tolerance, would cover much of the peninsula until the beginning of the 9th century.

As Iberia's Christians began the Reconquista (Reconquest) – the centuries-long campaign by Christian forces to reclaim the peninsula – the Muslims of Al-Andalus constructed a chain of fortified positions through the heart of Iberia. One of these forts was built by Muhammad I, emir of Córdoba, in 854, on the site of what would become Madrid.

The name they gave to the new settlement was Magerit (or Mayrit), which comes from the Arabic word *majira,* meaning water channel. At first, Magerit was merely one of a string of such forts across the so-called Middle March, a frontier land between the core of Al-Andalus in the south and the small Christian kingdoms of the north. The Middle March's capital was Toledo.

As the Reconquista gathered strength, forts such as Magerit grew in significance as part of a defensive line against Christian incursion. The garrison of Magerit became an island in a sea of hostile territory.

Wander down to the last remaining fragment of the Muralla Árabe (Arab Wall), below the modern Catedral de Nuestra Señora de la Almudena, and you can still get a sense of this isolated settlement surrounded by sweeping plains. In place of the Palacio Real stood the fort (*al-qasr* – hence the Spanish *alcázar*) which occupied the high ground, making it virtually impregnable from the north, west and south. Huddled behind the citadel walls to the south was a tiny tangle of lanes known as the *al-mudayna* (hence Almudena) in which soldiers lived with their families. The eastern side, where Plaza de Oriente is now, was more heavily fortified, thereby giving rise to Magerit's growing sense of insecurity.

Magerit's strategic location in the centre of the peninsula drew an increasing number of soldiers and traders. To accommodate the many newcomers, Magerit grew into a town.

1561	1702
Felipe II establishes his permanent court at Madrid, a town of 30,000 people	Felipe V is crowned, beginning the Bourbon dynasty that still rules Spain

South of what is now Calle de Segovia (then a stream), in the Vistillas area, emerged the busiest of the *arrabales* (suburbs beyond the city walls). To this day the warren of streets around Vistillas is known as the *morería* – Moorish quarter. The main mosque was built on what is now the corner of Calle Mayor and Calle de Bailén, although nothing remains of it.

When the emirate of Córdoba broke up into a series of smaller Muslim kingdoms called *taifas* in 1008, Magerit was attached to Toledo. Across Iberia, the armies of Muslim and Christian Spain battled for supremacy but Magerit was not considered one of the great prizes and for all its fortifications, it would pass into Christian hands without a fight. In 1085, Toledo's ruler gave Magerit to King Alfonso VI of Castile in return for assistance in capturing Valencia.

A MEDIEVAL CHRISTIAN OUTPOST

Madrid may have passed from one empire to another but it continued much as it had before. Little more than a large village, it was ruled over by less-than-interested and distant rulers and existed in the shadow of more established nearby cities such as Segovia and Toledo. Whereas other Castilian cities received generous *fueros* (self-rule ordinances), Madrid had to content itself with occasional, offhand royal decrees. Left largely to their own devices, a small number of local families set about governing themselves, forming Madrid's first town council, the Consejo de Madrid. Just as the city began to attain some semblance of second-rate respectability, the horrors of the Black Death in 1348 struck, devastating the population.

In the same year, the Castilian king began to tire of Madrid's growing independence and appointed *regidores* (governors) of Madrid and other cities in an attempt to tighten central control. A handful of families (the Luzóns, Vargases and others) began to monopolise local power, ruling as petty oligarchs through a feudal system of government, the Comunidad de Villa y Tierra, in which the *villa* (town) lorded it over the peasants who worked the surrounding *tierra* (land).

The travelling Cortes (royal court and parliament) sat in Madrid for the first time in 1309. This first sign of royal favour was followed by others – Madrid (or rather the *alcázar*) was an increasingly popular residence with the Castilian monarchs, particularly Enrique IV. They found it a relaxing base from which to set off on hunting expeditions, especially for bears in the El Pardo district.

Despite the growing evidence of royal attention, medieval Madrid remained dirt-poor and small-scale. As one 15th-century writer observed, 'in Madrid there is nothing except what you bring with you'. It simply bore no comparison with other major Spanish, let alone European, cities.

Beyond the small-world confines of Madrid, however, Spain was being convulsed by great events that would ultimately transform Madrid's fortunes. The marriage of Isabel and Fernando united Christian Spain for the first time. Together they expelled the last of the Muslim rulers from Granada, financed Christopher Columbus' voyages of American discovery and ordered the expulsion of Jews who would not convert to Christianity from Spain – all in 1492.

Carlos I, the grandson of Isabel and Fernando, became the King of Spain in 1516. Three years later he succeeded to the Habsburg throne and so became Carlos V, Holy Roman Emperor. His territories stretched from Austria to the Netherlands and from Spain to the American colonies, but with such a vast territory to administer, he spent only 16 years of his 40-year reign in Spain. The Spanish nobility were not amused and rose up in what came to be known as the rising of the *Comuneros*. In March 1520 Toledo rebelled and Madrid closely followed suit. After a year of fighting, Carlos and his forces prevailed, whereupon he retaliated by concentrating ever-more power in his own hands.

1808	1813
Napoleonic troops under General Murat march into Madrid and Joseph Bonaparte, Napoleon's brother, is crowned King of Spain	French troops expelled from Spain at the Battle of Vitoria

A CAPITAL CHOICE

When Felipe II decided to make Madrid Spain's capital in 1561, it was not the most obvious of choices and other cities seemed eminently more qualified. Madrid had a population of just 30,000 people, whereas Toledo and Seville could each boast more than 80,000. Even Valladolid, the capital of choice for Isabel and Fernando, had 50,000 inhabitants. What's more, in the 250 years since 1309, Madrid had hosted Spain's travelling road show of royalty – a custom necessitated by the demands of the Reconquista – just 10 times, far less than Spain's other cities of eminence.

Madrid's apparent obscurity may, however, explain precisely why Felipe II chose it as the permanent seat of his court. Valladolid was considered to be of questionable loyalty. Toledo, which like Madrid stands close to the geographical heart of Spain (Felipe II wanted the capital to be 'a city fulfilling the function of a heart located in the middle of the body'), was known for its opinionated nobles and powerful clergy who had shown an annoying tendency to oppose the king's whims and wishes. In contrast, more than one king had described Madrid as 'very noble and very loyal'. By choosing Madrid, Felipe II was choosing the path of least resistance.

The decision saved Madrid from a life of provincial obscurity. This was most evident in 1601 when Felipe III, tired of Madrid, moved the court to Valladolid. Within five years, the population of Madrid halved. The move was so unpopular that the king, realising the error of his ways, returned to Madrid. 'Sólo Madrid es corte' (roughly, 'Only Madrid can be home to the court') became the catchcry and thus it has been ever since.

A TALE OF TWO CITIES

By the time that Carlos' son and successor, Felipe II, ascended the Spanish throne in 1556, Madrid was surrounded by walls that boasted 130 towers and six stone gates, but these fortifications were largely built of mud and designed more to impress than provide any meaningful defence of the city.

Such modest claims to significance notwithstanding, Madrid was chosen by Felipe II as the capital of Spain in 1561.

Suddenly thrust into the spotlight, Madrid took considerable time to grow into its new role. Felipe II was more concerned with the business of empire and building his monastic retreat at San Lorenzo de el Escorial than developing Madrid. Despite a handful of elegant churches, the imposing *alcázar* and a smattering of noble residences, Madrid consisted, for the most part, of precarious, whitewashed houses that were little more than mud huts. They lined chaotic, ill-defined and largely unpaved lanes and alleys. The monumental Paseo del Prado, which now provides Madrid with so much of its grandeur, was nothing more than a small creek.

With more ostentatiousness than class, Madrid's indolent royal court retreated from reality and embarked on an era of decadence. Amid the squalor in which the bulk of Madrid's people toiled, royalty and the aristocracy gave themselves over to sickening displays of wealth and cavorted happily in their make-believe world of royal splendour. The sumptuous Palacio del Buen Retiro was completed in 1630 and replaced the *alcázar* as the prime royal residence (the Museo del Ejército building and Casón del Buen Retiro are all that now remain). Countless grand churches, convents and mansions were also built and, thanks to royal patronage, this was the golden age of art in Spain. Velázquez, El Greco, José de Ribera, Zurbarán, Murillo and Coello were all active in the 17th century. For the first time, Madrid began to take on the aspect of a city.

But for all its newfound wealth and status, Madrid suffered several handicaps compared with more illustrious capitals elsewhere in Europe: it was bereft of a navigable river,

Statue of King Felipe III (p66) in Plaza Mayor

1833	1860
King Fernando VII dies, leaving three-year-old Isabel II as heir-apparent	One quarter of Madrid's working populace is employed to serve in aristocratic households

port, decent road links or the slightest hint of entrepreneurial spirit; agricultural land around the town was poor; and the immense wealth from the Americas was squandered on wars and the court. Madrid was, in fact, little more than a large grubby leech, bleeding the surrounding provinces and colonies dry.

By the middle of the 17th century Madrid had completely outgrown its capacity to cope: it was home to 175,000 people, making it the fifth-largest city in Europe (after London, Paris, Constantinople and Naples). But if you took away the court the city amounted to nothing and when Pedro Texeiro drew the first map of the city in 1656, the place was still largely a cesspit of narrow, squalid lanes.

THE BOURBONS LEAVE THEIR MARK

After King Carlos II died in 1700 without leaving an heir, Europe was engulfed by the 12-year War of the Spanish Succession. While Europe battled over the Spanish colonial carcass, Felipe V (grandson of Louis XIV of France and Maria Teresa, a daughter of Felipe IV) ascended the throne. He may have founded the Bourbon dynasty which remains at the head of the Spanish state today, but he also presided over the loss of most of Spain's European territories and was left with just Spain over which to rule.

Thankfully, Felipe proved much more adept at nation-building than military strategy. His centralisation of state control and attempts at land reform are viewed by some historians as the first steps in making Spain a modern European nation. He preferred to live outside the noisy and filthy capital but when in 1734 the *alcázar* was destroyed in a fire, the king laid down plans for a magnificent new Palacio Real (Royal Palace) to take its place.

His immediate successors, especially Carlos III (r 1759–88), also gave Madrid and Spain a period of comparatively common-sense governance. Carlos (with the big nose – his equestrian statue dominates the Puerta del Sol) came to be known as the best 'mayor' Madrid had ever had. He cleaned up the city (by all accounts the filthiest in Europe), completed the Palacio Real, inaugurated the Real Jardín Botánico (Royal Botanical Gardens) and carried out numerous other public works. His stamp upon Madrid's essential character was also evident in his sponsorship of local and foreign artists, among them Goya and Tiepolo. Carlos III also expelled the backward-looking Jesuits in 1767 and embarked on a major road-building programme.

By the time Carlos III died in 1788, Spain and its capital were in better shape than ever. However, Spain remained, despite all the improvements, an essentially poor country with a big-spending royal court.

NAPOLEON & EL DOS DE MAYO

Within a year of Carlos III's death, Europe was in uproar as the French Revolution threatened to sweep away the old order. Through the machinations of Carlos IV, the successor to Carlos III, and his self-seeking minister, Manuel Godoy, Spain incurred the wrath of both the French and the British.

The consequences were devastating. First, Nelson crushed the Spanish fleet in the Battle of Trafalgar in 1805. Next, Napoleon convinced a gullible Godoy to let French troops enter Spain on the pretext of a joint attack on Portugal, whereby General Murat's French detachment took control of Madrid, easily defeating General Tomás de Morla's bands of hearty but unruly armed citizenry. By 1808 the French presence had become an occupation and Napoleon's brother, Joseph Bonaparte, was crowned king of Spain.

Madrid did not take kindly to foreign rule and, on the morning of 2 May 1808, Madrileños, showing more courage than their leaders, attacked French troops around the Palacio Real and what is now Plaza del Dos de Mayo. Murat moved quickly and by the end of the day the rebels were defeated. Goya's masterpieces, *El Dos de Mayo* and *El Tres de Mayo,* on display in the Museo del Prado, poignantly evoke the hope and anguish of the ill-fated rebellion.

1881	1873
The PSOE (Spanish Socialist Workers' Party) is founded	Spain is declared a republic

Joseph Bonaparte transformed Madrid with a host of measures necessary in a city that had grown up without any discernible sense of town planning. These measures included the destruction of various churches and convents to create public squares and widening streets. Sanitation was also improved and cemeteries were moved to the outskirts of the city.

Although the French were finally evicted from Spanish territory in 1813 as a result of the Guerra de la Independencia (War of Independence, or Peninsular War), in 1812 30,000 Madrileños died from hunger alone.

When the autocratic King Fernando VII returned in 1814, Spain was a country in disarray and, at one point, French troops even marched back into Spain to prop him up. Though Fernando was not given to frequent bouts of enlightenment, two of his projects would stand the test of time – he opened the renewed Parque del Buen Retiro, which had been largely destroyed during the war, to the public and founded an art gallery in the Prado (p83). When he died in 1833, Fernando left Spain little more than a three-year-old daughter to rule over them, a recipe for civil war, and an economy in tatters.

A COUNTRY DIVIDED

Isabel II, a toddler, was obviously not quite up to running the country, and power passed into the hands of her mother, María Cristina, who ruled as regent. Fernando's brother, Don Carlos, and his conservative supporters disputed Isabel's right to the throne so María Cristina turned to the liberals for help. Thus began what was known as the Carlist wars.

Political upheaval remained part of Madrid's daily diet, characterised by alternating coups by conservative and liberal wings of the army. Madrileños must have rued the day their city became capital of this deeply fragmented country.

Apart from anything else, Madrid was incredibly backward. A discernible middle class only began to make a timid appearance from the 1830s. It was aided when the government ordered the *desamortización* (disentailment) of Church property in 1837. A speculative building boom ensued – if you've lived in Madrid since the late 1990s, you'll see that history has a habit of repeating itself – and its beneficiaries constituted the emerging entrepreneurial class.

For 25 years after Isabel began to rule in her own right in 1843, Madrid was awash with coups, riots and general discontent. It is therefore remarkable that amid the chaos the city's rulers laid the foundations for modern Madrid's infrastructure. In 1851, the city's first railway line, between Madrid and Aranjuez, opened. Seven years later, the Canal de Isabel II, which still supplies the city with water from the Sierra de Guadarrama, was inaugurated. Street paving, the sewage system and rubbish collection were improved, and gas lighting was introduced. More importantly, foreign (mostly French) capital was beginning to fill the investment vacuum.

Signs that Madrid was finally becoming a national capital worthy of the name also began to appear with the construction of a national road network radiating from the capital, and public works, ranging from the reorganisation of the Puerta del Sol to the building of the Teatro Real, Biblioteca Nacional and Congreso de los Diputados (lower house of parliament), were carried out.

In the 1860s, the first timid moves to create an Ensanche, or extension of the city, were undertaken. The initial spurt of building took place around Calle de Serrano,

Alfonso XII's Mausoleum (p88), Parque del Buen Retiro

1898	1919
Spain loses its remaining colonies of Cuba, Puerto Rico and the Philippines to the USA	Madrid's first metro line starts running

where the enterprising Marqués de Salamanca bought up land and built high-class housing. Poor old Salamanca was ahead of his time and lost everything in his gamble – it was only after he died that Salamanca became one of Madrid's most exclusive barrios (districts).

In 1873, Spain was declared a republic, but the army soon intervened to restore the Bourbon monarchy. Alfonso XII, Isabel's son, assumed power.

In the period of relative tranquillity that ensued, the expansion of the Ensanche gathered momentum, the city's big train stations were constructed and the foundation stones of a cathedral were laid. Another kind of 'cathedral', the Banco de España, was completed and opened its doors in 1891. By 1898 the first city tramlines were electrified and in 1910 work began on the Gran Vía. Nine years later the first metro line started operation.

The 1920s were a period of frenzied activity, not just in urban construction but in intellectual life. As many as 20 newspapers circulated on the streets of Madrid and writers and artists (including Lorca, Dalí and Buñuel) converged on the capital, which hopped to the sounds of American jazz. The '20s roared as much in Madrid as elsewhere in Europe.

Against this backdrop of a culturally burgeoning city, however, dark clouds were gathering.

THE DESCENT INTO CIVIL WAR

Recession late in WWI and the disastrous Spanish campaign in Morocco in the 1920s had worsened things to such an extent that in 1923 the captain-general of Catalonia, General Miguel Primo de Rivera, launched a coup that would lead to an uneasy six-year dictatorship. Alfonso XIII had him removed in 1930 and Madrid erupted in joyful celebration. It would prove to be a false dawn, for the Spanish capital, now home to more than one million people, had become the seething centre of Spain's increasingly radical politics.

The rise of the socialists in Madrid and anarchists (especially popular among Barcelona's industrial workers and farmers in the south of the country) had sharpened social tensions throughout the country. Municipal elections in Madrid in April 1931 brought a coalition of republicans and socialists to power. Three days later a second republic was proclaimed and Alfonso XIII fled. The republican government opened up the Casa de Campo – until then a private royal playground – to the public and passed numerous reformist laws.

Divisions within the government enabled a right-wing coalition to assume power in 1933. The following year General Francisco Franco violently put down a miners' revolt in Asturias with merciless Spanish Foreign Legion troops.

Again the pendulum swung and in February 1936 the left-wing Frente Popular (Popular Front) just beat the right's Frente Nacional (National Front) to power. One of its first actions was to remove suspect generals – Franco was sent to the Canary Islands. With the army supporting the right-wing parties and the extreme left clamouring for revolution, the stage was set for a showdown.

In the end the army moved first. In July 1936, garrisons in North Africa revolted, quickly followed by others on the mainland. Three years of nasty warfare followed, characterised by horrendous atrocities carried out by both the republican and nationalist sides.

Having stopped nationalist troops advancing from the north, Madrid found itself in the sights of Franco's forces moving up from the south. By early November 1936 they were in the Casa de Campo. The government escaped to Valencia, but the resolve of the city's defenders, a mix of hastily assembled recruits, sympathisers from the ranks of the army and air force, the International Brigades and Soviet advisers, held firm. Fighting was heaviest in the northwest of the city, around Argüelles, but Franco's frontal assault failed for two and a half years.

Encircled on all sides and with much of Spain falling to Franco's forces, Madrileños lived a bizarre reality. People went about their daily business, caught the metro to work and got on with things as best they could. All the while, skirmishes continued around Argüelles

1923	1931
General Miguel Primo de Rivera launches a military coup and begins a six-year dictatorship	After nationwide municipal elections a republic is called and King Alfonso XIII flees

and nationalist artillery intermittently shelled the city, particularly Gran Vía (nicknamed 'Howitzer Alley'), from the Casa de Campo. On 28 March 1939, an exhausted Madrid finally surrendered.

FRANCO'S MADRID

A deathly silence fell over the city as the new dictator made himself at home. Mindful that he was occupying a city that had hardly welcomed him with open arms, Franco considered shifting the capital south to the more amenable Seville. As if to punish Madrid for its resistance, he opted instead to remake Madrid in his own image and transform the city into a capital worthy of its new master.

Franco and his right-wing Falangist Party maintained a heavy-handed repression and Madrid in the early 1940s was impoverished and battle-scarred, a 'city of a million cadavers', according to one observer.

In the Francoist propaganda of the day, the 1940s and 1950s were the years of *autarquía* (economic self-reliance, largely induced by Spain's international isolation after the end of WWII). For most Spaniards, however, these were the *años de hambre* (the years of hunger). Only in 1955 did the average wage again reach the levels of 1934.

Throughout the 1940s, many thousands of suspects, ranging from supporters of the Frente Popular to union members, were harassed, imprisoned, tortured and shot. Thousands of political prisoners were shipped off to Nazi concentration camps. Many of those who remained were put to work in deplorable conditions, most notably to construct the grandiose folly of Franco's Valle de los Caídos monument northwest of Madrid.

The dire state of the Spanish economy forced hundreds of thousands of starving *campesinos* (peasants) to flock to the capital, increasing the already enormous pressure for housing. Most contented themselves with erecting *chabolas* (shanty towns) in the increasingly ugly satellite suburbs that began to ring the city.

Opposition to Franco among university students and union members began to appear in the early 1950s, which Franco, with his highly developed sense of paranoia, blamed on freemasons, Jews, Basques, Catalans or communist plots. But he ultimately owed his survival to the Soviet Union. In 1953, the USA decided to grant economic aid to Franco's Spain in exchange for the use of Spanish air and naval bases during the Cold War.

By the early 1960s industry was taking off in and around Madrid. Foreign investment poured in and the services and banking sector blossomed. The grand, tree-lined Paseo de la Castellana took on much of its present aspect although many fine old palaces that once lined the roadside were demolished in the process. These were replaced by such buildings as the none-too-elegant Torres de Colón.

The 1960s were known as the *años de desarollo* (years of development), when Spain enjoyed something of an economic miracle. Madrid began to enjoy greater prosperity as investment soared. Factories of the American Chrysler motor company were Madrid's single biggest employers in the 1960s. In 1960 fewer than 70,000 cars were on the road in Madrid. Ten years later more than half a million clogged the capital's streets.

For all the signs of development in Madrid, Franco was never popular in his own capital and an increased standard of living did little to diminish their disdain for a man who held the capital in an iron grip. From 1965, opposition to Franco's regime became steadily more vocal. Again, the universities were repeatedly the scene of confrontation, but clandestine trade unions, such as Comisiones Obreras (CCOO; Workers Commissions) and the outlawed UGT, also began to make themselves heard again.

The waves of protest were not restricted to Madrid. In the Basque Country the terrorist group ETA began to fight for Basque independence. Their first important action outside the Basque Country was the assassination in Madrid in 1973 of Admiral Carrero Blanco, Franco's prime minister and designated successor.

Franco fell ill in 1974 and died on 20 November 1975.

1936	1939
The Spanish Civil War breaks out; Nationalist forces bombard Madrid from the Casa de Campo	Franco's troops finally enter Madrid in March, putting an end to the Civil War

A CITY OF IMMIGRANTS

In a country where regional nationalisms abound – even Barcelona, that most European of cities, is fiercely and parochially Catalan – Madrid is notable for its absence of regional sentiment. If you quiz Madrileños as to why this is so, they most often look mystified and reply, 'but we're *all* from somewhere else'.

It has always been thus in Madrid. In the century after the city became the national capital in 1561, the population swelled by 500%, from 30,000 to 150,000. Most were Spaniards (peasants and would-be nobles) who'd left behind the impoverished countryside and were drawn by the opportunities which existed on the periphery of the royal court.

During the first three decades of the 20th century, Madrid's population doubled from half a million to almost one million; in 1930, a study found that less than 40% of the capital's population was from Madrid. The process continued in the aftermath of the civil war and in the 1950s alone, more than 600,000 arrived from elsewhere in Spain.

In the late 20th century, the process of immigration began to take on a new form, as Spain became the EU's largest annual recipient of immigrants. By early 2006, more than 16.5% of Madrid's population were foreigners, some 536,000 out of 3.29 million inhabitants and more than double the national average.

Not surprisingly, true Madrileños are something of a rare breed. Those who can claim four grandparents born in the city are dignified with the name *gatos* (cats). Although you could be forgiven for thinking that it reflects their tendency to crawl around the city until all hours, the term actually dates from when one of Alfonso VI's soldiers artfully scaled Muslim Magerit's formidable walls in 1085. 'Look,' cried his comrades, 'he moves like a cat!'

History

THE TRANSITION TO DEMOCRACY

FROM THE BEGINNING

After the initial shock caused by the death of Franco, who had cast a shadow over Spain for almost four decades, Spaniards began to reclaim their country.

The PSOE, Partido Comunista de España (PCE; Spanish Communist Party), trade unions and a wide range of opposition figures emerged from hiding and exile. Franco's trusted advisors remained in control of both parliament and the armed forces but had neither the authority nor charisma necessary to hold back the tide of liberal optimism sweeping the country.

King Juan Carlos I, of the Bourbon family that had left the Spanish political stage with the flight of Alfonso XIII in 1931, had been groomed as head of state by Franco. But the king confounded the sceptics by entrusting Adolfo Suárez, a former moderate Francoist with whom he had long been in secret contact, with government in July 1976. With the king's approval, Suárez quickly rammed a raft of changes through parliament while Franco loyalists and generals, suddenly rudderless without their leader, struggled to regroup.

Suárez and his centre-right coalition won elections in 1977 and set about writing a new constitution in collaboration with the now-legal opposition. It provided for a parliamentary monarchy with no state religion and guaranteed a large degree of devolution to the 17 regions into which the country was now divided.

Spaniards got the fright of their lives in February 1981 when a pistol-brandishing, low-ranking Guardia Civil (Civil Guard) officer, Antonio Tejero Molina, marched into the Cortes in Madrid with an armed detachment and held parliament captive for 24 hours. Throughout a day of high drama, the country held its breath as Spaniards waited to see whether Spain would be thrust back into the dark days of dictatorship or whether the fledgling democracy would prevail. With the nation glued to their TV sets, King Juan Carlos I made a live broadcast denouncing Tejero and calling on the soldiers to return to their barracks. The coup fizzled out.

A year later, Felipe González' PSOE won the national elections. Spain's economic problems were legion – incomes were on a par with those of Iraq, ETA terrorism was claiming dozens of lives every year and unemployment was above 20%. But one thing that Spaniards had in abundance was optimism and when, in 1986, Spain joined the European Community (EC), as it was then called, the country had well and truly returned to the fold of modern European nations.

1968	1975
Basque separatist movement ETA launches armed campaign which will kill more than 800 people in 35 years	Franco dies in November after 36 years in power, opening the way for a return to democratic rule three years later

LA MOVIDA MADRILEÑA

What London was to the swinging '60s and Paris to 1968, Madrid was to the 1980s. After the long, dark years of dictatorship and conservative Catholicism, Spaniards, especially Madrileños, emerged onto the streets with all the zeal of ex-convent schoolgirls. Nothing was taboo as young Madrileños discovered the '60s, '70s and early '80s all at once. Drinking, drugs and sex suddenly were OK. All night partying was the norm, cannabis was virtually legalised and the city howled. All across the city, summer terraces roared to the chattering, drinking, carousing crowds and young people from all over Europe flocked here to take part in the revelry.

What was remarkable about *la movida* is that it was presided over by Enrique Tierno Galván, an ageing former university professor who had been a leading opposition figure under Franco and was affectionately known throughout Spain as 'the old teacher'. A Socialist, he became mayor in 1979 and, for many, launched *la movida* by telling a public gathering *'a colocarse y ponerse al loro',* which loosely translates as 'get stoned and do what's cool'. Not surprisingly, he was Madrid's most popular mayor ever and when he died in 1986, a million Madrileños turned out for his funeral.

But *la movida* was not just about rediscovering the Spanish art of *salir de copas* (going out to drink). It was also accompanied by an explosion of creativity among the country's musicians, designers and film-makers keen to shake off the shackles of the repressive Franco years.

The most famous of these was film director Pedro Almodóvar. Still one of Europe's most creative directors, his riotously colourful films captured the spirit of *la movida,* featuring larger-than-life characters who pushed the limits of sex and drugs. Although his later films such as *Todo Sobre My Madre* (All About My Mother) and *Mujeres al Borde de un Ataque de Nervios* (Women on the Verge of a Nervous Breakdown) became internationally renowned, his first film, *Pepi, Luci, Bom y Las Otras Chicas del Montón* (Pepi, Luci, Bom and All Those Other Girls), released in 1980, is where *la movida* really comes alive. When he wasn't making films, Almodóvar immersed himself in the spirit of *la movida,* doing drag acts in smoky bars that people-in-the-know would frequent.

Among the other names from *la movida* that still resonate, the designer Agatha Ruiz de la Prada (p161) stands out. Start playing anything by Alaska, Los Rebeldes, Radio Futura or Nacha Pop and watch Madrileños' eyes glaze over with nostalgia.

What happened to *la movida*? Many say that it died in 1991 with the election of the conservative Popular Party's José María Álvarez del Manzano as mayor. In the following years rolling spliffs in public became increasingly dangerous and creeping clamps (ie closing hours) were imposed on the almost lawless bars. Pedro Almodóvar was even heard to say that Madrid had become 'as boring as Oslo'.

Things have indeed quietened down a little, but only when compared with the 1980s. If only all cities were this 'boring'.

At a city level, a much-loved Socialist, Enrique Tierno Galván presided over Madrid Ayuntamiento (town hall) from 1979 until 1991, when the PP's José María Álvarez del Manzano finally broke the Socialists' monopoly on power. Álvarez del Manzano, who remained in power until 2003, became known as 'The Tunnelator' for beginning the ongoing mania of Madrid governments for semipermanent roadworks and large-scale infrastructure projects. He also has the dubious distinction of being credited with bringing an end to the hedonistic Madrid of the 1980s.

González and the PSOE remained in power at a national level until 1996 when the right-wing PP, which had been created by former Franco loyalists, picked up the baton under José María Aznar.

From 1996 until 2004, the three levels of government in Madrid (local, regional and national) remained the preserve of the PP, a dominance that prompted observers from other regions to claim that the PP overtly favoured development of the capital at the expense of Spain's other regions. Whatever the truth of such accusations, the city has moved ahead in leaps and bounds and as the national economy took off in the late 1990s, Madrid reaped the benefits. Extraordinary expansion programmes for the metro, highways, airport, outer suburbs and for inner city renewal are unmistakable signs of confidence. By one reckoning, up to 75% of inward foreign investment into Spain is directed at the capital. In the process, Madrid, defying its less-than-glorious history, has become one of Europe's most prosperous cities.

1986	2004
Spain joins European Community (EC)	Terrorist bombings kill 191 people and the PSOE government is elected to power three days later

Sights ■

Sights

Madrid may be Europe's most dynamic city, but because it has no signature Eiffel Tower, no Coliseum and no otherworldly Gaudí-esque flourishes, many first-time visitors wonder what there is to see in the Spanish capital. The answer is wonderful sights in abundance, so many in fact that few travellers leave disappointed with their menu of high culture and high-volume excitement.

For a start, Madrid has three of the finest art galleries in the world and if ever there was a golden mile of fine art, it has to be the combined charms of the Museo del Prado, Centro de Arte Reina Sofía and the Museo Thyssen-Bornemisza. There are so many works by the master painters in Madrid that masterpieces overflow from these three museums into dozens of museums and galleries across the city. The combination of stunning architecture and feel-good living has never been easier to access than in the beautiful plazas where *terrazas* (cafés with outdoor tables) provide a front-row seat for Madrid's fine cityscape and endlessly energetic street life. We challenge you to find a more spec-

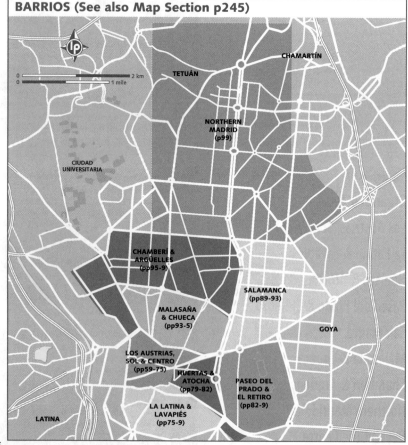

BARRIOS (See also Map Section p245)

tacular and agreeable setting for your coffee than the Plaza Mayor, Plaza de Santa Ana or Plaza de Oriente. Throw in some outstanding city parks (the Parque del Buen Retiro in particular) and areas such as Chueca, Malasaña, Lavapiés and Salamanca which each have their own alluring or intoxicating identity, and you'll quickly end up wishing, like Hemingway, that you never had to leave.

Madrid is divided up into *distritos* (districts) and these are subdivided into barrios (neighbourhoods), the official names of which are largely ignored by Madrileños. Indeed the word barrio has a very strong feel of local identity about it. Madrileños have their own city map in their heads and, since they know best, we follow them.

Los Austrias, Sol and Centro make up the bustling, compact and medieval heart of Madrid, where the village of Magerit came to life, and this area now yields an impossibly rich heritage of things to see, among them palaces, churches and grand squares. La Latina and Lavapiés, two of Madrid's oldest inner-city barrios are immediately south and southwest of the centre, and have plenty to see and even more to experience. East of here takes in Huertas and Atocha, with the former the home to a labyrinth of more vibrant nightlife than seems possible but also with its fair share of cultural sights that are well worth tracking down. Down the hill, Atocha is a gateway to the grand boulevard of the Paseo del Prado, a haven of culture boasting the city's finest museums. Part of the

IT'S FREE!

- Museo del Prado (free Sun; p83)
- Centro de Arte Reina Sofía (free Sat afternoon & Sun; p80)
- Museo Municipal de Arte Contemporáneo (free Tue-Sun; p94)
- Museo Arqueológico Nacional (free Sat afternoon & Sun; p91)
- Ermita de San Antonio de la Florida (free daily; p96)

same barrio, the Parque del Buen Retiro is a refuge made up of green parkland and gardens, and serves as an entry point to the exclusive barrio of Salamanca. West of Salamanca are two of modern Madrid's coolest barrios, Malasaña and Chueca, which have been transformed from gritty, working-class dives into cultural focal points. Neighbouring Chamberí and Argüelles have few sights to talk about but offer an ambience that is rapidly making them the barrios of choice for discerning Madrileños. The outer *distritos* of Madrid offer some parks and children's attractions, such as Warner Brothers Movie World.

Within each section, sights are listed in alphabetical order. See Transport (p202) for details of getting around Madrid.

ITINERARIES
One Day

Just one day in Madrid? What were you thinking?! You've got a hectic day ahead of you so make sure you plan it around the best places (and plazas) to relax and, in the process, sample café culture at its best. Begin in the **Plaza Mayor** (p65) with its architectural beauty, fine *terrazas* and endlessly fascinating passing Madrid parade. Wander down Calle Mayor, where you'll pass the delightful **Plaza de la Villa** (p64) en route, and head for the **Palacio Real** (p63). By then you're sure to be ready for a coffee or even something stronger and there's no finer place to rest than in the **Plaza de Oriente** (p65). Double back up towards the **Plaza de la Puerta del Sol** (p64) where Madrid is at its most clamorous, and the streets, lanes and squares are alive with colour, and vocal, gesticulating people. Forge on to lose yourself in the Huertas area around **Plaza de Santa Ana** (p82), the ideal place for a long, liquid lunch. After that, time for some high culture, so stroll down the hill to the incomparable **Museo del Prado** (p83), the home of a grand collection of predominantly Spanish Old Masters and one of the most outstanding art galleries in Europe. In anticipation of a long night ahead, catch your breath in the **Parque del Buen Retiro** (p87) before heading up along Gran Vía and into **Chueca** (p93) for some of Madrid's famously noisy and eclectic nightlife.

Sights

ITINERARIES

Three Days

Three days is, in our view, the bare minimum for getting to know and enjoy Madrid. That way you can not only take its pulse, as with the One Day itinerary, but get under its skin a little. Even if you're not an art buff, but especially if you are, you really should see one (or both) of the **Centro de Arte Reina Sofía** (p80) and **Museo Thyssen-Bornemisza** (p86). Never has so much fine art been so plentiful and so accessible, and that in itself can be a problem – there's so much to absorb that we suggest seeing one each morning. Pause in **Plaza de la Cibeles** (p88) to admire some of the best in Madrid architecture as you work your way north to the **Gran Café de Gijón** (p125), one of Madrid's grand old cafés. A quick metro ride across town to the Príncipe Pío stop puts you within striking distance of the astonishing Goya frescoes in the **Ermita de San Antonio de la Florida** (p96). While you're in the area, consider a chicken-and-cider meal at **Casa Mingo** (p128). On day three, head for La Latina and the great restaurants and tapas bars along **Calle de la Cava Baja** (p116) or some cod-and-*callos* tapas at **Casa Revuelta** (p114). If it's a Sunday; better still precede these outings with a wander through **El Rastro** (p76), one of the best flea markets in Europe. Another great place to explore is around Malasaña, where **Calle de Manuela Malasaña** (p123) offers rich pickings and the august and old-world **Café Comercial** (p123) is a fine pit stop at any time of the day.

TOP PLACES FOR CHILDREN

- Warner Brothers Movie World (p101)
- Teleférico (p98)
- Faunia (p100)
- Estadio Santiago Bernabéu (p99)
- Parque del Buen Retiro (p87)

One Week

Now you're talking. You've seen the biggest and best of Madrid's sights and by now you've probably already sorted out your favourite café for your morning cuppa and paper. Time for some shopping: Calle de Serrano in **Salamanca** (p161) has just about everything for the designer-conscious, while **Calle de Fuencarral** (p164) or Calle de Augusto Figueroa will appeal to those who want to choose from a range of goods whether it be fine Spanish shoes, great party gear or leather whips. Had an overdose of culture? Try two very different types of temples – the **Plaza de Toros** (p92) where the theatrical art of bullfighting is at its best and worst, and the **Estadio Santiago Bernabéu** (p99) where the glamour that is Real Madrid lives and breathes. Deepen your Madrid experience by wandering through medieval and multicultural **Lavapiés** (p77) or seeing a live flamenco performance, preferably at **Cardamomo** (p145). Hemingway hated leaving Madrid, but leave you should, partly because the longer you stay the harder it is to leave, but also so as not to miss out on the considerable charms of nearby **Toledo** (p181) and **Segovia** (p185). **Córdoba** (p192) may be 400km away but the high speed AVE train from Atocha station whisks you there and deep into Andalucía and Spain's Moorish past in less than two hours. Of the numerous royal residences in the vicinity of Madrid, the most impressive is **San Lorenzo de el Escorial** (p195), but **Chinchón** (p197) is an enchanted alternative with ramshackle village charm written all over its colonnaded Plaza Mayor.

DISCOUNTS & CLOSING TIMES

The Paseo del Arte ticket covers the big three galleries (Museo del Prado, Museo Thyssen-Bornemisza and Centro de Arte Reina Sofía) for €12 and is valid for up to 18 months (one visit to each). Never has €12 been better spent. For unlimited visits to either the Prado or the Reina Sofía, a year's ticket costs €36. A yearly ticket to both these galleries and eight other museums throughout the country is also available, although prices were under review at the time of writing.

A more extensive system of discounts is available if you buy the Madrid Card; see p211 for details.

Most, but not all, museums and monuments close on Monday (the Reina Sofía is an exception and closes on Tuesday). Many are also shut on Sunday afternoons, although the Prado and the Thyssen are notable exceptions. In July and August, some close parts of their displays for want of staff, most of whom take annual leave around this time. A few minor museums close entirely throughout August.

ORGANISED TOURS

Adventurous Appetites (☎ 63 933 10 73; www.adven turousappetites.com; 4-hr tour €40; ☻ 8pm Mon-Sat) English-language tapas tours through central Madrid from the bear statue in Puerta del Sol. Price includes the first drink.

Bike Spain (Map pp254–5; ☎ 91 522 38 99; www.bike spain.info; Calle del Carmen 17; day/night tours €25/30) English-language guided city tours by bicycle, plus longer expeditions to San Lorenzo de El Escorial (€75).

Descubre Madrid (Discover Madrid; ☎ 902 221 622; www .esmadrid.com; walking tours adult/child, student or senior €3.20/2.60, bus tours €6.20/4.85, bicycle tours €3.20/2.60 plus €6 bike rental) Conducts dozens of tours in Spanish and English. Walking tours include Madrid of the Bourbons, Velázquez & El Buen Retiro, Legends of Old Madrid, Traditional Shops & Taverns, Madrid of Cervantes and Madrid of the Habsburgs. Tours may change from season to season. Ask at the Centro de Turismo de Madrid (Tourist Office; Map pp254–5; Plaza Mayor 27) for details and departure times.

Madrid Bike Tours (☎ 680 581 782; www.madrid biketours.com; 4hr tours & picnic lunch €55 per person) Londoner Mike Chandler offers a guided two-wheel tour of Madrid as well as tours further afield.

Madrid Visión (☎ 91 779 18 88 or 91 765 10 16; www .madridvision.es; adult 1-/2-day ticket €14.50/19, child 7-16 & senior over 65 1-/2-day ticket €8/10, child under 7 free; ☻ 9.30am-midnight 21 Jun-20 Sep, 10am-7pm 21 Dec-20 Mar, 10am-9pm rest of the year) Hop-on, hop-off open-topped buses that run every 10 to 20 minutes along three routes: Historical Madrid, Modern Madrid and Monumental Madrid. Information, including maps, is available at tourist offices, most travel agencies and some hotels, and you can get tickets on the bus. The ticket also entitles you to a series of discounts at some museums, restaurants and shops.

Pullmantur (Map pp254–5; ☎ 91 541 18 07; www .pullmantur-spain.com; Plaza de Oriente 8; day/night tour from €19/12.50) One of several private companies offering bus tours of Madrid and excursions beyond, including to San Lorenzo de El Escorial and Valle de los Caídos.

Trapsatur (Map pp250–1; ☎ 91 542 66 66; www .trapsatur.com; Calle de Isabel la Católica; day/night tours from €17/12) Another private company serving Madrid and surrounding sights and cities.

LOS AUSTRIAS, SOL & CENTRO

Drinking p133, Eating p114, Nightlife p139, Shopping p157, Sleeping p169

From the tangle of streets tumbling down the hillside of Los Austrias and the busy shopping streets around the Plaza de la Puerta del

TOP SIGHTS IN LOS AUSTRIAS, SOL & CENTRO

- Plaza Mayor (p65)
- Palacio Real (p63)
- Plaza de la Villa (p64)
- Plaza de Oriente (p65)
- Convento de las Descalzas Reales (p61)
- Real Academia de Bellas Artes de San Fernando (p66)

Sol (the Gate of the Sun; more commonly known as Puerta del Sol) to the monumental Gran Vía, which marks the northern border of central Madrid, this is Madrid at its most diverse. This is where the splendour of Imperial Spain was at its most ostentatious and Spain's overarching Catholicism was at its most devout – think expansive palaces, elaborate private mansions, ancient churches and imposing convents amid the raucous clamour of modern Madrid.

The area that slopes down the hill south-west of the Plaza Mayor is Madrid at its most medieval and has come to be known as Madrid de los Austrias, in reference to the Habsburg dynasty, which ruled Spain from 1517 to 1700. The busy and bustling streets between the Puerta del Sol and Gran Vía, is the heart and centre of Madrid, a designation that extends west to the Palacio Real, the royal jewel in Madrid's considerable crown. At the hub is the splendour of the glorious Plaza Mayor.

For getting the most out of your time here, see boxed text, p170.

Orientation

The attractive and always busy hemisphere that makes up the Puerta del Sol is the navel of Madrid and Spain (a plaque marks the spot in front of the Casa de Correos). Although fascinating in its own right, it's a reference point for the centre of town and metro and bus lines radiate out from here across the city. To the east the avenues of Calle de Alcalá and Carrera de San Jerónimo head towards the Paseo del Prado.

Central Madrid is best explored by hopping from square to square, pausing for a coffee or something stronger at each while you plan your next move. A couple of hundred metres west of Puerta del Sol, the arcaded Plaza Mayor is the perfect place to get your bearings. Ringed by handy metro stops (Sol, Ópera, Tirso de Molina), it's a landmark you'll happily pass through again and again.

Not far southwest of the Plaza Mayor, the steep Calle Segovia leads down through the heart of Los Austrias, while Calle de la Cava Baja is your enchanting introduction to the wiles of La Latina.

To the north of Plaza Mayor the east–west Calle Mayor (Main St) is lined with apartments, shops and eateries. As it heads down the hill towards Calle de Bailén and the Palacio Real it passes Plaza de la Villa.

The other main axis through this part of central Madrid is Calle del Arenal, which spills into Plaza de Isabel II, home of the Teatro Real, which in turn yields to the majestic Plaza de Oriente and the Palacio Real. West of the palace and some way below it stretches what might be called the palatial backyard, the beautifully maintained and carefully studied Campo del Moro.

North of Calle del Arenal a web of streets rises gradually towards Gran Vía, a noisy avenue punched through the heart of Madrid early in the 20th century. The pedestrian streets around Calle de Preciados bristle with department stores and are thronged with shoppers, and there are several important convents scattered amid the modern temples to consumerism, most notably the Convento de las Descalzas Reales.

Like in any European city, the city centre has its share of seediness. Calle de la Montera is the home patch of hookers and pimps, while some of the streets dropping down to Plaza de España from Plaza de Santo Domingo have a slightly louche feel, too.

CAMPO DEL MORO Map pp246-7

☎ 91 454 88 00; Paseo de la Virgen del Puerto; ☒ 10am-8pm Mon-Sat, 9am-8pm Sun & holidays Apr-Sep, 10am-6pm Mon-Sat, 9am-6pm Sun & holidays Oct-Mar; Ⓜ Príncipe Pío

From this park you can gain an appreciation of Madrid in its earliest days – it was from here, in what would become known as Campo del Moro (Moor's Field), that an Almoravid army laid siege to the city in 1110. The troops occupied all but the fortress (where the Palacio Real now stands), but the Christian garrison held on until the Almoravid fury abated and their forces retired south. The 20 hectares of gardens that now adorn the site were laid in 1844, with alterations in 1890. The gardens' centre-

piece, the elegant **Fuente de las Conchas** (Fountain of the Shells), was designed by Ventura Rodríguez, the Goya of Madrid's 18th-century architecture scene. The only entrance is from Paseo de la Virgen del Puerto.

CATEDRAL DE NUESTRA SEÑORA DE LA ALMUDENA Map pp254-5

☎ 91 542 22 00; Calle de Bailén; ☒ 9am-9pm; Ⓜ Ópera

Paris has Notre Dame and Rome has St Peter's Basilica. In fact, almost every European city of stature has its signature cathedral, a stand-out monument to a glorious Christian past. Not Madrid. The Catedral de Nuestra Señora de la Almudena, south of the Palacio Real, is cavernous and largely charmless, its colourful, modern ceilings doing little to make up for the lack of the old-world gravitas that so distinguishes great cathedrals.

Carlos I first proposed building a cathedral here back in 1518 but building didn't actually begin until the 1880s. Other priorities got in the way and it wasn't finished until 1992. Not surprisingly, the pristine, bright white neo-Gothic interior holds no pride of place in the affections of Madrileños. Its only redeeming feature is that the exterior shares a certain aesthetic harmony with the neighbouring Palacio Real and the combined effect is striking from a distance.

Just around the corner in Calle Mayor, the low-lying ruins of Santa María de la Almudena (Map pp254–5) are all that remain of Madrid's first church, which was built on the site of Magerit's Great Mosque when the Christians arrived in the 11th century.

Catedral de Nuestra Señora de la Almudena (above)

CONVENTO DEL CORPUS CRISTI (LAS CARBONERAS) Map pp254-5

☎ 91 548 37 01; Plaza del Conde de Miranda; admission free; ⏰ 9.30am-1pm & 4-6.30pm; Ⓜ Ópera
Architecturally nondescript but culturally curious, this church hides behind sober modern brickwork on the western end of a quiet square. A closed order of nuns occupies the convent building around it and, when Mass is held, the nuns gather in a separate area at the rear of the church. They maintain a centuries-old tradition of making sweet biscuits that can be purchased from the entrance just off the square on Calle del Codo. You make your request through a grill and the products are delivered through a little revolving door that allows the nuns to remain unseen by the outside world (see p157 for more info).

CONVENTO DE LA ENCARNACIÓN

Map pp254-5

☎ 91 454 88 00; www.patrimonionacional.es in Spanish; Plaza de la Encarnación 1; adult/student & EU senior €3.60/2, EU citizens free Wed, combined ticket with Convento de las Descalzas Reales €6/3.40; ⏰ 10.30am-12.45pm & 4-5.45pm Tue-Thu & Sat, 10.30am-12.45pm Fri, 11am-1.30pm Sun & holidays; Ⓜ Ópera
Founded by Empress Margarita de Austria, this 17th-century mansion built in the Madrid baroque style (a pleasing amalgam of brick, exposed stone and wrought iron) is still inhabited by nuns of the Augustine order. The large art collection dates mostly from the 17th century and among the many gold and silver reliquaries is one that contains the blood of San Pantaleón, which purportedly liquefies each year on 28 June. The convent also sits on a pretty plaza with lovely views down towards the Palacio Real.

CONVENTO DE LAS DESCALZAS REALES Map pp254-5

☎ 91 454 88 00; www.patrimonionacional.es in Spanish; Plaza de las Descalzas 3; adult/student & EU senior €5/2.50, EU citizens free Wed, combined ticket with Convento de la Encarnación €6/3.40; ⏰ 10.30am-12.30pm & 4-5.30pm Tue-Thu & Sat, 10.30am-12.30pm Fri, 11am-1.30pm Sun & holidays; Ⓜ Callao
The grim, prison-like walls of this one-time palace keep modern Madrid at bay and offer no hint that behind the sober plateresque façade lies a sumptuous stronghold of the faith.

The compulsory guided tour (in Spanish) leads you up a gaudily frescoed Renaissance stairway to the upper level of the cloister. The vault was painted by Claudio Coello, one of the most important artists of the Madrid School (p23) of the 17th century and whose works adorn San Lorenzo de El Escorial.

You then pass several of the convent's 33 chapels – a maximum of 33 Franciscan nuns is allowed to live here (perhaps because Christ is said to have been 33 when he died) as part of a closed order. These nuns follow in the tradition of the Descalzas Reales (Barefooted Royals), a group of illustrious women who cloistered themselves when the convent was founded in the 16th century. The first of these chapels contains a remarkable carved figure of a dead, reclining Christ, which is paraded in a moving Good Friday procession each year. At the end of the passage is the antechoir, then the choir stalls themselves, where Doña Juana – the daughter of Carlos I and who in a typical piece of 16th-century collusion between royalty and the Catholic Church, commandeered the palace and had it converted into a convent – is buried. A *Virgen la Dolorosa* by Pedro de la Mena is seated in one of the 33 oak stalls.

In the former sleeping quarters of the nuns are some of the most extraordinary tapestries you're ever likely to see. Woven in the 17th century in Brussels, they include four based on drawings by Rubens. To produce works of this quality, four or five artisans could take up to a year to weave just 1 sq m of tapestry.

GRAN VÍA Map pp250-1

Ⓜ Gran Vía or Callao
It's difficult to imagine Madrid without Gran Vía, the grand boulevard that climbs through the centre of Madrid from Plaza de España down to Calle de Alcalá, but it has only existed since 1911 when it was bull-dozed through what was then a labyrinth of old streets. It may have destroyed whole neighbourhoods, but it is nonetheless considered one of the most successful examples of urban planning in central Madrid since the late 19th century.

Its short history has been eventful and its very existence was controversial from the start, sweeping away a lively inner-city community, including the house where Goya had once lived, to be replaced by the towering *belle époque* façades that lord it over the street below.

One eye-catching building, the **Carrión** (Map pp250–1), on the corner of Gran Vía and Calle de Jacometrezo, was Madrid's first tower-block apartment hotel and caused quite a stir when it was put up during the pre-WWI years. Also dominating the skyline about one-third of the way along Gran Vía stands the 1920s-era **Telefónica building** (Map pp254–5), which was for years the highest building in the city. During the Civil War, when Madrid was besieged by Franco's forces and the boulevard became known as 'Howitzer Alley' due to the artillery shells that rained down upon it, the Telefónica building was a favoured target.

Among the more interesting buildings is the stunning, French-designed **Edificio Metrópolis** (Map pp254–5; 1905), which marks the southern end of Gran Vía. The winged victory statue atop its dome was added in 1975 and is best seen from Calle de Alcalá or Plaza de Cibeles. A little up the boulevard is the **Edificio Grassy** (with the Piaget sign; Map pp254–5), built in 1916. With its circular 'temple' as a crown, and profusion of arcs and slender columns, it's one of the most elegant buildings on the Gran Vía.

Otherwise, Gran Vía is central Madrid in microcosm, proliferating with luxury hotels and cheap *hostales* (hotels), pinball parlours and dark old cinemas, as well as everything from jewellery stores, banks and high fashion to fast food and sex shops.

IGLESIA DE SAN GINÉS Map pp254–5
☎ 91 366 48 75; Calle del Arenal 13; admission free; ⊗ for services only; Ⓜ Sol or Ópera
Due north of Plaza Mayor, San Ginés is one of Madrid's oldest churches: it has been here in one form or another since at least the 14th century. It is speculated that, prior to the arrival of the Christians in 1085, a Mozarabic community (Christians in Muslim territory) lived around the stream that later became Calle del Arenal and that their parish church stood on this site. What you see

today was built in 1645 but largely reconstructed after a fire in 1824. The church houses some fine paintings, including an El Greco.

IGLESIA DE SAN NICOLÁS DE LOS SERVITAS Map pp254–5
☎ 91 548 83 14; Plaza de San Nicolás 6; admission free; ⊗ 8am-1.30pm & 5.30-8.30pm Mon, 8-9.30am & 6.30-8.30pm Tue-Sat, 9.30am-2pm & 6.30-9pm Sun & holidays; Ⓜ Ópera
Tucked away up the hill from Calle Mayor, this intimate little church is Madrid's oldest surviving building of worship. As such, it offers a rare glimpse of how medieval Madrid must have appeared before it took on the proportions of a city. It is believed to have been built on the site of Muslim Magerit's second mosque. The most striking feature is the restored 12th-century *mudéjar* (decorative style of Islamic architecture as used on Christian buildings) bell tower, although much of the remainder dates in part from the 15th century. The vaulting is late Gothic while the fine timber ceiling, which survived a fire in 1936, dates from about the same period. Other elements inside this small house of worship include plateresque and baroque touches although much of the interior is a study in simplicity. The architect Juan de Herrera (see p25), one of the great architects of Renaissance Spain, was buried in the crypt in 1597.

MURALLA ÁRABE Map pp246–7
Cuesta de la Vega; Ⓜ Ópera
Behind the cathedral apse and down Cuesta de la Vega is a disappointingly short stretch of the so-called Arab Wall, the city wall built by Madrid's early-medieval Muslim rulers. Some of it dates as far back as the 9th century, when the initial Muslim fort was raised. Other sections date from the 12th and 13th centuries, by which time the city had been taken by the Christians. The earliest sections were ingeniously conceived – the outside of the wall was made to look dauntingly sturdy, while the inside was put together with cheap materials to save money. It must have worked, as the town was rarely ever taken by force. In summer, the city council organises open-air theatre and music performances here.

PALACIO DE SANTA CRUZ Map pp254-5

☎ 91 379 95 50; Plaza de la Provincia; Ⓜ Sol
Just off the southeast corner of Plaza Mayor and dominating Plaza de Santa Cruz is this baroque edifice, which houses the **Ministerio de Asuntos Exteriores** (Ministry of Foreign Affairs) and hence can only be admired from the outside. A landmark with its grey slate spires, it was built in 1643 and initially served as the court prison.

PALACIO REAL Map pp254-5

☎ 91 454 88 00; www.patrimonionacional.es in Spanish; Calle de Bailén; adult/student & EU senior €9/3.50, adult without guide €8, EU citizens free Wed, Armería Real €3.40/1.70; ☽ 9am-6pm Mon-Sat, 9am-3pm Sun & holidays Apr-Sep, 9.30am-5pm Mon-Sat, 9am-2pm Sun & holidays Oct-Mar; Ⓜ Ópera
In their modern manifestation, the Bourbons who rule Spain are one of Europe's more modest royal families, but their predecessors lived far more sumptuous lifestyles.

You can almost imagine how the eyes of Felipe V, the first of the Bourbon kings, lit up when the *alcázar* (Muslim-era fortress) burned down in 1734 on Madrid's most exclusive perch of real estate. His plan? Build a palace that would dwarf all its European counterparts. The Italian architect Filippo Juvara (1678–1736), who had made his name building the Basilica di Superga and the Palazzo di Stupinigi in Turin, was called in but, like Felipe, he died without bringing the project to fruition. On Juvara's death, another Italian, Giovanni Battista Sacchetti, took over, finishing the job in 1764.

The result was an Italianate baroque colossus with some 2800 rooms, of which around 50 are open to the public. It's occasionally closed for state ceremonies and official receptions, but the present king is rarely in residence, preferring to live somewhere more modest.

The **Farmacia Real** (Royal Pharmacy), the first set of rooms to the right at the southern end of the **Plaza de la Armería** (Plaza de Armas) courtyard, contains a formidable collection of medicine jars and stills for mixing royal concoctions, suggesting that the royals were either paranoid or decidedly sickly. West across the plaza is the **Armería Real** (Royal Armoury), a hoard of weapons and striking suits of armour, mostly dating from the 16th and 17th centuries.

Changing of the guard at Palacio Real (left)

From the northern end of the Plaza de la Armería, the main stairway, a grand statement of imperial power, leads to the royal apartments and eventually to the **Salón del Trono** (Throne Room). The latter is nauseatingly lavish with its crimson-velvet wall coverings complemented by a ceiling painted by the dramatic Venetian baroque master, Tiepolo, who was a favourite of Carlos III. Nearby, the **Salón de Gasparini** has an exquisite stucco ceiling and walls resplendent with embroidered silks. The aesthetic may be different in the **Sala de Porcelana** but the aura of extravagance continues with myriad pieces from the one-time Retiro porcelain factory screwed into the walls. In the midst of it all comes the spacious **Comedor de Gala** (Gala Dining Room). Only students with passes may enter the **Biblioteca Real** (Royal Library).

If you're lucky, you might just catch the colourful changing of the guard in full parade dress. This takes place at noon on the first Wednesday of every month (except July and August) between the palace and the Catedral de Nuestra Señora de la Almudena.

The French-inspired **Jardines de Sabatini** (☽ 9am-9pm May-Sep, 9am-8pm Oct-Apr) lie along the northern flank of the Palacio Real. They were laid out in the 1930s to replace the royal stables that once stood on the site.

Work is underway on the **Museum of Royal Collections** (Map pp246–7) behind the Catedral de Nuestra Señora de la Almudena and adjacent to the Palacio Real, which is being built to house much of the Palace's collection.

THINGS THEY SAID ABOUT…PUERTA DEL SOL

During the first days I could not tear myself away from the square of the Puerta del Sol. I stayed there by the hour, and amused myself so much that I should like to have passed the day there. It is a square worthy of its fame; not so much on account of its size and beauty as for the people, life and variety of spectacle which it presents at every hour of the day. It is not a square like the others; it is a mingling of salon, promenade, theatre, academy, garden, a square of arms, and a market. From daybreak until one o'clock at night, there is an immovable crowd, a crowd that comes and goes through the ten streets leading into it, and a passing and mingling of carriages which makes one giddy.

Edmondo De Amicis, *Spain & the Spaniards* (1885)

PLAZA DE ESPAÑA Map pp250-1
Ⓜ Plaza de España

It's hard to know what to make of this curiously unprepossessing square. The 1953 **Edificio de España** (Spain Building) on the east side clearly sprang from the totalitarian recesses of Franco's imagination for it is strongly reminiscent of austere Soviet monumentalism, but there is also something strangely grand and pleasing about it. To the north stands the rather ugly and considerably taller 35-storey **Torre de Madrid** (Madrid Tower). Taking centre stage in the square is a statue of Cervantes. At the writer's feet is a bronze of his immortal characters, Don Quixote and Sancho Panza. The monument was erected in 1927. But Plaza de España is at its best down in its lower (western) reaches where abundant trees are remarkably successful in keeping Madrid's noise at bay.

PLAZA DE LA PUERTA DEL SOL
Map pp254-5
Ⓜ Sol

The official centrepoint of Spain is a gracious hemisphere of elegant façades and often overwhelming crowds. It is, above all, a crossroads. People here are forever heading somewhere else, on foot, by metro (three lines cross) or bus (many lines terminate and start here).

In Madrid's earliest days, the Puerta del Sol (the Gate of the Sun),was the eastern gate of the city and from here passed a road through the peasant hovels of the outer 'suburbs' en route to Guadalajara, to the northeast. The name of the gate appears to date from the 1520s, when Madrid joined the revolt of the Comuneros against Carlos I and erected a fortress in the east-facing arch in which the sun was depicted. The fort, which stood about where the metro station is today, was demolished around 1570.

The main building on the square houses the regional government of the Comunidad de Madrid. The **Casa de Correos**, as it is called, was built as the city's main post office in 1768. The clock, which marks a classic meeting place for Madrileños, was added in 1856. On New Year's Eve, people throng the square to wait impatiently for the clock to strike midnight, and at each gong swallow a grape – not as easy as it sounds! The semi-circular junction owes its present appearance in part to the Bourbon king Carlos III (r 1759–88), whose equestrian statue (the nose is unmistakable) stands in the middle.

Just to the north of Carlos, the statue of a bear nuzzling a *madroño* (strawberry tree) is not only the city's symbol but also another favourite meeting place.

PLAZA DE LA VILLA Map pp254-5
☎ 010; ☺ free guided tour of Ayuntamiento 5pm & 6pm Mon; Ⓜ Ópera

There are grander plazas, but this intimate little square is one of Madrid's prettiest. Enclosed on three sides by pleasing and wonderfully preserved examples of 17th-century Madrid-style baroque architecture *(barroco Madrileño)* – a fairly sober local version of the more flowery baroque seen elsewhere – it has been the permanent seat of Madrid's city government since the Middle Ages.

The 17th-century **Ayuntamiento** (town hall), on the western side of the square is a typical Habsburg edifice with Herrerian slate-tile spires. First planned as a prison in 1644 by Juan Gómez de Mora, who also designed the Convento de la Encarnación, its granite and brick façade is a study in sobriety. The final touches to the Casa de la Villa (as the town hall was also known) were only made to the building in 1693, and Juan de Villanueva, of the Museo del Prado fame, made some alterations a century later.

The Ayuntamiento offers free tours (in Spanish) through various reception halls and into the **Salón del Pleno** (council chambers). The latter were restored in the 1890s and again in 1986; the decoration is sumptuous neo-Classical with late 17th-century ceiling frescoes. Look for the ceramic copy of Pedro Teixera's landmark 1656 map of Madrid just outside the chambers.

On the opposite side of the square the 15th-century **Casa de los Lujanes** is more Gothic in conception with a clear *mudéjar* influence. The brickwork tower is said to have been 'home' to the imprisoned French monarch François I and his sons after their capture during the Battle of Pavia (1525). As the star prisoner was paraded down Calle Mayor, locals are said to have been more impressed by the splendidly attired Frenchman than they were by his more drab captor, the Spanish Habsburg emperor Carlos I.

The **Casa de Cisneros**, built in 1537 by the nephew of Cardinal Cisneros, a key adviser to Queen Isabel, is plateresque in inspiration, although it was much restored and altered at the beginning of the 20th century. The main door and window above it are what remains of the Renaissance-era building. It now houses the office of the *alcalde* (mayor) and is home to the **Salón de Tapices** (Tapestries Hall), adorned with exquisite 15th-century Flemish tapestries. It is visited as part of the Ayuntamiento tour.

About 100m east along Calle del Codo and across Plaza del Conde de Miranda is the bustling 19th-century **Mercado de San Miguel** (central produce market) in Plaza de San Miguel. One block southwest of Plaza de la Villa looms the 18th-century baroque remake of the **Iglesia del Sacramento**, the central church of the Spanish army.

Along Calle Mayor, as you approach Calle de Bailén, stands the **Palacio del Duque de Uceda** which is now used as a military headquarters (the Capitanía General). Designed by Juan Gómez de Mora in 1608 in the Madrid baroque style, the palacio replaced an earlier building, outside which five assassins, apparently with Felipe II's approval, killed Juan de Escobedo, envoy of Don John of Austria, on 31 May 1578.

If you duck down behind this massive mansion, you'll end up in Calle de la Villa. At No 2 was once the Estudio Público de Humanidades. This was one of Madrid's more important schools in the 16th century and Cervantes studied here for a while.

PLAZA DE ORIENTE Map pp254-5
Ⓜ **Ópera**

On a summer's evening, there's no finer place to be than the majestic Plaza de Oriente, which was given its present form under French occupation in the early 1800s. Overlooked by the Palacio Real, and enclosed by a semicircle of elegant (and superexpensive) apartment buildings, cafés and the Teatro Real, the square is one of Madrid's most open and agreeable. The square is dominated by an equestrian statue (designed by Velázquez) of Felipe IV and littered with 20 statues of mostly ancient monarchs who, local legend has it, get down off their pedestals at night and stretch their legs a bit.

If you were wondering how a heavy bronze statue of a rider and his horse rearing up can actually maintain that stance, the answer is simple – the hind legs are solid while the front ones are hollow. That idea was Galileo Galilei's.

The adjacent **Jardines Cabo Naval**, which is a great place to watch the sun set, adds to the sense of a sophisticated oasis of green in the heart of Madrid.

PLAZA DE RAMALES Map pp254-5
Ⓜ **Ópera**

Unfortunately this pleasant little triangle of open space was beset with major building works along its west side when we last passed through, but it's not without historical intrigue. Joseph Bonaparte ordered the destruction of the Iglesia de San Juanito to open up a pocket of fresh air in the then-crowded streets. It is believed Velázquez was buried in the church; excavations in 2000 revealed the crypt of the former church and the remains of various people buried in it centuries ago, but Velázquez was nowhere to be found.

PLAZA MAYOR Map pp254-5
Ⓜ **Sol**

The stunningly beautiful Plaza Mayor is an undoubted highlight of any visit to Madrid. The grandeur of its buildings – the uniformly ochre apartments with wrought-iron balconies offset by the exquisite frescoes of the 17th-century **Real Casa de la Panadería** (Royal Bakery) – is one thing, but this is a living, breathing entity, from the outdoor tables of the *terrazas* to the students strewn across the cobblestones on a sunny day.

Ah, the history the plaza has seen! Designed in 1619 by Juan Gómez de Mora and built in typical Herrerian style, of which the slate spires are the most obvious expression, its first public ceremony was suitably auspicious – the beatification of San Isidro Labrador (St Isidro the Farm Labourer), Madrid's patron saint. Thereafter it was as if all that was controversial about Spain took place in this square. Bullfights, often in celebration of royal weddings or births, with royalty watching on from the balconies and up to 50,000 people crammed into the plaza were a recurring theme until 1878. Far more notorious were the *autos-de-fe* (the ritual condemnation of heretics) followed by executions – burnings at the stake, deaths by garrotte on the north side of the square and hangings to the south. These continued until 1790 when a fire largely destroyed the square, which was subsequently reproduced under the supervision of Juan de Villanueva who lent his name to the building that now houses the Museo del Prado.

Not all the plaza's activities were grand events and just as it is now surrounded by shops, it was once filled with food vendors. In 1673, King Carlos II issued an edict allowing the vendors to raise tarpaulins above their stalls to protect their wares and themselves from the refuse and raw sewage that people habitually tossed out of the windows above! Well into the 20th century, trams ran through the Plaza Mayor.

In the middle of the present-day square stands an equestrian statue of the man who ordered its construction, Felipe III. Originally placed in the Casa de Campo, it was moved to the Plaza Mayor in 1848, whereafter it became a favoured meeting place for irreverent Madrileños who arranged to catch up 'under the balls of the horse'. The colourful frescoes on the Real Casa de la Panadería were painted in 1992, replacing earlier ones.

REAL ACADEMIA DE BELLAS ARTES DE SAN FERNANDO Map pp254-5

☎ 91 524 08 64; http://rabasf.insde.es in Spanish; Calle de Alcalá 13; adult/student/child under 18 & senior €2.40/1.20/free, free to all on Wed; ☉ 9am-7pm Tue-Fri, 9am-2.30pm Sat-Mon Sep-Jun, varied hours in Jul & Aug; Ⓜ Sevilla

In any other city, this gallery would be a stand-out attraction, but in Madrid it too often gets forgotten in the rush to the Prado, Thyssen or Reina Sofía. A visit here is a fascinating journey into another age of art, although when we tell you that Picasso and Dalí studied at this academy (long the academic centre of learning for up-and-coming artists), but found it far too stuffy for their liking, you'll get an idea of what to expect. A centre of excellence since Fernando VI founded the academy in the 18th century, it remains a stunning repository of works by some of the best-loved old Spanish masters.

The 1st floor, mainly devoted to a mix of 16th- to 19th-century paintings, is the most noteworthy of those in the academic gallery. Among relative scattered unknowns you come across a hall of works by Zurbarán – especially arresting is the series of full-length portraits of white-cloaked friars – and a *San Jerónimo* by El Greco.

At a 'fork' in the exhibition a sign points right to Rooms 11–16, the main one showcasing Alonso Cano (1601–67) and José de Ribera (1591–1652). In the others, a couple of minor portraits by Velázquez hang alongside the occasional Rubens, Tintoretto and Bellini, which have somehow been smuggled in. Rooms 17 to 22 offer a roomful of Bravo Murillo and last, but most captivating, more than a dozen pieces by Goya, including self-portraits, portraits of King Fernando VII and the infamous minister Manuel Godoy, along with one on bullfighting.

The 19th and 20th centuries are the themes upstairs. It's not the most extensive or engaging modern collection but you'll find drawings by Picasso as well as works by Joaquín Sorolla, Juan Gris, Eduardo Chillida and Ignacio Zuloaga, in most cases with only one or two items each.

TEATRO REAL Map pp254-5

☎ 91 516 06 60; www.teatro-real.com in Spanish; Plaza de Oriente; admission by guided tour (in Spanish) adult/student up to 26 years & senior €4/2; ☉ 1pm Tue-Fri, 11.30am-1.30pm Sat, Sun & holidays; Ⓜ Ópera

Backing onto the Plaza de Oriente, Madrid's signature opera house does not have the most distinguished of histories. The first theatre was built in 1708 on the site of the public washhouses. Torn down in 1816, its successor was built in 1850 under the reign of Isabel II, whereafter it was burned down and later blown up in the Civil War (when it was used as a powder store, resulting in

(Continued on page 75)

1 *Madrileño children in folk dress*
2 *A Spanish guard on horseback*
3 *Woman in traditional Spanish costume during the Fiestas de San Isidro Labrador (p10)* **4** *Guitarist at the Fiestas de San Isidro Labrador (p10)*

1 *Façade of the Palacio de Comunicaciones (p88)* **2** *Picasso's Guernica (p82), Centro de Arte Reine Sofía (p80)* **3** *Bustling Plaza Mayor (p65)*

...ntro de Arte Reina Sofía
...) **2** Palacio Real (p63)
...nset over Puerta de Alcalá
...)

1 *Ice-cream lovers at Giangrossi (p123)* **2** *Chocolates at Cacao Sampaka (p164)* **3** *Suckling pig at Restaurante Sobrino de Botín (p115)* **4** *Drinking on Plaza de Santa Ana (p82)*

1 *People eating chocolate y churros (p129)* **2** *Fine Spanish wines (p40)* **3** *Traditional Spanish paella (p126)* **4** *Gran Café de Gijón (p125)*

1 *Café La Palma (p114)* **2** *Clubbers at Cool (p139)* **3** *Flamenco dancing (p30)* **4** *Flamenco band at Cardamomo (p145)*

1 *Fans on display at El Rastro (p159)* 2 *Agatha Ruiz de la Prada designer store (p161)* 3 *Rosettes on sale for carnival time* 4 *Designer fashions on Calle De Serrano (p175)*

1 Campo del Moro (p60)
2 Alfonso XII's Mausoleum
(p88) overlooking the lake
Parque del Buen Retiro (p8
3 Real Jardín Botánico (p8

(Continued from page 66)

the inevitable fireworks). It finally took its present neo-Classical form in 1997 and, viewed from Plaza de Isabel II, it's a fine addition to the central Madrid cityscape; in Plaza de Oriente, however, it's somewhat overshadowed by the splendour of its surrounds. The 1997 renovations combined the latest in theatre and acoustic technology with a remake of the most splendid of its 19th-century décor. The guided tours take about 50 minutes. See also p147.

LA LATINA & LAVAPIÉS

Drinking p133, Eating p116, Nightlife p139, Shopping p159, Sleeping p171

With an identity all its own, Lavapiés is one of Madrid's oldest and most traditional barrios. There's something medieval about its steep streets, which are home to quirky bars, restaurants and alternative-cool shops. While for centuries, the rest of central Madrid had a fairly homogenous population, with poor Spaniards and immigrants banished to the burgeoning dormitory suburbs and towns to the north and south, Lavapiés has always been rundown and multicultural, a variegated community of migrants, legal and otherwise, that has lent the place a unique dimension. Black Africans, Moroccans, South Americans and Chinese live cheek by jowl with locals whose grandparents also lived here and who wouldn't live anywhere else. It's a gritty, fascinating and generally harmonious mix. To live in Lavapiés is a statement of attitude. To spend any time here is essential to understanding modern Madrid.

Lavapiés spills over into La Latina, which comes to life on weekends and throngs on Sundays with the Rastro crowd keen to savour one of Europe's most engaging flea markets. La Latina encompasses the onetime Moorish quarter of medieval Christian Madrid and still represents something of a meeting point between the old-world elegance of Madrid de los Austrias and working-class Lavapiés. It appeals not just to tourists – house prices here are soaring.

For advice on how to dive into the mix, see boxed text p172.

Orientation

La Latina forms a rough triangle bordered by Calle de Segovia, Ronda de Segovia and

TOP SIGHTS IN LA LATINA & LAVAPIÉS

- El Rastro (p76)
- Lavapiés (p77)
- Basílica de San Francisco El Grande (p76)
- Iglesia de San Andrés (p77)

Calle de Toledo, which separates it from Lavapiés. The web of lanes around Calle de Segovia and Calle de Bailén once constituted the Morería, the Moorish quarter of Magerit, while the medieval city walls once loosely followed Calles de la Cava Baja and de la Cava Alta. The sloping gardens of Vistillas at the western end of the barrio offer nice views west to the Sierra de Guadarrama. Just south of the gardens stands the fine baroque Basílica de San Francisco el Grande.

From Plaza de Tirso de Molina and Calle de la Magdalena a series of long narrow lanes drops downhill into Lavapiés. The barrio's most obvious nerve centre is the small triangular Plaza de Lavapiés (where the metro stop is); there's a hotchpotch of interesting bars and eateries close by. Further west, the streets of El Rastro, between Calle de los Embajadores and Ribera de los Curtidores are important thoroughfares.

Lavapiés is cordoned off to the south by Ronda de Toledo and Ronda de Atocha, noisy and ugly avenues that head east to Atocha station.

BASÍLICA DE NUESTRA SEÑORA DEL BUEN CONSEJO Map pp254-5

☎ 91 369 20 37; Calle de Toledo 37; ☷ 8am-noon & 6-8.30pm; Ⓜ Tirso de Molina

Towering above the northern end of bustling Calle de Toledo, which runs south from Plaza Major, is the imposing church that long served as the city's de facto cathedral until Nuestra Señora de la Almudena was completed in 1992.

Still known to locals as the Catedral de San Isidro, the austere baroque basilica was founded in the 17th century as the headquarters for the Jesuits and today is home to the remains of the city's main patron saint, San Isidro (in the third chapel on your left after you walk in). His body, apparently remarkably well preserved, is only removed from here on rare occasions, such as in 1896 and 1947 when he was paraded about town in the hope he would bring rain.

Next door, the **Instituto de San Isidro** once went by the name of Colegio Imperial and, from the 16th century on, was where many of the country's leading figures were schooled by the Jesuits. You can wander in and look at the elegant courtyard.

Just south of the church, the road forks. The left fork, Calle de los Estudios, leads into El Rastro. Calle de Toledo continues off to the right and leads 800m further downhill to the triumphal arch at the **Puerta de Toledo** (Map pp246–7) and beyond. Completed in 1817 to celebrate the defeat of Napoleon, it was actually begun by Joseph Bonaparte to celebrate a French victory! Beyond, the 18th-century **Puente de Toledo**, completed in 1732 by Pedro de Ribera and still Madrid's most elegant bridge, spans the Río Manzanares.

BASÍLICA DE SAN FRANCISCO EL GRANDE Map pp246-7

☎ 91 365 38 00; Plaza de San Francisco; admission €3; ☼ 11am-1pm & 5-7pm Tue-Sat; Ⓜ La Latina or bus 3, 60, 148

Lording it over the southwestern corner of La Latina, this imposing and recently restored baroque basilica is far enough away from the well-trodden tourist trail to give a sense of one of Madrid's grand old churches; it feels more like a local church (albeit a struggling one) than a tourist attraction. Beneath the frescoed cupolas (restored in 2000–01) and the appealing

Rooftop of the Basílica de San Francisco el Grande (above)

chapel ceilings by Francisco Bayeu, old women seem lost amid the empty pews as priests try to ignore the fact that church attendance in Spain is at an all-time low.

Legend has it that St Francis of Assisi built a chapel on this site in 1217. The current version – one of the city's largest – was designed by Francesco Sabatini, who also designed the Puerta de Alcalá and finished off the Palacio Real. He designed the church with a highly unusual floor plan: when you enter, the building arcs off to the left and right in a flurry of columns. Off this circular nave lie several chapels, while a series of corridors behind the high altar is lined with works of art. A guide usually directs you to the sacristy, which features fine Renaissance *sillería* – the sculpted walnut seats where the church's superiors would meet.

A 19th-century plan to create a grand linking square supported by a viaduct between this church and the Palacio Real never left the drawing board, but you can see a model in the Museo Municipal.

BASÍLICA DE SAN MIGUEL Map pp254-5

☎ 91 548 40 11; Calle de San Justo 4; ☼ 10.30am-12.30pm & 6-8.30pm Mon-Sat; Ⓜ La Latina or Sol

Hidden away off Calle de Segovia, this basilica is something of a surprise. Its convex, late-baroque façade sits in harmony with the surrounding buildings of old Madrid and among its fine features are statues representing the four virtues, and the reliefs of Justo and Pastor, the saints to whom the church was originally dedicated. The rococo and Italianate interior, completed by Italian architects in 1745, is another world altogether with gilded gold flourishes and dark, sombre domes.

EL RASTRO Map pp254-5

Ribera de los Curtidores; ☼ 8am-3pm Sun & holidays; Ⓜ La Latina

The crowded Sunday flea market was, back in the 17th and 18th centuries, largely dedicated to a meat market (the word *rastro*, which means 'stain', referred to the trail of blood left behind by animals dragged down the hill). The road leading to the market, Ribera de los Curtidores, translates as Tanners' Alley and further evokes this sense of a slaughterhouse past. On Sunday mornings, this is *the* place to be, with all of Madrid in all its diversity here in search of a bargain (see p159).

THINGS THEY SAID ABOUT... EL RASTRO

The Rastro was itself a curious place then, almost medieval. There was sold almost everything imaginable: used clothes, pictures, false teeth, books, medicines, chestnuts, coach wheels, trusses, shoes. There one met all types: Moors, Jews, blacks, travelling charlatans, rat-catchers and sellers of caged birds.

Pío Baroja, *Desde la última vuelta del Camino,* (1948)

IGLESIA DE SAN ANDRÉS Map pp254-5

☎ 91 365 48 71; Plaza de San Andrés; ⏲ 8am-1pm & 5.30-8pm; Ⓜ La Latina

This proud church is more imposing than beautiful and what you see today is the result of restoration work completed after the church was gutted during the Civil War. Like many of Madrid's churches, it's at its best when illuminated by night as a backdrop for local café life.

The interior is not without its appeal, most notably its extraordinary baroque altar. Stern, dark columns with gold-leaf capitals against the rear wall lead your eyes up into the dome, all rose, yellow and green, and rich with sculpted floral fantasies and cherubs poking out of every nook and cranny.

Across from the main entrance on Plaza de San Andrés is a deceptively realistic mural that rises three stories and will have you looking twice.

Around the back, on **Plaza de la Paja** (Straw Square), is the **Capilla del Obispo**, a hugely important site on the historical map of Madrid. It was here that San Isidro Labrador, patron saint of Madrid, was first buried. When the saint's body was discovered there in the late 13th century, two centuries after his death, decomposition had not yet set in. Thus it was that King Alfonso XI ordered the construction in San Andrés of an ark to hold his remains and a chapel in which to venerate his memory.

In 1669 (47 years after the saint was canonised), the last of many chapels was built on the site and that's what you see today. If you're allowed in (the chapel is generally closed except for temporary exhibitions), note the Gothic vaulting in the ceilings and the fine Renaissance reredos (screens), a combination that's quite rare in Madrid. But don't go looking for the saint's remains because San Isidro made his last move to the Basílica Nuestra Señora del Buen Consejo in the 18th century.

IGLESIA DE SAN PEDRO EL VIEJO

Map pp254-5

☎ 91 365 12 84; Costanilla de San Pedro; Ⓜ La Latina

Like the Iglesia de San Nicolás de los Servitas, this fine old church is one of the few remaining windows on medieval Madrid, most notably its clearly *mudéjar* bell tower. The church arose in the days when Madrid was still influenced by its Muslim occupation and the two churches are the only sites where traces of *mudéjar* Madrid remain *in situ*. Otherwise, you need to visit Toledo (p181), 70km south of Madrid, to visualise what Madrid once was like. The church interior (generally closed) is 15th-century Gothic, although largely disguised by 17th-century renovation.

LA CASA ENCENDIDA Map pp246-7

☎ 902 430 322; www.lacasaencendida.com in Spanish; Ronda de Valencia 2; ⏲ 10am-10pm; Ⓜ Embajadores

This cultural centre is utterly unpredictable, if only because of the quantity and scope of its activities – everything from exhibitions, cinema sessions, workshops and more. The focus is often on international artists or environmental themes.

LAVAPIÉS Map pp254-5

Ⓜ Lavapiés

There's nowhere quite like Lavapiés. It's not that there are specific tourist attractions worth seeing – in fact, there aren't any of note. Rather, coming here is about exploring a medieval street plan and immersing yourself in one of Madrid's most intriguing barrios. It's at once deeply traditional – when Madrileños dress up for the Fiestas de San Isidro Labrador (p11), they don the outfits of working-class *chulapos* and *manolas* who frequented Lavapiés in centuries past – and proudly multicultural, home to more immigrants than any other central Madrid barrio. It's quirky, alternative and a melting pot all in one and, despite the diversity, you get the rare sense of a community where everyone seems to know one another. People hang out the windows and talk (or shout) to one another across the washing hung out to dry over the narrow streets.

If Spain's emergence as a multi-ethnic, multifaith country works anywhere, it works here, perhaps because Lavapiés has had more practice at it than the rest of Spain. The name comes from *aba-puest* ('place of the Jews') because the bulk of the city's Jewish population once lived in the eastern half of Lavapiés (the existence, centuries ago, of at least one synagogue in the area is documented) in what was then known as the *Judería* (Jewish quarter). The bulk of them left after the Catholic Monarchs ordered the expulsion of Jews and Muslims from Spain in 1492. Those who remained behind became *conversos* (converts to Christianity).

Lavapiés is now home to a fascinating mix of working-class *gatos* (cats – slang for Madrileños), *gitanos* (Roma people) and migrants from far and wide. According to one count, people from over 50 countries are represented in an area made up of a couple of dozen streets. It remains a largely poor part of town with its fair share of run-down apartments, but house prices are rising, not least because of the bohemian attraction it holds for many young people.

If you need some direction for your wanderings, begin in the **Plaza de Lavapiés** and strike out into any of the surrounding streets. One building that catches the community spirit of this lively barrio is **La Corrala** (Map pp246–7; Calle de Mesón de Paredes 65), an intriguing traditional (if much tidied up) tenement block, built around a central courtyard, which functions now as a make-shift stage for (mainly summertime) theatre. The **Teatro Valle-Inclán**, on the southern edge of the Plaza de Lavapiés, and formerly

known as the Teatro Olímpico, is a stunning contemporary addition to the eclectic Lavapiés streetscape.

MUSEO DE SAN ISIDRO Map pp254-5
☎ 91 366 74 15; www.munimadrid.es/museo sanisidro; Plaza de San Andrés 2; admission free; ⏰ 9.30am-8pm Tue-Fri, 10am-2pm Sat & Sun; Ⓜ La Latina

Next door to the Iglesia de San Andrés is a modest building on the spot where they say San Isidro Labrador (the patron saint of Madrid) ended his days around 1172. Of great historical interest (though not much to look at) is the 'miraculous well' where the saint called forth water to slake his master's thirst. In another miracle, the son of the saint's master fell into a well, whereupon Isidro prayed and prayed until the water rose and lifted his son to safety.

The small museum is housed in a largely new building with a 16th-century Renaissance courtyard and a 17th-century chapel, and contains assorted archaeological finds from old Madrid. These include a mosaic found on the site of a Roman villa in Carabanchel, now a southern suburb of the city, as well as various Iron Age, Bronze Age and Roman artefacts dug up around the Río Manzanares as well as a few Visigothic and Muslim-era odds and ends. Another highlight is a model based on Pedro Teixera's 1656 map of Madrid. Most of the museum building is taken up with temporary exhibition space.

PLAZA DE LA CEBADA Map pp254-5
Ⓜ La Latina

Just west of La Latina metro station, the busy and bar-strewn corner of Madrid marked by the ill-defined 'Barley Square' is one of the key historical sites for understanding what medieval Madrid was like, although it requires a little imagination.

In the wake of the Christian conquest the square was, for a time, the site of a Muslim cemetery, and the nearby **Plaza de la Puerta de Moros** (Moors' Gate) underscores that this area was long home to the city's Muslim population. The square eventually became a popular spot for public executions – until well into the 19th century, the condemned would be paraded along Calle de Toledo, before turning into the square and mounting the gallows. In an era when decent entertainment was hard to come by, it appears Madrileños rather enjoyed a good execution.

The **Teatro de la Latina**, at the Calle de Toledo end of the elongated square, stands where one of Queen Isabel's closest advisers, Beatriz Galindo, built a hospital in the 15th century. A noted humanist, Galindo was known as 'La Latina' for her prodigious knowledge of Latin (which she taught Queen Isabel) and general erudition. Only Galindo's nickname reminds us of what once stood here.

Not far from the theatre, the narrow streets of **Calle de la Cava Alta** and **Calle de la Cava Baja** delineate where the second line of medieval Christian city walls ran. They continued up along what is now **Calle de los Cuchilleros** (Knifemakers St) and along the **Cava de San Miguel**, and were superseded by the third circuit of walls, which was raised in the 15th century. The *cavas* were initially ditches dug in front of the walls, later used as refuse dumps and finally given over to housing when the walls no longer served any defensive purpose.

VIADUCT & CALLE DE SEGOVIA
Map pp246-7
Ⓜ **Ópera**

Jardines de las Vistillas, the leafy area around and beneath the southern end of the viaduct that crosses Calle de Segovia is an ideal spot to pause and ponder the curious history of one of Madrid's oldest barrios.

Probably the best place to do this is just across Calle de Bailén where the *terrazas* of **Las Vistillas** offer one of the best vantage points in Madrid for a drink, with views towards the Sierra de Guadarrama. During the Civil War, Las Vistillas was heavily bombarded by Nationalist troops from the Casa de Campo, and they in turn were shelled from a republican bunker here.

The adjacent viaduct, which was built in the 19th century and replaced by a newer version in 1942, would also become a place associated with death, albeit of a different kind. It was the suicide launch-pad of choice until plastic barriers were erected in the late 1990s. They obscure the views but one assumes the local death rate has dropped, too.

Before the viaduct was built, anyone wanting to cross over was obliged to make their way down to Calle de Segovia and back up the other side. If you feel like re-enacting the journey, head down to Calle de Segovia and cross to the southern side.

Just east of the viaduct, on a characterless apartment block (No 21) wall, is one of the city's oldest **coats of arms**. The site once belonged to Madrid's Ayuntamiento. Take care when crossing the street because the pace of traffic is a far cry from the days when a punt ferried people across what was then a trickling tributary of the Manzanares.

Climbing back up the southern side from Calle de Segovia you reach Calle de la Morería. The area south to the Basílica de San Francisco el Grande and southeast to the Iglesia de San Andrés was the heart of the *morería* (Moorish quarter). The Muslim population of Magerit was concentrated here following the 11th-century Christian takeover. Strain the imagination a little and the maze of winding and hilly lanes even now retains a whiff of a North African medina.

Another option is to follow Calle de Segovia west, down to the banks of the Manzanares and a nine-arched bridge, the **Puente de Segovia**, which Juan de Herrera built in 1584. The walk is more pleasant than the river, a view shared by the writer Lope de Vega who thought the bridge a little too grand for the 'apprentice river'. He suggested the city buy a bigger river or sell the bridge!

HUERTAS & ATOCHA
Drinking p134, Eating p118, Nightlife p140, Shopping p160, Sleeping p172

The area around Calle de las Huertas is Madrid in a nutshell.

By day, it's a place to enjoy the height of sophisticated European café culture in the superb Plaza de Santa Ana. Down the hill, into the impossibly narrow and largely traffic-free streets, you'll find restaurants, quirky shops and a few landmarks to the days when Madrid's writers made this their home – the other name for this area is the Barrio de las Letras (Barrio of Letters). If you keep going down the hill, you'll end up at the Centro de Arte Reina Sofía, one of the finest contemporary art galleries in Europe and just across from the Atocha train station.

By night, Madrileños turn up the volume and the roar emanating from the area's countless bars, and jazz and flamenco venues rises up and spreads across the city. It's all very cultural, casual and, dare we say it, downright intoxicating.

For taking the pulse of this busy barrio, see boxed text p173.

TOP SIGHTS IN HUERTAS & ATOCHA

- Centro de Arte Reina Sofía (right)
- Plaza de Santa Ana (p82)
- Casa de Lope de Vega (right)

Orientation

The Huertas area owes its name to the mostly traffic-free Calle de las Huertas, which starts just southwest of the Plaza de Santa Ana and runs all the way down the hill to the Paseo del Prado. Other streets connect the centre of Madrid to the Paseo del Prado, most notably Calle de Atocha, which ends at the thundering roundabout of Plaza del Emperador Carlos V. This roundabout is flanked on one side by the Atocha train station, the 19th-century gateway into the capital, and on the other by the Centro de Arte Reina Sofía.

Heading north from the Plaza de Santa Ana, more intriguing, tightly packed streets lead towards the Carrera de San Jerónimo, which slips by the Congreso de los Diputados (lower house of the national parliament) on its way down to the Plaza de Neptuno.

ANTIGUA ESTACIÓN DE ATOCHA

Map pp246-7

Plaza del Emperador Carlos V; Ⓜ Atocha Renfe
Large areas of central Madrid may have been blighted by ill-conceived and downright ugly apartment blocks in the 1970s, but by the 1990s the city's developers had learned to make use of the elegant architecture of yesteryear. Nowhere is this more evident than at the Antiguo Estación de Atocha where the grand iron and glass relic from the 19th century was preserved and artfully converted in 1992 into a surprising tropical garden with more than 500 plant species. Around the greenery, various shops and Renfe information offices have been installed, along with a pretty mezzanine restaurant. The project was the work of architect Rafael Moneo, who is now behind the still more ambitious Gran Prado project. The tropical garden station certainly makes a pleasant, although slightly humid, departure or arrival point in Madrid and the cavernous ceiling resonates with the grand old European train stations of another age.

ATENEO CIENTÍFICO, LITERARIO Y ARTÍSTICO DE MADRID Map ppp254-5

☎ 91 429 17 50; Calle del Prado 21; Ⓜ Sevilla
Nestled away in the heart of what is unofficially known as the Barrio de las Letras, this venerable club of learned types was founded in the 19th century and has hardly changed since. It's not really open to the public, but no-one seems to mind if you wander into the foyer, which is lined with portraits of terribly serious-looking fellows. They may even let you amble upstairs to the library, a jewel of another age, with dark timber stacks, weighty tomes and creakily quiet reading rooms dimly lit with desk lamps.

CASA DE LOPE DE VEGA Map pp254-5

☎ 91 429 92 16; Calle de Cervantes 11; adult/student & senior €2/1, free Sat; ☿ 9.30am-2pm Tue-Fri, 10am-2pm Sat; Ⓜ Antón Martín
Lope de Vega may be little known outside the Spanish-speaking world, but he was one of the greatest playwrights ever to write in Spanish, not to mention one of Madrid's favourite and most colourful literary sons. What Real Madrid's footballers now are to Madrid's celebrity rumour mill, Lope de Vega was to scandalised Madrid society in the 17th century; he shared the house, where he lived and wrote for 25 years until his death in 1635, with a mistress and four children by three different women. Today the house, which was restored in the 1950s, is filled with memorabilia related to his life and times. Lope de Vega's house was a typical *casa de malicia* (roughly translated, 'sneaky house'). Out the back is a tranquil garden, a rare haven of birdsong in this somewhat claustrophobic district. It is believed that Cervantes, the author of Don Quixote and far less famous than Lope de Vega in his day, died a few doors up the road at No 2.

CENTRO DE ARTE REINA SOFÍA

Map pp254-5

☎ 91 774 10 00; www.reinasofia.es; Calle de Santa Isabel 52; adult/student/child under 12 & senior over 65 €6/4/free, free to all Sat 2.30-9pm & Sun, handset guide €3; ☿ 10am-9pm Mon & Wed-Sat, 10am-2.30pm Sun Ⓜ Atocha
Adapted from the shell of an 18th-century hospital, the Centro de Arte Reina Sofía houses the best Madrid has to offer in

modern Spanish art, principally spanning the 20th century up to the 1980s (for more recent works, visit the Museo Municipal de Arte Contemporáneo; p94). The occasional non-Spaniard artist makes an appearance at the Reina Sofía, but most of the collection is strictly peninsular.

While the stately grandeur of the 18th-century palace, which houses the Museo del Prado, is an essential part of the Prado's charm, the state-of-the-art Reina Sofía is a perfect showpiece for converting old-world architecture to meet the needs of a dynamic modern collection. This is especially the case in the stunning extension that spreads along the western tip of the Plaza del Emperador Carlos V and which hosts temporary exhibitions, auditoriums, the bookshop, a café and the museum's library.

The main gallery's permanent display ranges over the 2nd (Rooms 1 to 17) and 4th floors (Rooms 18 to 45). The gallery refers to the ground floor as the 1st floor and so on; we'll use its floor-numbering system here. As you skip from room to room and from floor to floor, the peaceful courtyard offers a peaceful respite from the clamour of Madrid, while the views over the city from the external glass lift, especially on the top floor, are outstanding.

The big attraction for most visitors is Picasso's *Guernica* (see boxed text, p82), in Room 6 on the 2nd floor, which is worth the entrance price even if you see nothing else. Alongside this masterwork is a plethora of the artist's preparatory sketches, offering an intriguing insight into the development of this seminal work.

Rush straight for it if you must, but don't make the mistake of neglecting the other outstanding works on show here.

Primary among the other stars in residence is the work of Joan Miró (1893–1983), which adorns Room 7, a long gallery adjacent to the Picasso collection. Amid his often delightfully bright primary-colour efforts are some of his equally odd sculptures. Since his paintings became a symbol of the Barcelona Olympics in 1992, his work has begun to receive the international acclaim it so richly deserves and this is the best place to get a representative sample of his innovative work.

In Room 9 you can see a couple of small canvasses by Vassily Kandinsky (1866–1944), one of the few foreigners on show here, but you'll want to rush to Room 10 to view the 20 or so canvases by Salvador Dalí (1904–1989), especially the surrealist extravaganza *El Gran Masturbador* (1929). Amid this collection is a strange bust of a certain *Joelle* done by Dalí and his pal Man Ray (1890–1976). Other surrealists, including Max Ernst (1891–1976), appear in Room 11.

If you can tear yourself away from the big names, the Reina Sofía proffers a terrific opportunity to learn more about 20th-century Spanish art, examples of which are littered throughout the gallery. Room 12, for example, concentrates on the Madrileño José Gutiérrez Solana (1886–1945). He depicts himself in gloomy fashion in *La Tertulia del Café de Pombo* (*The Circle of the Café Pombo;* 1920). Room 3 hosts works by the better-known Juan Gris, and these spill over into Room 4. Among the bronzes of Pablo Gargallo (1881–1934) in Room 5 is a head of Picasso. Also on the 2nd floor, in Room 1, you'll find the excellent works of the important Basque painter Ignazio Zuloaga (1870–1945).

Room 12 has a display dedicated to Buñuel, including a portrait of the filmmaker by Dalí and sketches by the poet Federico García Lorca. Room 13 hosts a long list of artists active in the turbulent decades of the 1920s and 1930s, including Benjamín Palencia. Luis Fernández (1900–73) dominates Room 14.

The collection on the 4th floor takes up the baton and continues from the 1940s until the 1980s. A new approach to landscapes evolved in the wake of the Civil

The eclectic Centro de Arte Reina Sofía (p80)

GUERNICA

Guernica is one of the most famous paintings in the world, a signature work of cubism whose disfiguration of the human form would become an eloquent symbol of a world's outrage at the horrors wrought upon the innocent by modern warfare.

Already associated with the Republicans when the Civil War broke out in 1936, Picasso was commissioned by the Republican government of Madrid to do the painting for the Paris Exposition Universelle in 1937. As news filtered out about the bombing of Gernika (Guernica) in the Basque Country by Hitler's Legión Condor, at the request of Franco, on 26 April 1937 (almost 2000 people died in the attack and much of the town was destroyed), Picasso shelved his earlier plans and committed his anger to canvas. To understand the painting's earth-shattering impact at the time, it must be remembered that the attack on Guernica represented the first use of airborne military hardware to devastating effect.

Guernica has always been a controversial work and was initially derided by many as being more propaganda than art. The 3.5m by 7.8m painting subsequently migrated to the USA and only returned to Spain in 1981, in keeping with Picasso's wish that the painting return to Spanish shores once democracy had been restored. The Basques believe that its true home is in the Basque Country and calls to have it moved there continue unabated, although such a move is unlikely to happen anytime soon.

War, perhaps best exemplified by the work of Juan Manuel Díaz Caneja (1905–88) in Room 18. In the following room you can study works by two important groups to emerge after WWII, Pórtico and Dau al Set. Among artists of the latter was Barcelona's Antoni Tàpies (b 1923), some of whose later pieces also appear in Rooms 34 and 35.

Rooms 20 to 23 offer a representative look at abstract painting in Spain. Among the more significant contributors are Eusebio Sempere (1923–85) and members of the Equipo 57 group (founded in 1957 by a group of Spanish artists in exile in Paris), such as Pablo Palazuelo. Rooms 24 to 35 leads you through Spanish art of the 1960s and 1970s. Some external reference points, such as works by Francis Bacon (1909–92) and Henry Moore (1831–95), both in Room 24, are thrown in to broaden the context.

Closer to the present day, Room 38 is given over to work by Eduardo Arroyo, while beautiful works of the Basque sculptor Eduardo Chillida (1924–2002) fill Rooms 42 and 43.

CONGRESO DE LOS DIPUTADOS

Map pp254-5

☎ 91 390 60 00; Plaza de las Cortes; admission free; ◷ guided tours 10am-noon Sat; Ⓜ Sevilla
Spain's lower house of parliament was originally a Renaissance building, but it was completely revamped in 1843 and given a façade with a neo-Classical portal. The modern extension tacked onto it seems a rather odd afterthought. Bring your passport if you want to visit.

PLAZA DE SANTA ANA Map pp254-5

Ⓜ Sevilla, Sol or Antón Martín
The Plaza de Santa Ana is a delightful confluence of elegant architecture and irresistible energy. What it lacks in distinguished history, it makes up for as a focal point of music (there are smoky flamenco bars in the surrounding streets and street performers love the plaza itself), culture (from the Teatro Español to the favourite haunts of bullfighters), daytime café sophistication and nocturnal, full-volume hedonism.

Sure, it was discovered long ago by resident and visiting *guiris* (foreigners). And true, some *gatos* haughtily avoid it for that very reason. But many a true-blue *gato* winds up here for an afternoon coffee or a long, long evening.

PASEO DEL PRADO & EL RETIRO

Eating p120, Sleeping p174

If you've just come down the hill from Huertas, you'll feel like you've left behind a mad house for an oasis of greenery, fresh air and culture. The Museo del Prado and the Museo Thyssen-Bornemisza are among the richest galleries of fine art in the world and plenty of other museums lurk in the quietly elegant streets just behind the Prado. Rising up the hill to the east are the stately gardens of the supremely enjoyable Parque del Buen Retiro.

For more ideas on enjoying Paseo del Prado & El Retiro, see boxed text p174.

Orientation

The Paseo del Prado – which becomes the Paseo de los Recoletos and then the Paseo de la Castellana further north – cuts through the heart of modern Madrid. Once, it was a stream that marked the city's eastern extremity. The *prado* (field) was the preserve of gardens and palaces that were green playgrounds for Madrid's swollen nobility.

ERMITA DE SAN ISIDORO Map pp246-7

Cnr Calle O'Donnell & Avenida de Menéndez Pelayo; Ⓜ Príncipe de Vergara

As you ramble through the northeastern corner of the Parque del Buen Retiro, keep an eye out for the remnants of this small country chapel, which is noteworthy as one of the few, albeit modest, examples of Romanesque architecture to be found in Madrid. Parts of the wall, a side entrance and part of the apse were restored in 1999 and are all that remain of the 13th-century building. When it was built, Madrid was a little village more than 2km away.

IGLESIA DE SAN JERÓNIMO EL REAL

Map p257

☎ 91 420 35 78; Calle de Ruiz de Alarcón; Ⓜ Atocha or Banco de España

Tucked away behind the Museo del Prado, this lavish chapel was traditionally favoured by the Spanish royal family. Here, amid the mock-Isabelline splendour, King Juan Carlos I was crowned in 1975 upon the death of Franco. The interior is actually a 19th-century reconstruction that took its cues from the Iglesia de San Juan de los Reyes in Toledo; the original was largely destroyed during the Peninsular War. Being a chapel of royal choice did little to protect it from the Museo del Prado's inexorable expansion – what remained of the cloisters next door was demolished (despite vociferous local protests) to make way for the Gran Prado extension.

TOP SIGHTS IN PASEO DEL PRADO & EL RETIRO

- Museo del Prado (right)
- Museo Thyssen-Bornemisza (p86)
- Parque del Buen Retiro (p87)
- Plaza de la Cibeles (p88)

MUSEO DE ARTES DECORATIVAS

Map p257

☎ 91 532 64 99; http://mnartesdecorativas.mcu.es; Calle de Montalbán 12; adult/student/senior €2.40/1.20/free, free to all on Sun; ⏰ 9.30am-3pm Tue-Sat, 10am-3pm Sun & holidays; Ⓜ Retiro

This niche museum won't appeal to everyone but those who love sumptuous period furniture, ceramics, carpets, tapestries and the like, will find themselves spending a worthwhile hour or two here. The exhibits span the 15th to the late-19th centuries and are spread over five floors.

There's plenty to catch your eye and the ceramics from around Spain are a definite feature, while the surprisingly varied recreations of kitchens from several regions are particularly curious. Reconstructions of regal bedrooms, women's drawing rooms and 19th-century salons also help shed light on how the privileged classes of Spain have lived through the centuries.

MUSEO DEL PRADO Map p257

☎ 91 330 28 00; http://museoprado.mcu.es; Paseo del Prado; adult/student/child under 18 & senior over 65 €6/4/free, free to all Sun, headset guide €3; ⏰ 9am-8pm Tue-Sun; Ⓜ Banco de España

Welcome to one of the best and most important art galleries anywhere in the world. The more than 7000 paintings held in the Museo del Prado's collection (although less than half are currently on display) are like a window on the historical vagaries of the Spanish soul, at once grand and imperious in the royal paintings of Velázquez, darkly tumultuous in the *pinturas negras* (black paintings) of Goya and outward-looking with sophisticated works of art from all across Europe. Spend as long as you can at the Prado or, better still, plan to make a couple of visits because it can all be a little overwhelming if you try to absorb it all at once. Either way, it's an artistic feast that is many visitors' main reason for visiting Madrid.

Part of the Prado's appeal is the fact that the building in which it is housed is itself a masterpiece, although its early days were less than momentous. Completed in 1785, the neo-Classical Palacio de Villanueva was conceived as a house of science but served, somewhat ignominiously, as a cavalry barracks for Napoleon's troops during their occupation of Madrid between 1808 and 1813.

Sights

PASEO DEL PRADO & EL RETIRO

In 1814 King Fernando VII decided to use the palace as a museum, although his purpose was more about finding a way of storing the hundreds of royal paintings gathering dust than any high-minded civic ideals – his was an era where art was a royal preserve. Five years later the Museo del Prado opened with 311 Spanish paintings on display. The Prado has never looked back.

You can enter the Prado by the southern Puerta de Murillo, but we suggest that you climb the stairs and enter through the northern Puerta de Goya. Entering this way thrusts you immediately into the grandeur of this former palace as well as into the middle of its priceless collection.

After crossing the entrance area, you begin a rich journey through the main hall once presided over by Spanish kings and queens. The first section, Room 24 contains some vivid, almost surreal works by the 16th-century master El Greco (see boxed text, p183), whose figures are characteristically slender and tortured, and whose pride of place contrasts to the painter's rejection by Felipe II as a court painter. Also nearby are works by Titian who was preferred by Felipe II. Put together, these two artists are a wonderful introduction to the Prado's astonishing collection.

About halfway along the main hall, turn left into Room 12 where you'll encounter the extraordinarily life-filled paintings of one of the greatest figures of Spanish art. Of the many paintings by Diego Rodriguez de Silva y Velázquez (p22) that so distinguish the Prado by their presence, *Las Meninas* is what most people come to see. Completed in 1656, it is more properly known as *La Família de Felipe IV (The Family of Felipe IV)*. It depicts Velázquez himself on the left and, in the centre, the infant Margarita. There is more to it than that: the artist in fact portrays himself painting the king and queen, whose images appear, according to some experts, in mirrors behind Velázquez. His mastery of light and colour is never more apparent than here. An interesting detail of the painting, aside from the extraordinary cheek of painting himself in royal company, is the presence of the cross of the Order of Santiago on his vest. The artist was apparently obsessed with being given a noble title. He got it shortly before his death, but in this oil painting, he has awarded himself the order years before it would in fact be his!

There are more fine works by Velázquez in Rooms 14 and 15, but don't fail to return to the main hall, where Room 29 is framed by his stunning paintings of various members of royalty – Felipe II, Felipe IV, Margarita de Austria (a younger version of whom features in *Las Meninas*), El Príncipe Baltasar Carlos and Isabel de Francia – on horseback; but you could pick any work of Velázquez and not be disappointed. By now you'll have become accustomed to the subtle but strategically placed lighting of the Prado and high ceilings that together combine to make this one of the world's premier exhibition spaces where the paintings seem to spring off the canvas.

Room 32 is your introduction to Francisco José de Goya y Lucientes (p23), who is the most extensively represented of the Spanish masters in the Prado. To capture Goya's magic in the best-loved paintings of this prolific master, we suggest a selective approach. Head for Room 22, where you'll find what are probably his best-known and most intriguing oils, *La Maja Vestida* and *La Maja Desnuda*. These portraits of an unknown woman commonly believed to be the Duquesa de Alba (who may have been Goya's lover) are identical save for the lack of clothing in the latter. You can enjoy the rest of Goya's works later (he fills Rooms 19 to 22 and his early preparatory paintings for tapestries, religious paintings and drawings are on the 2nd floor) but make your way to Room 39, where pride of place is given to the dramatic *El Dos de Mayo* and *El Tres de Mayo*. Two of Madrid's most emblematic paintings, they bring to life the 1808 anti-French revolt and subsequent execution of insurgents in Madrid.

By now you should be ready for more dark and disturbing works of Goya's later years, his *Pinturas Negras* (Black Paintings; Rooms 35 to 38), so-called because of the dark browns and black that dominate, and the distorted animalesque appearance of their characters. The Prado's administrators have displayed these wonderfully, with dimmer lights to suit the sombre mood the paintings evoke. Among the most disturbing of these works is *Saturno Devorando a Su Hijo (Saturn Devouring His Son)*, but to capture the essence of Goya's genius, *La Romería de San Isidro* and *El Akelarre (El gran cabrón)* are unrivalled. The former evokes a writhing mass of tortured humanity, while the latter is dominated by the compelling

ONLY IN MADRID

Spaniards love to take to the streets, whether it be to demonstrate against the war in Iraq, protest against social reforms by the government of the day, or to march in solidarity with the victims of terrorism. But Madrid must be the only city in the world where a near-riot was caused by an art exhibition.

John Hooper in his fine book *The New Spaniards* tells the story of how in 1990 the Prado brought an unprecedented number of works by Velázquez out of storage and opened its doors to the public. The exhibition was so popular that more than half a million visitors came to see the rare showing. Just before the exhibition was scheduled to end, the Prado announced that they would keep the doors open for as long as there were people wanting to enter. When the doors finally shut at 9pm, several hundred people were still outside waiting in the rain. They chanted, they shouted and they banged on the doors of this august institution with their umbrellas. The gallery was re-opened, but queues kept forming and when the doors shut on the exhibition for good at 10.30pm, furious art-lovers clashed with police. At midnight, there were still almost 50 people outside chanting 'We want to come in'.

individual faces of the condemned souls of Goya's creation. The two paintings face off against each other in Room 38.

Having captured the essence of the Prado, you're now free to select from the diverse masterpieces that remain. If Spanish painters have piqued your curiosity, the stark figures of Francisco de Zurbarán dominate Rooms 17A and 18A, while Bartolomé Esteban Murillo (Rooms 28 and 29) and José de Ribera (Room 16) should also be on your itinerary.

Another alternative is the Prado's outstanding collection of Flemish art. The fulsome figures and bulbous cherubs of Peter Paul Rubens (1577–1640) provide a playful antidote to the darkness of many of the other Flemish artists and can be enjoyed in Rooms 8 to 11. His signature *Las Tres Gracias (The Three Graces)* is in Room 9, while the stand-out *Adoración de los Reyes Magos* is in Room 9B. Other fine works in the vicinity include those by Anton Van Dyck (Rooms 9B, 10A and 10B) and on no account miss Rembrandt in Room 7.

But, without doubt, there is no more weird-and-wonderful painting in the Prado than *The Garden of Earthly Delights* by Hieronymus Bosch (c1450–1516), which can be found in Room 56, downstairs on the ground floor. No-one has yet been able to provide a definitive explanation for this hallucinatory work, although many have tried. While it is, without doubt, the star attraction of this fantastical painter's collection, all his work rewards inspection. The closer you look, the harder it is to escape the feeling that he must have been doing some extraordinary drugs.

Also on the ground floor is the Prado's nod to the Italians of the Renaissance.

Among the plethora of Madonnas with babes and Christ in many poses, are some sensational works worth checking out, like *The Story of Nastagio degli Onesti* in three parts by Botticelli. There's classic chiaroscuro from Caravaggio, while Tintoretto and Titian play with perspectives. You'll also find a couple of paintings by the German artist Albrecht Dürer (1471–1528) in Room 55B.

The Prado is undergoing a major extension project that could last for years, although it's unlikely to change the major exhibition spaces for some years, if at all. The work of architect Rafael Moneo (p27), the €50 million Gran Prado extension project involves adapting what were the cloisters of the Iglesia de San Jerónimo El Real, and connecting them to the main building via a subterranean passage. Administration will move to the new building and a new library, drawings gallery, temporary exhibition space and seminar centre will also be set up there. That part of the project was nearing completion at the time of research, but at a later stage some of the thousands of paintings currently in storage (known as the 'Hidden Prado') will also adorn what was until recently the Museo del Ejército (Army Museum), making this world-class gallery even better.

MUSEO NAVAL Map p257

☎ 91 379 52 99; www.museonavalmadrid.com in Spanish; Paseo del Prado 5; admission free; ☽ 10am-2pm Tue-Sun; Ⓜ Banco de España
A block south of Plaza de la Cibeles, this museum will appeal to those who love their ships or who have always wondered what the Spanish armada really looked like.

On display are quite extraordinary models of ships from the earliest days of Spain's maritime history to the 20th century. Lovers of antique maps will also find plenty of interest, especially Juan de la Cosa's parchment map of the known world, put together in 1500. The accuracy of Europe is quite astounding, and it's supposedly the first map to show the Americas (albeit with considerably greater fantasy than fact). Littered throughout this pleasant and rarely cluttered exhibition space are dozens of uniforms, arms, flags (including a Nazi flag from the German warship *Deutschland*, which was bombed by Republican planes off Ibiza in 1937) and other naval paraphernalia.

MUSEO THYSSEN-BORNEMISZA

Map pp254–5

☎ 91 369 01 51; www.museothyssen.org; Paseo del Prado 8; adult/student & senior €6/4, temporary exhibitions adult/student & senior/child under 12 €5/3/free, headset guide €3; ⏰ 10am-7pm Tue-Sun; Ⓜ Banco de España

Perhaps the most wide-ranging private collection of predominantly European art in the world, the Museo Thyssen-Bornemisza is the favourite art gallery of many visitors to Madrid. If you want to study the body of work of a particular artist in depth, head to the Museo del Prado or Centro de Arte Reina Sofía. But the Thyssen has something for everyone with a breathtaking breadth of artistic styles from the masters of medieval art down to the zany world of contemporary painting. All the big names are here, sometimes with just a single painting, but the Thyssens' gift to Madrid and the art-loving public is to have them all under one roof. Its easy-to-follow floor plan also makes it one of the most easily navigable galleries in Madrid and means that you can be selective about your viewing by heading straight to the paintings where your interest lies.

The unique collection is the legacy of Baron Hans Heinrich Thyssen-Bornemisza, a German-Hungarian magnate. Spain managed to acquire the prestigious collection primarily when the baron married Carmen Tita Cervera, a former Miss España and ex-wife of Lex Barker (of *Tarzan* fame). The deal was sealed when the Spanish government offered to overhaul the neo-Classical Palacio de Villahermosa specifically to house the collection. Almost 800 works have hung here since October 1992 and although the baron died in 2002, his glamorous wife has shown that she has learned much from the collecting nous of her late husband. In early 2000 the museum acquired two adjoining buildings, which have been joined to the museum to house approximately half of the collection of Carmen Thyssen-Bornemisza.

The collection is spread out over three floors, with the oldest works on the top floor down to the contemporary scene on the ground floor.

The 2nd floor, which is home to medieval art, is probably of least interest to the casual visitor, although there are some real gems hidden among the mostly 13th- and 14th-century and predominantly Italian, German and Flemish religious paintings and triptychs. To guide your exploration, we suggest pausing in Room 5 where you'll find one work by Italy's Piero della Francesca (1410–92) and the instantly recognisable *Henry VIII* by Holbein the Younger (1497–1543), before continuing on to Room 10 for the Brueghel-like and evocative 1586 *Massacre of the Innocents* by Lucas Van Valckenberch.

Room 11 is dedicated to El Greco (with three pieces) and his Venetian contemporaries Tintoretto and Titian, while Caravaggio and the Spaniard José de Ribera dominate Room 12. A single painting each by Murillo and Zurbarán add more of a Spanish flavour in the two rooms that follow, while the exceptionally rendered views

The unsurpassable Museo Thyssen-Bornemisza (above)

of Venice by Canaletto (1697–1768) should on no account be missed.

But best of all on this floor is the extension (Rooms A to H) built to house the burgeoning collection with more Canalettos hanging alongside Monet, Sisley, Renoir, Pissarro, Degas, Constable and Van Gogh.

Before heading downstairs, a detour to Rooms 19 through to 21 will satisfy those devoted to 17th-century Dutch and Flemish masters, Anton van Dyck, Jan Brueghel the Elder and Rembrandt (one painting).

If all that sounds impressive, the 1st floor is where the Thyssen is truly elevated into the ranks of great art galleries. English visitors may want to pause in Room 28 where you'll find a Gainsborough, but if you've been skimming the surface of this at times overwhelming collection, Room 32 is the place to linger over each and every painting. The astonishing texture of Van Gogh's *Les Vessenots* is a masterpiece, but the same could be said for *Woman in Riding Habit* by Manet, *The Thaw at Véthueil* by Monet and Pissarro's quintessentially Parisian *Rue Saint-Honoré in the Afternoon*.

Rooms 33 to 35 play host to Modigliani, Picasso, Cezanne, Matisse and Egon Schiele, while the baronness' eye for quality is nowhere more evident than in the extension (Rooms I to P). Juan Gris, Matisse, Picasso, Kandinsky, Georges Braque, Toulouse-Lautrec, Degas, Sorolla, Sisley and Edward Hopper are all present, but our favourites include the rich colours of Gauguin's *Mata Mua*, Monet's dreamlike *Charing Cross Bridge* and the rare appearance of Edvard Munch with *Geese in an Orchard*. Quite simply, it's an outrageously rich collection.

On the ground floor, the foray into the 20th century that you began in the 1st-floor extension takes over with a fine spread of paintings from cubism through to pop art. Like much modern art, some of it may be an acquired taste, but bypassing most of it would be a grievous error.

In Room 41 you'll see a nice mix of the big three of cubism, Picasso, Georges Braque and Madrid's own Juan Gris, along with several other contemporaries. Picasso pops up again in Room 45, another one of the gallery's stand-out rooms. Its treasures include works by Marc Chagall, Kandinsky, Paul Klee and Joan Miró.

Room 46 is similarly rich with the splattered craziness of Jackson Pollock's *Brown and Silver I* and the deceptively simple

but strangely pleasing *Green on Maroon* by Mark Rothko taking centre stage. In Rooms 47 and 48, the Thyssen builds to a stirring climax, with Salvador Dalí, Francis Bacon, Roy Lichtenstein, Edward Hopper and Lucian Freud, Sigmund's Berlin-born grandson, all represented. The latter's distinguished *Portrait of Baron HH Thyssen-Bornemisza*, the man who made it all possible, is a nice way to finish.

PALACIO DE LINARES & CASA DE AMÉRICA Map p257

☎ 91 595 48 00; www.casamerica.es in Spanish; Paseo de los Recoletos 2; admission free; ⏰ 11am-2pm & 5-8pm Tue-Sat, 11am-2pm Sun & holidays; Ⓜ Banco de España

So extraordinary is the Palacio de Comunicaciones on Plaza de la Cibeles that many visitors fail to notice this fine 19th-century pleasuredome that stands watch over the northeastern corner of the plaza. Built in 1873, it's a worthy member of the line-up of grand façades on the plaza, while its interior is notable for the copious use of Carrara marble. Unfortunately, much of it is closed to the public so you may have to content yourself with a visit to the **Casa de América**, a modern exhibition centre in the palace's grounds, which also hosts all sorts of events and concerts. All of which sounds fairly straightforward were it not for the legend that says the palace has a curse on it. The first duke of Linares is said to have had a bastard daughter, with whom his son later fell in love. They only found out she was his half-sister after they were wed – quite a scandal in Madrid's gossipy noble circles.

PARQUE DEL BUEN RETIRO Map p257

admission free; ⏰ 6am-midnight May-Sep, 6am-10pm Oct-Apr; Ⓜ Retiro, Príncipe de Vergara or Atocha

The wonderful gardens of El Retiro are as enjoyable as any you'll find in a European city. Littered with marble monuments, landscaped lawns, the occasional elegant building and abundant greenery, it's quiet and contemplative during the week, but is transformed on weekends.

Once the preserve of kings, queens and their intimates, the park is now open to all and, whenever the weather's fine and on Sunday in particular, Madrileños from all across the city gather here to stroll, read the Sunday papers in the shade, take a boat ride (€4 for 45 minutes) or take a cool drink at the numerous outdoor *terrazas*. Weekend buskers, Chinese masseurs and tarot readers ply their trades, while art and photo exhibitions are sometimes held at the **Palacio de Exposiciones**. Puppet shows for the kids are another summertime feature (look for **Tiritilandia**, or Puppet Land).

Most of the activity takes place around the artificial lake *(estanque)*, but the park is large enough to allow you to escape the crowds (apart from the lovers under trees locked in seemingly eternal embraces).

The lake is watched over by the massive ornamental structure of **Alfonso XII's mausoleum** on the east side of the lake, complete with marble lions. If you want to catch the essence of Madrid's seemingly endless energy, come here as sunset approaches on a summer Sunday's afternoon – as the crowd grows, bongos sound out across the park and people start to dance.

On the western side of the lake, the odd structure decorated with sphinxes is the **Fuente Egipcia** (Egyptian Fountain) and legend has it that an enormous fortune buried in the park by Felipe IV in the mid-18th century rests here. Park authorities assured us that we could put away our spade and that the legend is rot.

The **Palacio de Cristal** (☎ 91 574 66 14; 🕙 11am-8pm Mon-Sat, 11am-6pm Sun & holidays May-Sep, 10am-6pm Mon-Sat, 10am-4pm Sun & holidays Oct-Apr), a charming metal and glass structure to the south of the lake, was built in 1887 as a winter garden for exotic flowers. It's also the scene of occasional exhibitions. Just north of here, the **Palacio de Velázquez** (☎ 91 573 62 45; 🕙 11am-8pm Mon-Sat, 11am-6pm Sun & holidays May-Sep, 10am-6pm Mon-Sat, 10am-4pm Sun & holidays Oct-Apr) was built in 1883 for a mining exposition and is now used for temporary exhibitions. Another building occasionally used for temporary exhibitions is the **Casa de Vacas** (☎ 91 409 58 19; 🕙 11am-10pm).

At the southern end of the park, near **La Rosaleda** (Map pp246–7; Rose Gardens), on a roundabout, is a statue of **El Ángel Caído** (Map p257; the Fallen Angel, aka Lucifer), one of the few statues to the devil anywhere in the world.

In the southwest corner of the park, is the moving **Bosque de los Ausentes** (Forest of the Absent), an understated memorial to the 191 victims of the 11 March 2004 train bombings. For each victim stands an olive or cypress tree. About 200m north of the monument is the **Bosque de los Ausentes information office** (🕙 10am-2pm & 4-7pm Sat, Sun & holidays).

PLAZA DE LA CIBELES Map p257

Ⓜ Banco de España

Of all the grand roundabouts that punctuate the elegant boulevard of Paseo del Prado, Plaza de la Cibeles most evokes the splendour of imperial Madrid.

The jewel in the crown is the astonishing **Palacio de Comunicaciones**. Built between 1904 and 1917 by Antonio Palacios, Madrid's most prolific architect of the *belle époque*, it combines elements of the North American monumental style of the period with Gothic and Renaissance touches. Newcomers find it hard to accept that this is merely the central post office, although the city council are soon to take it over as the Ayuntamiento (town hall). Other landmark buildings around the perimeter include the **Palacio de Linares** and **Casa de América**, the **Palacio de Buenavista** and the national **Banco de España** (1891). The views east towards the Puerta de Alcalá or west towards the Edificio Metrópolis are some of Madrid's finest.

The spectacular fountain of the goddess Cybele at the centre of the plaza is also one of Madrid's most beautiful. Ever since it was erected in 1780 by Ventura Rodríguez, it has been a Madrid favourite. Carlos III liked it so much that he tried to have it moved to the gardens of the Granja de San Ildefonso, on the road to Segovia, but the Madrileños kicked up such a fuss that he let it be.

For all its popularity, symbolism of ancient mythology and role as exemplar of centuries-old public art, Cibeles endures Madrileños affection as hard love. Ever since the Spanish national football competition got under way at the beginning of the last century, the Cibeles fountain has been the venue for joyous and often destructive celebrations by players and supporters of Real Madrid whenever the side has won anything of note. In recent years the frenzy of clambering all over the fountain and chipping bits off as souvenirs has seen the city council board up the statue and surround it with police on the eve of important matches.

A stony-faced Neptune in the Plaza de Neptuno (below)

PLAZA DE NEPTUNO Map p257

Ⓜ Banco de España or bus 10, 14, 27, 34, 37, 45
Officially known as Plaza de Cánovas del
Castillo, the next roundabout south of Cibeles is something of a crossroads of Spanish nobility. The Ritz and the Palace, two of
Madrid's longest standing and most exclusive hotels, glower at each other across
the plaza with self-righteous grandeur,
while the Museo Thyssen-Bornemisza and
the Prado do likewise in competition for
the title of Madrid's best loved repository
of fine art. The centrepiece is an ornate
fountain and 18th-century sculpture of
Neptune, the sea god, by Juan Pascual de
Mena. But Madrileños, never the most rev-
erent lot, know it better as the celebration
venue of choice for fans of Atlético Madrid
who lose all sense of decorum when their
team wins a major trophy. The last time
this happened, in 1996, the hundreds of
thousands of success-starved Atlético fans
celebrated in anything but noble style
and Neptune was relieved of a few fingers.
Charges are still pending.

REAL FÁBRICA DE TAPICES Map pp246-7

☎ 91 434 05 50; www.realfabricadetapices.com in
Spanish; Calle de Fuenterrabía 2; admission €2.50;
🕑 10am-2pm Mon-Fri Sep-Jul; Ⓜ Menéndez
Pelayo
If a wealthy Madrid nobleman wanted to
impress, he came here to the Royal Tapestry
Workshop where royalty commissioned the
pieces that adorned their palaces and private
residences. Spain and the Vatican were the
biggest patrons of the tapestry business:
Spain alone is said to have collected four million tapestries. With such an exclusive clientele, it was a lucrative business and remains
so, 300 years after the factory was founded.
Its connections to the Madrid of the 18th
century become even more important when
it is remembered that Goya began his career
here, first as a cartoonist and later as a tapestry designer. Given such an illustrious history,
it is, therefore, somewhat surprising that
visiting here today feels like visiting a carpet
shop with small showrooms strewn with
fine tapestries and carpets. If you know your
stuff, however, you'll soon see that what's on
display is of the highest quality (with prices
to match). If you're lucky, you'll get to see
how they're made.

REAL JARDÍN BOTÁNICO Map p257

☎ 91 420 30 17; Plaza de Bravo Murillo 2; adult/
student/child under 11 & senior €2/1/free; 🕑 10am-
9pm May-Aug, 10am-8pm Apr & Sep, 10am-7pm Oct
& Mar, 10am-6pm Nov-Feb; Ⓜ Atocha
Although not as expansive or as popular as
the Parque del Buen Retiro, Madrid's botanical gardens are another leafy oasis in the
centre of town. With some 30,000 species
crammed into a relatively small 8-hectare
area, it's more a place to wander at leisure
than laze under a tree, although there are
benches dotted throughout the gardens
where you can sit.

In the centre stands a **statue of Carlos III**
who in 1781 moved the gardens here
from their original location at El Huerto de
Migas Calientes, on the banks of the Río
Manzanares. In the **Pabellón Villanueva**, on the
northern flank of the gardens, art exhibitions are frequently staged – the opening
hours are the same as for the park and the
exhibitions are usually free.

SALAMANCA

Drinking p135, Eating p121, Nightlife p140, Shopping p161,
Sleeping p175
The theme of grand and rarely restrained
elegance continues in the barrio of Salamanca, Madrid's most exclusive quarter.
Salamanca resonates with old money and is
thus a world away from gritty Lavapiés or
the all-things-to-all-people busyness of the

Sights

SALAMANCA

city centre. Salamanca is a place to put on your finest clothes and be seen (especially along Calle de Serrano), to stroll into shops with an affected air and resist asking the prices, or to promenade en route between the fine museums and parks that make you wonder whether you've arrived at the height of civilisation.

For more earthy delights, the Plaza de Toros and Museo Taurino to the east of the barrio is the spiritual home of Spanish bullfighting.

For more ideas on enjoying Salamanca, see boxed text, p175.

Orientation

Paseo de los Recoletos and its continuation, Paseo de la Castellana delineates the western end of Salamanca's neat grid of streets tacked on to the northern and eastern sides of the Parque del Buen Retiro. Calle de María de Molina, Calle de Francisco Silvela and Calle del Doctor Esquerdo rule Salamanca off neatly to the north and east. The posher parts of Salamanca centre around Calle de Alcalá, Calle de Serrano, Calle Príncipe de Vergara and Calle de Goya. Four blocks east of the Retiro is one of the city's main hospitals, the Hospital General Gregorio Marañón.

BIBLIOTECA NACIONAL & MUSEO DEL LIBRO Map p252

☎ 91 580 78 05; www.bne.es; Paseo de los Recoletos 20; admission free; 🕑 10am-9pm Tue-Sat, 10am-2pm Sun; Ⓜ Colón

One of the most outstanding of the many grand edifices erected in the 19th century on the avenues of Madrid, the 1892 Biblioteca Nacional (National Library) dominates the southern end of Plaza de Colón. The reading rooms are more for serious students but the sections given over to the fascinating Museo del Libro – if it ever reopens after renovations – are imaginatively presented and a worthwhile stop for any bibliophile yearning to see a variety

of Arabic texts, illuminated manuscripts, centuries-old books of the Torah and still more. If your Spanish is up to it, the displays should come to life with interactive video commentaries.

CASA DE LA MONEDA Map pp246-7

☎ 91 566 65 44; www.fnmt.es; Calle del Doctor Esquerdo 36; admission free; 🕑 10am-5.30pm Tue-Fri, 10am-2pm Sat & Sun & holidays; Ⓜ O'Donnell

The national mint (literally the 'house of coin') is a collectors' treasure-trove of coins from Ancient Greece and Roman Spain and proceeds through the Byzantine, Visigothic and Islamic periods in Spain. The latter period is particularly well represented. Coins from the days of the Catholic Monarchs abound, and the collection continues through to the establishment of the peseta as the Spanish currency – only recently consigned to history by the euro. Paper money ranges from a 14th-century Chinese note to revolutionary Russian cash. Also on display is an extensive collection of prints and *grabados* (etchings), lottery tickets since 1942 and stamps. You can also follow the processes involved in coining money and even strike your own medal. If all this ancient money has whetted your appetite, consider a visit to the Plaza Mayor (p65) on Sunday morning when the porticoes are crowded with dealers selling coins, stamps and banknotes.

FUNDACIÓN JUAN MARCH Map pp246-7

☎ 91 435 42 40; www.march.es; Calle de Castelló 77; admission depends on exhibition; 🕑 11am-8pm Mon-Sat, 11am-3pm Sun & holidays; Ⓜ Núñez de Balboa

This foundation organises some of the better temporary exhibitions in Madrid each year and it's always worth checking the listings pages of local papers or *What's On in Madrid* (from the tourist office) to see what exhibitions are happening. The foundation also stages concerts and other events throughout the year (see p147 for more info).

FUNDACIÓN LA CAIXA Map p252

☎ 902 223040; www.fundacio.lacaixa.es in Spanish; Calle de Serrano 60; 🕑 11am-8pm Mon & Wed-Sat, 11am-2.30pm Sun & holidays; Ⓜ Serrano

The Catalan building society, La Caixa, has extensive art archives and treasures, some

---

TOP SIGHTS IN SALAMANCA

- Plaza de Toros & Museo Taurino (p92)
- Museo Arqueológico Nacional (opposite)
- Museo de la Escultura Abstracta (opposite)

SALAMANCA'S DIFFICULT BIRTH

Salamanca, with its expensive boutiques, high-class restaurants and luxury apartments, was born with a silver spoon in its mouth. When Madrid's authorities were looking to expand beyond the now-inadequate confines of the medieval capital, the Marqués de Salamanca, a 19th-century aristocrat and general with enormous political clout, heard the call. He threw everything he had into the promotion of his barrio, buying up land cheaply, which he later hoped to sell for a profit. He was ahead of his time – the houses he built contained Madrid's first water closets, the latest in domestic plumbing and water heating for bathrooms and kitchens, while he also inaugurated horse-drawn tramways. In the year of his death, 1883, the streets got electric lighting. Hard as it is now to imagine, there was little enthusiasm for the project and the marques quickly went bankrupt. Towards the end of his life, he wrote: 'I have managed to create the most comfortable barrio in Madrid and find myself the owner of 50 houses, 13 hotels and 18 million feet of land. And I owe more than 36 million reales on all of this. The task is completed but I am ruined.' It was only later that Madrileños saw the error of their ways.

of which it puts on show every now and then at this gallery. The emphasis is on contemporary art, whether local or international, and it's always worth ringing or checking the local papers to see what's on.

MUSEO ARQUEOLÓGICO NACIONAL

Map p252

☎ 91 577 79 12; www.man.es in Spanish; Calle de Serrano 13; adult/student/senior €3/1.50/free, free to all from 2.30pm Sat & all day Sun; ⏰ 9.30am-8.30pm Tue-Sat, 9.30am-2.30pm Sun & holidays; Ⓜ Serrano

On the east side of the building housing the Biblioteca Nacional, the rather forbidding-looking entrance to the National Archaeology Museum bears little resemblance to what lies within. With typical Spanish flair for presentation – lighting is perfect and the large collection of artefacts is never cluttered – this delightful collection spans everything from prehistory to the Iberian tribes, Imperial Rome, Visigothic Spain, the Muslim conquest and specimens of Romanesque, Gothic and *mudéjar* handiwork.

The ground floor is the most interesting. Highlights include the stunning mosaics taken from Roman villas across Spain (the 4th-century *Mosaico de las Musas* from Navarra in Room 24 and the incomplete *Triumph of Bacchus* in Room 22 will particularly catch the eye); the stunning gilded *mudéjar*-domed ceiling in Room 35 and the arches taken from Zaragoza's Aljafería; and the more sombre Christian Romanesque and later-Gothic paraphernalia of Room 33. Elsewhere, sculpted figures such as the *Dama de Ibiza* and *Dama de Elche* reveal a flourishing artistic tradition among the Iberian tribes – no doubt influenced by contact with Greek, Phoenician and Carthaginian civilisation. The

latter bust continues to attract controversy over its authenticity, a century after it was found near the Valencian town.

The basement contains displays on prehistoric man and spans the Neolithic period to the Iron Age – it's probably more of interest to dedicated archaeological buffs. Modest collections from ancient Egypt, Etruscan civilisation in Italy, classical Greece and southern Italy under Imperial Rome take their place alongside the ancient civilisations in the Balearic and Canary Islands.

The 1st floor contains all sorts of items pertaining to Spanish royalty and court life from the 16th to the 19th centuries.

Outside, stairs lead down to a partial copy of the prehistoric cave paintings of Altamira (Cantabria).

MUSEO DE LA ESCULTURA ABSTRACTA Map p252

www.munimadrid.es/museoairelibre/; Paseo de la Castellana; Ⓜ Rubén Darío

This fascinating open-air collection of 17 abstracts includes works by the renowned Basque artist Eduardo Chillida, the Catalan master Joan Miró as well as Eusebio Sempere and Alberto Sánchez, one of Spain's foremost sculptors of the 20th century. The sculptures are beneath the overpass where Paseo de Eduardo Dato crosses Paseo de la Castellana. All but one are on the eastern side of Paseo de la Castellana.

MUSEO LÁZARO GALDIANO

Map pp246-7

☎ 91 561 60 84; www.flg.es in Spanish; Calle de Serrano 122; adult/student €4/3, free Wed; ⏰ 10am-4.30pm Wed-Mon; Ⓜ Gregorio Marañón

This is the sort of place you expect to find in Calle de Serrano, with an imposing early

20th-century Italianate stone mansion set just back from the street, and Don José Lázaro Galdiano (1862–1947), a successful and cultivated businessman, was just the sort of man you'd expect to find in Salamanca. A patron of the arts, he built up an outstanding private collection that he bequeathed to the state upon his death. It was no mean inheritance with some 13,000 works of art and *objets d'art*, a quarter of which are on show at any time. The highlights are the works by Van Eyck, Bosch, Zurbarán, Ribera, Goya, Claudio Coello, El Greco, Gainsborough and Constable.

The ground floor is largely given over to a display setting the social context in which Galdiano lived, with hundreds of curios on show. The 1st floor is dominated by Spanish artworks up until Goya, the 2nd floor continues with Goya and paintings from the rest of Europe. The top floor is jammed with all sorts of ephemera (such as Mrs Galdiano's fan collection). A lawyer and journalist, Galdiano also collected a library of some 20,000 volumes.

The ceilings were all painted according to their room's function. The exception is Room 14, which features a collage from some of Goya's more famous works, among them *La Maja* and the frescoes of the Ermita de San Antonio de la Florida, in honour of the genius.

PLAZA DE TOROS & MUSEO TAURINO Map p244

☎ 91 556 92 37; www.las-ventas.com in Spanish; Calle de Alcalá 237; ⏱ museum 9.30am-2.30pm Mon-Fri Oct-May, 9.30am-2.30pm Tue-Fri & 10am-1pm Sun Jun-Sep; Ⓜ Las Ventas

The Plaza de Toros Monumental de Las Ventas (often known simply as Las Ventas) is not the most beautiful bullring in the world – that honour probably goes to Ronda in Andalucía – but it is the most important.

A classic example of the neo-*mudéjar* style, it was opened in 1931 and hosted its first *corrida* (bullfight) three years later. Like all bullrings, the circle of sand enclosed by four storeys, which can seat up to 25,000 spectators, evokes more a sense of a theatre than a sports stadium, which, given the spectacle on offer, is perhaps appropriate. (It also hosts concerts; see p149) To be carried high on the shoulders of aficionados out through the grand and decidedly Moorish Puerta de Madrid is the ultimate dream

of any *torero* (bullfighter) – if you've made it at Las Ventas, you've reached the pinnacle of the bullfighting world. The gate is known more colloquially as the gate of glory.

If your curiosity is piqued, wander into the **Museo Taurino**, a collection of paraphernalia, costumes, photos and other bullfighting memorabilia up on the top floor above one of the two courtyards by the ring. During the bullfighting season it also opens at the weekend. Tours take place between 10am and 2pm from Tuesday to Sunday.

The area where the Plaza de Toros is located is known as Las Ventas because, in times gone by, several wayside taverns (*ventas*), along with houses of ill repute, were to be found here.

PUERTA DE ALCALÁ Map p257

Plaza de la Independéncia; Ⓜ Retiro

This stunning triumphal gate was once the main entrance to the city (its name derives from the fact that the road that passed under it led to Alcalá de Henares) and was surrounded by the city's walls. It was here that the city authorities controlled access to the capital and levied customs duties.

The first gate to bear this name was built in 1599, but Carlos III was singularly unimpressed and had it demolished in 1764 to be replaced by another, the one you see today. It originally lay in the Puerta del Sol, then Plaza de la Cibeles, but was moved in the late 19th century to its present spot on Plaza de la Independencia as the city grew. The city authorities later gave up trying to keep pace with Madrid's inexorable eastward expansion and its purpose is now purely decorative. It is best viewed from Plaza de la Cibeles to the west from where it complements the grandeur of the Palacio de Comunicaciones as part of one of

Madrid's most attractive vistas. From the east, the views through the arch down towards central Madrid are similarly special. Our only complaint? It could do with a clean. Twice a year, in autumn and spring, cars abandon the roundabout and are replaced by flocks of sheep being transferred in an age-old ritual from their summer to winter pastures (and vice versa).

MALASAÑA & CHUECA

Drinking p136, Eating p123, Nightlife p141, Shopping p164, Sleeping p176

The funky inner-city barrios of Malasaña and Chueca are emblematic of the new Madrid – formerly down-at-heel and narrow streets that have been transformed into some of the capital's coolest. Streets are cobbled, bars are plentiful and Chueca is unmistakeably and proudly gay in every sense of the word. This is a ghetto with a difference – tolerant, open to all and upwardly mobile. Yes, there's a pervasive atmosphere of decay in much of the district, but this is decay with charm, a lively, feel-good area with some great bars, shops, restaurants and a few museums. The streets surrounding Plaza del Dos de Mayo (Malasaña) and Plaza de Chueca are the focal points of the day- and night-time action, while the streets around the Antiguo Cartel de Conde Duque conceal secret gems that few but Madrileños know.

Unless you're into designer labels (Salamanca) or big department stores (Centro), Chueca is the best place to go shopping in Madrid, especially along Calle de Fuencarral, Calle del Almirante and Calle de Piamonte with an astonishing variety of bright, challenging and downright quirky fashion boutiques. For something completely different, the Café Comercial, on the Glorieta de Bilbao roundabout, is all that remains of the area's vibrant literary-café scene.

This area is not without its problems, especially in the small, seedy red-light zone

around Calle de la Luna. But after the craziness of the years of *la movida*, there's a powerful sense that new blood and life is being injected into the area and any edginess is just enough to lend it a little extra colour and flavour.

If you're keen to get an essential flavour of Malasaña and Chueca, see boxed text p176.

Orientation

Malasaña is enclosed by Gran Vía (south), Calle de la Princesa (west), Calle de Alberto Aguilera (north) and Calle de Fuencarral (east). The heart of Chueca starts not far east of the latter street and pretty much extends down as far as the Paseo de los Recoletos, with Gran Vía and Calle de Genova enclosing Chueca to the south and north, respectively. The major, roughly north–south thoroughfares through the area are Calle de San Bernardo, Calle de Fuencarral and Calle de Hortaleza. For Chueca, the metro stop of the same name deposits you in the middle of the action, while other useful stops for both barrios include Tribunal, Noviciado, San Bernardo, Bilbao and Alonso Martínez.

ANTIGUO CUARTEL DEL CONDE DUQUE Map pp250-1

☎ 91 588 57 71; Calle del Conde Duque 9-11;
Ⓜ Noviciado or San Bernardo

Dominating the western edge of Malasaña is this grand former barracks. Nowadays it has a day job housing government archives, libraries, the Hemeroteca Municipal (the biggest collection of newspapers and magazines in Spain) and the Museo Municipal de Arte Contemporáneo. Now and then in summer the one-time barracks becomes a music venue. In the gardens outside the northeast side of the building, you'll often find old men playing *petanca (pétanque)* under the trees like a scene from Madrid's village past.

MUSEO DE CERA Map p252

☎ 91 319 26 49; www.museoceramadrid.com;
Paseo de los Recoletos 41; adult/child under 7
€12/8; Ⓨ 10am-2.30pm & 4.30-8.30pm Mon-Fri,
10am-8.30pm Sat-Sun & holidays; Ⓜ Colón

If wax museums are your thing, this is a fairly standard version of the genre. Some 450 characters have been captured in the sticky stuff, although some are less convincing than others. Subjects are a typical hotchpotch from Princess Diana (known to Spaniards as Lady Di) to Cervantes, Dalí and Picasso, and from the dark days of the Inquisition to Freddy Krueger. In addition, you can board the Tren del Terror (€3) or the Simulador (€3) – the latter shakes you up a bit, as though you were inside a washing machine. Another sideshow is the Multivisión animated 'experience' (€2). All a bit dire really, although it might amuse the kids.

MUSEO MUNICIPAL Map pp250-1

☎ 91 588 86 72; www.munimadrid.es/museomunicipal; Calle de Fuencarral 78; admission free; ✆ 9.30am-8pm Tue-Fri, 10am-2pm Sat & Sun Sep-Jun, 9.30am-2.30pm Tue-Fri, 10am-2pm Sat & Sun Jul & Aug, closed holidays; Ⓜ Tribunal
The entrance of this fine museum is extraordinary – an elaborate and restored baroque entrance, raised in 1721 by Pedro de Ribera. The interior is dominated by paintings and other memorabilia charting the historical evolution of Madrid, of which the highlights are Goya's *Allegory of the City of Madrid* and *San Fernando ante la Virgen (St Ferdinand before the Virgin Mary)*, by the Neapolitan baroque artist Luca Giordano (1634–1705). The latter lies in the chapel, all that remains of the building's original purpose as a hospice. Before you step into the chapel proper, you will

see two sculpted sepulchres. The one on the right is of Beatriz Galindo (see p79) and the other of her husband, Francisco Ramírez.

On the ground floor, Madrid de los Austrias (Habsburg Madrid) is brought to life with paintings and by an absorbing and expansive model of 1830s Madrid. Note especially the long-disappeared bullring next to the Puerta de Alcalá and the absence of the Gran Vía through the centre of Madrid. On the 1st floor, the various rooms take you from Bourbon Madrid through to the final years of the 19th century. The top floor is set aside for temporary exhibits and a room devoted to the satirist and artist Enrique Herreros (1903–77). The selected drawings take an ironic look at the Madrid of the 1950s and 1960s.

Not all sections may be open as renovations at the museum are taking place in sections, although it plans to stay open throughout the works.

MUSEO MUNICIPAL DE ARTE CONTEMPORÁNEO Map pp250-1

☎ 91 588 59 28; www.munimadrid.es/museoartecontemporaneo; Calle del Conde Duque 9-11; admission free; ✆ 10am-2pm & 5.30-9pm Tue-Sat, 10.30am-2.30pm Sun & holidays; Ⓜ Noviciado or San Bernardo
Spread over two floors, this is a rich collection of modern Spanish art, mostly

Intricate detail on the façade of the Museo Municipal (above)

paintings, along with some photography. Running throughout much of the gallery are works showcasing creative interpretations of Madrid's cityscape. It is curious to see, side by side, avant-garde splodges and almost old-fashioned visions of modern Madrid. Some examples of the latter include Juan Moreno Aquado's (b 1954) *Chamartín* (2000), Luis Mayo's *Cibeles* (1997) and a typically fantastical representation of the Cibeles fountain by Ouka Lele. The 1st floor is a mix of works acquired between 1999 and 2001, while the 2nd floor contains a chronological display (starting with the 1920s). The many talented artists represented here include Eduardo Arroyo and Basque sculptor Jorde Oteiza.

MUSEO ROMÁNTICO Map pp250-1
Calle de San Mateo; M Tribunal
This museum has been closed for years as seemingly interminable renovations take place. We include it here in case it reopens. The late-18th-century building was converted into a museum by the Marqués de la Vega-Inclán (who was involved in the creation of the chain of luxury hotels known as the *paradores*) in 1924. Prior to its closure, it housed a minor treasure-trove of mostly 19th-century paintings, furniture, porcelain, books, photos and other bits and bobs from a bygone age and offered an insight into what upper-class houses were like in the 19th century.

PALACIO BUENAVISTA & CASA DE LAS SIETE CHIMENEAS Map pp254-5
Plaza de la Cibeles; M Banco de España
Set back amid gardens on the northwest edge of Plaza de la Cibeles stands the Palacio Buenavista, now occupied by the army. It once belonged to the Alba family, and the young Duchess of Alba, Cayetana, who was widely rumoured to have had an affair with the artist Goya, lived here for a time.

A block behind it to the west, on the tiny Plaza del Rey, is the Casa de las Siete Chimeneas, a 16th-century mansion that takes its name from the seven chimneys it still boasts and which gives a tantalising glimpse of the sort of residences that once lined the Paseo de la Castellana. They say that the ghost of one of Felipe II's lovers still runs about here in distress on certain evenings. Nowadays, it's home to the Ministry of Education, Culture and Sport.

PALACIO DE LIRIA Map pp250-1
☎ 91 547 53 02; Calle de la Princesa 20; admission on guided visit by prior arrangement only; ⏰ 11am & noon Fri; M Ventura Rodríguez
This 18th-century mansion, rebuilt after fire in 1936, is typical of Madrid in that it nestles amid the modern architecture just north of Plaza de España as a reminder of the days when the streets were lined with residences like these. It holds an impressive collection of art, period furniture and *objets d'art*. To join a guided visit you need to send a formal request with your personal details to the palace, which is home to the Duke and Duchess of Alba, one of the grandest names in Spanish nobility. The waiting list is long and most mortals content themselves with staring through the gates into the grounds.

SOCIEDAD GENERAL DE AUTORES Y EDITORES Map pp250-1
www.sgae.es; Calle de Fernando VI 4; M Alonso Martínez
This swirling, melting wedding cake of a building is as close as Madrid comes to the work of Antoni Gaudí, which so illuminates Barcelona. It's a joyously self-indulgent ode to Modernismo and virtually one of a kind in Madrid. Casual visitors are actively discouraged, although it's far more impressive from the street. The only exception is on the first Monday of October, which is International Architecture Day.

CHAMBERÍ & ARGÜELLES
Eating p127, Nightlife p142, Shopping p165, Sleeping p177

They call Chamberí, north of the city centre, the most *castizo* part of Madrid, which roughly translates as the most typically Madrileño area of the capital. At once traditional and sophisticated, this leafy barrio has in recent years become the most sought-after address in Madrid for Madrileños in the know and prices have even begun to surpass those of Salamanca. In the early 19th century the barrio was an insignificant village beyond the then city boundaries – Napoleon himself is believed to have spent the night here in December 1808, in the early months of his occupation of Spain.

TOP SIGHTS IN CHAMBERÍ & ARGÜELLES

- Ermita de San Antonio de la Florida (right)
- Museo de América (opposite)
- Templo de Debod (p98)
- Faro de Madrid (right)

You don't come here for the sights – there's little more than a couple of curious museums – but it's an outstanding place to eat and drink with cool new places opening up all the time. More than that, Chamberí may be fairly well off today, but it lacks the snootiness of Salamanca and it's here that you get a sense of Madrid as the Madrileños experience it away from the tourist crowds. The same could be said for quiet Argüelles, which runs into the pretty Parque del Oeste at its western boundary.

Orientation

For the purposes of this book, Chamberí stretches westward from Paseo de la Castellana in the east to Calle de la Princesa. Argüelles spreads west from Calle de la Princesa and doglegs south. Sloping parkland along Paseo del Pintor Rosales closes off the area to the west. The Parque del Oeste also drops away from Argüelles, while the Teleférico cable car sets off from a nearby perch for its little jaunt across to the Casa de Campo. Nearby, across the Avenida del Arco de la Victoria, are Museo de América and the Faro, an observation tower open to the public. The area is extremely well connected by metro and other forms of transport; important metro stops include Moncloa, Bilbao and Quevedo.

CEMENTERIO DE LA FLORIDA Map pp246-7

Calle de Francisco; Ⓜ Príncipe Pío
Across the train tracks from the Ermita de San Antonio de la Florida is the cemetery where 43 rebels executed by Napoleon's troops lie buried. They were killed on the nearby Montaña del Príncipe Pío in the pre-dawn of 3 May 1808, after the Dos de Mayo rising. The event was immortalised by Goya and a plaque placed here in 1981. The forlorn cemetery, established in 1796, is usually closed.

ERMITA DE SAN ANTONIO DE LA FLORIDA Map pp246-7

☎ 91 542 07 22; Glorieta de San Antonio de la Florida 5; admission free; ☺ 10am-2pm & 4-8pm Tue-Fri, 10am-2pm Sat & Sun (varied hours Jul-Aug); Ⓜ Príncipe Pío
Simply extraordinary: the frescoed ceilings of the Ermita de San Antonio de la Florida are one of Madrid's most surprising secrets, not least because this humble hermitage is small and otherwise modest from the outside. Recently restored – and also known as the Panteón de Goya – the southern of the two chapels is one of the few places to see a Goya in its original setting, as painted by the master 1798 on the request of Carlos IV.

Figures on the dome depict the miracle of St Anthony. The saint, who lived in Padua in Italy, heard word from his native Lisbon that his father had been unjustly accused of murder. The saint was whisked miraculously to his hometown from northern Italy, where he tried in vain to convince the judges of his father's innocence. He then demanded that the corpse of the murder victim be placed before the judges. Goya's painting depicts the moment in which St Anthony calls on the corpse (a young man) to rise up and absolve his father. Around them swarms a typical Madrid crowd. It was customary in such works that angels and cherubs appear in the cupola, above all the terrestrial activity, but Goya, never one to let himself be confined within the mores of the day, places the human above the divine.

The painter is buried in front of the altar. His remains were transferred in 1919 from Bordeaux (France), where he had died in self-imposed exile in 1828. Oddly, the skeleton that was exhumed in Bordeaux was missing one important item – the head.

On 13 June every year, it is a Madrid tradition for young people to come here to pray for a partner.

FARO DE MADRID Map pp246-7

☎ 91 544 81 04; Avenida de los Reyes Católicos; lift €1.20; ☺ 10am-2pm & 5-7pm Tue-Sun; Ⓜ Moncloa
The odd tower (lighthouse) just in front of the Museo de América is the place to go for panoramic views of Madrid. It was built in 1992 to commemorate the 500th anniversary of the discovery of America and to celebrate Madrid's role that year as the

European Cultural Capital. There is no café up here, so be warned, and before paying for your lift ticket, take a look out to the horizon – it's probably not worth the €1.20 if it's a hazy day.

MUSEO DE AMÉRICA Map pp246-7

☎ 91 549 26 41; http://museodeamerica.mcu.es in Spanish; Avenida de los Reyes Católicos 6; adult/student/child under 18 & senior €3/1.50/free, free to all Sun; 🕙 9.30am-3pm Tue-Sat, 10am-3pm Sun & holidays; Ⓜ Moncloa

Empire may have become a dirty word but it defined how Spain saw itself for centuries. Spanish vessels crossed the Atlantic to the Spanish colonies in Latin America carrying adventurers one way and gold and other looted artefacts from indigenous cultures on the return journey. These latter pieces – at once the heritage of another continent and a fascinating insight into Imperial Spain – are the subject of this excellent, if largely unselfcritical museum.

The two levels of the museum show off a representative display of ceramics, statuary, jewellery and instruments of hunting, fishing and war, along with some of the paraphernalia of the colonisers. The display is divided into five thematic zones: El Conocimiento de América (which traces the discovery and exploration of the Americas), La Realidad de America (a big-screen summary of how South America wound up as it has today) and others on society, religion and language, which each explore tribal issues, the clash with the Spanish newcomers and its results. The Colombian gold collection, dating as far back as the 2nd century AD, and a couple of shrunken heads are particularly eye-catching.

Temporary exhibitions with various Latin-American themes are regularly held here.

MUSEO DE CERRALBO Map pp250-1

☎ 91 547 36 46; http://museocerralbo.mcu.es in Spanish; Calle de Ventura Rodríguez 17; adult/student €2.40/1.20, free Wed & Sun; 🕙 9.30am-3pm Tue-Sat, 10am-3pm Sun & holidays Oct-May, 10am-1pm Mon, 9.30am-2pm Tue-Sat, 10am-2pm Sun & holidays Jun-Sep; Ⓜ Ventura Rodríguez

Huddled beneath the modern apartment buildings northwest of Plaza de España, this noble old mansion is like an apparition of how wealthy Madrileños once lived. The former home of the 17th Marqués de Cerralbo (1845–1922) – politician, poet and archaeologist – it's a study in 19th-century opulence.

The upper floor of the museum boasts a gala dining hall and a grand ballroom. The mansion is jammed with the fruits of the collector's eclectic meanderings – from Oriental pieces to religious paintings and clocks.

On the main floor are spread suits of armour from around the world and dating as far back as the 15th century, while the Oriental room is full of carpets, Moroccan kilims, tapestries, musical instruments, 18th-century Japanese suits of armour and items from Turkey, much of it obtained at auction in Paris in the 1870s. The music room is dominated by a gondola of Murano

FORGETTING FRANCO?

The megalomaniacal pretensions of dictators know no bounds and Franco was no exception. Casting an eye over the triumphal arches built by kings in their own honour elsewhere in Madrid, Franco decided that he wanted one of his own. To commemorate his victorious troops' entry into Madrid, he built the Arco de la Victoria in 1956 and adorned it with references to his triumphs. After Franco's death in 1975 when fascism became a dirty word in Spain, all references to Franco were removed from the gate and just the *quadriga* (a chariot drawn by four horses) on the summit remains of the dictator's decoration. It is now known by locals in somewhat less grandiose terms as the Puerta de Moncloa (Moncloa Gate) on the Plaza de la Moncloa (Map pp246–7) and seems marooned amid the gridlocked traffic around 200m southeast of the Faro de Madrid.

The fate of Franco's grand project is symptomatic of his place in the public memory, but not so much as you'd expect. Travellers are often surprised by the fact that monuments to Franco remain *in situ* across Spain. It is only in recent years, under the Socialist government that took power in March 2004, that the statues have started coming down, often accompanied by vocal protests by diehard Franco supporters. Until March 2005 an equestrian statue of Franco stood on Plaza de San Juan de la Cruz (Map p245) outside the Nuevos Ministerios complex of government offices in northern Madrid and similar statues were taken down around the same time in Santander and Guadalajara. However, at last count, more than 150 streets in Madrid still bear the name of Franco and senior members of his government.

glass and pieces of Bohemian crystal. The house is also replete with porcelain, including Sèvres, Wedgwood, Meissen and local ceramics. Clearly the marques was a man of diverse tastes and it can all be a little overwhelming, especially once you factor in artworks by Zurbarán, Ribera, van Dyck, and El Greco's *Éxtasis de San Francisco*.

MUSEO SOROLLA Map pp246-7

☎ 91 310 15 84; http://museosorolla.mcu.es in Spanish; Paseo del General Martínez Campos 37; adult/student/child under 18 & senior €2.40/1.20/free; ☒ 9.30am-3pm Tue-Sat, 10am-3pm Sun & holidays; Ⓜ Iglesia

The Valencian artist Joaquín Sorolla immortalised the clear Mediterranean light of the Valencian coast. His Madrid house, a quiet mansion surrounded by lush gardens that he designed himself, was inspired by what he had seen in Andalucía and now contains the fullest collection of the artist's works.

On the ground floor you enter a cool *patio cordobés*, an Andalucían courtyard off which is a room containing collections of Sorolla's drawings. The 1st floor, with the main salon and dining areas, was mostly decorated by the artist himself. On the same floor are three separate rooms that Sorolla used as studios. In the second one is a collection of his Valencian beach scenes. The third was where he usually worked. Upstairs, works spanning Sorolla's career are organised across four adjoining rooms.

Water feature in the garden of the Museo Sorolla (above)

PARQUE DEL OESTE Map pp246-7

Avenida del Arco de la Victoria; Ⓜ Moncloa

Sloping down the hill behind the Moncloa metro station, Parque del Oeste (Park of the West) is quite beautiful, with plenty of shady corners where you can recline under a tree in the heat of the day, and fine views out to the west towards Casa de Campo. It has been a Madrileño favourite ever since its creation in 1906, and one of the country's greatest ever writers, Benito Pérez Galdós (p28), took his last ride in Madrid here in August 1919. He soon fell ill and died in his house in Salamanca in January 1920.

In recent years, the park has become the unofficial base of some new Madrileños, the large Latin-American community who gather here on weekend afternoons in large numbers to pass the time or for barbecues and impromptu football games.

Until a few years ago, the Paseo de Camoens, a main thoroughfare running through the park, was lined with prostitutes by night. To deprive the prostitutes of clients, the city authorities now close the park to wheeled traffic from 11pm on Friday until 6am on Monday.

TELEFÉRICO Map pp246-7

☎ 91 541 74 50; www.teleferico.com in Spanish; adult one-way/return €3.25/4.65, child 3-7 years one-way/return €3/€3.80; ☒ hours vary; Ⓜ Argüelles

One of the world's most horizontal cable cars (it never hangs more than 40m above the ground) putters out from the slopes of La Rosaleda, 2.5km across into the depths of the Casa de Campo, Madrid's enormous green (in summer more a dry olive hue) open space to the west of the city centre. Although not the most exciting ride around, it's relaxing and a very local thing to do. Try to time it so you can settle in for a cool lunch or evening tipple on one of the *terrazas* along Paseo del Pintor Rosales.

TEMPLO DE DEBOD Map pp246-7

☎ 91 366 74 15; www.munimadrid.es/templodebod/; Paseo del Pintor Rosales; admission free; ☒ 10am-2pm & 6-8pm Tue-Fri, 10am-2pm Sat & Sun Apr-Sep, 9.45am-1.45pm & 4.15-6.15pm Tue-Fri, 10am-2pm Sat & Sun Oct-Mar; Ⓜ Ventura Rodríguez

Yes this is an Egyptian temple in downtown Madrid. No matter which way you look at it, there's something incongruous about finding the Templo de Debod in the Parque de la Montaña northwest of Plaza de España. How did it end up in Madrid? The temple was saved from the rising waters of Lake Nasser in southern Egypt as Egyptian president Gamal Abdel Nasser built the Aswan High Dam. After 1968 it was sent block by block to Spain as a gesture of thanks to Spanish archaeologists in the Unesco team that worked to save the extraordinary monuments that would otherwise have disappeared forever.

Begun in 2200 BC and completed over many centuries, the temple was dedicated to the god Amon of Thebes, about 20km south of Philae in the Nubian desert of southern Egypt. According to some authors of myth and legend, the god Isis gave birth to Horus in this very temple.

The views from the surrounding gardens towards the Palacio Real are quite special.

NORTHERN MADRID
Eating p130, Nightlife p142

Madrileños like to keep business and play separate and, one of the world's most famous football stadiums notwithstanding, northern Madrid thinks far more of business than it does of play. Most of the gracious old palaces and mansions that once lined the Paseo de la Castellana were long ago replaced by high-rise office buildings and residential apartments; pretty much everything that you see has appeared since the 1940s. Everywhere you turn, there's a pervasive sense of money being made, especially on the more commercial, west side of Paseo de la Castellana. There are a few megabars around Calle de Orense, but largely it's a mix of offices and suburban quiet. If you stray west towards Calle de Bravo Murillo, in Tetuán, you'll end up in a working-class barrio of tight and ragged lanes, which are something of a magnet for Latin-American immigrants.

Come to northern Madrid to see Real Madrid play or to visit the Museo de la Ciudad, but you're unlikely to linger much beyond that. That said, there are a few worthwhile bars, restaurants and even the odd gem of a hotel.

Orientation
Just about everything you're likely to need in northern Madrid is on, or just off, Paseo de la Castellana, which runs through the striking Torres Puerta de Europa on Plaza de Castilla close to its northern end. These remarkable leaning towers are 115m high and with a 15° tilt, and have become a symbol of modern Madrid. Just northeast of the towers is the Chamartín train station.

ESTADIO SANTIAGO BERNABÉU
Map p245

☎ 91 398 43 00 or 902 291 709; www.realmadrid .com; Avenida de Concha Espina 1; tour adult/child under 14 €9/7, admission Exposición de Trofeos only €7/5; ⏰ 10.30am-6.30pm except day of or after game, Exposición de Trofeos only on match days, up to 5hr before kick-off & the day after matches; Ⓜ Santiago Bernabéu

Football fans and budding Madridistas (Real Madrid supporters) will want to stop by the Estadio Santiago Bernabéu (see p151 for additional info), a temple to all that is extravagant and successful in football. Not much is off-limits, so for details on tours of the stadium, turn to p15. A highlight is the Exposición de Trofeos, an extraordinary array of league trophies, European Cups and the intercontinental trophies. Check out Raul's personal collection of awards in the Rincón de Raúl.

MUSEO DE LA CIUDAD Map p244

☎ 91 588 65 99; www.munimadrid.es/museo delaciudad/; Calle del Príncipe de Vergara 140; admission free; ⏰ 10am-2pm & 4-7pm Tue-Fri & 10am-2pm Sat & Sun Sep-Jun, 10am-2pm Tue-Fri & 10am-2pm Sat & Sun Jul-Aug; Ⓜ Cruz del Rayo

The highlights of this museum, which spreads over five floors, are the scale models of various Madrid landmarks, among them the Plaza de Toros and equestrian statues of Felipe IV and Carlos III. Other models cover whole barrios or features such as Plaza de la Villa and Paseo de la Castellana. The theme running throughout the museum is 'Discover your city' and it's a topic well worth exploring as the exhibits take you from Madrid and its beginnings to the Enlightenment, through the 19th century, and to the present. The displays on the airport and how the gas, electricity and telephone systems work, however, are as dry as dust and offer just a bit too much discovery for our taste.

BEYOND THE CENTRE

The attractions beyond Madrid's central barrios are spread pretty far and wide. With the exception of the Casa de Campo, west of the Manzanares (and home to the city zoo and amusement park), there's little reason to do anything other than see the sight and come back.

Orientation

You'll find the Casa de Campo west of the city centre, while the Dehesa de la Villa is northeast of the Ciudad Universitaria in the city's northwest. The Parque del Capricho and Parque Juan Carlos I are east of the city near the airport and the Zoo Aquarium de Madrid lies to the southeast. The Museo del Ferrocarril is about 1km south of Atocha station in the former Las Delicias train station. South of Madrid near the town of San Martín de la Vega is Madrid's answer to Disney World: Warner Brothers Movie World.

CASA DE CAMPO Map pp246-7

Ⓜ Batán

Sometimes called the 'lungs of Madrid', this 17-sq-km semiwilderness stretches west of the Río Manzanares. There are prettier and more central parks in Madrid but such is its scope that there are plenty of reasons to visit. And visit the Madrileños do, nearly half a million of them every weekend, celebrating the fact that the short-lived republican government of the 1930s opened the park to the public (it was previously the exclusive domain of royalty).

For city-bound Madrileños with neither the time nor the inclination to go further afield, it has become the closest they get to nature, despite the fact that cyclists, walkers and picnickers overwhelm the

TRANSPORT TO OUTLYING SIGHTS

The most efficient way to get to the sights in this chapter (with the exception of Warner Brothers Movie World, which requires a regional train) is by metro. In some cases you have a short walk afterwards but overall it's quicker than taking the bus or even driving. The appropriate metro stations are indicated in each entry.

byways and trails that crisscross the park. There are tennis courts and a swimming pool, as well as a zoo (Zoo Aquarium de Madrid) and an amusement park (Parque de Atracciones). At Casa de Campo's southern end, restaurants specialise in wedding receptions, ensuring plenty of bridal parties roam the grounds in search of an unoccupied patch of greenery where they can take photos. Also in the park, the Andalucían-style ranch known as Batán is used to house the bulls destined to do bloody battle in the Fiestas de San Isidro Labrador.

But as diverse as the attractions of Casa de Campo are, something has definitely been lost from the days before 2003 when unspoken intrigues surrounded the small **artificial lake** (Ⓜ Lago) where several lakeside *terrazas* and eateries were frequented by an odd combination of punters, working girls and clients. By night, prostitutes jockeyed for position while punters kept their places around the lakeside *chiringuitos* (open-air bars or kiosks) as though nothing out of the ordinary was happening. The traffic in the middle of the night here was akin to rush hour in the city centre. In late 2003, the police shut this scene down. There are no more louche nocturnal traffic jams but how long will the ban last?

DEHESA DE LA VILLA

🕒 9am-dusk; Ⓜ Francos Rodríguez

If you're keen to escape the tourist invasion of the city centre, this relaxing green space is strewn with *terrazas* and families out for a Sunday stroll far from the city's hustle and bustle.

FAUNIA

☎ 91 301 62 10; www.faunia.es in Spanish; Avenida de las Comunidades 28; adult/child under 12 & senior €19/13; 🕒 10am-5pm Wed-Sun, open later in summer; Ⓜ Valdebernardo or bus 8, 71, 130

This modern animal theme park takes you through a range of thematic areas, including an aviary, an insectarium, a parade of more than 70 penguins in the snow, an Amazon jungle scene (complete with simulated tropical storm) and performing dolphins and sea lions. It's also a good place to see the highly endangered Iberian lynx. Faunia is located east of the M-40, about 7km from the centre.

TOP SIGHTS BEYOND THE CENTRE

- Warner Brothers Movie World (right)
- Casa de Campo (opposite)
- Parque del Capricho (right)
- Parque de Atracciones (below)
- Faunia (opposite)

MUSEO DEL FERROCARRIL

☎ 902 228 822; www.museoferrocarril.org; Paseo de las Delicias 61; adult/student & senior €4/2.50, free Sat; ⏱ 10am-3pm Tue-Sun Sep-Jul; Ⓜ Delicias

You don't have to be a trainspotter to enjoy this railway museum – you'll see as many kids as anoraks – but it helps. Housed in the disused 1880s Estación de Delicias south of Lavapiés, this museum has about 30 pieces of rolling stock lined up along the platforms, ranging from the earliest steam locomotives to a sleeping car from the late 1920s and the Talgo II, which ran on the country's long-distance routes until 1971. Several rooms off the platforms are set aside for dioramas of train stations, memorabilia, station clocks and the like. There are plenty of model trains and tracks at the shop on the way out.

PARQUE DE ATRACCIONES

☎ 91 463 29 00; www.parquedeatracciones.es; Casa de Campo; admission €6.20, unlimited-rides stamp adult/child under 8 €23.50/13.20, single-ride tickets €2; ⏱ hours vary; Ⓜ Batán

There's not much that's especially Spanish about this amusement park, but it's got the usual collection of high-adrenaline rides, shows for the kids and kitsch at every turn. In the Zona de Máquinas (the rather ominous sounding Machines Zone) are most of the bigger rides, such as the Siete Picos (Seven Peaks, a classic roller coaster), the Lanzadera (which takes you up 63m and then drops you in a simulated bungee jump), La Máquina (a giant wheel that spins on its axis) and the favourite of all, the Tornado, a kind of upside down roller coaster that zips along at up to 80km/h. Strictly for those with cast-iron stomachs.

After all that gut-churning stuff, you'll be grateful for the Zona de Tranquilidad, where you can climb aboard a gentle

Ferris wheel, take a theme ride through the jungle or just sit back for a snack. Of course, tranquillity is relative – El Viejo Caserón (haunted house) is not for the nervous among you (in our experience, it's the adults who get spooked. La Zona de la Naturaleza (Nature Zone) offers, among other things, Dodgems and various water rides.

Finally, in the Zona Infantil, younger kids can get their own thrills on less hair-raising rides, such as a Ford-T, the Barón Rojo (Red Baron) and Caballos del Oeste (Horses of the Wild West).

The park, in the Casa de Campo, has all sorts of timetable variations so it is always a good idea to check before committing yourself.

PARQUE DEL CAPRICHO

Avenida de Logroño; ⏱ 9am-9pm Sat-Sun & holidays Apr-Sep, 9am-5pm Sat-Sun & holidays Oct-Mar; Ⓜ Canillejas

Inspired by Versailles, this incongruous place has pretensions to grandeur that it never quite fulfils. The motley smattering of buildings and the labyrinth have been restored after lying semi-abandoned for decades – the highlight is probably the neomedieval hermitage. It's a fairly short walk north of the metro station.

PARQUE JUAN CARLOS I

☎ 91 721 00 79; ⏱ 9am-dusk; Ⓜ Campo de las Naciones

Just west of the Parque del Capricho is this massive green area laid out near the city's main trade fair. Well-kept gardens are sprinkled between open fields, although it's largely a modern creation, needs time to mature and doesn't have the sense of decadent wellbeing that so distinguishes the Parque del Buen Retiro or Parque del Oeste. That said, there's plenty of space to lounge in the shade and fly kites. For €3.50 you can ride in a catamaran, on a little train and check out the Estufa Fría (a modern greenhouse).

WARNER BROTHERS MOVIE WORLD

☎ 91 821 12 34; www.warnerbrospark.com; San Martín de la Vega; adult/child & senior €33/25; ⏱ from 10am, closing hours vary; *cercanías* train (line C3 for Pinto) from Atocha stops in park near San Martín de la Vega (around 20 min)

Disney World it ain't but this movie theme-park, 25km south of central Madrid, has much to catch the attention. Kids will love the chance to hang out with Tom and Jerry, while the young-at-heart film buffs among you will be similarly taken with the Wild West or remakes of the studio sets for such Beverly Hills greats as *Police Academy*. Entrance to the park is via Hollywood Boulevard, not unlike LA's Sunset Boulevard, whereafter you can choose between Cartoon World, the Old West, Hollywood Boulevard, Super Heroes (featuring Superman, Batman and the finks of Gotham City) and finally Warner Brothers Movie World Studios. It's all about the stars of the silver screen coming to life as life-sized cartoon characters roam the grounds, and rides and high-speed roller coasters (up to 90km/h!) distract you if attention starts to wane. There are also restaurants and shops.

To get here by car, take the N-IV (the Carretera de Andalucía) south out of Madrid and turn off at Km22 for San Martín de la Vega, about 15km east of the exit. Follow the signs to the car park, where parking is available for €5.

Opening times are complex and do change – check before heading out.

ZOO AQUARIUM DE MADRID

☎ 91 512 37 70; www.zoomadrid.com; adult/child 3-7 years & senior €14.90/12.20; ☼ 10.30am-dusk; Ⓜ Batán

Madrid's zoo, in the Casa de Campo about 300m from the Parque de Atracciones, is your fairly standard European city zoo and home to about 3000 animals (ranging from koalas to wolves). Exhibits range from Emperor scorpions to scary green mambas, as well as zebras, giraffes, rhinoceroses, leopards, flamingos, grey kangaroos and rattlesnakes. There's also a fine aquarium and you can watch dolphins and sea lions get up to their tricks in the Delfinario. Shows are held at least a couple of times a day. The 3000-sq-m Aviario (aviary) contains some 60 species of eagle, condor and vulture.

Walking Tours

Walking Tours

Exploring Madrid on foot is a great way of getting to know the city, although judicious use of the city's excellent metro system can help you avoid some of the surprisingly steep hills. The following walks offer quite different visions of the city. The time you spend will depend greatly on whether you stop to visit sights or have a coffee along the way. Times given are for an estimated nonstop stroll.

OLD MADRID

Start in the pulsating, geographic centre of Spain, the **Plaza de la Puerta del Sol 1** (Puerta del Sol; p64), then head northwest along Calle de Preciados. The second street on the left will bring you out onto Plaza de las Descalzas, home to the **Convento de las Descalzas Reales 2** (p61) which is austere from the outside and anything but within. Moving southwest, you come to the **Iglesia de San Ginés 3** (p62) in Calle de los Bordadores, the site of one of Madrid's oldest places of Christian worship. Behind it is the wonderful **Chocolatería de San Ginés 4** (p129), place of worship for lovers of *churros y chocolate* (a deep-fried stick of plain pastry immersed in thick hot chocolate).

Continue up to and across Calle Mayor until you reach the grand **Plaza Mayor 5** (p65), before turning westward and heading down the hill to the historic Plaza de la Villa, home of Madrid's 17th-century **Ayuntamiento 6** (town hall; p64). On the same square stand the 16th-century **Casa de Cisneros 7** (p65) and the Gothic **Casa de los Lujanes 8** (p65), one of the oldest surviving buildings in Madrid.

Take the street down the left side of the Casa de Cisneros, cross Calle del Sacramento at the end, go down the stairs and follow the cobbled Calle del Cordón out onto the Calle de Segovia. Almost directly in front of you is the *mudéjar* (an architectural style developed by the Moors) tower of the 15th-century **Iglesia de San Pedro El Viejo 9** (p77), whereupon the narrow, almost medieval streets of Old Madrid close in and twist their way down the hill. Proceeding up Costanilla de San Pedro, you reach the **Museo de San Isidro 10** (p78). Next door is the **Iglesia de San Andrés 11** (p77), where the Madrid's patron saint, San Isidro Labrador, was interred.

From here, twist down through lanes which time forgot to Calle de Bailén and head north to the wonderful, if expensive

ALONG THE WAY

Before you get started, we suggest you wander into La Mallorquina (p129) for a scrummy pastry and a cup of coffee. It's the perfect way to start any day. If you're feeling peckish around the Plaza Mayor, head for a *bocadillo de calamares* (calamari roll) at **Cervecería Compano** (p115) or a more substantial meal at **Restaurante Sobrino de Botín** (p115), the world's oldest restaurant. A more chic option is **La Turuleta** (p117), while the nearby **Bonanno** (p133) is a groovy place for a drink. If hunger doesn't develop until after you've left the Plaza de Oriente, try **Taberna La Bola** (p116) for Madrid specialities.

Restaurante Sobrino de Botín (p115)

terrazas (outdoor cafés) on the edge of the **Jardines de las Vistillas 12** (p79) where you can contemplate the sweeping views out towards the Sierra de Guadarrama.

After enjoying a nice, soothing *cerveza* (beer), follow the viaduct north to the **Catedral de Nuestra Señora de la Almudena 13** (p60), the **Palacio Real 14** (p63) and the supremely elegant **Plaza de Oriente 15** (p65). The eastern side of the plaza is closed off by the **Teatro Real 16** (p66).

Return to the west side of the square and follow the walkway extension of Calle de Bailén which leads into **Plaza de España 17** (p64), with its statue of Don Quixote and monumental towers. Calle de Ferraz leads northwest to the curious mansion of the **Museo de Cerralbo 18** (p97) and then the ancient Egyptian **Templo de Debod 19** (p98), from where there are more fine views.

Return to Plaza de España, the eastern flank of which marks the start of Gran Vía, a Haussmannesque boulevard that was slammed through the tumbledown slums to the north of Sol in the 1910s and 1920s. Today it is a busy thoroughfare, choked with traffic and humming with passers-by darting in and out of side streets, shops and eateries. About halfway along is the mighty **Telefónica building 20** (p62), still easily visible from its hill-top perch. Head down past the elegant façades to the superb dome of the **Edificio Metrópolis 21** (p62) where Gran Vía meets Calle de Alcalá. Down the hill is **Plaza de la Cibeles 22** (p88), Madrid's favourite roundabout. Look out especially for the late-19th-century **Banco de España 23** (p88) on your right as you approach and, on your left, the **Palacio de Buenavista 24** (p88). Impossible to miss is the ornate **Palacio de Comunicaciones 25** (p88) facing you in all its glory across the square.

ARTISTIC MADRID

Before setting out on your art exploration of the city, pause in the splendid old **Café Comercial 1** (p123), on the Glorieta de Bilbao and a favoured haunt of writers, artists and intellectuals for more than a century. From here, walk northeast along Calle de Luchana, northwest up Calle de Santa Engracia and then down the hill of Paseo del General Martínez Campos to the **Museo Sorolla 2** (p98), home to the works of Joaquín Sorolla, one of the major Spanish painters of the early 20th century.

Continue on down to Paseo de la Castellana and the **Museo de la Escultura Abstracta 3** (p91), an outdoor exhibition of fine modern sculptures by some of the big names of Spanish contemporary art. As you continue wending your way south along this grand boulevard – you should shun the outer footpaths and wander under the shade of the trees which run almost through the centre – pause at either the **Café-Restaurante El Espejo 4** (p137) or **Gran Café de Gijón 5** (p125),

WALK FACTS

Start Café Comercial
Finish Centro de Arte Reina Sofía
Distance 5km
Duration Two hours, plus gallery time
Transport to Ⓜ Bilbao
Transport from Ⓜ Atocha

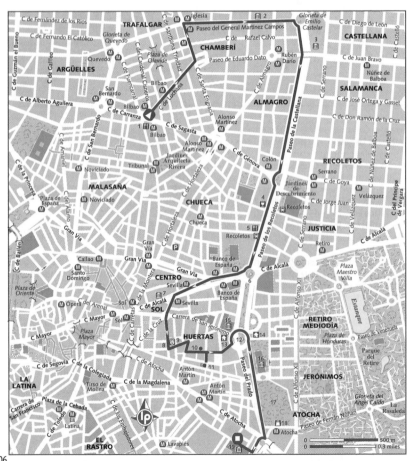

both of which are steeped in history, atmosphere and the ghosts of writers and artists past.

At **Plaza de la Cibeles 6** (p88), turn right up the hill to **Real Academia de Bellas Artes de San Fernando 7** (p66). Cross the elegant Plaza de Canalejas and keep going along Calle del Principé to **Plaza de Santa Ana 8** (p82), where a statue of the poet Federico García Lorca looks towards the **Teatro Español 9** (p147). From the plaza, take Calle del Prado, turn right on Calle de León, then left down Calle de Cervantes. Number 11 is the **Casa de Lope de Vega 10** (p80), the playwright's house. You're now in the heart of the Barrio de las Letras, where many famous Spanish writers spent their days, and just

ALONG THE WAY

Apart from the already mentioned **Gran Café de Gijón** (p125) and **Café-Restaurante El Espejo** (p137), **La Finca de Susana** (p120) is a fine place to stop for lunch and **Viva Madrid** (p135) is good for a restorative drink. **Zerain** (p120) is another good lunch option. If you're a fan of Lope de Vega, you may even want to stay in the **Hotel Lope de Vega** (p173) which is themed on the writer's works. To finish the day, try a *bocadillo* (bread roll) in **El Brillante** (p119), or head towards Lavapiés along Calle de Argumosa where you'll find good bars (p133) and restaurants (p116).

around the corner (Calle de Quevedo, then Calle de Lope de Vega) is the 17th-century **Convento de las Trinitarias 11** (Map pp254–5), where writer Miguel de Cervantes is buried (it's closed to the public).

Return to Calle de Cervantes and turn left at the grand **Plaza de Neptuno 12** (Plaza de Cánovas del Castillo; p89) roundabout – which is watched over by the two grand old dames of the Madrid hotel scene, the **Palace 13** (p175) and the **Hotel Ritz 14** (p175) – for the extraordinary **Museo Thyssen-Bornemisza 15** (p86). Diagonally across the plaza is the gracious, low-slung Palacio Villanueva, better known to art-lovers as the peerless **Museo del Prado 16** (p83) where you could spend hours or even days. Behind the Prado is the verdant **Real Jardín Botanico 17** (p89), then the long-standing **Cuesta de Moyana Bookstalls 18** (p159), both of which are pleasant detours as you continue south en route to Madrid's other extraordinary gallery, the **Centro de Arte Reina Sofía 19** (p80).

A TAPAS SUNDAY

Half of Madrid might well be out partying until the small hours on a Saturday night, but the other half gets up (relatively) early and heads to **El Rastro 1** (p76), arguably the largest flea market in Europe. Treasure-hunt and inch your way through the crowds sated by this typically Madrileño start to a Sunday, and then head out along Plaza de la Cebada to **Plaza de la Puerta de Moros 2** (p78) and **Plaza de San Andrés 3** (p77), where a bohemian post-Rastro crowd drums up a storm as well as an infectiously festive atmosphere. The storeys-high mural on the east side of the plaza always prompts a double-take from first-time visitors.

By late morning the bars are open and your first stop should be **Taberna Algorta 4** (p116), along Calle de la Cava Baja; it's home to some of the most imaginative Basque *pintxos* (tapas) in town. Tempting as most of the choices are, pace yourself because you won't want to miss the sublime *bacalao* (cod) that they serve up at **Casa Revuelta 5** (p114). If you're lucky, there'll be an impromptu band playing outside to entertain you while you wait for an opening to appear at the door.

Suitably fortified and needing to shed some weight, skirt the **Plaza Mayor 6** (p65) and head up to Plaza de Santa Cruz and then along Calle de Atocha to Plaza de Jacinto Benavente, from where Calle de las Huertas leads down to **Casa Alberto 7** (p134). At this

ALONG THE WAY

Just before Plaza de Jacinto Benavente, pop into **Hammam Medina Mayrit** (p154) and make an appointment for a heavenly Turkish bath and massage to aid recovery from all this walking. In Huertas, the sweet tooths among you will relish the old-world charm and delicious pastries of **Antigua Pastelería del Pozo** (p129).

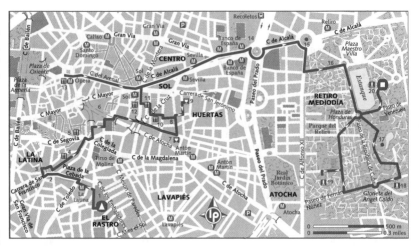

engaging old *taberna* (tavern), timing is everything because it's famous at 1pm for its vermouth on tap – taking a tipple at this hour on a Sunday is an essential initiation into living like a Madrileño. Cross **Plaza de Santa Ana 8** (p82) and down Calle de Echagaray where **La Venencia 9** (p135) serves sherry straight from the barrels which adorn this atmospheric place. Return to Plaza de Santa Ana and head down into the lanes which writhe down towards Sol. Don't miss **Las Bravas 10** (p119) on Callejón

de Álvarez Gato for the best-in-town fried potatoes with spicy tomato sauce, while the rustic **La Oreja del Oro 11** (p119) on Calle de Victoria is the place for *oreja* (pig's ear) – trust us, it's surprisingly good – and a glass of white Ribeiro wine from Galicia. If you're not feeling *that* adventurous, try **La Casa del Abuelo 12** (p119), directly opposite, which has terrific prawns.

To continue your tapas tour of the capital, pass through the monumental Puerta del Sol and head down Calle de Arenal to the cool and artsy **Café del Real 13** (p114), where the coffee is rather good and the carrot or chocolate cakes are as tasty as the ambience is cosy and cool.

By now it's time for some serious walking, so retrace your steps up Calle de Arenal, cross Sol again and make your way back up Calle de Alcalá to **Plaza de la Cibeles 14** (p88). From here, you can see the monumental **Puerta de Alcalá 15** (p92), one of the grand old gateways to the city. Be sure to keep it in sight, because that's where you're headed. It stands alongside the gate to the **Parque del Buen Retiro 16** (p87), a magnificent park with grand old gardens that were once the sole preserve of royalty, but Madrileños now reclaim it with a vengeance on Sundays when the weather's fine and the whole of Madrid comes out to play. Laze on the lawns with the Sunday papers, take a boat ride or explore this expansive park's many attractions, among them the **Palacio de Cristal 17** (p88) and the statue of **El Ángel Caído 18** (p88), one of the world's few statues of the devil. During your rounds, don't fail to pay homage to the fallen of the 11 March 2004 train bombings at the peaceful **Bosque de los Ausentes 19** (p88). As it gets nearer to sunset, make your way back to the lake and to **Alfonso XII's Mausoleum 20** (p88). If the weather is fine, the young and energetic take over this grand monument for impromptu drum-and-dance sessions that greet the night with a bang.

THE PICK OF THE PLAZAS

You learn a lot about Madrid from its plazas (squares) and the most enjoyable lesson is that no city in Europe has a finer café culture than the Spanish capital. When the weather's warm, taking up an outdoor chair amid the elegant and bustling surrounds of a Madrid bar or café is one of life's greatest and most indulgent pleasures, especially if you've a glass of La Rioja wine to nurse and the city's inventive street performers are out and about.

The perfect place to start is the **Plaza de Santa Ana 1** (p82), which is Madrid in microcosm – beautiful, brimful of charm and invariably thronging with a mixed local and international crowd. The plaza is the heartbeat of Huertas, that party-going corner of Madrid that never seems to sleep, but you'll be equally at home with a coffee on a relatively quiet afternoon.

You may never want to leave, but you've only scratched the surface of what Madrid has to offer. To truly understand Madrid, wind your way south from Plaza de Santa

WALK FACTS

Start Plaza de Santa Ana
Finish Plaza de Chueca
Distance 6km
Duration Three hours
Transport to Ⓜ Sevilla, Sol or Anton Martín
Transport from Ⓜ Chueca

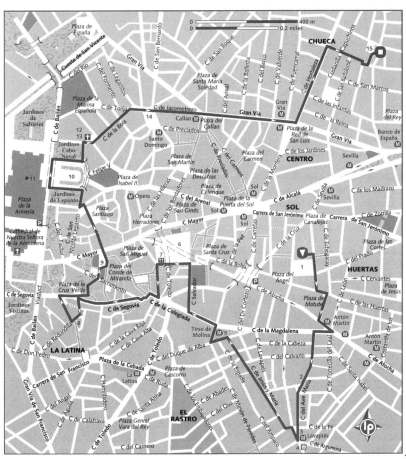

ALONG THE WAY

If beer's your thing (and even if it's not), we suggest **Cervecería Alemana** (p135) on Plaza de Santa Ana. While down in Lavapiés **El Eucalipto** (p134), **La Inquilina** (p134) and **Casa Montes** (p134) are the places where the barrio lives, drinks and enjoys. Plaza de la Paja is best enjoyed with a cake or a *mojito* (Cuban rum-based cocktail) from **Delic** (p116), while **Ene Restaurante** (p117 is funky with a capital F. On Plaza de Oriente, our vantage point of choice is **Café de Oriente** (Map pp254–5; Plaza de Oriente 2; ☺ 9am-midnight). In Chueca, we love **Café Belén** (p137) while for a meal look no further than **Calle de Libertad** (p123).

Ana. As soon as you cross Calle de Atocha, you'll notice that the ambience has changed – it's quieter, more multicultural, older and far more ramshackle than the more polished Huertas. Welcome to **Lavapiés 2** (p77), a community barrio if ever there was one and a place distinguished by its scruffy elegance and vibrant pulse. You could wander at will down the hill along the quiet, little lanes, but Calle del Avenida Marta, then Calle de Avenida María provide the easiest access to the **Plaza de Lavapiés 3** (p78), one of Madrid's most eclectic. There's not much to see, apart from the state-of-the-art **Teatro Valle-Inclán 4** (p147), but it's all about the buzz of a diverse community. If you enjoy late-night revelry, you'll likely be back in Lavapiés before long.

Calle de Jesús y Marta climbs the hill to **Plaza de Tirso de Molina 5** (Map pp254–5), another triangle of rustic charm, but keep on moving to the **Plaza Mayor 6** (p65) – we defy you to find a more beautiful city square anywhere in the world. Take a seat; the cafés surrounding the cobblestones are all wonderful vantage points for watching the passing Madrid streetlife but they're all expensive. If the prices send a shiver down your spine, grab an ice cream from **Los Caprichos de Martina 7** (p126) and occupy one of the benches that encircle the plaza's lamp-posts. Before sitting, look closely and you'll the see the story of the plaza's fascinating history carved into the backrests – bullfights and the Inquisition are recurring themes.

Suitably rested, head down Calle de Segovia and up to sloping **Plaza de la Paja 8** (p77), one of La Latina's many hidden secrets. You could be in a quiet Spanish *pueblo* (village) here. Dip down again to Calle de Segovia and then wind your way up to the pleasing and intimate **Plaza de la Villa 9** (p64). Descending down Calle Mayor takes you to the stunning **Plaza de Oriente 10** (p65) with its marble statues of Spanish kings, and green hedges, not to mention the magnificent **Palacio Real 11** (p63).

Off the northeast corner of the plaza, **Plaza de la Encarnación 12** (p61) has fine views back towards the Palacio Real and is notable for the **Convento de la Encarnación 13**. You could easily take the metro to continue (line 2 from Santo Domingo to Ópera, then change to line 3, where it's three stops to Chueca), but the walk up to the nondescript **Plaza de Santo Domingo 14** (Map pp250–1), along Gran Vía and then Calle de Hortaleza allows you to appreciate the subtle transformation of the city's personality from Royal Madrid, through the busy shopping streets and into the extravagantly gay milieu of Chueca. **Plaza de Chueca 15** (Map pp250–1) is possibly Madrid's busiest plaza by night and is infused with the personality of the gay community who've made this barrio their own. There are dozens of bars and restaurants where you can rest those weary feet.

The Plaza de Santa Ana (p82) is a top spot for some café culture

Eating ▮

Eating

Madrid has become a magnet for outstanding cooking, and eating out in the Spanish capital is a real treat.

There's everything to be found here, not least the rich variety of regional Spanish specialities from across the country. You could travel to the bastions of fine Spanish cooking – the chefs of the Basque Country and Catalonia have particularly rich traditions and are leading the new wave of progress – to sample the endless delights in their natural setting. But only in Madrid will you find it all within a short walk or metro ride from your hotel door. Throw in some outstanding restaurants serving international cuisine from South America to Japan and you'll quickly discover that the choice of where to eat is almost endless.

There is not a barrio in Madrid where you can't find a great meal. Restaurants in Malasaña, Chueca, La Latina and Huertas range from stunning old *tabernas* (taverns) to chic, sophisticated and clean-lined boutique restaurants that won't break the bank. For more classically classy surrounds, Paseo del Prado, El Retiro, Salamanca and northern Madrid are generally pricey but of the highest standard and ideal for a special occasion or for spotting royalty and celebrities. But wherever you go in Madrid, you'll find delicious tapas in the most unlikely looking bars, for to drink without eating is just not doing things the Madrileño way.

If you're eager to know more about what distinguishes and excites the palate of Madrileños, and for general information about Spanish food, see the Food & drink chapter. And if you speak Spanish and want some local opinions on the restaurants covered in this guide, *La-Netro* (www.lanetro.com) has numerous customer-generated restaurant reviews.

Almost more than the myriad tastes on offer, however, it is the buzz that accompanies eating in Madrid that elevates the city into the ranks of the great culinary capitals of the world. In Madrid, eating is not a functional pastime to be squeezed in between other more important tasks; instead it is one of life's great pleasures, an end in itself to be enjoyed for hours on end with friends and a glass or two of wine, an event to be savoured like all good things in life.

Opening Hours

Most restaurants and other types of eateries open their kitchens from 1pm to 4pm (lunch) and again between 8.30pm to midnight (dinner). However, few locals would sit down to lunch before 2pm, or dinner before 10pm and some places stay open until 1am on weekends. Bars and cafés that offer tapas generally adhere to similar hours as far as food goes,

---

WOULD YOU LIKE SMOKE WITH THAT, SIR?

Those of you who remember with nostalgia the days of smoke-filled Spanish restaurants or the days when you could be served by a smoking Madrid bank teller are in for a rude shock.

Since 1 January 2006, all Spanish bars, restaurants, offices and other enclosed public places have become subject to strict antismoking legislation. Smoking is now banned in all workplaces, schools (like they had to ban this?), public transport, sports and cultural centres and on public transport. The law also extends to bars and restaurants although these have an opt-out clause. Those establishments over 100 sq m must have designated smoking areas, while smaller bars must make a choice – ban smoking or make the bar off limits to children.

Despite the Spanish reputation for lighting up whenever and wherever possible, polls show that a majority of Spaniards supports the law, although about the same percentage don't expect their compatriots to comply. At one level, their scepticism appears to have been misplaced – restaurants, offices, shops and public transport are all now largely smoke free or have *zonas de fumadores* (smoking sections). Little seems to have changed, however, when it comes to bars and nightclubs or at least not so that you'd notice. We've found only a handful of bars that have elected to become smoke free and, of the rest, families still bring their children to bars thick with smoke.

although you'll sometimes find something still at the bar outside normal meal times. Cafés tend to open from 8am or 9am through to at least 9pm, and often to midnight or beyond if they double as bars. Most restaurants are shut on Christmas Eve and many on New Year's Eve (or Christmas Day and New Year's Day). Some close over Easter and a good many shut for at least part of August as well.

For more details on how Madrileños eat, see p38.

For more details on how Madrileños eat, see p38.

How Much?

In the following pages a 'meal' is understood to mean a starter, main course and dessert, including a little modestly priced wine. Prices have risen pretty steadily in Madrid over the past few years and you may find that eating out in Madrid is not a whole lot cheaper than any other major European city. This latter phenomenon is most noticeable in the mid-range places although Madrid's top dining experiences are, compared with eating out in places such as London, Paris or Milan, refreshingly easier on your personal fortune.

One great way to cap prices at lunch-time on weekdays is to take *menú del día*, a full set meal (usually with several options), water and wine. These meals generally start from around €9. Many restaurants listed in this chapter, where you might otherwise pay much more *a la carta*, offer this cost-saving midday option meaning that some places may fit more easily within your budget than they first appear.

> ## EATING PRICE CATEGORIES
>
> Throughout this chapter, restaurants are listed according to the barrio (area of Madrid), then by price range, followed by alphabetical order. Each place is accompanied by one of the following symbols:
>
> | | |
> |---|---|
> | € | less than €15 a meal per person |
> | €€ | €16-45 a meal per person |
> | €€€ | more than €45 a meal per person |

At some of the fancier restaurants, you sometimes have the option of a *menú de degustación*, a set tasting meal of several different dishes. This can be a great way to sample the broad range of tastes the restaurant offers and it also has the advantage of having a fixed price.

Booking Tables

At many of the midrange restaurants and simpler taverns with *comedores* (dining rooms) you can generally turn up and find a spot without booking ahead. At better restaurants and for dinner especially it is safer to make a booking; you should always reserve a table at sit-down restaurants on Friday and Saturday night.

Tipping

A service charge is generally calculated into most bills in Madrid, so any further tipping is a matter of personal choice. Spaniards themselves are pretty stingy when it comes to tipping and often leave no more than €1 per person or nothing more than small change. If you're particularly happy, 5% on top would be fine.

Self-catering

Making your own snacks is the cheapest way to keep body, soul and finances together. Although there are produce markets in barrios across Madrid, some of the larger ones include: **Mercado de San Miguel** (Map pp254–5; ☼ 9am-2.30pm & 5.15-8.15pm Mon-Fri, 9am-2.30pm Sat; Ⓜ Sol) on the square of the same name, just off Plaza Mayor; **Mercado de la Cebada** (Map pp254–5; ☼ 9am-2pm & 5-8pm Mon-Fri, 9am-2.30pm Sat; Ⓜ La Latina), on the square of the same name; and **Mercado de la Paz** (Map p252; ☼ 9am-8pm Mon-Sat; Ⓜ Serrano). For freshly baked bread, head for a *panadería* (bakery).

For a gourmet touch, the basement at **El Corte Inglés** (p157) department store has some tempting local and imported goodies. Other specialist gourmet food stores include **Hespen**

DO IT YOURSELF – TOP EAT STREETS

- Calle de la Cava Baja (p116) Medieval streetscape, great tapas and fine old-style dining.
- Calle de la Libertad (p123) Lined with small boutique restaurants serving up innovative tastes.
- Calle de Manuela Malasaña (p123) A feel-good vibe and delicious nouveau cuisine.
- Around Plaza de Lavapiés & Calle de Argumosa (p116) Flavours and diners as eclectic as the barrio of Lavapiés.
- Plaza de la Paja & Calle de Almendro (p116) Cosy and super-trendy restaurants hide in the labyrinthine lanes of old Madrid.

& Suárez (p164), **Maison Blanche** (p165) and **Mantequería Bravo** (p163). For a wonderful selection of Spanish and other European cheeses, **Poncelet** (Map pp250–1; ☎ 91 308 02 21; www.poncelet.es; Calle de Argensola 27; ☺ 10.30am-8.30pm Mon-Sat; Ⓜ Alonso Martínez) should be your first stop.

For all things British, try **Things You Miss** (Map pp250–1; ☎ 91 447 07 85; www.thethingsyoumiss.com; Calle de Juan de Austria 11; ☺ 9.30am-2.30pm & 5.30-8.20pm Mon-Fri, 10am-2.30pm Sat; Ⓜ Iglesia or Bilbao), while Americans will feel right at home at **Taste of America** (Map p245; ☎ 91 562 16 32; Calle de Serrano 149; ☺ 9am-9pm Mon-Fri, 10am-9pm Sat; Ⓜ República Argentina) with its Aunt Jemima's syrup, Duncan Hines cake frosting and frozen bagels. Lovers of homemade French products should head for **Sabores de Francia** (Map pp250–1; ☎ 91 445 96 77; www.saboresdefrancia.com; Calle de Gonzalo de Córdoba 6; ☺ 11am-2pm & 5-8.30pm Tue-Fri, 11am-2pm Sat; Ⓜ Quevedo); Saturday is the day to pick up your freshly baked croissants.

There are plenty of purveyors of fine Spanish wines, but none finer than the old corner shops of **Reserva & Cata** (p165) and **María Cabello** (p161), while **Lavinia** (p162) has a large range of Spanish and international bottles.

LOS AUSTRIAS, SOL & CENTRO

Old Madrid has a little bit of everything, from the world's oldest restaurant and hearty Madrileño cooking in places rich in history and character, to fine regional tapas and Asian flavours. It also offers some wonderful little cafés from which to watch the passing parade.

CAFÉ DEL REAL Map pp254-5 Café €
☎ 91 547 21 24; Plaza de Isabel II 2;
☺ 9am-1am Sun-Thu, 10am-2am Fri & Sat;
Ⓜ Ópera

One of the nicest cafés in central Madrid, this place serves top-notch chocolate or carrot cakes (€6.50) and a rich variety of creative coffees to the soundtrack of chill-out music. The best seats are upstairs where the low ceilings, wooden beams and leather chairs are a great place to pass an afternoon with friends. It gets busy at night and is a favourite staging post for Madrileños on their Sunday afternoon stroll, but also makes a pleasant spot for breakfast.

CASA REVUELTA Map pp254-5 Tapas €
☎ 91 366 33 32; Calle de Latoneros 3; meal €10-15;
☺ lunch & dinner Tue-Sat, lunch Sun; Ⓜ Sol or La Latina

Casa Revuelta puts out Madrid's finest tapas of *bacalao* (cod) bar none. While aficionados of Casa Labra may disagree, the fact that the old owner painstakingly extracts every fish bone in the morning and serves as a waiter in the afternoon wins the argument for us. Early on a Sunday afternoon, as the Rastro crowd gathers here, it's filled to the rafters with that inexplicable feel-good Madrid buzz. It's also the sort of place where old local men who've been coming here for decades always manage to find room.

CERVECERÍA 100 MONTADITOS
Map pp254-5 Bocadillos €
☎ 902 197 494; Calle Mayor 22; meal €10; Ⓜ Sol

This bar serves up no less than 100 different varieties of mini-*bocadillos* (filled rolls, usually without butter) that span the full range of Spanish staples, such as chorizo (seasoned pork sausage), *jamón* (ham), tortilla, a variety of cheeses and seafood, in more combinations than you could imagine. Each one costs a princely €1. You fill out your

Eating

LOS AUSTRIAS, SOL & CENTRO

order, take it up to the counter and your name is called in no time. Other branches of this bar can be found all over town.

CERVECERÍA COMPANO
Map pp254-5 — Bocadillos €
Calle de Botaneros; bocadillos €2; ⏰ **lunch & dinner until late;** Ⓜ **Sol**
Spanish bars don't come any more basic than this, but it's the purveyor of an enduring and wildly popular Madrid tradition – a *bocadillo de calamares* (a large roll stuffed with deep-fried calamari) at any hour of the day or night. There are similar bars in the vicinity.

BANGKOK CAFÉ Map pp254-5 — Thai €€
☎ **91 559 16 96; 1st fl, Calle Bordadores 15; meal €15-20;** Ⓜ **Sol or Ópera**
Great Thai food, reasonable prices (the *menú del día* goes for €9), good service and a subtly stylish dining area make for a terrific meal in the heart of town. If you're lucky, you'll get one of the tables overlooking the busy street life of Calle de Arenal. Unusually for Madrid, it's a nonsmoking restaurant.

CASA LABRA Map pp254-5 — Tapas & Spanish €€
☎ **91 531 00 81; Calle de Tetuán 11; meal €25-30;** ⏰ **noon-3.30pm & 5.30-11pm Mon-Sat (restaurant), daily (bar);** Ⓜ **Sol**
One of the favourite tapas bars of Madrileños, Casa Labra has been going

A Madrileño favourite, Casa Labra (above)

strong since 1860, an era that the décor strongly evokes. Locals love their *bacalao* and ordering it here is a Madrid rite of initiation. This is also a bar with history – it was here that the Spanish socialist party was formed and it was a favourite of Lorca, the poet, as well.

CASA PACO Map pp254-5 — Madrileño €€
☎ **91 366 31 66; Plaza de la Puerta Cerrada 11; meal €25-30;** ⏰ **Mon-Sat Sep-Jul;** Ⓜ **La Latina**
The gaily painted exterior of this old Madrid tavern is hard to miss and harder to resist, especially in winter when the local Madrid specialities – *callos* (tripe), *cocido* (stew)and succulent steaks – come into their own. The bar area is also a good place for tapas or a wine.

LA VIUDA BLANCA
Map pp254-5 — Creative €€
☎ **91 548 75 29; Calle de Campomanes 6; meal €25;** ⏰ **Tue-Sat, lunch Mon;** Ⓜ **Ópera**
Calle de Campomanes is quickly becoming one of central Madrid's coolest streets and La Viuda Blanca is an essential part of its charm. The dining room is flooded with sunshine through the glass roof, the crowd is young and trendy, and the cooking spans wok dishes and baked salmon to more traditional rice concoctions. After the kitchen closes, it transforms into the equally cool La Viuda Negra bar (p133).

MUSASHI Map pp254-5 — Japanese €€
☎ **91 559 29 39; Calle de las Conchas 4; meal €15-20;** ⏰ **Tue-Sun;** Ⓜ **Santo Domingo**
Unlike their Chinese counterparts, Japanese restaurants in Madrid have a reputation for being pricey, but this compact little restaurant is an exception. The food is so good that the prince and his new bride reportedly dined here not long after their wedding and there's the full range of sushi, tempura and rice dishes to choose from.

RESTAURANTE SOBRINO DE BOTÍN
Map pp254-5 — Spanish €€
☎ **91 366 42 17; Calle de los Cuchilleros 17; meal €35-45;** Ⓜ **La Latina or Sol**
This place is famous for many reasons. For a start, the Guinness Book of Records has recognised it as the oldest restaurant in the world (1725). And then there's the fact that it has appeared in many novels about

115

Madrid, most notably Hemingway's *The Sun Also Rises*. The secret of their endurance is fine *cochinillo* (suckling pig) and *cordero asado* (roast lamb) cooked in wood-fired ovens, and eating in the vaulted cellar is a treat. If we had one criticism, it would be that, with one eye on the tourist market, staff are keen to keep things ticking over and there's little chance to linger.

TABERNA DEL ALABARDERO

Map pp254-5   Tapas & Spanish €€
☎ 91 547 25 77; Calle de Felipe V 6; meal €40-45; Ⓜ Ópera
This fine old Madrid *taberna* is famous for its *montaditos de jamón* or *bonito* (small rolls of cured ham or tuna) in the bar while out the back the more classic cuisine includes fine *croquetas* (croquettes), *morcilla* (blood sausage) and *rabo de toro* (bull's tail, usually in a stew). The atmosphere is cosy and elegant with period photos and old-style service.

TABERNA LA BOLA

Map pp254-5   Madrileño €€
☎ 91 547 69 30; Calle de la Bola 5; meal €30-35; Ⓥ Mon-Sat, lunch Sun; Ⓜ Santo Domingo
In any poll of food-loving locals seeking the best and most traditional Madrid cuisine, Taberna La Bola (going strong since 1880) always features near the top. We're inclined to agree and if you're going to try *cocido a la Madrileña* (Madrid stew; €16.80) at some stage while you're in Madrid, this is a good place to do so. It's busy and noisy and very Madrid.

LA LATINA & LAVAPIÉS

La Latina ranks up there with Malasaña and Chueca for fine, superstylish dining and you could just about take your pick of any of the restaurants around Calle de la Cava Baja and Plaza de la Paja and not leave disappointed. There's an emphasis on cool, stylish interiors and equally cool and casual clientele, but you'll also find your fair share of throwbacks to another Madrid era, with atmospheric old *tabernas* that have been perfecting traditional Madrileño cuisine for decades.

Lavapiés is more eclectic and multicultural and, generally speaking, the further down the hill you go, the better it gets, especially around Plaza de Lavapiés and Calle de Argumosa.

TOP TAPAS VENUES
- Biotza (p121)
- Bocaito (p124)
- Sagarretxe (p129)
- Taberna Algorta (below)
- La Trucha (p120)

BAR MELO'S Map pp254-5   Bocadillos & Tapas €
☎ 91 527 50 54; Calle de Ave María; meal €10-15; Ⓥ 9pm-2am Tue-Sat; Ⓜ Lavapiés
One of those Spanish bars that you'd normally walk past without a second glance, Bar Melo's is famous across the city for its *zapatillas* (great, spanking *bocadillos* of *lacón* – cured shoulder of pork – and cheese). They're big, they're greasy and they're damn good; the place is packed on a Friday or Saturday night when a *zapatilla* is the perfect accompaniment to a night of drinking.

DELIC Map pp254-5   International €
☎ 91 364 54 50; Costanilla de San Andrés 14; meal €15; Ⓥ 11am-2am Wed-Sat, 11am-midnight Sun, 8pm-2am Mon; Ⓜ La Latina or bus 31, 50, 65
There's no finer way to spend a summer's afternoon or evening than nursing a *mojito* at Delic's Plaza de la Paja *terraza*; it also offers a delicious range of cakes (€4.50 to €6) and international food in the chilled and cosy indoor dining area.

EL GRANERO DE LAVAPIÉS

Map pp254-5   Vegetarian €
☎ 91 467 76 11; Calle de Argumosa 10; meal €10-15; Ⓥ 1-4pm Mon-Thu & Sat, 1-4pm & 8.30-11pm Fri; Ⓜ Lavapiés
This simple but cosy vegetarian restaurant feels like eating at home, with just one dining room and friendly, family-style service. The food (all vegetarian) is home-cooked and tasty, making it a great choice for lunch and, unusually, it has a *menú del día* on Saturday (€10) as well as weekdays (€8.50).

TABERNA ALGORTA Map pp254-5   Tapas €
☎ 91 366 48 77; Calle de la Cava Baja 26; meal €15; Ⓥ Tue-Sat, lunch Sun; Ⓜ La Latina
The Basques have turned tapas (or *pintxos* as they call them) into an art form and Taberna Algorta is one of the finest exponents.

The cooks call their abundant offerings 'high cuisine in miniature' – the first part is true, but these are some of the biggest *pintxos* you'll find and some are a meal in themselves. They also do wonderful things with seafood and potatoes.

CASA LUCIO Map pp254-5 · Madrileño €€
☎ 91 365 32 52; Calle de la Cava Baja 35; meal €35-45; ☺ Sun-Fri, dinner Sat Sep-Jul; Ⓜ La Latina

Lucio has been wowing Madrileños with his light touch, quality ingredients and home-style local cooking for ages – think seafood, roasted meats and, a Lucio speciality, eggs in abundance – which is the main reason the king is known to frequent this place. There's also *rabo de toro* (bull's tail) during the Fiestas de San Isidro Labrador and plenty of rioja to wash away the mere thought of it.

EL ESTRAGÓN Map pp254-5 · Vegetarian €€
☎ 91 365 89 82; Plaza de la Paja 10; meal €20-25; Ⓜ La Latina or bus 31, 50, 65

A delightful spot for crepes and other vegetarian specialities, El Estragón is undoubtedly one of Madrid's best vegetarian restaurants, although attentive vegans won't appreciate the use of butter. It's also on one of old Madrid's quieter and more delightful squares.

ENE RESTAURANTE
Map pp254-5 · Fusion €€
☎ 91 366 25 91; Calle del Nuncio 19; meal €25-30; Ⓜ La Latina

Just across from Iglesia de San Pedro El Viejo, one of Madrid's oldest churches, Ene is anything but old-world. The design is cutting-edge and stylish with the dining area awash with reds and purples, while the young and friendly waiters circulate to the tune of lounge music. The food is Spanish-Asian fusion and there are also plenty of *pintxos* to choose from. The weekday *menú del día* costs €11. The chill-out beds downstairs are great for an after-dinner cocktail.

LA BUGA DEL LOBO
Map pp254-5 · Spanish €€
☎ 91 467 61 51; Calle de Argumosa 11; meal €20-25; ☺ 11am-2am Wed-Mon; Ⓜ Lavapiés

One of the 'in' places in cool and gritty Lavapiés, the popularity of La Buga del Lobo shows no sign of abating. The atmosphere is bohemian and chilled, with funky, swirling murals and jazz or lounge music. The food's good – the *chorizo frío de sidra* (cold chorizo in cider) or *pimientos rellenos* (stuffed pepper) are a highlight – but it's best known for its groovy vibe at any time of day or night.

LA BURBUJA QUE RÍE
Map pp254-5 · Asturian €€
☎ 91 366 51 67; Calle del Ángel 16; meal €20; Ⓜ La Latina

'The Laughing Bubble' is an excellent Asturian tavern that serves up nourishing and hearty dishes with cider; the *patatas con cabrales* (potato with blue cheese) is a fine order. All right, you can have beer or wine too, if you must insist, but it takes the fun out of the proceedings! Either way the atmosphere is good-naturedly rollicking.

LA TURULETA
Map pp254-5 · Gourmet Spanish & Tapas €€
☎ 91 364 26 66; Calle de Almendro 25; meal €15-20; ☺ Wed-Mon; Ⓜ La Latina

One of the many cool places to have opened up in this food-rich corner of La Latina, La Turuleta has simple designer décor, great food and an ambience that's friendly, laid-back and classy all at once. The food ranges from the basic (*tostas*; toasts) to the inventive (*milhojas de escalibada*; red capsicum in pastry served with eggplant and raviolis filled with cod).

MALACATÍN Map pp254-5 · Madrileño €€
☎ 91 365 52 41; Calle de Ruda 5; meal €25-30; ☺ Mon-Fri, lunch Sat; Ⓜ La Latina

If you want to see discerning Madrileños enjoying their favourite local food, this is arguably the best place to do so. The clamour of conversation – an essential part of the Madrileño eating experience – bounces off the tiled walls of the compact dining area which is adorned with bullfighting memorabilia. The speciality is as much *cocido* (stew) as you can eat (€18). Their *degustación de cocido* (taste of *cocido*; €5) at the bar is a great way to try Madrid's favourite dish without going all the way, although locals would argue that doing that is like smoking without inhaling.

MEIGAS Map pp254-5
Galician €€

☎ 91 354 08 84; Calle de Humilladero 4; meal €20-25; Ⓜ La Latina

This bright and vaguely minimalist Galician restaurant is an excellent place to eat, just off the well-worn La Latina track. It's all about friendly service and more types of seafood than you knew existed, including mussels, octopus, cockles and razor clams. Prices tend to be a touch lower here and dishes are a little more creative than at the longer-standing Galician restaurants.

OLIVEROS Map pp254-5
Madrileño €€

☎ 91 354 62 52; Calle de San Milán 4; meal €15-20; ☾ 1-5pm & 8pm-midnight Tue-Sat, noon-6pm Sun mid-Sep–mid-Aug; Ⓜ La Latina

If you're looking for one of the famous old *tabernas* of Madrid, you can do much worse than coming here. In the Oliveros family since 1921, this tiny, warm, bottle-lined den doesn't disappoint with its local dishes of *cocido a la Madrileña* or *callos de la Abuela* (grandma's tripe).

POSADA DE LA VILLA
Map pp254-5
Madrileño €€

☎ 91 366 18 60; Calle de la Cava Baja 9; meal €35-40; ☾ Mon-Sat, lunch Sun Sep-Jul; Ⓜ La Latina

The Posada is a wonderfully restored 17th-century inn (*posada*) that reeks of conservatism (Popular Party bigwigs love the place) and is something of a local landmark. The atmosphere is formal, the decoration sombre and traditional, (heavy timber and brickwork) and the cuisine decidedly local – *cocido*, *callos* and *sopa de ajo* (garlic soup).

RESTAURANTE JULIÁN DE TOLOSA
Map pp254-5
Navarran €€

☎ 91 365 82 10; Calle de la Cava Baja 8; meal €35; ☾ Mon-Sat, lunch Sun; Ⓜ La Latina

Where many restaurants serving authentic regional Spanish cooking go for dark and traditional décor, this fine Navarran restaurant has a subtly modern aesthetic to accompany its excellent, meat-dominated menu – the *chuletón* (basically a huge chop of top-quality, juicy meat) for two is outstanding. Fine Navarran wines and *alubias rojas de Tolosa* (red beans from Tolosa) are other highlights.

Fire up the appetite at Posada de la Villa (left)

VIUDA DE VACAS Map pp254-5
Spanish €€

☎ 91 366 58 47; Calle de la Cava Alta 23; meal €15-25; ☾ Fri-Wed; Ⓜ La Latina

With its quaint old wooden façade, wooden stools, checked tablecloths and terracotta floor, the 'Cow Widow' is an atmospheric old tavern that draws a knowledgeable local crowd. When the place is full, as it usually is, the noise bounces off the tiled walls to create an agreeable clamour. The specialities include *bacalao* (cod), *besugo al horno* (baked red bream) and *gallina en pepitoria* (chicken in almond sauce).

HUERTAS & ATOCHA

Late-night (or all-night) drinking is a Huertas forté, but there are also plenty of good restaurants. The pick of the places is in the lanes between Puerta del Sol and Plaza de Santa Ana, while down the hill around Calle del Prado promises equally rich pickings. Whether you prefer Spanish, *nouvelle cuisine*, tapas, vegetarian, Galician, Basque or Cuban flavours, you'll find them in Huertas.

CÍRCULO DE BELLAS ARTES
Map pp254-5
Café €

☎ 91 521 69 42; Calle de Alcalá 42; ☾ 9am-1am; Ⓜ Sevilla

This daring, convoluted structure, designed by Antonio Palacios Ramilo in 1919, boasts a wonderful *belle époque* café replete with chandeliers and the charm of a bygone era. You have to buy a temporary club membership (€1) to drink here, but it's worth every cent, even if the service is a tad stuffy.

EL BRILLANTE Map p257 Bocadillos €

☎ 91 528 69 66; Calle del Doctor Drumén 7; bocadillos €3-5; ⏱ 6.30am-12.30am; Ⓜ Atocha
Just by the Centro de Arte Reina Sofía, this breezy, no-frills bar-eatery is a Madrid institution for its *bocadillos* (the *bocadillo de calamares* is an old favourite) and other snacks (*raciones* cost €6 to €10). It's also famous for *chocolate con churros* or *porras* (deep-fried doughnut strips) in the wee hours after a hard night on the tiles. There's another branch (Map pp246–7; ☎ 91 448 19 88; Calle de Eloy Gonzalo 14; Ⓜ Quevedo) in Chamberí.

LA BIOTIKA Map pp254-5 Vegetarian €

☎ 91 429 07 80; Calle del Amor de Dios 3; meal €10-15; Ⓜ Antón Martín
The macrobiotic, café-style La Biotika, out the back of a health food shop, is an enduring vegetarians' paradise, where you can opt for such faves as *seitan* ('wheat meat'), tofu-based dishes and generous salads. The emphasis is on simplicity and healthy eating with not too many creative twists.

LA NEGRA TOMASA Map pp254-5 Cuban €

☎ 91 523 58 30; Calle de Cádiz 9; meal €15; ⏱ noon-3.30am Sun & Mon, noon-5.30am Tue-Sat; Ⓜ Sol
Bar, restaurant and magnet for all things Cuban, La Negra Tomas is a boisterous meeting place for the Havana set with waitresses dressed in traditional Cuban outfits (definitely pre-Castro), decent food such as *cojimar* (shrimps in a tomato sauce with rice and slices of banana fritter) and typical drinks of the Caribbean such as *mojitos*.

LA OREJA DEL ORO Map pp254-5 Tapas €

Calle de la Victoria 9; meal €10-15; ⏱ Wed-Sun; Ⓜ Sol
In Spain they say, 'we eat everything from the pig, except the walk' and here's proof.

TOP SPOTS FOR REGIONAL SPANISH SPECIALITIES

- Casa Hortensia (p125) – Asturias region.
- Restaurante Julián de Tolosa (opposite) – Navarra.
- Zerain (p120) – Basque Country.
- Restaurante Extremadura (p126) – Extremadura.
- Mardrid (p122) – Galicia.

Oreja (pig's ear) is something of a delicacy and great mounds of it are on offer at this basic little Galician bar. It's a bit gristly but surprisingly good and is even better washed down with a glass of refreshing white Ribeiro wine. Another good order from the many Galician specialities available are the *pimientos de padrón* (small green peppers).

LAS BRAVAS Map pp254-5 Tapas €

☎ 91 532 26 20; Callejón de Álvarez Gato 3; meal €15; ⏱ 10am-11.30pm; Ⓜ Sol
Las Bravas has long been the place for a *caña* (small glass of beer) and the best *patatas bravas* (fried potatoes with a spicy tomato sauce) in town. The antics of the bar staff are enough to merit a stop, and the distorting mirrors are a minor Madrid landmark. Elbow your way to the bar and be snappy about your orders.

EL CENADOR DEL PRADO

Map pp254-5 Spanish Creative €€
☎ 91 429 15 61; Calle del Prado 4; meal €35-40; ⏱ Mon-Sat, lunch Sun; Ⓜ Antón Martín
Amid the constant casual chatter of Huertas, El Cenador del Prado is a discreet and quietly elegant oasis, ideal for a romantic meal. It has fairly traditional Spanish cooking with a few international twists and turns, such as the *chipirones rellenos de butifarra guisados con almejas* (baby squid stuffed with Catalan sausage and cooked with clams).

GULA GULA Map pp254-5 Nouvelle Cuisine €€

☎ 91 420 29 19; Calle del Infante 5; meal €15-20; ⏱ 9am-3am Tue-Sun; Ⓜ Antón Martín
One of the first designer restaurants to hit Madrid back in the mid-1990s, Gula Gula continues to offer fun food. The bare brick walls, parquet floor, stage lighting and sexily dressed waiting staff help to create an ambience that's camp and snappy. The food is a mixed bag but leans towards vegetarian (the salad buffet is excellent) in this meat-loving city. There's another branch at Gran Vía 1 (Map pp254–5).

LA CASA DEL ABUELO

Map pp254-5 Tapas €€
☎ 91 521 23 19; Calle de la Victoria 12; meal €15-25; ⏱ 11.30am-3.30pm & 6.30-11.30pm; Ⓜ Sol
The 'House of the Grandfather' is an ageless, popular place where the traditional order

Eating

HUERTAS & ATOCHA

is a *chato* (small glass) of the heavy, sweet El Abuelo red wine (made in Toledo province) and the heavenly *gambas a la plancha* (grilled prawns) or *gambas al ajillo* (prawns sizzling in garlic on little ceramic plates).

LA FINCA DE SUSANA

Map pp254-5   Mediterranean €€

☎ 91 369 35 57; Calle de Arlabán 4; meal €15-20; Ⓜ Sevilla

Just because you're paying relatively low prices for your meal doesn't mean that you have to dine in *cutre* (rough-and-ready) surrounds. The classy dining area of soft lighting and plenty of greenery is matched by a mix of innovative and traditional food that draws a hip young crowd. The *fideua con ali-oli* (small pasta noodles with seafood and garlic mayonnaise) is a fine choice. It doesn't take reservations and there's often a queue outside.

LA TRUCHA Map pp254-5   Tapas €€

☎ 91 532 08 82; Calle de Núñez de Arce 6; meal €20-25; Ⓣ Tue-Sat; Ⓜ Sol

'The Trout' is one of Madrid's great tapas bars. The counter is loaded with enticing choices and the bar staff will have their own idea about what's good to try – listen to them because they know their tapas. If it's too crowded, try the other branch (☎ 91 429 58 33; Calle de Manuel Fernández y González 3) nearby.

LHARDY Map pp254-5   Gourmet Spanish €€

☎ 91 522 22 07; Carrera de San Jerónimo 8; meal €35-45; Ⓣ Mon-Sat, lunch Sun; Ⓜ Sevilla

This Madrid landmark (since 1839) is an elegant treasure-trove of delicatessen items that's ideal for those planning a dinner party of gourmet tapas. You can also sit down to full meals (the house specialities are Madrid dishes such as *callos* and *cocido*, as well as *perdiz estofado* – partridge stew).

MACEIRA Map pp254-5   Galician €€

☎ 91 429 15 84; Calle de Jesús 7; meal €15-20; Ⓣ Tue-Sun, dinner Mon; Ⓜ Antón Martín

Get in here early as the simple wooden benches and tables creak under the weight of so much attention. Get stuck into classic *raciones* of Galician seafood, such as *pulpo a la gallega* (boiled octopus; €8.25) downed with a crisp white Ribeiro. It has another branch (☎ 91 429 58 18; Calle de Huertas 66) around the corner.

ZERAIN Map pp254-5   Basque €€

☎ 91 429 79 09; Calle de Quevedo 3; meal €30-35; Ⓣ Mon-Sat; Ⓜ Antón Martín

In the heart of the Barrio de las Letras, this sophisticated Basque restaurant is one of the best places in the area to sample Basque cuisine. The essential staples include cider, *bacalao* and wonderful steaks, while there are also a few splashes of creativity thrown in (the secret's in the sauce).

PASEO DEL PRADO & EL RETIRO

In the discreet residential enclave between the Parque del Buen Retiro and the Museo del Prado you'll find a handful of fairly exclusive restaurants where eating is taken seriously, elegant, classic charm is the pervasive atmosphere and limousines wait outside to ferry the well-heeled back home.

BALZAC Map p257   Innovative Madrileño €€€

☎ 91 420 06 13; Calle de Moreto 7; meal €70-80; Ⓣ Mon-Sat; Ⓜ Banco de España or Atocha

While Basque and Catalan chefs have been capturing the world's attention for their *nouvelle cuisine*, Madrid's Andrés Madrigal has been quietly gathering plaudits. His faithfulness to traditional Madrileño cooking has been fused to what he calls 'inno-

LATE BITES & DAWN DINING

Way past midnight and your stomach's growling? If you know where to look, meals are available in Madrid up to 2am, and sometimes later. In Huertas try **La Negra Tomasa** (p119) or **Gula Gula** (p119). Around Plaza Mayor, **Cervecería Compano** (p115) serves *bocadillos de calamares* until the wee hours, while the kitchen might still be open at **Delic** (p116) down on Plaza de la Paja. In Lavapiés, the bocadillos of **Bar Melo's** (p116) are a Madrid institution while **La Inquilina** (p134) and **La Buga del Lobo** (p117) are also possibilities. In Malasaña, **Casa Do Compañeiro** (p124) stays open till 2am, as does **Giangrossi** (p123) on Friday and Saturday for ice creams. For a *chocolate con churros* at any time of night, **Chocolatería San Ginés** (p129) is legendary, while Chinese vendors often set up snack stalls at all hours along Gran Vía (Map pp250–1) on weekends.

vation, risk-taking and rebellious spirit'. The results are stunning, such as *canelones de rabo de toro con infusión de cardamomo y las ultimas trufas negras de invierno* (cannelloni of bull's tail with an infusion of cardamom and the freshest black truffles of winter). The service is also impeccable.

CLUB 31 Map p257 — Spanish €€€

☎ 91 532 05 11; Calle de Alcalá 58; meal €50-60; Ⓜ Retiro

An old Madrid classic, Club 31 has a vaguely contemporary design with long black seats, leaning wall mirrors and bright white designer lamps hanging from the ceiling, but the cuisine is classic. The accent is on fish and venison, with the occasional modern touch (such as the lobster *soufflé*). You could set your watch by the old-style, professional service. Last time we were here, royalty were at the next table.

SALAMANCA

Eating out in Salamanca is traditionally as exclusive as the shops that fill the barrio, the sort of places where the keys to Jags and BMWs are left for valet parking, and prices and quality are high. We've listed a few of them, but Salamanca is also home to some of Madrid's best-kept eating secrets, from Madrid's best hot dogs and Basque tapas (*pintxos*) to fusion restaurants and intimate dens of creative home-cooking.

CAFETERÍA GALATEA

Map pp246-7 — Tapas & Hot Dogs €

☎ 91 431 15 01; Calle de Príncipe de Vergara 4; meal €5-10; Ⓨ 7am-midnight Sun-Thu, 7am-1am Fri & Sat; Ⓜ Príncipe de Vergara

In a city of such rich culinary pickings, it may seem strange to list a place known for its hot dogs, but they come with lashings of mustard and tomato sauce and, if you wish, cheese, tomato and onion. Madrileños swear by them and, admittedly, they're a meal in themselves, especially the *gigantes* (gigantics). Most remarkably, it's in Salamanca.

FAST GOOD Map p252 — Healthy Fast Food €

Calle de Juan Bravo 3; meal €10; Ⓨ noon-midnight; Ⓜ Núñez de Balboa

When Ferran Adrià, the star Catalan chef, became concerned about Spaniards' grow-

Try quick and healthy food at Fast Good (below)

ing obsession with fast food, he decided to do something about it. Fast Good is a wonderfully simple concept (food that's fast but healthy) and it's a terrific place to get a freshly prepared hamburger, roast chicken or panini with a creative twist. We enjoyed the panini of *champiñones frescos con gorgonzola* (fresh mushrooms and gorgonzola cheese) almost as much as the curvy white and lime-green décor.

BIOTZA Map p252 — Basque Tapas €€

☎ 91 781 03 13; Calle de Claudio Coello 27; meal €25; Ⓨ 9am-midnight Mon-Thu, 9am-2am Fri & Sat; Ⓜ Serrano

This superstylish and breezy Basque tapas bar is one of the best places in Madrid to sample the creativity of bite-sized *pintxos* (tapas) as only the Basques can make them. It's the perfect combination of San Sebastián bars laden with food and Madrid style in the pale-green tile decoration and unusual angular benches. The *pintxos* cost around €3 apiece, but we suggest one of the *degustación de pintxos* (tasting menus; €11 to €16) where you get a selection.

LA GALETTE

Map p252 — Vegetarian & European €€

☎ 91 576 06 41; Calle del Conde de Aranda 11; meal €30; Ⓨ Mon-Sat, lunch Sun; Ⓜ Retiro

Walk into this lovely little restaurant and you could be in the south of France with its delightfully intimate little dining area. The food is a revelation, with around half the dishes 'baroque vegetarian', as the owner calls them. It is creative cooking at its best, and it feels like it's emerging from your grandma's kitchen. The *croquetas de manzana* (apple croquettes) are a house speciality, but everything on the extensive menu is good.

LE CAFÉ Map p252 — Spanish €€
☎ 91 781 15 86; Calle de los Recoletos 13; meal €25-30; Ⓜ Retiro
It can be almost impossible to get a table here at lunchtime on a weekday when locals stream in from surrounding homes and offices for the buzzing atmosphere and supermodern, supercool orange décor. The food is largely traditional Spanish fare (rice dishes are a recurring theme) and they're done well.

MARDRID Map pp246-7 — Galician €€
☎ 91 309 12 80; Plaza de Manuel Becerra 19; meal €20-25; Ⓨ Mon-Sat, lunch Sun; Ⓜ Manuel Becerra
En route to or from Las Ventas bullring, consider this innovative Galician restaurant where the décor is white and fishy, and the food is dominated by seafood – as is the Galicians' wont. The *salpicón de centolla* (salad of spider crab) is superb and paying just €10 for the *menú del día* in such a classy place feels like you've just won the lottery.

MUMBAI MASSALA Map p252 — Indian €€
☎ 91 435 71 94; Calle de los Recoletos 14; meal €30-35; Ⓜ Retiro
Enter through the heavy red curtain and into a brightly coloured and beautifully decorated Indian world where the food and service are good and the ambience laid-back. Servings aren't enormous, but they're superbly done with dishes spanning the subcontinent from southern India (think spicy) to Pakistan. If you can't decide, the *menú de degustación* (tasting menu) for €27.50 is a fine banquet.

TEATRIZ Map p252 — Fusion €€
☎ 91 577 53 79; Calle de la Hermosilla 15; meal €30-40; Ⓜ Serrano
Designed by Philippe Stark, the former Teatro Beatriz has an eerily lit bar right on the stage and it's the kind of place where you'll need to look like George Clooney to fit in. The food follows the fashion, ranging from Made in Spain to Fusion. While you're there, check out the loos, where you leave luminous footprints!

EL AMPARO Map p252 — Basque & Creative €€€
☎ 91 431 64 56; Calle de Puigcerdà 8; meal €80-100; Ⓨ Mon-Fri, dinner Sat; Ⓜ Serrano
Hidden away down a charming alley in the heart of Salamanca, El Amparo is one of the more exclusive restaurants in Madrid. The cuisine has been variously described as Basque and *nueva cocina Madrileña* (nouvelle Madrid cuisine), which indicates that you can expect a bit of a mix – the *cigala salteadas con raviolis de queso, miel y romero* (sauteed crayfish with cheese, honey and rosemary raviolis) for example. The service and wine list are admirable, and the food is generally excellent. Some of the homemade desserts are simply divine.

PARADIS ERRE EFE
Map p257 — Innovative €€€
☎ 91 575 45 40; Paseo de los Recoletos 2; meal €50-60; Ⓨ Mon-Fri, dinner Sat; Ⓜ Banco de España
Housed in the Casa de América in Palacio Linares, this unique place offers the minimalist décor that exudes modishness and where Barcelonan chef Ramón Freixa offers 'interactive' cooking. You want a veal fillet? Fine, now you choose what goes with it. The elegant main dining room, dominated by whites and blacks, is surrounded by smaller annexes.

TOP MADRID SPECIALITIES AND WHERE TO FIND THEM
- *Cocido a la Madrileña* (Madrid stew) – **Taberna La Bola** (p116), **Malacatín** (p117) or **Lhardy** (p120)
- *Callos a la Madrileña* (tripe casserole with chorizo and chillies) – **Casa Paco** (p115) or **Oliveros** (p118)
- *Sopa de ajo or sopa castellana* (garlic broth with floating egg and bread) – **Posada de la Villa** (p118)
- *Chocolate con churros* (deep-fried doughnut strips dipped in hot chocolate) – **El Brillante** (p119) or **Chocolatería San Ginés** (p129)
- *Bocadillo de calamares* (a roll stuffed with calamari) – **Cervecería Compano** (p115)

THAI GARDENS Map p252   Thai €€€
☎ 91 577 88 84; Calle de Jorge Juan 5; meal €45-50; Ⓜ Serrano

This sophisticated restaurant is awash with greenery and is a favoured haunt of Spain's celebrities and well-to-do. The food is exquisite, the service faultless and the staff say that the ingredients are flown in weekly from Thailand. At lunchtime it offers a good set menu for €25, while bookings are essential on weekends.

MALASAÑA & CHUECA

Unless you're particularly after the exclusivity of fine and expensive dining, Malasaña and Chueca have some of the best places to eat in Madrid. Old *tabernas* abound, each with its speciality, but there are also plenty of places where nouvelle Spanish cuisine is served in lively, stylish and anything-but-pretentious surroundings. Wandering around the two barrios, you're sure to find your own favourite, but there are two streets that stand out – Calle de Manuela Malasaña and, in Chueca, Calle de la Libertad.

CAFÉ COMERCIAL Map pp250-1   Café €
☎ 91 521 56 55; Glorieta de Bilbao 7; ⊙ 8am-1am Sun-Thu, 8am-2am Fri & Sat; Ⓜ Bilbao

This glorious old Madrid café proudly fights a rearguard action against progress with heavy leather seats, abundant marble and old-style waiters. As close as Madrid came to the intellectual cafés of Paris' Left Bank, the cafés of the Glorieta de Bilbao were in the 1950s and 1960s a centre of coffee-house intellectualism. Café Comercial is the last to remain and has changed little since those days, although the clientele has broadened to include just about anyone.

CHIACCHERE Map pp250-1   Italian €
☎ 91 521 26 90; Calle de la Libertad 9; meal €10-15; ⊙ noon-8pm Mon-Thu, noon-midnight Fri & Sat; Ⓜ Chueca

Amid the gastronomic excess and creativity of Calle de la Libertad, they keep it simple at Chiacchere, a favoured haunt of Madrid's Italian community. It has a bright, coffee-shop ambience and the lunch set meal of bruschetta, pasta of the day, coffee and a soft drink costs €11.50.

TOP PLACES FOR INTERNATIONAL CUISINE

- Thai Gardens (left) – Thai
- Mosaiq (p129) – Middle Eastern
- Nagoya (p129) – Japanese
- Mumbai Massala (opposite) – Indian
- Kim Bu Mbu (p125) – African

FRESC CO Map pp250-1   Salad & Pasta Buffet €
☎ 91 521 60 52; Calle de Sagasta 30; meal €8-10; ⊙ 12.30pm-1am; Ⓜ Alonso Martínez

If you just can't face deciphering another Spanish menu or are in dire need of a do-it-yourself salad, Fresc Co is a fresh, well-priced and all-you-can-eat antidote. An extensive choice of self-service salads, soups, pasta and pizza are on offer and the price includes a drink. Queues often go out the door at lunchtime.

GIANGROSSI
Map pp250-1   Homemade Ice Cream €
☎ 900 555 009; Calle de Alberto Aguilera 1; ⊙ 9am-1am Mon-Thu, 9am-2am Fri & Sat, noon-1am Sun; Ⓜ San Bernardo

Ice cream never tasted so good as in this stylish and supermodern café with deep leather chairs and high ceilings. Far more than just your chocolate-strawberry-and-vanilla ice creamery, there are dozens of flavours (and milkshakes) to choose from, coffee is outstanding and the cakes and chocolates are divine. There's a smaller branch (Map p252; Velázquez 44) in Salamanca.

LA TABERNA DE SAN BERNARDO
Map pp250-1   Tapas €
☎ 91 445 41 70; Calle de San Bernardo 85; meal €15; ⊙ 2.30-4.30pm & 8.30pm-2.30am; Ⓜ San Bernardo

Stick your head in the door and there's not a lot to catch your attention, but pass by here on a Saturday night when it's buzzing with locals and pause long enough to read the menu and you'll be hooked. The *raciónes* (€6 to €8) include plenty of Spanish staples (potatoes, *chistorra,* eggs and *bacalao* are plentiful) with a few surprising twists thrown in – the *berenjenas con mile de caña* (deep-fried eggplant with honey) is brilliant.

TOP SPOTS FOR VEGETARIANS & VEGANS

- La Isla del Tesoro (opposite)
- La Galette (p121)
- El Granero de Lavapiés (p116)
- El Estragón (p117)
- La Biotika (p119)

TETERÍA DE LA ABUELA

Map pp250-1   Tea Room €

Calle del Espíritu Santo 19; crepes €5-7; 5pm-2am Tue-Sun; Tribunal

This enchanting tea room with tiny marble-top tables, rickety wooden seats and an old-fashioned till is where the 19th century meets the 1960s. It's old-world, friendly, and home to a great range of teas and delicious crepes.

WAGABOO Map pp250-1   Creative Asian €

91 531 65 67; Calle de Gravina 18; meal €15; Chueca

Serving an almost exclusively gay clientele, Wagaboo offers cheap and cheerful pasta and noodle dishes (the tagliatelle Stolichnaya is an acquired taste, though) and an unmistakeable *frisson* ripples across the room whenever the door opens.

A BRASILEIRA Map pp250-1   Brazilian €€

91 308 36 25; Calle de Pelayo 49; meal €20-25; Chueca

Never tried Brazilian food? Here's a great place to start. Only one problem? It's too popular for its own good so finding a table is a challenge. Once seated, the rice dishes are terrific (the *vatapá* – mixed seafood – is especially good) and the meat is inevitably a feature. The long list of cocktails makes it a good starting point for your Chueca night of revelry.

ANTIGUA CASA ÁNGEL SIERRA

Map pp250-1   Tapas €€

91 531 01 26; Calle de Gravina 11; meal €15-20; 12.30pm-1am; Chueca

Famous for its *boquerones* (anchovies) and *empanadas* (savoury pies), this historic old *taberna* is the antithesis of modern Chueca chic – it has hardly changed since it opened in 1917 and thankfully that includes the wonderful façade. Fronting onto the Plaza de Chueca, it can get pretty lively of an evening.

BAZAAR

Map pp250-1   Mediterranean Nouvelle Cuisine €€

91 523 39 05; Calle de la Libertad 21; meal €20-25; Chueca

Occupying a privileged corner location, with hardwood floors, grand windows, theatre lighting and comfy leather seats, Bazaar is invariably packed with a casual young crowd who come for the fresh tastes and mixed meat and fish menu. It doesn't take reservations so get here early.

BOCAITO Map pp250-1   Tapas €€

91 532 12 19; Calle de la Libertad 4-6; meal €15-20; Mon-Fri, dinner Sat; Chueca or Banco de España

Film-maker Pedro Almodóvar finds this bar and restaurant in the traditional Madrid style 'the best antidepressant'. Forget about the sit-down restaurant and just jam into the bar, order a few *raciones* off the menu, slosh them down with some gritty red or a *caña* and enjoy the theatre in which these busy barmen excel.

BOGA BAR

Map pp250-1   Seafood & Rice Dishes €€

91 532 18 50; Calle del Almirante 11; meal €35-40; Mon-Sat, lunch Sun; Chueca

Boga Bar is right at home in this exclusive corner of Madrid – this is where Chueca creativity meets Salamanca designer shops – and the round arches, fire-red walls and deep-green fronds make for one of the barrio's most agreeable dining atmospheres. The seafood is outstanding and popular, and the desserts are quite heavenly.

CASA DO COMPAÑEIRO

Map pp250-1   Galician Tapas €€

91 521 57 02; Calle de San Vicente Ferrer 44; meal €15-25; 1.30pm-2am; Tribunal

Tucked away in the streets just up from Plaza Dos de Mayo, this old Madrid *taberna* has a wonderful tiled and wood façade, basic wooden stools and marble-top tables. It's renowned for its *pulpo a la gallega* (Galician-style octopus), *pimientos de padrón* (grilled little green peppers) and *lacón*.

CASA HORTENSIA

Map pp250-1   Asturian €€

☎ 91 539 00 90; 2nd fl, Calle de la Farmacia 2; meal €20-30; 🕑 lunch Tue-Sat; Ⓜ Tribunal or Gran Vía

With all the innovations happening elsewhere in Madrid, it's good to know that some things don't change. Casa Hortensia is better than it looks from the outside and is an old favourite for huge plates of Asturian specialities such as *fabada asturiana* (white-bean stew with pork and blood sausage) or *tacos de merluza rebozadaos* (tacos of hake in breadcrumbs).

CASA PERICO Map pp250-1   Spanish €€

☎ 91 532 81 76; Calle de la Ballesta 18; meal €25; 🕑 Mon-Fri, lunch Sat; Ⓜ Callao

With little passing traffic to attract (the street is not one of Madrid's finest), this old Madrid legend is restricted to a clientele consisting entirely of people in-the-know. Even when you push open the door it's not entirely clear you're in a restaurant – the handful of check-cloth–covered tables are huddled behind a mess of wine bottles, crates and God knows what else. What's special is the house specialities such as *arroz a lo cutre* ('grotty rice', actually a delicious creamy rice dish). A great, quirky place to eat.

CON DOS FOGONES

Map pp250-1   International €€

☎ 91 559 63 26; Calle de San Bernardino 9; meal €25-30; Ⓜ Plaza de España

A welcome addition to the Madrid culinary scene, Con Dos Fogones is cool and classy with bright colours softly lit by designer lamps. The food is everything from salads and quality hamburgers to great slabs of fine Argentinean beef. The *menú del día* is a bargain €9, while, unusually, they have an evening menu for €14.80

CRÊPERIE MA BRETAGNE

Map pp250-1   Crepes €€

☎ 91 531 77 74; Calle de San Vicente Ferrer; meal €20-25; 🕑 8.30pm-1am Thu-Sun, 8.30pm-2am Fri & Sat; Ⓜ Tribunal

What a wonderful little place this is – dark, candlelit and all about delicious crêpes. After eating these exquisite delights (a meal in themselves) from the rustic wooden tables, there are more crepes, this time sweet, for dessert. You'll never want to see a crepe again after eating here, but over-indulgence in such a cosy atmosphere is a great way to go out.

GRAN CAFÉ DE GIJÓN

Map p252   Café & Spanish €€

☎ 91 521 54 25; Paseo de los Recoletos 21; meal €30; 🕑 7am-2am; Ⓜ Chueca or Banco de España

This graceful old café has been serving coffee and meals since 1888 and has long been a favourite with Madrid's literati for a drink or a meal. The latter is a bit of a national smorgasbord, ranging from *cabrito asado a la segoviana* (roast kid goat) to *bacalao al pil pil* (the typically steamed Basque cod in a garlic sauce).

KIM BU MBU Map pp250-1   African €€

☎ 91 521 26 81; Calle de Colmenares 7; meal €20; Ⓜ Chueca or Banco de España

Stepping inside this fine African restaurant, with stunning African décor and a tranquil air, is like entering another world. The *menú de degustación* (€21; tasting menu) is a good way to get acquainted with the perhaps unfamiliar Senegalese and other unusual tastes. Then again, the *gambas con mango y batata dulce* (prawns with mango and sweet potato) are pretty self-explanatory and very good.

LA COQUETA Map pp250-1   Spanish €€

☎ 91 523 06 47; Calle de la Libertad 3; meal €25-30; 🕑 Mon-Sat; Ⓜ Chueca or Banco de España

Calle de la Libertad is probably Chueca's culinary queen and La Coqueta well deserves its place alongside the many fine restaurants along this street. Popular with a gay crowd, its clean lines and contrasting colour schemes are stylish while dishes such as the *arroz cremoso a la marinera con mejillones y sepia* (creamy seafood rice with mussels and squid) are excellent.

LA ISLA DEL TESORO

Map pp250-1   Vegetarian €€

☎ 91 593 14 40; Calle de Manuela Malasaña 3; meal €30; Ⓜ Bilbao

This place wins our vote for Madrid's best vegetarian restaurant. The décor is funky, intimate and as inventive as the food. The *ensalada boskimana* (salad of goat's cheese,

THE BEST ICE CREAM IN MADRID

- Giangrossi (p123) Delicious homemade ice cream amid décor that evokes a chic Madrid bar.
- Bajo Cero (opposite) Hip surrounds and boutique ice cream and milkshakes.
- Palazzo (Map pp254–5; ☎ 91 532 26 42; Gran Vía 32; ⏰ 11am-10pm; Ⓜ Gran Vía) The best vanilla ice cream with a hint of lemon.
- Los Caprichos de Martina (Map pp254–5; ☎ 91 365 04 19; Calle de Toledo 4; ⏰ 11am-2am; Ⓜ Sol) Just down the steps from Plaza Mayor and good for homemade ice cream.

dates, honey and other assortments) sets the tone for cooking that's fresh and always surprising, and you'll be served by friendly, turquoise-clad waiters who have English-language menus. A great choice in a great barrio.

LA MUSA   Map pp250-1   Cutting Edge €€
☎ 91 448 75 58; Calle de Manuela Malasaña 18; meal €25-30; ⏰ 9am-5pm & 7pm-midnight; Ⓜ Bilbao or San Bernardo

A local favourite of Malasaña's hip young crowd, La Musa has designer décor, lounge music on the sound system and food that will live long in the memory. The fried green tomatoes with strawberry jam and great meat dishes are fun and filled with flavour. It doesn't take reservations so sidle up to the bar, put your name on the waiting list and soak up the ambient buzz of Malasaña at its best. The same owners run Ojaláa (Map pp250–1; ☎ 91 523 27 47; Calle de San Andrés 1; ⏰ 9am-12.30am Sun-Wed, 9am-1.30am Thu, 9am-2pm Fri & Sat), which has an equally cool vibe and menu, and stays open longer. It's to the south of La Musa.

LA PAELLA DE LA REINA
Map pp254-5   Rice Dishes €€
☎ 91 531 18 85; Calle de la Reina 39; meal €20-30; Ⓜ Banco de España

Madrid is not renowned for its paella (Valencia is king in that regard), but Valencianos who can't make it home are known to frequent La Paella de la Reina. Like any decent paella restaurant, you need two people to make an order but once that requirement is satisfied, you've plenty of choice. The typical Valencia paella is cooked

with beans and chicken but there are also plenty of seafood varieties on offer.

LAYDOWN REST CLUB
Map pp250-1   Innovative €€
☎ 91 548 79 37; Plaza Mostenses 9; meal €30; ⏰ 2-4pm & 9.30pm-2.30am Tue-Fri, 9.30pm-2.30am Sat & Sun, 2-4pm Mon; Ⓜ Plaza de España or Noviciado

The name says it all and this place has to be seen to be believed. Part of a new craze in concept-dining, Laydown Rest Club is whiter-than-white and completely devoid of tables – you eat Roman-style while reclining on beds and are served by toga-clad waiters with huge feather fans. It's all the rage at the moment and is a dining experience unlike any other. Incredible. The menu changes daily, but for a taste, try the weekday *menú* at lunchtime for just €11. It can be difficult to find – from Plaza Mostenses, head east along Calle del General Mitre then take the first lane on the right.

NINA   Map pp250-1   Nouvelle Cuisine €€
☎ 91 591 00 46; Calle de Manuela Malasaña 10; meal €25-30; Ⓜ Bilbao

This is one of our favourite restaurants in Madrid with fantastic food, great service and a subtly stylish dining area. The cooking is similarly stylish (English-language menus are available) and the *foie fresco a la plancha* (grilled foie gras) is rich and divine. Popular with a sophisticated local crowd, Nina can be a hard place to get a table and booking on weekends is essential (the two sittings are at 9.15pm and 11.15pm). It also does a fine brunch (€18) on weekends.

RESTAURANTE EXTREMADURA
Map pp250-1   Extremaduran €€
☎ 91 531 88 82; Calle de la Libertad 13; meal €30; Ⓜ Chueca

The hearty, meat-dominated cooking from the Spanish interior that you'll find here is especially good in winter when you'll better understand the Iberian love for *caza* (game) and other meat, which is usually accompanied by full volume conversation. *Jamón* is a key fixture (some of the best *jamón* comes from Extremadura) and the roast lamb *(cordero asado)* is well worth trying.

RESTAURANTE MOMO

Map pp250-1   Cutting Edge €€

☎ 91 532 73 48; Calle de la Libertad 8; meal €25;
☺ Mon-Sat; Ⓜ Chueca

Momo may have moved from its famous
location a few blocks away, but it remains a
Chueca beacon of reasonably priced, inventive cuisine. This was one of the first restaurants to take Chueca dining to a new level
and it still has its deservedly loyal following
among the gay, straight and arts crowds.
The *pavo con salsa de pistachos* (turkey with
pistachio sauce) is merely one highlight
among many and the *menú del día* is one of
Madrid's best bargains.

SALVADOR Map pp250-1   Madrileño €€

☎ 91 521 45 24; Calle de Barbieri 12; meal €25;
☺ Mon-Sat Sep-Jul; Ⓜ Chueca

This old Hemingway favourite is typical of
many old Madrid classics – walking past,
you wouldn't give it a second look. Since
the dark days of 1941 locals have been
coming to the 'Saviour' for lashings of
hearty Madrid cooking and among them
are plenty of aficionados and *toreros* (bullfighters, or matadors as they are popularly
known outside Spain) especially during the
Fiestas de San Isidro Labrador. Ordering a
plate of *rabo de toro* (bull's tail) is a way to
win friends, while the remainder is simple,
no-nonsense fare.

TABERNA ÁRABE LA GRANJA DE

SAID Map pp250-1   Moroccan €€

☎ 91 532 87 93; Calle de San Andrés 11;
meal €15-20; ☺ 1pm-2am; Ⓜ Tribunal

If you've ever spent any time in North
Africa or the Middle East, this place is a
sensory feast sure to bring back memories.
There's *tagine* (stew cooked in a ceramic
pot), couscous, plenty of vegetarian options, lots of exotic teas to choose from,
dimly lit Moroccan décor and a heady in-
cense haze. It's a fine late-night alternative
to the hedonism elsewhere in the barrio.

WOKCAFE Map pp254-5   Innovative Asian €€

☎ 91 522 90 69; Calle de las Infantas 44; meal €25;
☺ Mon-Sat; Ⓜ Chueca or Plaza de España

Step inside here, with its blood-red décor,
conical dangling lampshades, bordello
mirrors and grand windows, and you could
be in Barcelona, Sydney or New York. The
hip ambience attracts a chirpy, inner-urban

Wokcafe (below) is a fine place for wining and dining

crowd who fill the place at lunchtimes, but
the *menú express* (€9) ensures you won't
have to wait long for a table.

CHAMBERÍ & ARGÜELLES

At first glance, Chamberí and Argüelles
seem more residential than great places to
go out. With so many young and upwardly
mobile Madrileños clamouring to live
here, however, there are some outstanding
choices if you know where to look. Another
advantage is that there's rarely another tourist in sight and you'll feel much more a part
of the barrio than in the town centre.

BAJO CERO Map pp246-7   Ice Cream €

☎ 900 191 191; Glorieta de Quevedo 6; ☺ 8am-
midnight Mon-Thu, 8am-1am Fri, 9am-1am Sat,
9am-midnight Sun; Ⓜ Quevedo

You can tell that a barrio is going upmarket when even its ice creameries have a
super-cool style. Curvaceous chairs, bright
colours, friendly service and a sophisticated
vibe (not to mention brilliant ice creams,
milkshakes and cakes) are what it's all
about.

BODEGA DE LA ARDOSA

Map pp246-7   Tapas €

☎ 91 446 58 94; Calle de Santa Engracia 70; meal
€10-15 ☺ 10am-3.30pm & 7-11pm Thu-Tue;
Ⓜ Iglesia

Tucked away in a fairly upscale and modern corner of Chamberí, this fine old relic
has the typical tiled façade of old Madrid.

Locals have been coming here for their morning tipple for decades and for some of the best *patatas bravas* (fried potatoes with a spicy tomato sauce) in Madrid. It also has vermouth on tap.

CACHABACHA Map pp250-1   Bocadillos €
☎ 690 265 556; Calle de Gonzalo de Córdoba; meal €5-10; 🕑 9am-11pm Mon-Fri & 11am-11pm Sat; Ⓜ Quevedo

Wandering around Chamberí and you can't face a three-course Spanish meal? Cachabacha has a bar ambience with bright colours and brick arches, and an excellent meal of soup, *bocadillo* and drink for €6.50. The service is relaxed and friendly.

CASA MINGO Map pp246-7   Asturian €
☎ 91 547 79 18; Paseo de la Florida 34; meal €10-15; 🕑 11am-midnight; Ⓜ Príncipe Pío

Built in 1916 to feed workers building the Príncipe Pío train station, Casa Mingo is a large Asturian cider house known by just about every Madrileño, most of whom agree that it's the best place to order *pollo asado* (roast chicken) and a bottle of cider. There are also a few Asturian specialities such as *chorizo a la sidra* (chorizo in cider), tortilla and *queso de cabrales* (aged blue cheese).

LOCANDITA Map pp250-1   Tapas €
☎ 91 444 00 74; Calle de Fuencarral 148; meal €10-15; 🕑 7am-10.30pm Mon-Thu, 9am-10.30am Fri-Sun; Ⓜ Quevedo

Good for a breakfast pastry, *menú del día* (€9.90) or a drink at any hour of the day, this friendly little bar is a bright place to rest during your Chamberí explorations.

CASA RICARDO Map pp246-7   Spanish €€
☎ 91 447 61 19; Calle de Fernando el Católico 31; meal €15-20; 🕑 Mon-Sat, lunch Sun; Ⓜ Argüelles or Quevedo

This brilliant little 1930s-era *taberna* is tucked away in residential Chamberí but well worth venturing out for. Their speciality is *callos* but there's plenty more to choose from, including the outstanding *calamares en su propia tinta* (calamari in its own ink). Like any old Spanish bar worth its salt, it's cramped and adorned with bullfighting photos, and is aimed at aficionados rather than tourists.

EL PEDRUSCO Map pp246-7   Spanish €€
☎ 91 446 88 33; Calle de Juan de Austria 27; meal €25-30; 🕑 lunch Mon-Thu, lunch & dinner Fri & Sat; Ⓜ Iglesia

If you haven't time to visit one of the *asadors* (restaurants specialising in roasted food, particularly meat) of Segovia (p188), head to this fine restaurant where the roasted meats are as good as any in Madrid. The *menú segoviano* (€23) includes succulent roast lamb, while the *menú pedrusco* (€25) has some vegetable respite, at least until the steak arrives.

LA PLAYA Map pp246-7   Creative €€
☎ 91 446 01 07; Calle de Magallanes 24; meal €15-25; 🕑 Tue-Sat, lunch Sun; Ⓜ Quevedo

When Madrileños go out to lunch, especially during the week, they often like to eat what their grandmothers used to cook. There aren't many better places to do this than at La Playa, where the dining room is 1950s (this isn't a style choice – that's how it's been left), the waiters likewise, and the food simple and hearty. Examples include *albóndigas de carne de cebón con salsa* (meatballs with sauce) or *alcachofas del tiempo con almejas* (artichokes of the season with clams). It's always packed.

MOMA 56 Map pp246-7   Fusion €€
☎ 91 399 48 73, 91 395 20 59; Calle de José Abascal 56; meal €30-35; Ⓜ Gregorio Marañon

Still one of *the* places to be seen at the moment, Moma 56 is two diverging options in one (see p142). Momabar is to the left, where you can perch on slippery metallic bar stools or take a table for Basque *pintxos*. To the right is the classily designed Asia Lounge where Thai, Cantonese and Vietnamese options abound. The buzz about Moma is considerable and it's always packed, although food critics with whom we spoke felt that it's not quite worth the rave.

TOP INNOVATIONS
- Laydown Rest Club (p126)
- Ene Restaurante (p117)
- Fast Good (p121)
- Balzac (p120)
- Paradis Erre Efe (p122)

MADRID FOR THE SWEET TOOTH

Tapas may be a Spanish institution, but what Madrileños really love are their pastries, especially at breakfast but any excuse will do. These are our favourite classic Madrid pastry shops, which we were forced to visit (purely for research purposes, you understand).

Antigua Pastelería del Pozo (Map pp254–5; ☎ 91 522 38 94; Calle del Pozo 8; ☽ 9.30am-2pm & 5-8pm Mon-Sat, 9.30am-3pm Sun; Ⓜ Sol) Has lost none of its old charm in turning out all sorts of great pastries. It has been in operation since 1830, making it the city's oldest dealer in tooth-decaying items.

Chocolatería San Ginés (Map pp254–5; ☎ 91 365 65 46; Pasadizo de San Ginés 5; ☽ 6pm-7am; Ⓜ Sol) Perhaps the best known of Madrid's *churros y chocolate* vendors. You can stop by in the evening for one of these calorific bombs, but its main market is clubbers with the munchies, pouring out of the city's nearby dance palaces.

Horno de San Onofre (Map pp250–1; ☎ 91 532 90 60; Calle de San Onofre 3; ☽ 8am-9pm; Ⓜ Gran Vía) and **Horno de Santiguesa** (Map pp254–5; ☎ 91 559 62 14; Calle Mayor 73; ☽ 8am-9pm; Ⓜ Ópera) These are owned by the same family and everything's a speciality, from cakes and pastries to bitesized sweets and Christmas *turrón* (a nougat-like sweet). The interiors are decorated in a classically elegant, old-world Madrid style.

La Mallorquina (Map pp254–5; ☎ 91 521 12 01; Puerta del Sol 8; ☽ 9am-9.15pm; Ⓜ Sol) Another classic pastry shop that's packed to the rafters by Madrileños who just couldn't pass by without stopping. Treat yourself to a takeaway *ensaimada* (a light pastry dusted with icing sugar) from Mallorca or climb to the upstairs café where the world-weary, bow-tied waiters are part of a journey back in time.

Niza (Map pp250–1; ☎ 91 308 13 21; Calle de Argensola 24; ☽ 10am-2.30pm & 5.30-8.30pm Mon-Sat, 10am-2.30pm Sun, Sep-Jul; Ⓜ Alonso Martínez) It may be small but it's home to the most astonishing, old-Madrid interior decoration and it's worth a visit here just to admire the stunning ceiling and other fittings, even if you don't buy anything. But buy you should, especially the *rusos* (cream-filled pastries) and delicious *tarta de niza*.

MOSAIQ Map pp250-1   Middle Eastern €€
☎ 91 308 44 46; Calle de Caracas 21; meal €30-35; Ⓜ Alonso Martínez or Iglesia

Excellent Middle Eastern and North African cuisine is the order of the day at this atmospheric place. Stepping inside the door is like entering an Arabian bazaar, with Moroccan lamps, colourful tilework and abundant cushions. The food is varied and tasty, and choices such as *tagine de cordero* (lamb cooked in a ceramic pot with plums) are among the highlights.

NAGOYA Map pp250-1   Japanese €€
☎ 91 448 69 07; Calle de Trafalgar 7; meal €20-25; Ⓜ Bilbao

Madrid finally has its fair share of Japanese restaurants, but you won't find any finer than this one. The service is friendly and fast, and the food is outstanding – from the tempura and sushi to the *kami yaki soba* (duck with noodles and teriyaki sauce). Ask for your *maki* with *sesamo por fuera* (sesame on the outside) and you'll be in heaven.

RUO Map pp246-7   Asian €€
☎ 91 559 83 27; Calle de Martín de los Heros 31; meal €15-20; ☽ Mon-Sat; Ⓜ Ventura Rodríguez

If you're heading for the cinema (or are hungry afterwards), you could do a lot worse than check out this excellent Chinese–Thai–Vietnamese restaurant where the food is terrific and the prices a steal (the *menú del día* goes for €7.80). If you can't choose between your *pad thai* or *rollitos vietnamitas* (Vietnamese spring rolls), try one of the *menús de degustación,* which cost just €16.50.

SAGARRETXE Map pp246-7   Basque Tapas €€
☎ 91 446 25 88; Calle de Eloy Gonzalo 26; meal €15-20; ☽ noon-5pm & 7pm-midnight Sun-Wed, noon-5pm & 7pm-12.30am Thu, noon-5pm & 7pm-1am Fri & Sat; Ⓜ Iglesia

One of the best Basque *pintxos* bars in Madrid, Sagarretxe takes the stress out of taking tapas. Simply point and they'll put any of the wonderful selection on a plate for you. Better still, order the *surtido de 8/12 pintxos* (your own selection of 8/12 tapas) for €12/16. There's a more expensive but equally good restaurant downstairs.

WOK Map p252   Asian €€
☎ 91 319 18 62; Calle de Genova 27; meal €15-20; Ⓜ Colón

If the crowds and queues are anything to go by, Madrileños have been crying out for reasonably priced Asian food but in a classier setting than most Chinese restaurants in

Madrid can muster. Just about everything is wok-cooked here and there are a handful of vegetarian options, but don't expect anything too spicy. Service is fast and furious at lunchtime on weekdays so go elsewhere if you're after a long, lazy lunch.

JOCKEY Map p252   Spanish €€€
☎ 91 319 24 35; Calle de Amador de los Ríos 6; meal €70-100; ☯ lunch & dinner Sep-Jul; Ⓜ Colón
Fine Spanish cooking, with the occasional nod to French sophistication, and celebrities and royalty dotted around the dining room (Prince Felipe, heir to the Spanish throne, and Letizia Ortiz chose the Jockey chefs for their wedding banquet in May 2004) make for a top-quality dining experience. If we could choose one dish, it would probably be lobster ragout with truffles and fresh pasta.

LA BROCHE Map pp246-7   Creative €€€
☎ 91 399 34 37; Calle de Miguel Ángel 29; meal €80; Ⓜ Gregorio Marañón
Sergi Arola, a young Catalan acolyte of the world-renowned Ferran Adrià, has made his own splash in this hotel restaurant in the busy uptown area of Madrid. He mixes his ingredients carefully, without necessarily going overboard and the dining room is an intimate, minimalist white.

NORTHERN MADRID

If you want to see the state of Spain's economy, visit any restaurant in northern Madrid. The business and well-heeled clientele know their food and are happy to pay for it. Often it's a fair metro or taxi ride north of the centre, but well worth it for a touch of class.

SUKOTHAY Map p245   Japanese & Thai €€
☎ 91 598 03 56; Paseo de la Castellana 105; meal €25-40; ☯ Mon-Sat Sep-Jul; Ⓜ Santiago Bernabéu
With not a red Chinese lantern to be seen, this stylish Asian restaurant has terrific food (the full gamut from sashimi to a lightly spiced *pad thai*). Thursday nights (when its stays open until 2am) is sushi-*cava* night – for €22 you can enjoy a selection of sushi and wash it down with bubbly.

SANTCELONI Map p245   Basque-Navarran €€€
☎ 91 210 88 40; Paseo de la Castellana 57; meal €90-110; Ⓜ Gregorio Marañón
The Michelin-starred Santceloni is one of Madrid's best restaurants with luxury Asian-inspired décor and food that wins plaudits from discerning food lovers from across Spain and abroad. Each dish is exquisite – try for example the *jarrete de ternera* (veal shanks with glazed vegetables) or try the chef's showpiece *menú gastronómico* (€110).

ZALACAÍN Map p245   Basque-Navarran €€€
☎ 91 561 48 40; Calle de Álvarez de Baena 4; meal €70-100; ☯ Mon-Fri, dinner Sat Sep-Jul; Ⓜ Gregorio Marañón
There is a seamless, quiet efficiency about this classy home of the best in traditional cooking. Everyone who's anyone in Madrid, from the king down, has eaten here since the doors opened in 1973. The pig's trotters filled with mustard and candied potato are a house speciality. The wine list is purported to be one of the best in the city (they stock an estimated 35,000 bottles) and you should certainly dress to impress (men will need a tie).

Nightlife

Drinking & Nightlife

You've seen the great paintings, have eaten an outstanding meal and, if you have any sense, you'll have taken your siesta. Now it's time for your initiation into Europe's most dynamic nightlife. To get an idea of how much Madrileños like to go out and have a good time, there is one simple statistic: Madrid has more bars than any city in the world, six, in fact, for every 100 inhabitants. And what Hemingway wrote of Madrid in the 1930s remains true to this day: 'To go to bed at night in Madrid marks you as a little queer. For a long time your friends will be a little uncomfortable about it. Nobody goes to bed in Madrid until they have killed the night.'

People here live fully for the moment. Today's encounter can be tomorrow's distant memory, but you need to know how things work here. Don't even think of starting your night until after midnight (most Madrileños will be too busy eating up to that point anyway), hence our suggestion of a late afternoon siesta. The nonexistent closing hours of Madrid in the 1980s may be a thing of the past (most bars close by 3am on weekends or 2am on school nights), but when the bars close, the clubs kick in and keep going until dawn. At any hour after midnight, don't be surprised if you find yourself stuck in a traffic jam of cars and people that happens only in Madrid.

Although you'll find pulsating nightlife in the most unlikely corners of town, some barrios definitely offer more *marcha* (action) than others. Huertas and Chueca are undoubtedly Madrid's hedonism centres; the former attracts a local and international crowd just about any night of the week, while Chueca is exuberantly and extravagantly gay, although everyone's welcome. Malasaña, the spiritual home of *la movida Madrileña* (the sociocultural movement set off by the explosion of liberties after the death of Franco; see boxed text, p54), has never really grown up and is the barrio (district) of choice for grunge-rockers, sideburns and an eclectic crowd. Lavapiés and, to a lesser extent, La Latina are gritty, groovy and cool all at once, and definitely among night-time Madrid's best-kept secrets.

This chapter is divided into 'Drinking' and 'Clubs & Discos', although in Madrid the two usually overlap. Some bars and clubs also have live music, but you'll find the best live music venues listed in the Entertainment chapter (p148).

FIND YOUR BARRIO STYLE

FIND YOUR BARRIO STYLE

For…
- *pijos* and *pijas* (beautiful people) – head to Salamanca (p135)
- Madrid rockers – head to Malasaña (p136)
- the gay scene – head to Chueca (p136)
- *guiris* (foreigners) – head to Huertas (p134)
- community barrio feel – head to Lavapiés (opposite)

Live music at Café La Palma (p141)

What's On

The Spanish-language *Guía del Ocio*, a weekly magazine sold at newsstands for €1, contains listings of many clubs and bars as well as a guide to the week's concerts, special events and movies. Also check out the monthly *Salir Urban*. The best gay guide is *Shanguide*, which you can pick up for free in bars around Chueca or at the **Berkana bookstore** (Map pp250–1; ☎ 91 522 55 99; Calle de Hortaleza 64; Ⓜ Chueca). Bar staff are also mines of information on where the action's moving after their bar closes.

DRINKING

Madrileños seem up for a drink almost any time of the day or night, but few allow themselves to get blind drunk. They love a tipple – and blimey, the tipples are generous – but they keep it under control. It's a well-honed survival technique, as most Madrileños have learned that pacing themselves is the key to lasting until dawn. It's a key strategy for making the most of your Madrid night.

For advice on what to order, whether it be wine, beer or spirits, see p40. Classic clubbing drinks here include gin and tonics, *cubatas* (rum with Coke), *maribú piñas* (coconut rum with pineapple juice) and vodka mixed with just about anything. Another typically Madrid order is a Cuban *mojito* (rum with sugar and lashings of mint) or a Brazilian *caipirinha* (made with *cacheca*, a spirit similar to rum).

Early in the night you'll pay as little as €4 for a mixed drink, but as it gets later the prices go up.

LOS AUSTRIAS, SOL & CENTRO

Old taverns and the odd hidden gem populate Madrid's centre and, as a general rule, the further you stray from the Plaza Mayor, the more prices drop and the fewer tourists you'll see.

LA VIUDA NEGRA Map pp254-5

Black Widow; ☎ 91 548 75 29; Calle de Campomanes 6; ☯ 5-9pm Sun & Mon, 9pm-2am Tue & Wed, 9pm-3am Thu-Sat; Ⓜ Ópera

This all-dressed-in-orange, loungelike cocktail bar is minimalist enough for Manhattan and genuinely cool enough to satisfy the sophisticated new-Madrid crowd. If you're the sort that likes to settle in for the night, you can eat first at sister restaurant La Viuda Blanca (p115) next door, then ease over to the bar for funky house music until late. Sunday afternoons are jazzy and very mellow.

TABERNA DE CIEN VINOS Map pp254-5

☎ 91 365 47 04; Calle del Nuncio 17; ☯ 1-3.45pm & 8pm-1am Tue-Sat, 1-4pm Sun; Ⓜ La Latina

This unpretentious wine bar is one of the best-known in town and as fashions come and go elsewhere, the classic décor and friendly service has fostered a loyal following of regulars. You can order by the glass or by the bottle.

LA LATINA & LAVAPIÉS

Two different barrios, two very different vibes. On summer weekend nights (and many Sunday afternoons), crowds of happy Madrileños spill from the bars of La Latina down the slopes, turning otherwise medieval streets into bonhomie central. The pick of the bars are in the area roughly framed by Calle de la Cava Baja, Plaza de la Cebada, Plaza de la Paja and Calle de Segovia.

Lavapiés is a completely different kettle of fish altogether – working-class and quirky, with a very strong sense of community. If you're after an unmistakeably Madrid night but with nary a tourist in sight, Lavapiés is the place to find it.

AGUARDIENTE Map pp254-5

☎ 639 324 439; Calle de la Fé; ☯ 4pm-2am; Ⓜ Lavapiés

A small and busy bar that's as good for *copas* (alcoholic drinks) as for coffee, Aguardiente is a regular stop for many revellers on a typical Lavapiés night. There's not a lot to distinguish it from the other bars in the barrio, but it's a crowded place where you'll catch the Lavapiés vibe and find out where the crowd's heading next.

ALMENDRO 13 Map pp254-5

☎ 91 365 42 52; Calle de Almendro 13; ☯ 1-4pm & 7.30pm-12.30am Mon-Fri, 1-5pm & 8pm-1am Sat & Sun; Ⓜ La Latina

You could easily come here for the tapas but it's standing room only most nights, especially on weekends when locals come here for the fine wines and manzanilla (dry sherry), and the convivial buzz of a happy and discerning Madrid crowd. Step outside and you're in the heart of medieval Madrid.

BONANNO Map pp254-5

☎ 91 366 68 86; Plaza del Humilladero 4; ☯ noon-2am; Ⓜ La Latina

Newcomers to Madrid often wonder what all the fuss surrounding Madrid's nightlife is about, but that's because they start too early. If you're suffering from this affliction, head for Bonanno, a stylish cocktail bar that's popular with young professional Madrileños from early evening onwards. Be prepared to snuggle up close to those around you if you want a spot at the bar.

CAFÉ DEL NUNCIO Map pp254-5

☎ 91 366 09 06; Calle de Segovia 9; ⏰ noon-2am Sun-Thu, noon-3am Fri & Sat; Ⓜ La Latina

A sprawling bar, the Café del Nuncio straggles down a stairway passage to Calle de Segovia. You can drink on one of several cosy levels inside or, better still in summer, enjoy the outdoor seating. On summer weekends, this place hums with the sort of clamour that newcomers to Madrid (and plenty of long-standing residents) find irresistible.

CASA MONTES Map pp254-5

☎ 91 527 00 64; Calle de Lavapiés 40; ⏰ noon-3.30pm & 8pm-1am Tue-Sun; Ⓜ Lavapiés

Lavapiés is the sort of community where old-fashioned bars such as Casa Montes have been around so long that it's cool again to be seen here. César, the owner, is something of a local identity and he lends his bar much warmth and character. If you read Spanish you'll enjoy his handwritten poems attached to the wine bottles (great wines by the way) behind the bar. It's that sort of place.

EL EUCALIPTO Map pp254-5

Calle de Argumosa 4; ⏰ 6pm-2am Mon-Sat, 1pm-2am Sun; Ⓜ Lavapiés

You'd be mad not to at least pass by this fine little bar with its love of all things Cuban: from the music to the clientele and the Caribbean cocktails. Not surprisingly, the *mojitos* are a cut above the average and the streetside tables put you in the path of the fascinating Lavapiés street life.

EL VIAJERO Map pp254-5

☎ 91 366 90 64; Plaza de la Cebada 11; ⏰ 1pm-12.30am Tue-Thu & Sun, 1pm-1am Fri & Sat; Ⓜ La Latina

This upstairs bar requires the patience of a saint – it's busy and nigh-on impossible to get a table unless you're prepared to wait. But wait you should because El Viajero is

always buzzing and has been for years. On a summer's night, head up to the rooftop terrace where the views overlooking the plaza and the Iglesia de San Pedro are unbeatable.

LA INQUILINA Map pp254-5

☎ 627 511 804; Calle de Ave María 39; ⏰ 7pm-2am Tue-Thu, 1-4pm & 8pm-3am Fri-Sun; Ⓜ Lavapiés

An integral part of the often sophisticated, sometimes earthy charm of Lavapiés, La Inquilina is a wonderful bar that's ideal for taking the pulse of this increasingly cool barrio. People come from all over Madrid to drink here and it's very much a part of the local community. Contemporary artworks by budding local artists adorn the walls and you can either gather around the bar or take a table out the back.

LA VENTURA Map pp254-5

☎ 91 521 48 54; Calle del Olmo 21; ⏰ 10.30pm-3am Thu-Sun; Ⓜ Antón Martín

One of many Lavapiés secrets hidden behind nondescript doors, La Ventura is a smoky, underground-cool bar with a cut-off- from-the-outside-world feel that grows on you the longer you stay. It's always filled with locals and people-in-the-know, and don't believe everything you read – we've been there long after closing time, but we didn't tell you that.

HUERTAS & ATOCHA

The maze of streets around Huertas and the Puerta del Sol is a treasure chest of lively bars and nightspots, and you won't be hard-pressed to find a place to revel in the atmosphere with a drink in hand. Simply mention Huertas and chances are people think of Cervecería Alemana, a classic beer bar on Santa Ana, or the sherry at La Venencia. If you're staying around here, there's no point even trying to sleep so if you can't beat them…

CASA ALBERTO Map pp254-5

☎ 91 429 93 56; Calle de las Huertas 18; ⏰ noon-midnight Tue-Thu, noon-1.30am Fri & Sat; Ⓜ Antón Martín

Now here's an old Madrid landmark. Since 1827 Madrileños have been getting their vermouth from this elegant bar, where the hard stuff is served on tap. The tapas are good but come here on Sunday at 1pm and you're halfway towards being considered an honorary Madrileño.

TOP SPOTS FOR A DRINK

For…

- on-tap vermouth – **Casa Alberto** (right)
- a barrio feel – **La Inquilina** (right)
- a classy-feeling wine bar – **El Lateral** (p136)
- spotting famous faces – **Museo Chicote** (p138)
- cosy and intimate – **El Jardin Secreto** (p137)

LA HORA DEL VERMUT

Sunday. One o'clock in the afternoon. A dark bar off Calle de la Cava Baja. In any civilised city the bar would be shut tight at such an hour, but in Madrid the place is packed because it's *la hora del vermut* (vermouth hour), when friends and families head out for a quick apéritif before Sunday lunch. Sometimes referred to as *ir de Rastro* (going to the Rastro) because so many of the traditional vermouth bars are in and around the Rastro market, this Sunday tradition is deeply engrained in Madrileño culture. Some of the best bars for vermouth are along Calle de la Cava Baja (ie between El Rastro and Plaza Mayor), while **Casa Alberto** (opposite) is another legendary part of this fine tradition.

CERVECERÍA ALEMANA Map pp254-5

☎ 91 429 70 33; Plaza de Santa Ana 6;
🕑 11am-12.30am Sun-Thu, 11am-2am Fri & Sat,
closed August; Ⓜ Antón Martín or Sol

If you've only got time to stop at one bar on Plaza Santa Ana, let it be this classic *cervecería* (beer bar), renowned for its cold, frothy beers. It's fine inside, but snaffle a table outside in the plaza on a summer's evening and you won't be giving it up without a fight. This was one of Hemingway's haunts, and neither the wood-lined bar nor the bow-tied waiters have changed since his day.

LA VENENCIA Map pp254-5

☎ 91 429 73 13; Calle de Echegaray 7;
🕑 1-3.30pm & 7.30pm-1.30am Sun-Thu, 1-3.30pm & 7.30pm-2.30am Fri & Sat; Ⓜ Sol

This is how sherry bars should be – old world, and drinks poured straight from the wooden barrels. La Venencia is a barrio classic, with fine Jeréz sherry for just €1.35. There's no music, no flashy decorations; it's all about you, your *fino* (sherry) and your friends.

ØLSEN Map pp254-5

☎ 91 429 36 59; Calle del Prado 15; 🕑 1-4pm & 8pm-2am Tue-Sun; Ⓜ Antón Martín

This classy and clean-lined bar is a temple to Nordic minimalism and comes into its own after the Scandinavian restaurant out the back closes. We think the more than 80 varieties of vodka are enough to satisfy most tastes, while the vodka cocktails (€7 to €9) are also great. You'll hate vodka the next day, but Madrid is all about living for the night.

TABERNA ALHAMBRA Map pp254-5

☎ 91 521 07 08; Calle de Victoria 9;
🕑 10am-2am; Ⓜ Sol

There can be a certain sameness about the bars between Sol and Huertas, which is why this fine old *taberna* (tavern) stands out. The striking façade, *mudéjar* (Moorish architecture) decoration and exquisite tilework of the interior are quite beautiful; however, this place is anything but stuffy and the vibe is cool, casual and busy. Late at night, there are some fine flamenco tunes.

VIVA MADRID Map pp254-5

☎ 91 429 36 40; www.barvivamadrid.com;
Calle de Manuel Fernandez y González 7;
🕑 1pm-2am Sun-Thu, 1pm-3am Fri & Sat;
Ⓜ Antón Martín or Sol

A beautifully tiled bar, some of the best *mojitos* in town, a friendly atmosphere, crowded bars, a mixed crowd and scattered tables – what more could a Madrileño want? Not much apparently, Viva Madrid is famous on the Huertas late-night scene.

SALAMANCA

Salamanca is the land of the beautiful people and it's all about gloss and glamour: heels for her and hair gel for him. As you glide through the *pijos* (beautiful people), keep your eyes peeled for Real Madrid players, celebrities and designer clothes. If nothing else, you'll see how the other half lives.

CENTRO CUBANO DE ESPAÑA Map p252

☎ 91 575 82 79; www.elcentrocubano.com; Calle de Claudio Coello 41, 1st fl; 🕑 2pm-2am Sun-Wed, 2pm-2.30am Thu-Sat; Ⓜ Serrano

Always dreamed of Havana, Cuba? Come here and you'll be a whole lot closer. This is where Cubans from all over Madrid come to be reminded of the flavours (in the restaurant) and fine rum-based drinks (in the bar) of their homeland. They're a friendly lot and they're joined by plenty of Spaniards for whom the *mojitos* are unrivalled in Madrid. Once the Cubans start dancing to the music, you'll feel inadequate by comparison.

Drinking & Nightlife

DRINKING

TOP SPOTS FOR MARCHA

For…

- terrace drinking and lots of English speakers – **Plaza de Santa Ana** (Map pp254–5)
- a gay-friendly (or just plain friendly) scene – around **Plaza de Chueca** (Map pp250–1)
- eclectic bars and intimate clubs – Conde Duque, especially around **Calle de la Palma** (Map pp250–1)
- mega-clubs and a young crowd – around **Calle del Arenal** (Map pp254–5)
- classic bars with tapas, vermouth and flamenco – around **Calle de la Cava Baja** (Map pp254–5)

COLETTE CAFÉ Map p252

☎ 91 578 06 83; Calle de Serrano 45; ☿ 12.30pm-3am Mon-Fri, 7.30pm-3am Sat; Ⓜ Serrano or Nuñez de Balboa

This place wears its whiter-than-white minimalism on its sleeve and the patrons definitely belong to the too-cool-for-Lavapiés set. Dressed to kill and keen to be seen, the chic crowd loosens up a little as the night wears on, the cocktails kick in and the lights get dimmed. The somewhat grim entrance notwithstanding, this place is *so* Salamanca.

EL LATERAL Map p252

☎ 91 435 06 04; Calle de Velázquez 57; ☿ 10am-1am Sun-Thu, until late Fri & Sat; Ⓜ Velázquez or Nuñez de Balboa

It doesn't get much more *pijo* than this chic wine bar, where hair gel seems to be required for entry. Don't bother coming here after work's out unless you're in an Armani suit; at other times, the excellent wines and other drinks loosen up the crowd (if not the ties) more than you'd think. There are other branches at Paseo de la Castellana 132 and Fuencarral 43.

MALASAÑA & CHUECA

The two inner-city barrios of Malasaña and Chueca are two of Madrid's most eclectic, although they're worlds apart in terms of personality. Nocturnal Malasaña is home to those who would relive the anything-goes, rock-heavy days of *la movida Madrileña* (see boxed text, p54), which means a rebellious spirit during noisy, clamorous nights that seem to last forever. Chueca, on the other hand, caters more to the black-clad and stylish, making it the home barrio of

Madrid's considerable gay community. Chueca bars are, of course, gay-friendly; however, they're anything but exclusive and also attract a straight crowd who love the buzz that pervades the barrio.

ANTIK CAFÉ Map pp250-1

☎ 620 427 168; Calle de la Hortaleza 4 & 6; ☿ 10am-3am; Ⓜ Gran Vía

If you peer in at Antik Café from the street, you won't see a thing – the dark interior is all about intimacy and discretion. Once inside, the décor is chic, the clientele sophisticated and speaking in hushed conversations, and the drinks menu includes coffee laced with something a little stronger amid the range of spirits.

AREIA Map pp250-1

☎ 91 310 03 07; Calle de la Hortaleza 92; ☿ noon-3am; Ⓜ Chueca

The ultimate lounge bar by day (cushions and chill-out music abound and there are dark and secluded corners where you can hear yourself talk, or even snog quietly), this place is equally enjoyable by night when groovy DJs take over (from 11pm Sunday to Wednesday, and from 9pm the rest of the week) with deep and chill house, nu jazz, bossa and electronica. It's cool, funky and low-key all at once.

BAR COCK Map pp254-5

☎ 91 532 28 26; Calle de la Reina 16; ☿ 7pm-3am Mon-Thu, 7pm-3.30am Fri & Sat; Ⓜ Gran Vía

With a name like this, Bar Cock could go either way, but it's definitely cock as in 'rooster' so the atmosphere is elegant and classic rather than risqué. It's lively, notwithstanding the fact that the décor resembles an old gentleman's club. It's a popular weekend haunt of A-listers and a refined older crowd looking for good drinks and funky music.

CAFÉ ACUARELA Map pp250-1

☎ 91 522 21 43; Calle de Gravina 10; ☿ 11am-2am Sun-Thu, 11am-3am Fri & Sat; Ⓜ Chueca

Right on Plaza de Chueca and long a centre-piece of gay Madrid – a huge statue of a nude male angel guards the doorway – this is an agreeable, dimly-lit salon for quiet conversation and catching the weekend buzz as people plan their forays into the more clamorous bars in the vicinity.

CAFÉ BELÉN Map pp250-1

☎ 91 308 24 47; Calle de Belén 5; ☽ 3.30pm-3am; Ⓜ Chueca

Café Belén is cool in all the right places – lounge and chill-out music, dim lighting, a great range of drinks (the *mojitos* are as good as you'll find in Madrid and that's saying something) and a low-key crowd that's the height of casual sophistication.

CAFÉ PEPE BOTELLA Map pp250-1

☎ 91 522 43 09; Calle de San Andrés 12; ☽ 11am-2.30am; Ⓜ Bilbao or Tribunal

Pepe Botella has hit on a fine formula for success. As good in the wee small hours as it is in the afternoon, it's a classy bar with green velvet benches, marble-topped tables, and old photos and mirrors covering the walls. The faded elegance gives the place the charm that's made it one of the most popular and enduring drinking holes in the barrio.

CAFÉ-RESTAURANTE EL ESPEJO

Map p252

☎ 91 308 23 47; Paseo de los Recoletos 31; ☽ 8am-midnight; Ⓜ Colón

Once a haunt of writers and intellectuals, this place could well overwhelm you with all the mirrors, chandeliers and discreet charm of another era; but persevere, as the outdoor tables are some of Madrid's most popular drinking *terrazas* (venue with outdoor seating) on a warm summer's evening.

EL BANDIDO DOBLEMENTE ARMADO Map pp250-1

☎ 91 522 10 51; Calle de Apodaca 3; ☽ 5pm-1am Mon-Wed, 5pm-2am Thu-Sat; Ⓜ Bilbao or Tribunal

Part cool cocktail bar and part bookshop (the combination works), this attractive little bar is popular with an artsy crowd keen to keep abreast of the literary scene (this place is the focus for numerous literary events) and drawn by the smoky, funky music.

EL CAFÉ SIN NOMBRE Map pp250-1

☎ 655 760 715; Calle de Conde Duque 10; ☽ 10am-1pm & 5pm-3am Mon-Fri, 8pm-3am Sat; Ⓜ Plaza de España or Ventura Rodríguez

The 'Café With No Name' is one of Conde Duque's many well-kept secrets, the sort of place where Madrileños in-the-know gravitate while the tourists go elsewhere. With its exposed brickwork and wooden beams, it's

a classy place that comes alive late at night with the dull roar of Madrileños at play.

EL JARDIN SECRETO Map pp250-1

☎ 91 541 80 23; Calle de Conde Duque 2; ☽ 5.30pm-12.30am Sun-Thu, 6.30pm-2.30am Fri & Sat; Ⓜ Plaza de España

One of our favourite drinking places, 'The Secret Garden' has a hip café-style ambience in a barrio that is one of Madrid's best-kept secrets. It's at its best on a summer's evening but the atmosphere never misses a beat – candlelit, cosy and intimate with a real buzz among the young, professional crowd.

EL MOJITO Map pp250-1

Calle del Duque Osuna 6; ☽ 9.30pm-2.30am Sun-Thu, 9.30pm-3.30am Fri & Sat; Ⓜ Plaza de España

El Mojito is a modern temple to one of Madrileños' favourite drinks. In fact, they don't really serve much else, but the crowd is oh-so-cool and all dressed in black, and the music (it's live on Thursdays) is as Cuban as the *mojitos*. Space is always at a premium (the wall-to-ceiling mirrors make this place look larger than it is).

LA PALMERA Map pp250-1

Calle de la Palma 67; ☽ 9am-2am Tue-Sat; Ⓜ Tribunal

Tucked away in the barrio known as Conde Duque, this tiny place is well worth seeking out. Covered in blue and yellow tiles, La Palmera draws an artsy crowd who come to sit at the small wooden tables and nurse a drink or two. The atmosphere is very low-key.

LA VACA AUSTERA Map pp250-1

☎ 91 523 14 87; Calle de la Palma 20; ☽ 10pm-late Mon-Sat; Ⓜ Tribunal

Old habits die hard at this veteran bar which became famous during the heady days of *la movida* in the 1980s and is still going strong. It's what Spaniards like to call *cutre* (which roughly translates as rough-and-ready) and its warehouse feel won't be to everyone's taste, but it's a local icon and a totally unpretentious place to hear alternative rock music.

LA VÍA LACTEA Map pp250-1

☎ 91 446 75 81; Calle de Velarde 18; ☽ 7.30pm-3am; Ⓜ Tribunal

Another living, breathing and somewhat grungy relic of *la movida,* La Vía Lactea remains a Malasaña favourite for a mixed, informal crowd who seem to live for the 1980s – eyeshadow for boys and girls is a recurring theme. There are plenty of drinks to choose from and by early on Sunday morning anything goes. Expect long queues to get in on weekends.

LIBERTAD 8 Map pp250-1
☎ 91 532 11 50; Calle de la Libertad 8; ⏰ 4pm-2.30am Mon-Thu, 4pm-3am Fri & Sat; Ⓜ Chueca

Here's a novelty you won't find elsewhere – at 9pm every night a storyteller does their stuff, often role-playing into the bargain. The audience love to get involved and usually stay on for plenty more drinks afterwards. Even if you don't understand the story, it's a fine theatre accompaniment to your early evening drinks.

MAMÁ INÉS Map pp250-1
☎ 91 523 23 33; Calle de la Hortaleza 22; ⏰ 10am-2am Sun-Thu, 10am-3.30am Fri & Sat; Ⓜ Gran Vía or Chueca

A gay male meeting place with its low lights and low music, this café-bar is never sleazy and has a laid-back ambience by day and a romantic air by night. By day you can get breakfast, yummy pastries and all the gossip on where that night's hot spot will be.

MUSEO CHICOTE Map pp254-5
☎ 91 532 67 37; Gran Vía 12; ⏰ 8am-4am Mon-Sat; Ⓜ Gran Vía

The founder of this Madrid landmark is said to have invented more than a hundred cocktails, which the likes of Hemingway, Sophia Loren and Frank Sinatra all enjoyed at one time or another. It's still frequented by film stars and top socialites, and it's at its best after midnight when a lounge atmosphere takes over, couples cuddle on

Settle in for beer and tapas at Stop Madrid (below)

the curved benches and some of the city's best DJs do their stuff (CDs are available).

STOP MADRID Map pp250-1
☎ 91 521 88 87; Calle de la Hortaleza 11; ⏰ 12.30-4pm & 6.30pm-2am; Ⓜ Gran Vía

The name may be incongruous but this terrific old *taberna* is friendly, invariably packed with people, and wins the vote of at least one Lonely Planet author for the best sangria in Madrid.

THE QUIET MAN Map pp250-1
☎ 91 523 46 89; Calle de Valverde 44; ⏰ 6pm-2am Mon-Thu, 2pm-3.30am Fri-Sun; Ⓜ Tribunal or Chueca

Themed Irish pubs may have come to rule the world, but this Madrid institution was here long before the others and was one of the first bars outside Ireland to serve Guinness. It's a spacious, dark bar where you can play darts, have a seat on the refined velvet benches or park yourself at the bar.

CLUBS & DISCOS

Don't expect the dance clubs or *discotecas* (nightclubs) to really get going until at least 1am, and some won't even bat an eyelid until 3am, when the bars elsewhere have closed.

Club prices vary wildly, depending on the time of night you enter, the way you're dressed and the number of people inside. Most charge between €8 and €12 to enter, though megaclubs such as Palacio Gaviria and swanky places such as Moma 56 charge a few euros more. Discounts are possible if you keep your eyes open for the stamped tickets lying in bars about town.

TOP SPOTS FOR A MOJITO

It may be a taste of Havana, Cuba, but the *mojito* has been adopted by Madrid as its own. For ambience and quality, you can't beat the following:

- Centro Cubano de España (p135)
- Café Belén (p137)
- Delic (p116)
- El Mojito (p137)
- El Eucalipto (p134)

No barrio in Madrid is without a decent club or disco, but the most popular dance spots are between Gran Vía and Plaza Mayor. Classics such as the Palacio Gaviria, Teatro Joy Eslava, El Son, Ohm and Cool are all nearby. For intimate dancing or quirky décor, head to Chueca or Malasaña.

TOP CLUBS

For…

- spotting beautiful people – **Moma 56** (p142)
- downtempo grooves – **El Juglar** (p140)
- live shows – **Café la Palma** (p141)
- lounge music – **Stromboli Café** (p142)
- dancing till dawn – **Room at Stella** (p140)

LOS AUSTRIAS, SOL & CENTRO

COOL Map pp250-1

☎ 902 499 994; Calle Isabel la Católica 6; ☽ midnight-late Thu-Sat; Ⓜ Santo Domingo
Cool by name, cool by nature. One of the hottest clubs in the city, the curvy white lines, discreet lounge chairs in dark corners and pulsating dance floor is peopled by gorgeous people, gorgeous clothes and a strict entry policy; if a famous DJ is on the bill, expect to pay at least €30. The sexy, well-heeled crowd includes a lot of sleek-looking gay men and model-like women.

EL SON Map pp254-5

☎ 91 532 32 83; Calle de la Victoria 6; ☽ 7pm-late; Ⓜ Sol
If you're looking for salsa, merengue or some sexy tangos, look no further than El Son. This is the top place in town for Latin music, and it's very popular with Madrid's South and Central American population. Live Cuban music from Monday to Thursday keeps the place packed all week long.

OHM Map pp250-1

Sala Bash; ☎ 91 531 01 32; Plaza del Callao 4; ☽ midnight-6am Tue-Sun; Ⓜ Callao
The DJs who get you waving your hands in the air like you just don't care have made this club one of the most popular for Madrid's gay community, although the crowd is mixed. Thursday there's house music, while the latest R&B, lounge and hip-hop are regular features. You'll leave this place shaking your head – this is where Madrileños party like there's no tomorrow and some go straight to work the next morning.

PALACIO GAVIRIA Map pp254-5

☎ 91 526 60 69; Calle del Arenal 9; ☽ 11pm-4am Mon-Wed, 10.30pm-5.30am Thu-Sat, 8.30pm-2am Sun; Ⓜ Sol
An elegant palace converted into one of the most popular dance clubs in Madrid,

this is the kind of place where you're guaranteed to meet the locals, whether you want to or not. The crowd can be pretty young and boisterous, the queues long, and Thursday is international student and house music night – international relations have never been so much fun.

SUITE Map pp254-5

☎ 91 521 40 31; Calle de la Virgen de los Peligros 4; ☽ 9pm-2am Mon-Thu, 9pm-3am Fri & Sat; Ⓜ Sevilla
This retro bar is one of the trendiest in the area (as a glance at the slickly dressed and mainly gay crowd will show) with DJs cooking up some seriously funky sounds. On weekends, the dance floor is as tightly packed as any in Madrid.

TEATRO JOY ESLAVA Map pp254-5

☎ 91 366 37 33; Calle del Arenal 11; ☽ 11.30pm-5.30am Sun-Thu, 11.30pm-6am Fri & Sat; Ⓜ Sol
The only things guaranteed at this grand old Madrid dance club (housed in a 19th-century theatre) are a crowd and the fact that they'll be open (they claim to have opened every single day for the past 25 years). The music and the crowd are a mixed bag but queues are long and invariably include locals and tourists, and even the occasional *famoso* (celebrity).

LA LATINA & LAVAPIÉS

DEEP Map pp246-7

Sala Divino; ☎ 91 470 24 61; Paseo de la Ermita del Santo 48; ☽ midnight-6am Fri; Ⓜ Puerta del Ángel
The superclub of the Madrid scene, Deep is vast and the club of choice for a mainly younger crowd. This is where you will see Madrid's enduring addiction to house music in action and it doesn't relent until daybreak, moving to the mixes of some of the best local and international DJs.

EL JUGLAR Map pp254-5

☎ 91 528 43 81; Calle de Lavapiés 37;
⏰ 9pm-3.30am; Ⓜ Lavapiés

One of the hottest spots in Lavapiés at the moment, this great bar is for a largely bohemian crowd with downtempo jazz and soul beats, with some fiery nods to flamenco at 10pm every Sunday and on the first Wednesday of every month. It's busy all night, but the after-midnight Latin tunes are funky and get everyone dancing. There are more frenetic Madrid nightspots, but none more agreeable.

LA LUPE Map pp254-5

☎ 91 527 50 19; Calle Torrecilla del Leal 12;
⏰ 5pm-2am; Ⓜ Antón Martín

Madrileños in the know have been coming here to this fun and funky dance spot for years and there's no sign of its popularity abating. It's mostly the latest dance tunes with cosy and impromptu dance floors so packed that you'll struggle to make your way to the bar. Other places stay open later, but this place will really get your night off on the right foot. If you've a Chueca night in mind, there's another La Lupe at Calle de Hortaleza 51 (Map pp250–1; Ⓜ Chueca).

HUERTAS & ATOCHA

DUCADOS CAFÉ Map pp254-5

☎ 91 360 00 89; Plaza de Canalejas 3;
⏰ 8.30am-2am; Ⓜ Sevilla

If there's a constant here, it's the promise that the music, whatever the style, will get you groovin'. DJs roll through hip-hop, house, funk and soul but always find a way to keep the crowd happy and the dance

floor filled. The upstairs bar is open all day for tapas or snacks, though at night it becomes a chilled bar. Since there's no cover charge, this is a great place to start the night.

KAPITAL Map p257

☎ 91 420 29 06; Calle de Atocha 125; ⏰ 5.30-11pm Fri-Sun & midnight-6am Thu-Sun; Ⓜ Atocha

This massive seven-storey nightclub is one of Madrid's biggies with something for everyone: from cocktail bars and dance music to karaoke, salsa and hip-hop. The crowd is sexy, well-heeled and up for a good time. On Sundays, 'Sundance' (otherwise known as 'Kapital Love') is definitely for those who have no intention of appearing at work or university on Mondays. The afternoon sessions are for a younger crowd, while nights belong more to the Real Madrid set.

ROOM AT STELLA Map pp254-5

☎ 91 531 63 78; Calle de Arlabán 7; ⏰ 1-6am Thu-Sat; Ⓜ Sevilla

Don't even think about arriving at this club after 3am – there simply won't be room and those inside have no intention of leaving until dawn. DJ Ángel García is one of Madrid's best and the great visuals will leave you cross-eyed if you weren't already in this vibrant, heady place.

SALAMANCA

ALMONTE Map p246-7

☎ 91 563 25 04; Calle de Juan Bravo 35; ⏰ 9.30pm-5am; Ⓜ Nuñez de Balboa or Diego de León

If flamenco has captured your soul, but you want to do more than just watch, head to Almonte where the whitewashed façade

---

TOP CLUBS FOR COSY, MINIMALIST COOL

If megaclubs are not your scene, but you like your clubs to be chic in all the right places (curves and clean lines in both the furniture and clientele), the following places will fit the bill:

- House music with jazz inflections from DJs Kalero and Mikeel Molina gets things going at **Capote** (Map pp250–1; ☎ 91 319 01 38; Calle de Santa Teresa 3; ⏰ midnight-late; Ⓜ Alonso Martínez).
- House DJs make **Café Sambhad** (Map pp250–1; Calle de Duque de Osuna 4; ⏰ 6pm-2.30am Mon-Thu, 6pm-4am Fri & Sat; Ⓜ Plaza de España) a good place to end your Conde Duque night.
- Pop, rock and fusion in Warholesque surrounds are on offer at **Costello Café & Nightclub** (Map pp254–5; Calle del Caballero de Gracia 10; ☎ 6.30pm-3am Sun-Wed, 6.30pm-4am Thu-Sat; Ⓜ Gran Vía).
- Soul, disco and deep house draws a predominantly gay crowd to **Local Café Bar Lounge** (Map pp250–1; ☎ 91 532 76 10; Calle de la Libertad 28; ⏰ 5pm-3am; Ⓜ Chueca).
- Heartbreakingly sleek and oh-so-cool **Gaia** (Map pp254–5; ☎ 91 547 47 19; Calle de Amnistía 6; ⏰ 6pm-2.30am Tue-Sat, 6pm-1am Sun; Ⓜ Ópera) has great lounge music.

tells you that this is all about Andalucía, the home of flamenco. The young and the beautiful who come here have *sevillanas* (flamenco dance-style that originated in Seville) in their soul and in their feet, so head downstairs to see the best dancing, and dance if you dare.

GARAMOND Map p252

☎ 91 578 19 74; Calle de Claudio Coello 10; ☽ 6pm-3.30am Sun-Thu, 6pm-4.30am Fri & Sat; Ⓜ Retiro

Better look snazzy, 'cause they have what's known as a *puerta rigurosa*, which translates roughly as 'we won't let you in unless you look like you belong in Salamanca'. Although it's aimed at a 30-plus crowd, the atmosphere can get pretty charged and there seem to be enough hormones here to fill a school disco.

MALASAÑA & CHUECA

CAFÉ LA PALMA Map pp250-1

☎ 91 522 50 31; Calle de la Palma 62; ☽ midnight-4am Thu-Sat; Ⓜ Noviciado

It's amazing how much variety the Café la Palma has packed into its labyrinth of rooms. Live shows featuring hot local bands are held at the back, while DJs mix up the front. Some rooms have a café style, while others look like an Arab tearoom, pillows on the floor and all. Every night is a little different, so expect to be surprised.

EL JUNCO JAZZ CLUB Map pp250-1

☎ 91 319 20 81; Plaza de Santa Bárbara 10; ☽ 11pm-6am; Ⓜ Alonso Martínez

Night owls who are tired of the house music that pervades so many Madrid clubs will love the nightly live jazz concerts, followed by DJs spinning funk, nu jazz and innovative groove beats. The emphasis is on black music (a term that covers music from the American south) and the crowd is classy and casual.

EÓ Map pp250-1

☎ 91 521 73 79; Calle de Almirante 12; ☽ 10pm-3am Tue-Sat; Ⓜ Chueca

If you could bottle the energy of Chueca with the sophistication of Salamanca, you'd end up with EÓ. The cocktails are first-rate, there seems to be a door policy of only admitting the beautiful people of Madrid and,

Pump up the beer at Café La Palma (left)

though mainly Spanish, there are enough beautiful foreigners to lend the place an international feel.

LAYDOWN REST CLUB Map pp250-1

☎ 91 548 79 37; Plaza Mostenses 9; ☽ 11.30pm-2.30am Tue-Fri, 9.30pm-2.30am Sat & Sun; Ⓜ Plaza de España or Noviciado

This astonishing restaurant (p126) morphs into a nightclub after the meal is over and you can join them on the dance floor or lie down on one of the beds that fill the club. The DJs ensure that there's no danger of falling asleep.

PACHÁ Map pp250-1

☎ 91 447 01 28; Calle de Barceló 11; ☽ 12.30-5am Thu-Sat; Ⓜ Tribunal

This megaclub is one of the international chain of clubs that earned its fame in Ibiza; and as serious clubbers have moved on, the oh-my-gosh, barely-out-of-school set still turn up in droves for the fun mixture of house, Latin and Spanish music, and mix it with 30-somethings who never grew up.

PENTA BAR Map pp250-1

☎ 91 447 84 60; Calle de la Palma 4; ☽ 9pm-3am; Ⓜ Tribunal

A night-out here and you could be forgiven for believing that *la movida* never died down. It's an informal place where you can groove to the '80s music you love to hate;

141

but don't even think of turning up before midnight, especially from Thursdays to Saturdays, when the house DJ keeps the tunes hopping.

STROMBOLI CAFÉ Map pp250-1
☎ 91 319 46 28; Calle de Hortaleza 96;
🕑 6pm-3am; Ⓜ Chueca or Tribunal
One of Chueca's best café-clubs, Stromboli somehow manages to stay hip and happening with its lounge, nu jazz and deep house beats from some of the best local DJs who love the cosy, lounge feel almost as much as the punters do. Truly one of *the* places to be seen in Chueca.

TUPPERWARE Map pp250-1
☎ 91 446 42 04; Corredera Alta de San Pablo 26;
🕑 8pm-3.30am Sun-Wed, 9pm-3.30am Thu-Sat;
Ⓜ Tribunal
The atmosphere here is the ultimate in kitsch (huge eyeballs stuck to the ceiling, and plastic TVs with action-figure dioramas lined up behind the bar) but the atmosphere is fun and friendly, and appealing more to a 30-something crowd. Tupperware has been around for a while and the DJs are still pumping out a mix of soul, indie rock, and classics from the '60s and '70s.

WHY NOT? Map pp250-1
Calle de San Bartolomé 7; 🕑 10.30pm-late;
Ⓜ Chueca
Narrow and packed with bodies, gay-friendly Why Not? is the sort of place where nothing's left to the imagination (the gay and straight crowd who come here are

pretty amorous) and it's full nearly every night of the week. Pop and top-40 music are the standard here, and the dancing crowd is mixed and as serious about having a good time as they are about heavy petting.

CHAMBERÍ & ARGÜELLES

MOMA 56 Map pp246-7
☎ 91 395 20 59; Calle de José Abascal 56;
🕑 midnight-6am Thu-Sun; Ⓜ Gregorio Marañón
Two words: beautiful people. Get your Prada gear on and that studied look of sophistication, and join the small-time celebrities and owners of the flashy sports cars parked out front. The décor (red padded walls, red lighting) is as sleek as the too-cool crowd who shake off their pretensions once the live percussion fuses into DJ house. There's really nowhere quite like it in Madrid, so expect to pay around €15 for the privilege. Many people start the night here at the restaurant of the same name (p128) and continue until very late without need of anything else.

NORTHERN MADRID

LIVING Map p245
☎ 629 671582; Avenida del Brasil 5; 🕑 10pm-late Thu-Sat; Ⓜ Santiago Bernabéu
With its bright décor and clean-lined look, Living's chic atmosphere goes well with the fashionable, 30-something crowd that hangs out here. Dance and mingle downstairs or head up to a chill lounge where you can talk with a drink in hand. It's the most sophisticated (but never stuffy) of the many nightclubs that are clustered shoulder-to-shoulder along this street.

SPACE OF SOUND Map p245
Plaza Estación de Chamartín; 🕑 10am-6pm Sun;
Ⓜ Chamartín
If you can't bear your Saturday night to end, head to Space of Sound, the sort of place that makes Madrid unlike any other city in the world. This all-day Sunday dance club is a magnet for those who never want to go home and the DJs pump out energetic progressive house for a crowd as diverse as Madrid itself.

Entertainment

Entertainment

Madrid may not have the reputation of London or Paris when it comes to vibrant cultural life, but don't underrate Madrid's entertainment appeal. The clamorous days of *la movida Madrileña* (the sociocultural movement set off by the explosion of liberties after the death of Franco; see boxed text, p54) spilled over into the cultural sphere and those energetic days of the 1980s grew into something more mature by the time the city was named the European Capital of Culture in 1992. Now the best place in the world to see Spanish drama (both classical and modern) and *zarzuela* (a Madrid cross between opera and dance), Madrid also boasts fine flamenco venues, the world's most famous football club, the most prestigious bullring in Spain, excellent classical music programmes and live music whether it be in a dark Huertas bar or a mega-venue with a big-name world act. There are also plenty of activities for fitness fanatics or fine spas and relaxation centres for those who prefer to be pampered.

What's On

To find information on the current showings at Madrid's theatres, cinemas and concert halls, your best bet is the *Guía del Ocio,* a Spanish-only weekly magazine available for €1 at a news kiosk. It's website (www.guiade locio.com in Spanish) is a virtual version of the same publication. Also helpful is the comprehensive La Netro (http://madrid .lanetro.com), with information in Spanish. The Madrid page of www.whatsonwhen .com covers the highlights (in English) of sports and cultural activities, and has some information on getting tickets. The town hall's website (www.munimadrid.com) has practical details for the city's theatres and stages.

Also keep an eye out for the monthly Salir Urban (www.salirsalir.com). It's in Spanish, costs €1.80 and covers both Madrid and Barcelona. The monthly English expat publication In Madrid (www.in-madrid.com) is given out free at some hotels, original-version cinemas (where films are shown in their original language with Spanish subtitles), Irish pubs and English bookshops, and has lots of information about what to see and do in town. Not as helpful but free and in English are *Vive Madrid* and *Es Madrid Magazine,* both available at tourist offices and in some hotels.

The local press is always a good bet, with daily listings of films, concerts, football matches, bullfights and special events. On Fridays pick up *El Mundo*'s supplement magazine, *Metropoli,* for additional information on the week's offerings. Sports-only dailies such as *Marca* and *AS* are wildly popular and will give you the inside scoop on upcoming matches and events, provided you read basic Spanish.

> ## BOOKING CONCERT & THEATRE TICKETS
>
> There are plenty of outlets that sell tickets for concerts, theatre and other live performances, and many of these enable you to book online from anywhere in the world. For details on getting tickets for sporting events, see the Activities section (p150).
>
> Phone numbers that begin with 902 can only be dialled from within Spain.
>
> Madrid's major ticket vendors include:
>
> **Caixa Catalunya's Tel-Entrada** (☎ 902 101 212; www.telentrada.com)
>
> **El Corte Inglés** (☎ 91 379 80 00, 902 400 222; throughout city; ⏰ 10am-9pm Mon-Sat)
>
> **Entradas.com** (☎ 902 221 622)
>
> **FNAC** (☎ 91 595 62 00)
>
> **Localidades Galicia** (Map pp254–5; ☎ 91 531 27 32, 91 531 91 31; www.eol.es/lgalicia/; Plaza del Carmen 1; ⏰ 9.30am-1pm & 4.30-7pm Tue-Sat; Ⓜ Sol)
>
> **Servicaixa** (☎ 902 332 211) You can also get tickets in Servicaixa ATMs.
>
> **Tick Tack Ticket** (☎ 902 150 022)

FLAMENCO

Flamenco aficionados from Andalucía may look down their noses at the Madrid flamenco scene, but it was here that this most Spanish of art forms gained a broader following and international attention, and the city has long been a platform for some of flamenco's top dancers, guitarists and singers. For more information on flamenco as an art form, see p30.

The most accessible flamenco shows are in *tablaos* (small-stage theatres that usually double as restaurants) and are geared toward tourists. Although they're pricey (around €25 plus meal prices), you'll see all three elements of the art (dancing, singing and guitar) and you'll probably be sitting close enough to the stage to see the sweat dripping off the dancers. For something more informal, there are numerous flamenco bars and *peñas flamencas* (flamenco associations) scattered throughout Huertas, Lavapiés and La Latina. This is where performers hang out, and although shows aren't planned, some spontaneous music may start up after midnight. Festivals are another place to find flamenco; February's Festival Flamenco (p9), mostly held in the **Teatro Albéniz** (p146) is the city's biggest flamenco bash.

For those of you who want to dance your own version of the *sevillana* (flamenco dance-style that originated in Seville), **Al Monte** (p141) will get your heart racing, while **El Juglar** (p140) is a nightclub that hosts well-known flamenco performers on the first Wednesday of every month at 10pm, as well as another flamenco session on Sundays.

You can usually buy same-day tickets at the door, though on a springtime Saturday night or during a holiday weekend you'll need to book ahead. Hotels can sometimes help you find a spot at sold-out shows.

CAFÉ DE CHINITAS Map pp250-1

☎ 91 559 51 35; Calle de Torija 7; admission €28.50; 9pm-2.30am Mon-Sat, show 10.30pm; Santo Domingo

For a high-end flamenco show in an elegant setting, this traditional *tablao* is the perfect choice. It attracts top performers and big crowds, so book in advance. There's a minimum meal charge of €15.80 in addition to the admission.

Flamenco jam session at Cardamomo

CANDELA Map pp254-5

☎ 91 467 33 82; Calle del Olmo 2; 10.30pm-late; Antón Martín

Many of Madrid's young performers hang out at this informal bar, and spontaneous music often breaks out late in the evening. To see Candela at its best, come after 1am and respect the atmosphere.

CARDAMOMO Map pp254-5

☎ 913 69 07 57; Calle de Echegaray 15; admission free; 9pm-4am; Sevilla

If you believe that flamenco is best enjoyed in a dark, smoky bar where the crowd is predominantly local and where you can dance, clap and even sing along (the crowd is so thick no-one will mind), Cardamomo is ideal. Flamenco and flamenco-fusion tunes are played until late, and on Wednesday nights there are live shows around 10.30pm.

CASA PATAS Map pp254-5

☎ 91 369 04 96; www.casapatas.com; Calle de Cañizares 10; admission about €30 (for shows); noon-5pm & 8pm-3am, shows 10.30pm Mon-Thu, 9pm & midnight Fri & Sat; Antón Martín

One of the top flamenco stages in Madrid, this restaurant and *tablao* is a good place for an introduction to the art. Although it's geared toward tourists, locals stop by for a soul-filling session of passionate music and dance. They also hold classes here.

CORRAL DE LA MORERÍA Map pp254-5

☎ 91 365 84 46; www.corraldelamoreria.com; Calle de la Morería 17; admission from €30; 8.30pm-2am, show 10pm; Ópera

For a top-quality show that doesn't take itself too seriously, head to the Corral, one of the better meal-and-show places in Madrid. The stage area has a rustic feel, and tables are pushed up close to the small stage.

LA SOLÉA Map pp254-5

☎ 91 366 05 34; Calle de la Cava Baja 34; ⏰ 10pm- 5am Mon-Sat; Ⓜ La Latina

This long-standing flamenco bar has an authentic flamenco atmosphere that's filled with knowledgeable punters and regular performances by a soulful cast.

LAS CARBONERAS Map pp254-5

☎ 91 542 86 77; www.tablaolascarboneras.com; Plaza del Conde de Miranda 1; admission from €29; ⏰ 9pm-10.30pm Mon-Thu, 9-11pm Fri & Sat; Ⓜ Ópera, Sol or La Latina

Like most of the restaurants/tablaos around town, this place sees far more tourists than locals, but the quality is top-notch. It's not the place for gritty, soul-moving spontaneity, but it's still an excellent introduction.

LAS TABLAS Map pp250-1

☎ 91 542 05 20; Plaza de España 9; admission €6-20; ⏰ 7pm-1am, show 10.30pm; Ⓜ Plaza de España

One of the more recent newcomers to Madrid's flamenco scene, Las Tablas has quickly earned a reputation for classic flamenco. Most nights you'll see a classic flamenco show, with plenty of throaty singing and soul-baring dancing.

DANCE & BALLET

Spain's lively Compañía Nacional de Danza (☎ 91 354 50 53; http://cndanza.mcu.es/), under director Nacho Duato, performs worldwide and has won accolades for its marvellous technicality and style. The company, made up mostly of international dancers, performs original, contemporary pieces and is considered a main player on the international dance scene.

Madrid is also home to the Ballet Nacional de España (☎ 91 517 46 86; http://balletnacional.mcu.es/), a classical company that's known for its unique mix of ballet and traditional Spanish styles such as flamenco and zarzuela.

Both companies perform more often abroad than at home. When in town their works are staged in major venues; check newspapers for listings.

THEATRE

Madrid's theatre scene is a year-round affair, but it really gets going in autumn. Most shows are in Spanish, but those who don't speak the language may still enjoy musicals or zarzuela, Spain's own singing and dancing version of musical theatre. Tickets for all shows start at around €10 and run up to around €50. Most of the time you can get tickets at the box office on the day of the performance, but for new, popular or weekend shows you'll need to book ahead. Note that box offices are usually closed on Mondays and sometimes Tuesdays, when there are no shows. Other days, they are generally open from about 10am until 1pm and again from 5pm until the start of the night's show.

CENTRO CULTURAL DE LA VILLA

Map p252

☎ 91 575 60 80; Plaza de Colón; Ⓜ Colón or Serrano

Located under the waterfall at Plaza de Colón, the Centro Cultural has exhibition and performance space where it stages everything from classical concerts to comic theatre, opera and quality flamenco.

TEATRO ALBÉNIZ Map pp254-5

☎ 91 531 83 11, 902 488 488; Calle de la Paz 11; Ⓜ Sol

One of the premier venues for popular Spanish dramas with well-known casts, the Albéniz also hosts the Caja Madrid

LA ZARZUELA

What began in the late 17th century as a way to amuse King Felipe IV and his court has become one of Spain's most unique theatre styles. With a light-hearted combination of music and dance, and a focus on everyday people's problems, zarzuelas quickly became popular in Madrid, which remains the genre's undoubted capital. Although you're likely to have trouble following the storyline (zarzuelas are notoriously full of local references and jokes), seeing a zarzuela gives an entertaining look into local culture. One of the best places to catch a show is at the Teatro de la Zarzuela (opposite).

flamenco festival in late winter and many events during the Festival de Otoño.

TEATRO ALFIL Map pp250-1
☎ 91 521 45 41; Calle del Pez 10; Ⓜ Noviciado
Staging a broad range of alternative and experimental Spanish-language theatre, Teatro Alfil is a good place to catch up-and-coming Spanish actors and comedians, and mingle with an eclectic crowd.

TEATRO CALDERÓN Map pp254-5
☎ 91 420 37 97; Calle de Atocha 18;
Ⓜ Sol or Antón Martín
Big budget musicals take the stage in this grand old theatre and stay for months. Recent shows include *Queen* and *Fame*.

TEATRO COLISEUM Map pp250-1
☎ 91 547 66 12; Gran Vía 78; Ⓜ Plaza de España
One of the larger theatres in the city, here you can expect to see major musicals, often Broadway or West End hits but usually with an all-Spanish cast.

TEATRO DE LA ZARZUELA Map pp254-5
☎ 91 524 54 00; Calle de Jovellanos 4;
Ⓜ Banco de España
This theatre, built in 1856, is the premier place to see *zarzuela* (see boxed text, opposite). It also hosts mainstream shows, as well as a smattering of classical music and opera. Tickets range from €12 to €36.

TEATRO ESPAÑOL Map pp254-5
☎ 91 360 14 80; Calle del Príncipe 25;
Ⓜ Sevilla or Antón Martín
This theatre has been here since the 16th century and is still one of the best places to catch mainstream Spanish drama.

TEATRO PAVÓN Map pp254-5
☎ 91 528 28 19; Calle de los Embajadores 9;
Ⓜ La Latina or Tirso de Molina
The home of the National Classical Theatre Company, this theatre has a regular calendar of classical shows by Spanish and European playwrights.

TEATRO VALLE-INCLÁN Map pp254-5
☎ 91 505 88 00; Plaza de Lavapiés; Ⓜ Lavapiés
The stunning refurbishment of this theatre has brought new life (and innovative plays) to this once run-down corner of Lavapiés.

CLASSICAL MUSIC & OPERA

Yes, Madrid loves to party, but scratch just beneath the surface and you'll find a thriving city of high culture, with venues dedicated to year-round opera and classical music. Orchestras from all over Europe perform regularly here and Madrid's own Orquesta Sinfónica (www.osm.es) is a splendid orchestra that normally performs (or accompanies) in the Teatro Real or Auditorio Nacional de Música.

AUDITORIO NACIONAL DE MÚSICA
Map p244
☎ 91 337 01 00; www.auditorionacional.mcu.es;
Calle del Príncipe de Vergara 146; Ⓜ Cruz del Rayo
When it's not playing the Teatro Real, Madrid's Orquesta Sinfonía plays at this modern venue, which also attracts conductors from all over the world. It's usually fairly easy to get your hands on tickets at the box office.

FUNDACIÓN JUAN MARCH Map pp246-7
☎ 91 435 42 40; Calle de Castelló 77;
Ⓜ Nuñez de Balboa
A foundation dedicated to promoting music and culture (as well as exhibitions; see p90), the Juan March stages free concerts throughout most of the year. Performances range from solo concerts to themed concerts dedicated to a single style or composer.

TEATRO MONUMENTAL Map pp254-5
☎ 91 429 12 81, 91 429 81 19; Calle de Atocha 65;
Ⓜ Antón Martín
The main concert season runs from October to March, when concerts and occasional operas or *zarzuelas* show off this modern theatre's fabulous acoustics.

TEATRO REAL Map pp254-5
☎ 902 244848; Plaza de Oriente; Ⓜ Ópera
After spending €100 million-plus on a long rebuilding project, the Teatro Real is as technologically advanced as any venue in Europe, and is the city's grandest stage for elaborate operas and occasional ballets. You'll pay as little as €15 for a spot so far away you will need a telescope, although the sound quality is consistent throughout. For the best seats, don't expect change from €100.

CINEMA

Madrileños are some of Europe's most devoted movie-goers and on Sunday evenings just about every *sala* (venue) in town is packed and queues stretch down the street. Most people buy tickets at the door, but turning up a couple of hours early or ringing the cinema to make a booking can be a good idea. Regular tickets cost about €5.80, rising to €6 on weekends, though on the *día de espectador* (spectator's day), which varies according to theatre but is usually Wednesday, there's a discount.

The highest concentration of Spanish-language cinemas are on Gran Vía and Calle Fuencarral, but plenty of cinemas offer VO (*versión original*, or original version) films which are shown in the original language with Spanish subtitles. The best place to start looking is around Plaza de Emilio Jiménez Millas (better known by locals as Plaza de los Cubos), just northwest of Plaza de España. The major Spanish newspapers have full film listings. The following are the best original-version cinemas.

Alphaville (Map pp250–1; ☎ 91 559 38 36; Calle de Martín de los Heros 14; Ⓜ Plaza de España) A small cinema with a penchant for the quirky.

Cine Doré (Map pp254–5; ☎ 91 369 11 25; Calle de Santa Isabel 3; Ⓜ Antón Martín) A wonderful old cinema that's home to the Filmoteca Nacional (national film library) and shows classics past and present for just €1.50. Four movies are shown nightly, the first one at 5.30pm and the last around 10pm.

La Enana Marrón (Map pp250–1; ☎ 91 308 14 97; www.la enanamarron.org; Travesía de San Mateo 8; Ⓜ Alonso Martínez) It shows artsy and alternative (mostly Spanish) programme from documentaries to animated films, international flicks and oldies.

Princesa (Map pp250–1; ☎ 91 541 41 00; Calle de Princesa 3; Ⓜ Plaza de España) One of the larger of the original-version cinemas.

Renoir (Map pp250–1; ☎ 91 541 41 00; Calle de Martín de los Heros 12; Ⓜ Plaza de España) Offers plenty of latest-release films but some interesting documentaries and Asian flicks as well.

Verdi (Map pp246–7; ☎ 91 447 39 30; Calle de Bravo Murillo 28; Ⓜ Canal or Quevedo) This is an excellent neighbourhood cinema that cherry-picks the best of the big-budget art-house movies.

Yelmo Cineplex Ideal (Map pp254–5; ☎ 91 369 25 18, 902 220 922; Calle de Doctor Cortezo 6 28; Ⓜ Tirso de Molina) It's close to Plaza Mayor and offers a wide selection of films.

The classic Cine Doré (left)

LIVE MUSIC

The quality of live shows in Madrid is getting better every year, and there's more variety and more international headliners than ever. Summer is undoubtedly the best time to see the big names at an outdoor venue; keep an eye on the *Guía del Ocio* and newspapers from May through to early August. Although many bars and clubs have occasional live shows, the places listed here are known primarily for their concerts. Ticket prices will vary wildly according to the venue and who's performing there. For ticket and reservation information, see boxed text, p144.

MEGA-VENUES

Madrid is a major stop on the European tour circuit with big-name performers from Spain, the USA, the UK and Latin America making regular appearances.

AUDITORIO PARQUE JUAN CARLOS I
☎ 91 721 00 79; Avenida de Logroño; Ⓜ Campo de las Naciones

A large and modern amphitheatre-like auditorium in the midst of the green expanse of the Parque Juan Carlos I, this is a popular venue for big-name concerts.

ESTADIO DE LA COMUNIDAD DE MADRID

☎ 91 720 24 00; Avenida de Arcentales; Ⓜ Las Musas
They reserve the 20,000-seat 'La Peineta' (the stadium's nickname referring to the comblike shape of the central stage) for the biggies – Bruce Springsteen and Bon Jovi are just a couple of the rockers who've taken the stage here.

PALACIO DE LOS DEPORTES

Map pp246-7
☎ 91 258 60 16, 91 523 09 51; Calle de Jorge Juan 99; Ⓜ Goya or O'Donnell
After the old Palacio de los Deportes burned to the ground in 2001, the city authorities built a state-of-the-art, multipurpose venue in its place. It reopened in 2006 and can seat up to 18,000 people.

PLAZA DE TOROS MONUMENTAL DE LAS VENTAS Map p244

☎ 91 356 22 00; Calle de Alcalá 237; Ⓜ Ventas
Madrid's main bullring makes a great venue for outdoor concerts but it's off-limits to musicians when the bulls are in town (see p92 for more info). Recent top performers have included Chambao and Shakira.

JAZZ

Madrid has a handful of world-class jazz venues. Calle 54 is the place to be for Latin jazz, while Café Central has classical and fusion shows every night of the week. For more of a nightclub feel, try Clamores, while Populart has the intimate ambience of a knowledgeable jazz crowd. You'll pay about €10 to get into most places, but special concerts can run up to €20 or more.

CAFÉ CENTRAL Map pp254-5

☎ 91 369 41 43; Plaza del Ángel 10; ☿ 1.30pm-2.30am Sun-Thu, 1.30pm-3.30am Fri & Sat; Ⓜ Antón Martín or Sol
This Art-Deco bar is a great spot for an early-evening drink and, if you're clever, you'll stay until 10pm when Café Central morphs into one of Madrid's best jazz venues. Performances include everything from Latin jazz to fusion, tango and classic jazz at the nightly shows, and prices hover between €8 to €12 depending on who's playing.

CALLE 54 Map p245

☎ 90 214 14 12, 91 561 28 32; Paseo de la Habana 3; ☿ 7pm-late; Ⓜ Nuevos Ministerios or Santiago Bernabeu
Offering soul-satisfying Latin jazz, Calle 54 is responsible for putting Madrid on the international Latin-jazz circuit. It's an upscale (ie pricey) place that attracts a mixed audience of musicians, film stars and locals. Although the venue remains true to its Latin-jazz roots, you'll also hear other fusion performances, including occasional flamenco inflections. Live shows start around 11pm.

CLAMORES Map pp250-1

☎ 91 445 79 38; Calle de Alburquerque 14; ☿ 6pm-3am Sun-Thu, 6pm-4am Fri & Sat; Ⓜ Bilbao
Clamores is a classic jazz café that doesn't mind mixing pop, Brazilian or flamenco; the fusion sounds here always make for an interesting night and the lively crowd of locals only adds to the energy. The stained

---

A CULT CLUB FROM A CULT MOVIE

Film director Fernando Trueba, one of *the* names in Spanish cinema, gained a cult following among jazz aficionados after making the 2000 documentary movie *Calle 54*, a passionate and inspiring chronicle of Latin jazz. The Grammy-nominated film was shown in major film festivals all over the world, was dubbed the *Buena Vista Social Club* of Latin jazz and is still a name of worldwide legend for jazz aficionados.

But Trueba wasn't content with simply recording the genre he loves; he went one step further and created Calle 54 in Madrid, a club where the Latin-jazz spirit of the movie lives on. It has been an enormous success, thanks in no small part to the support of the legendary artists featured in the film, and has put Madrid firmly on the international Latin-jazz circuit. Greats such as Bebo Valdés, Chano Domínguez and Roy Hargrove have all taken the stage here, playing for appreciative audiences that often include Trueba's film pals, most notably Pedro Almodóvar and Penélope Cruz.

walls and yellowed photographs hanging on them show just how long this place has been putting on shows. Live shows can begin as early as 9pm but sometimes really get going after 1am on weekends.

POPULART Map pp254-5

☎ 91 429 84 07; Calle de las Huertas 22; 🕑 6pm-2.30am Mon-Fri, 6pm-3.30am Fri & Sat; Ⓜ Antón Martín or Sol

One of Madrid's classic jazz clubs, this place offers a low-key atmosphere and top-quality music. The shows start at 11pm, but if you want a seat get here early. There's no cover charge, and drinks cost €7 and up.

ROCK & BEYOND

Many of these concert venues double as clubs, making it possible to start off the night with a great concert and stay on to party until late. Ticket prices vary enormously, but expect to pay €10 to €15 for small or relatively unknown bands, and up to €50-plus for internationally known groups that occasionally make appearances at these intimate clubs.

GALILEO GALILEI Map p244

☎ 91 534 75 57; www.salagalileogalilei.com; Calle de Galileo 100; 🕑 6pm-4.30am; Ⓜ Islas Filipinas

There's no telling what they'll stage here next. With Jackson Browne, Niña Pastori and a team of Egyptian belly-dancers all among the recent performers.

HONKY TONK Map pp250-1

☎ 91 445 68 86; Calle de Covarrubias 24; 🕑 9.30pm-5.30am; Ⓜ Alonso Martínez

Despite the name, this is a great place to see local rock 'n' roll, though many acts have a little country or some blues thrown into the mix too. It's a fun vibe in a small-ish club, so arrive early as the place fills up fast.

LA BOCA DEL LOBO Map pp254-5

☎ 91 523 13 91; Calle de Echegaray 11; 🕑 9.30pm-3am; Ⓜ Sol

Known for offering mostly rock and alternative concerts, La Boca del Lobo (Wolf's Mouth) has broadened its horizons, adding country and jazz to the line-up. Concerts are held two to three times a week, usually on Wednesdays, Thursdays and/or Fridays.

LA RIVIERA Map pp246-7

☎ 91 365 24 15; Paseo Bajo de la Virgen del Puerto; 🕑 midnight-6am Tue-Sun; Ⓜ Puerta de Angel

A dance club and concert venue all in one, this sprawling Art-Deco monolith down by the Manzanares hosts some of the biggest names in rock and electronic music. Recent performers include James Brown and Van Morrison. In summer, the roof disappears and you can dance under the stars until early morning.

MOBY DICK Map p245

☎ 91 555 76 71; Avenida del Brasil 5; 🕑 9.30pm-5am Mon-Sat; Ⓜ Santiago Bernabéu

In the heart of a corner of Madrid that works hard by day and parties even harder on weekends, Moby Dick is a stalwart of the live-music scene. It's mostly rock but there's a pretty eclectic mix and there are plenty of dance bars alongside if the music's not to your liking.

SALA CARACOL Map pp246-7

Snail Room; ☎ 91 527 35 94; Calle de Bernardino Obregón 18; 🕑 8pm-2am; Ⓜ Embajadores

The Sala Caracol is a cosy venue (despite its industrial décor) which plays host to everything from jazzy flamenco and world music to heavy metal.

ACTIVITIES

Real Madrid and bullfighting – two of the Spanish icons which are best known beyond the country's borders – are Madrid's major sporting drawcards but there's also high-quality basketball as well as tennis to enjoy if you're in town at the right time.

For those who prefer getting all sweaty and making their own sport, there are gyms and health centres scattered throughout the city. Wonderful spas and massage centres represent the height of pampering for those keen not to get too active.

WATCHING SPORT
Football

El Estadio Santiago Bernabéu is a temple to football and one of the world's great football arenas; watching a game here is akin to a pilgrimage for sports fans. Real Madrid has more big-name stars (if not recent trophies) than any team in the world and when they click it's as close as you'll come to footballing perfection. When they do so with 80,000 passionate Madrileños in attendance, you'll get chills down your spine. If you're fortunate enough to be in town when Real Madrid win a major trophy, head to **Plaza de la Cibeles** and wait for the all-night party to begin.

The city's other big club, Atlético de Madrid, may have long existed in the shadow of their more illustrious city rivals, but it has been one of the most successful teams in Spanish football history in its own right.

For more information on football in Madrid, see p15.

TICKETS & RESERVATIONS

Tickets for football matches in Madrid start at around €10 and run up to the rafters for major matches – you pay in inverse proportion to your distance from the pitch. For bigger games, such as Real Madrid against Barcelona or Atlético de Madrid or a Champions League game, *entradas* (tickets) are nigh-on impossible to find unless you're willing to take the risk with scalpers. For less important matches, you shouldn't have too many problems.

Unless you book your Real Madrid ticket through a ticket agency, your best chance is to turn up at the **ticket office** (Map p245) at Gate 42 on Calle de Conche de Espina early in the week before a scheduled game (eg a Tuesday morning for a Sunday game). The all-important telephone number for booking tickets (which you later pick up at Gate 42) is ☎ 902 324 324, which only works if you're calling from within Spain.

If you're booking from abroad, there are numerous websites that sell tickets to Real Madrid games. While we're unable to z vouch for their good business practices, we can pass along the Web addresses of a few; www .madrid-tickets.net, www.madrid-tickets .com or www.ticket-finders.com.

To see an Atlético de Madrid game, try calling ☎ 91 366 47 07, but you're most likely to manage a ticket if you turn up at the ground a few days before the game. Otherwise, try **Localidades Galicia** (Map pp254–5; ☎ 91 531 27 32, 91 531 91 31; www.eol .es/lgalicia/; Plaza del Carmen 1; ⏰ 9.30am-1pm & 4.30-7pm Tue-Sat; Ⓜ Sol).

ESTADIO SANTIAGO BERNABÉU

Map p245

☎ 91 398 43 00, 90 232 43 24; www.realmadrid .com; Calle de Concha Espina 1; ⏰ to visit 10.30am-6.30pm except day of or after game; Ⓜ Santiago Bernabéu

Holding 80,000 delirious fans, the Santiago Bernabéu (named after the long-time club president) is a mecca for Madridistas (Real Madrid football fans) worldwide. Those

Silverware on display at Real Madrid's Estadio Santiago Bernabéu (above)

who can't come to a game in the legendary stadium can at least stop by for a tour (adult/child €9/7, entry at Gate 40), a peek at the trophies exhibit (match days only) or to buy Real Madrid memorabilia in the club shop. See also p99.

ESTADIO VALLECAS TERESA RIVERO

☎ 91 478 22 53; Calle de Payaso Fofó; Ⓜ Portazgo
Madrid's third football club is firmly rooted in the working-class barrio of Vallecas and it may not win all that often, but its fans know how to have a good time.

ESTADIO VICENTE CALDERÓN Map p244

☎ 91 366 47 07; www.at-madrid.com; Calle de la Virgen del Puerto; Ⓜ Pirámides
The home of Atlético de Madrid isn't as large as Real Madrid's (Vicente Calderón seats fewer than 60,000), but what it lacks in size it makes up for in raw energy. A game at the Estadio Vicente Calderón has a passionate, more carnivalesque feel to it than you could ever experience at a Real Madrid game.

Bullfighting

From the Fiestas de San Isidro Labrador in mid-May until the end of October, Spain's top bullfighters come to swing their capes in Las Ventas bullring. During the six weeks of the fiesta's main bullfighting season, there are *corridas* (bullfights) almost every day. If *toreros* (matadors) make a name for themselves here, they enter the annals of bullfighting legend, as this is the most demanding and prestigious bullfighting arena in the world.

For more information on this compelling but often disturbing spectacle, see p16.

TICKETS & RESERVATIONS

Tickets are divided into *sol* (sun) and *sombra* (shade) seating, the former being considerably cheaper than the latter. Ticket sales begin a couple of days before the fight, at Las Ventas ticket office (🕑 10am-2pm & 5-8pm). A few ticket agencies sell before then, tacking on an extra 20% for their trouble; one of the best is Localidades Galicia (p151). You can also get tickets at the authorised sales offices (La Central Bullfight & Football Ticket Office; Map pp254–5) on Calle de la Victoria. For most bullfights, you'll have no problem getting a ticket at the door, but

during the Fiestas de San Isidro or when a popular *torero* comes to town, book ahead.

The cheapest tickets (€3.80) are for standing-room *sol*, though on a broiling hot summer day it's infinitely more enjoyable to pay the extra €3 for *sombra* tickets. The very best seats – on the front row in the shade – are the preserve of celebrities and cost more than €100.

For information on who'll be in the ring, pay attention to the colourful posters tacked around town and check the daily newspapers.

PLAZA DE TOROS MONUMENTAL DE LAS VENTAS Map p244

☎ 91 356 22 00; Calle de Alcalá 237; Ⓜ Ventas
One of the largest rings in the bullfighting world, Las Ventas has a grand *mudéjar* (a Moorish architectural style) exterior and a suitably coliseum-like arena surrounding the broad sandy ring. For more information, see p92.

Basketball

Basketball has a loyal following in Madrid and its two major teams, Adecco Estudiantes and Real Madrid, likewise. The season runs, like the football, from September through to the second half of May. Real Madrid plays at the recently rebuilt and state-of-the-art Palacio de los Deportes, while Adecco Estudiantes plays at the Madrid Arena in Casa del Campo.

TICKETS & RESERVATIONS

Tickets range from about €15 to €50 for regular season games. You can buy Estudiantes tickets through El Corte Inglés (p144) or at the Polideportivo Magariños (Map p245; ☎ 91 562 40 22; Calle de Serrano 127; 🕑 10am-2pm & 4-8pm). Real Madrid tickets go on sale two hours before the game and you can buy them directly at the stadium box office.

ADECCO ESTUDIANTES

☎ 91 588 93 85; Madrid Arena, Calle de las Aves; Ⓜ Lago or Alto de Extremadura
The Estudiantes are Madrid's most popular team, and games in the excellent Madrid Arena (which also hosts the Tennis Masters series in October) are usually played in front of a packed house.

REAL MADRID
☎ 91 258 60 16, 91 523 09 51; www.realmadrid
.com/baloncesto/portada_eng.htm; Palacio de los
Deportes, Calle de Jorge Juan 99;
Ⓜ Goya or O'Donnell
The Real Madrid basketball team has a
hugely successful history and, as Madrid's
most glamorous team, it's a great team to
watch live. Tickets are usually easy to come
by on the day of the game.

HEALTH & FITNESS
Swimming
CANAL DE ISABEL II Map p244
☎ 91 554 51 53; Avenida Filipinas 54;
admission €3.50; ⊙ 11am-8pm Jun-early Sep;
Ⓜ Ríos Rosas or Canal
Open only in summer, this large outdoor
pool is easily accessible by metro from the
centre. It also has a football field, basketball
court and weights room.

CASA DEL CAMPO
☎ 91 463 00 50; Avenida Ángel; pool €4;
⊙ 11.30am-9pm summer, 9am-noon & 3-7pm
& 9-10pm winter; Ⓜ Lago
The large, outdoor pools at this sprawling
park get a little overwhelmed in summer,
while the rest of the year (October to April)
swimming is indoors.

PISCINA MUNICIPAL PEÑUELAS
Map pp246-7
☎ 91 474 28 08; Calle de Arganda; admission €4;
⊙ 11am-9pm Jun-Aug; Ⓜ Acacias, Pirámides or
Embajadores
With two gloriously cool pools and a
smaller, infants' pool, this outdoor complex
south of the city centre is a popular place
for a summer dip, but like any place where
there's water in Madrid, it gets excessively
crowded on summer weekends.

Tennis
POLIDEPORTIVO VIRGEN DEL
PUERTO Map pp246-7
☎ 91 366 28 40; Paseo de la Virgen del Puerto;
court rental from €5; ⊙ 8.30am-8.30pm;
Ⓜ Príncipe Pío
Run by the municipal government, this
modern sports centre near the Puente de

Segovia has eight regulation-size tennis
courts, eight paddle-ball courts and 12
table-tennis tables.

Skiing
MADRID XANADÚ
☎ 902 361309;Calle Puerto de Navacerrada,
Arroyomolinos; ⊙ 10am-7pm Mon-Fri,
10am-6pm Sat & Sun
Far out to the east of Madrid, you'll find the
largest covered ski centre in Europe. Open
year-round, it's kept at a decidedly cool -2°C
so rug up before hitting the surprisingly
good slopes. Within the same complex is a
mammoth mall, a 15-screen movie theatre,
a kart track and an amusement park. To get
here, take bus No 529, 531 or 536 from the
Méndez Álvaro transportation hub.

Gyms & Fitness Clubs
Public gyms and indoor pools (normally for
lap swimming only) are scattered throughout Madrid. They generally charge a modest €3 to €6 for one-day admission. If you're
looking for swankier options, head to one
of Madrid's privately owned health centres.
You'll pay €8 to €12 for a day's admission,
but you'll usually find less-crowded workout rooms.

POLIDEPORTIVO LA CHOPERA
Map p257
☎ 91 420 11 54; Parque del Buen Retiro;
admission €4.50; ⊙ 9am-8pm Mon-Fri; Ⓜ Atocha
With a fine new workout centre, several
football fields and a few tennis courts, this
sports centre in the southwestern corner of
El Retiro is one of Madrid's most attractive
and central *polideportivos* (sports centre
and gym).

POLIDEPORTIVO LA LATINA
Map pp254-5
☎ 91 365 80 31; Plaza de la Cebada; pool
adult/child €3.80/2.15; ⊙ 8.15am-7pm Mon-Thu,
8.15am-6pm Fri, 10am-8.30pm Sat & Sun;
Ⓜ La Latina
One of the most central municipal gyms
(and one of the few that has a pool, though
it's for indoor lap-swimming only), this gym
is busy day and night. While not all that
new or clean, it offers decent weight and
workout rooms.

Yoga

CITY YOGA Map p245

☎ 91 553 47 51; Calle de Artistas 43; classes from €13; ☼ 10am-10pm Mon-Fri, 10am-2pm Sat; Ⓜ Cuatro Caminos or Nuevos Ministerios

This yoga centre is one of the most popular in the city, with a variety of classes suiting all styles and ability levels. There's a one-off joining fee of €30.

Day Spas & Salons

CHI SPA Map p252

☎ 91 578 13 40; www.thechispa.com; Calle del Conde de Aranda 6; ☼ 10am-9pm Mon-Fri, 10am-6pm Sat; Ⓜ Retiro

Wrap up in a robe and slippers and prepare to be pampered in one of Europe's best day spas. There are separate areas for men and women, and services include a massage (€65 per hour), facial (€55 to €95), body peeling (€60 to €90), manicure (€25) or pedicure (€35). Now what was it you were stressed about?

HAMMAM MEDINA MAYRIT

Map pp254-5

☎ 902 333 334; www.medinamayrit.com; Calle de Atocha 14; ☼ 10am-midnight; Ⓜ Sol

Madrid only recently started to come to terms with its Arab origins and this is the finest product of the new accommodation. Using excavated cellars of old Madrid, this is an imitation, traditional Arab bath with massages and aromatherapy beneath the elegantly restored arches. There's also a Moroccan-style tearoom and restaurant. Prices start from around €34, although that can drop to €24 between 10am and 4pm Monday to Friday. Reservations are required.

ZENSEI Map pp246-7

☎ 91 549 60 49; Calle de Blasco de Garay 64; ☼ 10am-10pm Mon-Sat; Ⓜ Moncloa or Quevedo

This Japanese relaxation centre promises the ultimate in Zen massage, acupuncture, reiki, shiatsu and yoga, not to mention origami or Japanese tea-ceremony classes. Prices mostly range from €25 to €75 and you'll come out floating on air.

Shopping ■

Shopping

Madrid is a fantastic place to shop and Madrileños are some of the finest exponents of the art.

Although there are excellent English-language bookshops, gourmet food stores, shops selling chic modern furnishings and home accessories dotted around the city, when it comes to fashion each barrio has its own distinctive style. As a result, some planning is essential to making the most of your shopping time in Madrid.

Salamanca is the home of upmarket fashions, with lavish and chic boutiques lining up to showcase the best that Spanish and international designers have to offer. They all come with a luxury price tag attached, but prices are reasonable when you consider the quality and originality of what's on offer. Many of the Spanish designers have made a name for themselves internationally, but nowhere else can you find so many to suit your look in just a few city blocks. For more information on Spanish fashion, see p14.

Chueca and, to a lesser extent, Malasaña are Salamanca's alter ego; home to fashion that's as funky as it is offbeat and ideal for that studied underground look or alternative club wear that will fit right in with Madrid's hedonistic after-dark crowd.

Central Madrid – whether it's Sol, Huertas or La Latina – offers plenty of individual surprises although there's little uniformity in what you'll find. That sense is multiplied a hundred-fold in El Rastro market where Madrileños converge in epic numbers on Sundays to pick through the junk in search of treasure.

The peak shopping season is during *las rebajas,* the annual winter and summer sales, when prices are slashed on just about everything. The winter sales begin around 7 January, just after Three Kings' Day, and last well into February. Summer sales begin in early July and last into August.

The shopping day starts at about 10am and is often broken up by a long lunch from 2pm to 5pm. Shops re-open after lunch and stay busy until 8pm or even later. Shops selling music and books, as well as some convenience stores, are the only outlets allowed to open every Sunday, although all shops may (and most usually do) open on the first Sunday of every month and throughout December.

Visitors are entitled to a refund of the 16% IVA (value-added tax) on purchases costing more than €90.16, from any shop, if you take the goods out of the EU within three months. For details on claiming your refund upon departure from Spain, see p216.

Funky footwear at Mercado Fuencarral (p165)

> ## TOP MADRID SHOPPING STREETS
>
> For...
> - glamour – **Calle de Serrano; Calle de José Ortega y Gasset** (Map p252)
> - quirky and alternative cool – **Calle de Fuencarral** (Map pp250–1)
> - discounted designer shoes – **Calle de Agusto Figueroa** (Map pp250–1)
> - exclusive accessories – **Calle de Piamonte** (p165)

LOS AUSTRIAS, SOL & CENTRO

While you might go to Salamanca for high-class shopping or to Malasaña and Chueca for the quirky and alternative, the maze of streets around the Plaza Mayor and extending up toward Gran Vía have something for everyone, and it's a fine place to window-shop unless you're after something specific.

ADOLFO DOMINGUEZ

Map pp254-5   Fashion, Clothes & Shoes

☎ 91 522 65 65; Gran Vía 11; ☽ 10am-9pm Mon-Sat; Ⓜ Gran Vía

The stylish shop of this inventive Spanish designer has a grand chandelier and gorgeous winding staircase, and there's classy evening wear with nods to classic style throughout. There's another branch (Map pp250–1; ☎ 91 523 39 38; Calle de Fuencarral 5) where utterly modern, colourful and cool designs dominate.

ANTIGUA CASA TALAVERA

Map pp250-1   Ceramics

☎ 91 547 34 17; Calle de Isabel la Católica 2; ☽ 10am-1.30pm & 5-8pm Mon-Fri, 10am-1.30pm Sat; Ⓜ Santo Domingo

The extraordinary tiled façade of this wonderful old shop conceals an Aladdin's Cave of ceramics from all over Spain. This is not the mass-produced stuff aimed at a tourist market, but comes from the small family potters of Andalucía and Toledo, ranging from the decorative (tiles) to the useful (plates, jugs and other kitchen items). The old couple who run the place are delightful.

CASA DE DIEGO

Map pp254-5   Accessories

☎ 91 522 66 43; www.casadediego.com; Plaza de la Puerta del Sol 12; ☽ 9.30am-8pm Mon-Sat; ☎ Sol

This classic shop has been around since 1858, selling and repairing Spanish fans, shawls, umbrellas and canes. Service is old style and occasionally grumpy, but the fans are works of antique art.

CASA DEL LIBRO

Map pp254-5   Books

☎ 91 524 19 00; Gran Vía 29; ☽ 9.30am-9.30pm Mon-Sat, 11am-9pm Sun; Ⓜ Gran Vía

Spain's answer to Barnes & Noble, this sprawling mega-bookshop has titles on just about any topic you can think of. There's a large English and foreign-language literature section on the ground floor at the back, and nonfiction books in English are elsewhere mixed alongside Spanish titles.

CASA HERNANZ

Map pp254-5   Shoes

☎ 91 366 54 50; Calle de Toledo 18; ☽ 9am-1.30pm & 4.30-8pm Mon-Fri, 10am-2pm Sat; ☎ La Latina or Sol

The comfy, rope-soled *alpargatas,* Spain's traditional footwear, are worn by everyone from the King of Spain to the Pope, and you can buy your own pair at this humble workshop; you can even get them made to order.

CONVENTO DEL CORPUS CRISTI (LAS CARBONERAS)

Map pp254-5   Food & Drink

Plaza del Conde de Miranda 3; ☽ 9.30am-1pm & 4-6.30pm Mon-Sat, 11am-1pm & 4-6.30pm Sun; Ⓜ Ópera, La Latina or Sol

If you're after heavenly cookies and sweets, there's no substitute for the nuns of the Convento del Corpus Cristi, a closed order that makes and sells moist, rich pastries made with almonds and egg yolks. To the right of the convent's main entrance is a small door with a call button. Ring the nuns, and they'll let you into a small, dark room with a rotating countertop so that the nuns never see their customers.

EL ARCO ARTESANÍA

Map pp254-5   Designer Souvenirs

☎ 91 365 26 80; www.elarcoartesania.com; Plaza Mayor 9; ☽ 11am-9pm Mon-Sat; Ⓜ Sol or La Latina

This superstylish shop in the southwestern corner of Plaza Mayor sells an outstanding array of homemade designer souvenirs, from stone and glasswork to jewellery and home fittings. The papier mâché figures are gorgeous, but there's so much else here to turn your head.

EL CORTE INGLÉS

Map pp254-5   Department & Convenience Stores

☎ 91 418 88 00; www.elcorteingles.es; Calle de Preciados 3; ☽ 10am-10pm Mon-Sat; Ⓜ Sol

In the great tradition of department stores the world over, there's everything you need here from food and furniture to clothes, appliances, toiletries, electronics, books and music. Although you'll pay extra for the convenience of one-stop shopping, the after-sales service is better than most. Branches are scattered throughout the city.

EL FLAMENCO VIVE Map pp254-5   Music
☎ 91 547 39 17; Calle Conde de Lemos 7;
🕙 10.30am-2pm & 5-9pm Mon-Sat; Ⓜ Ópera
This temple to flamenco has it all, from guitars and songbooks to CDs, polka-dotted dancing costumes, shoes, colourful plastic jewellery and literature about flamenco. The knowledgeable staff can also point you in the direction of Madrid's best flamenco *tablaos* (small-stage theatres that usually double as restaurants) as well.

FLIP Map pp254-5   Fashion, Clothes & Accessories
☎ 91 366 44 72; Calle Mayor 19;
🕙 10.30am-9pm Mon-Sat; Ⓜ Sol
Too cool for its own good, Flip is funky and edgy with its designer T-shirts and G-Star jeans, as well as a groovy and often offbeat collection of belts, caps and bags. Staff are as hip as the clothing and always ready with advice. The changing rooms, however, require a contortionist's flexibility.

FNAC Map pp254-5   Books & Music
☎ 91 595 61 00; Calle de Preciados 28; 🕙 10am-9.30pm Mon-Sat, noon-9.30pm Sun; Ⓜ Callao
This four-storey megastore has a terrific range of CDs, DVDs, electronics and books; English-language books are on the 3rd floor. There's also a news kiosk downstairs with a good range of magazines.

JOSÉ RAMÍREZ Map pp254-5   Music
☎ 91 531 42 29; Calle de la Paz 8;
🕙 10am-2pm & 4.30-8pm; Ⓜ Sol
José Ramírez is widely considered to be one of Spain's best guitar makers and his guitars have been strummed by a host of flamenco greats and international musicians (even the Beatles). In the back of this small shop is a little museum with guitars dating back to 1830.

JUSTO ALGABA Map pp254-5   Specialist Store
☎ 91 523 35 95; Calle de la Paz 4; 🕙 10am-2pm & 5-8pm Mon-Fri, 10am-2pm Sat; Ⓜ Sol
Always wanted to be a torero but just didn't have a thing to wear? This is where Madrid's toreros come to have their *traje de luces* (suit of lights, the traditional glittering bullfighting suit) made in all their intricate

---

<table>
<tr><td>

TOP PLACES FOR QUALITY SPANISH GIFTS

Tired of bull postcards and tacky flamenco posters? Convinced that your discerning friends back home have taste that extends beyond a polka-dot flamenco dress? That's fine, you just need to know where to look.

- Antigua Casa Talavera (p157)
- Antigüedades Hom (p166)
- El Arco Artesanía (p157)
- Gil (p160)
- México (p161)

</td></tr>
</table>

---

excess. A custom-made suit starts at €2500 while the sexy pink tights are a steal at €50.

LA LIBRERÍA Map pp254-5   Books
☎ 91 541 71 70; Calle Mayor 80; 🕙 10am-2pm & 4.30-8pm Mon-Fri, 11am-2pm Sat; Ⓜ Ópera or Sol
This bookshop may be small, but it's the place to find books (almost all in Spanish) covering everything to do with Madrid, from coffee-table books to histories of every barrio in the capital.

PETRA'S INTERNATIONAL BOOKSHOP
Map pp254-5   Books
☎ 91 541 72 91; Calle de Campomanes 13;
🕙 11am-9pm Mon-Sat; Ⓜ Ópera or Santo Domingo
A wonderful little bookshop (with mostly second-hand stock), Petra's has a great selection in all major languages and across most major genres; it's also something of a meeting place for the lively expat community. The friendly owners can point you in the direction of activities in English and other languages. We also like a bookshop with a cat – Safi is its name.

SALVADOR BACHILLER
Map pp250-1   Fashion & Accessories
☎ 91 559 83 21; Gran Vía 65; 🕙 10am-9pm Mon-Thu, 10am-9.30pm Fri & Sat; Ⓜ Plaza de España or Santo Domingo
The stylish and high-quality leather bags, wallets, suitcases and other accessories of Salvador Bachiller are a staple of Spanish shopping aficionados. This is leather with a typically Spanish twist – the colours are dazzling in bright pinks, yellows and greens. Sound garish? You'll change your mind once you step inside.

LA LATINA & LAVAPIÉS

Shopping in La Latina is all about the quirky – from designer boutiques in the most unlikely little streets to curio shops so specialised that you wonder how they ever keep going. The immigrant population of Lavapiés has fostered a fascinating mix of ethnic shops (Asian food markets, Muslim meat shops and stores selling gifts imported from China) and the barrio's working-class origins are reflected in the cheap clothing shops that line many streets. It all meets in El Rastro.

CERERÍA ORTEGA
Map pp254-5   Antiques & Crafts
☎ 91 365 60 19; Calle de Toledo 43; ⏰ 9am-1.30pm & 5-8pm Mon-Fri; Ⓜ La Latina
You probably wouldn't give this place a second look from the outside, but it's a wonderful family-run business where the

Ortegas have been making old-fashioned wax candles since 1893. The dimly lit little shop smells of warm wax, and you can see the artisan candlemakers hard at work.

DEL HIERRO Map pp254-5   Fashion & Accessories
☎ 91 364 58 91; Calle de la Cava Baja 6; ⏰ 11am-2pm & 5-9pm Mon-Sat, 1-3pm Sun; Ⓜ La Latina or Tirso de Molina
If you're looking for a handbag that captures the essence of chic, modern Spain, then this small boutique has an exceptional selection from designers such as Iñaki Sampedro, Quique Mestre and Carlos de Caz. The look is sophisticated but colourful.

EL RASTRO Map pp254-5   Market
Calle de la Ribera de Curtidores; ⏰ 8am-2pm Sun; Ⓜ La Latina, Puerta de Toledo or Tirso de Molina
A Sunday morning at El Rastro is a Madrid institution. You could easily spend an entire morning inching your way down the Calle

EL RASTRO & THE FLEA MARKETS OF MADRID

Flea Markets, fresh markets, crafts markets…bargain hunters will have a field day in Madrid. The city's biggest and best-known market is **El Rastro** (above), a thriving mass of vendors, buyers, pickpockets and the generally curious. This classic flea market, open on Sunday mornings only, has been an open-air market for half a millennium and is considered the largest in Europe.

The madness begins at the Plaza de Cascorro, near La Latina metro stop, and worms its way downhill along the Calle de la Ribera de Curtidores and the streets off it. The shopping starts at about 8am and lasts until 2pm or 3pm, but for many Madrileños the best of El Rastro comes after the stalls have shut and everyone crowds into nearby bars for an *aperitivo* (appetizer) of vermouth and tapas. In fine weather, El Rastro Madrileños seem loath to return home and either bar-hop until sated or head for the Plaza de San Andrés where a light-hearted bohemian crowd fills the area with bongo music and dancing, or to the **Parque del Buen Retiro**. For advice on following in the Sunday footsteps of locals, turn to p107.

Apart from El Rastro, other curious local markets include the following:

Art Market (Plaza Conde de Barajas; ⏰ 10am-2pm Sun; Ⓜ Sol) Local art and prints of the greats.

Cuesta de Moyano Bookstalls (Map p257; Calle Claudio Moyano; ⏰ 9am-dusk Mon-Sat, 9am-2pm Sun; Ⓜ Atocha) Second-hand and new books in many languages.

Mercadillo Marqués de Viana (El Rastrillo; Map p245; Calle del Marqués de Viana; ⏰ 9am-2pm Sun; Ⓜ Tetuán) A calmer version of El Rastro in northern Madrid.

Mercado de Monedas y Sellos (Plaza Mayor; ⏰ 9am-2pm Sun; Ⓜ Sol) Old coins and stamps.

de la Ribera de Curtidos and through the maze of streets that hosts the Rastro flea market every Sunday morning. Cheap clothes, luggage, antiques, old photos of Madrid, old flamenco records, faux designer purses, grungy T-shirts, household goods and electronics are the main fare, but for every 10 pieces of junk, there's a real gem waiting to be found.

A word of warning: pickpockets love El Rastro as much as everyone else, so keep a tight hold on your belongings and don't keep valuables in easy-to-reach pockets.

HELENA ROHNER

Map pp254-5   Fashion & Jewellery

☎ 91 365 79 06; www.helenarohner.com; Calle de Almendro 4; ⏰ 9am-6pm Mon-Fri; Ⓜ La Latina or Tirso de Molina

One of Europe's most creative jewellery designers, Helena Rohner has a spacious and chic boutique in La Latina. Working with silver, stone and Murano glass, her work is inventive and a regular feature of Paris fashion shows.

LA LIBRERÍA DE LAVAPIÉS

Map pp254-5   Books

☎ 91 527 89 92; Calle de Argumosa 39; ⏰ 10am-10pm; Ⓜ Lavapiés or Atocha

If you value personal service, a community feel and the sort of cosy ambience that lends itself to browsing, this alternative bookshop is perfect. There's a carefully chosen English section as well as contemporary literature, the arts and books for families and children. They also do special orders.

HUERTAS & ATOCHA

You don't come to Huertas just for the shopping but it's a fun area to browse as you move from bar to restaurant or as you make your way down towards the Paseo del Prado.

CASA MIRA Map pp254-5   Food & Drink

☎ 91 429 88 95; Carrera de San Jerónimo 30; ⏰ 10am-2pm & 5-9pm Mon-Sat; Ⓜ Sevilla

The revolving, wedding cake–like display in the window is laden with sweets, cakes, fat pastries and candied fruits. It's all freshly baked or sugared on site and the shop is especially known for its *turrónes* (fudge-like Christmas candy).

FLAMENCO WORLD Map pp254-5   Music

☎ 91 360 08 65; www.flamenco-world.com; Calle de las Huertas 62; ⏰ 11.30am-2.30pm & 5-8.30pm Mon-Fri, 9.30am-1.30pm Sat; Ⓜ Antón Martín

For a terrific range of flamenco CDs and other flamenco-related items, this is one of the better shops in Madrid for immersing yourself in this intriguing sub-culture. The staff is knowledgeable and can help track down hard-to-find CDs.

GIL Map pp254-5   Jewellery, Perfume & Accessories

☎ 91 521 25 49; Carrera de San Jerónimo 2; ⏰ 9.30am-1.30pm & 4.30-8pm Mon-Fri, 9.30am-1.30pm Sat; Ⓜ Sol

You don't see them much these days, but the exquisite fringed and embroidered *mantones* and *mantoncillos* (traditional Spanish shawls worn by women on grand occasions) and delicate *mantillas* (Spanish veils) are

---

TOP SHOPS FOR CHILDREN

- Stunning handmade children's dolls, all beautifully attired, are proffered at **Así** (Map pp250–1; ☎ 91 548 28 28; Gran Vía 47; ⏰ 10am-8.30pm Mon-Sat; Ⓜ Santo Domingo or Callao). There are also intricate dolls' houses, where every single item (eg furniture, saucepans etc) can be purchased individually.

- This is a wonderfully personal toy shop with creative toys, books and games; they treat kids respectfully at **Imaginarium** (Map p252; ☎ 91 781 33 37; Calle de Claudio Coello 45; ⏰ 10am-8.30pm Mon-Sat; Ⓜ Serrano), with separate entrances for kids and adults.

- Classy children's clothes artfully fill **Mellymello** (Map p252; ☎ 91 431 23 66; Calle de Claudio Coello 97; ⏰ 10.30am-2.30pm & 4.30-8.30pm Mon-Sat; Ⓜ Núñez de Balboa). It's designer Salamanca wear for kids.

- Although a small shop (or maybe because of it), **Los Bebés de Chamberí** (Map pp250–1; ☎ 91 535 13 25; Calle de Gonzalo de Córdoba 7; ⏰ 10am-2pm & 5-8.30pm Tue-Fri, 11am-3pm Sat, 5-8.30pm Mon; Ⓜ Quevedo or Bilbao) highlights that wonderful individuality of Spanish children's clothes; you'll leave laden with bags for your own kids and for friends back home.

- If you're running out of books for the kids, you'll find a fine range in English and Spanish at **Biblioketa** (Map pp250–1; ☎ 91 391 00 99; Calle de Justiniano 4; ⏰ 10.30am-8pm Mon-Sat; Ⓜ Alonso Martínez).

stunning and uniquely Spanish gifts. Inside this dark shop, dating back to 1880, the sales clerks still wait behind a long counter to attend to you; it's like another age.

MARÍA CABELLO Map pp254-5   Food & Drink
☎ 91 429 60 88; Calle de Echegaray 19;
🕑 9.30am-3pm & 5.30-9pm Mon-Fri, 9.30am-3pm & 6-9.30pm Sat; Ⓜ Sol or Antón Martín
You just don't find wine stores like this any more – family-run, friendly, with knowledge-able staff, and still decorated in the original 1913 style with wooden shelves and even a ceiling fresco. There are fine wines in abundance (mostly Spanish, and a few foreign bottles) with some 500 labels on show or tucked away out the back.

MÉXICO Map pp254-5   Specialist Store
☎ 91 429 94 76; Calle de las Huertas 20;
🕑 9am-2pm & 5-8pm Mon-Fri, 9am-2pm Sat; Ⓜ Tirso de Molina, Antón Martín or Sol
A treasure chest of original old maps, this is a great place to find a unique souvenir of Spain. Some 160 folders hold antique, original maps of Madrid, Spain and the rest of the world. These are all originals or antique copies, not modern reprints, so prices range from a few hundred to thousands of euros.

SALAMANCA
Salamanca is Madrid's designer central, home to the richest concentrations of exclusive boutiques anywhere in Spain. Shopping here is a social event where people put on their finest just to go into the shops and where asking the price is not really the done thing. Service is often impeccable, if a little stuffy at times, but the fashions range from classically elegant to cool and cutting edge. Above all, this is the barrio to take the pulse of Spanish fashion and you're likely to find it in rude health. Throw in a sprinkling of stores for children, gourmet foods and designer home-wares and you could easily spend days doing nothing else but shopping.

AGATHA RUIZ DE LA PRADA
Map p252   Fashion, Clothes & Shoes
☎ 91 319 05 01; Calle de Serrano 27;
🕑 10am-8.30pm Mon-Sat; Ⓜ Serrano
This boutique has to be seen to be believed with pinks, yellows and oranges every-

where you turn. It's fun and exuberant, but it's not just for kids. It also has serious and highly original fashion; Agatha Ruiz de la Prada is one of the enduring icons of Madrid's 1980s outpouring of creativity known as *la movida Madrileña* (see boxed text, p54).

AMAYA ARZUAGA
Map p252   Fashion, Clothes & Shoes
☎ 91 426 28 15; Calle de Lagasca 50;
🕑 10.30am-8.30pm Mon-Sat; Ⓜ Velázquez
Amaya Arzuaga is one of Spain's top designers, with sexy, bold options. She loves mixing black with bright colours (one season it's 1980s fuchsia and turquoise, the next it's orange or red) and has earned a reputation as one of the most creative designers in Spain today.

ARMAND BASI
Map p252   Fashion, Clothes & Shoes
☎ 91 577 79 93; Calle de Claudio Coello 52;
🕑 10am-8.30pm Mon-Sat; Ⓜ Serrano
With hip, urban designs for men and women, this is the place to go when you want to look fashionable but carelessly casual; the fashion from here is ideal for a night out in the city's bars, especially in Chueca.

BOMBONERÍA SANTA
Map p252   Food & Drink
☎ 91 576 86 46; Calle de Serrano 56;
🕑 10am-3pm & 3.30-8.30pm Mon-Sat; Ⓜ Serrano
If your sense of style is every bit as refined as your palate, the exquisite chocolates in this tiny shop are guaranteed to satisfy. The packaging is every bit as pretty as the bonbons that fill them, but they don't come cheap – a large box will cost you at least €120!

CAMPER Map p252   Fashion, Shoes
☎ 91 578 25 60; www.camper.es; Calle de Serrano 24; 🕑 9.30am-8.30pm Mon-Fri, 9.30am-9pm Sat; Ⓜ Serrano
Spanish fashion is not all *haute couture* and this world-famous cool and quirky shoe brand from Mallorca has shops all over Madrid. The designs are bowling-shoe chic with colourful, fun designs that are all about comfort. There are other outlets throughout the city.

Shopping
SALAMANCA

CLOTHING SIZES

Measurements approximate only, try before you buy

Women's Clothing

Aus/UK	8	10	12	14	16	18
Europe	36	38	40	42	44	46
Japan	5	7	9	11	13	15
USA	6	8	10	12	14	16

Women's Shoes

Aus/USA	5	6	7	8	9	10
Europe	35	36	37	38	39	40
France only	35	36	38	39	40	42
Japan	22	23	24	25	26	27
UK	3½	4½	5½	6½	7½	8½

Men's Clothing

Aus	92	96	100	104	108	112
Europe	46	48	50	52	54	56
Japan	S		M	M		L
UK/USA	35	36	37	38	39	40

Men's Shirts (Collar Sizes)

Aus/Japan	38	39	40	41	42	43
Europe	38	39	40	41	42	43
UK/USA	15	15½	16	16½	17	17½

Men's Shoes

Aus/UK	7	8	9	10	11	12
Europe	41	42	43	44½	46	47
Japan	26	27	27½	28	29	30
USA	7½	8½	9½	10½	11½	12½

Designer fashions at Sybilla (p164)

DE VIAJE Map p252　　Books & Travel
☎ 91 577 98 99; Calle de Serrano 41; ☾ 10am-8pm
Mon-Fri, 10.30am-2.30pm & 5-8pm Sat; Ⓜ Serrano
Whether you're after a guidebook, coffee-table tome or travel literature, De Viaje probably has it. Covering every region of the world, they have mostly Spanish titles, but plenty in English as well. Staff are knowledgeable and friendly, and there's also a travel agency, a travel gear section and occasionally exhibitions of travel photos.

HABITAT Map p252　　Design, Homewares & Gifts
☎ 91 181 26 00; www.habitat.net; Calle de
Hermosilla 18; ☾ 10.30am-8.30pm Mon-Sat;
Ⓜ Serrano
If you live in Madrid but your heart's in Soho, then Habitat has the kinds of clean-lined couches, lamps and bedspreads you'll love, with a preppy, colourful twist. Prices are more reasonable than you might expect.

LAVINIA Map p252　　Food & Drink
☎ 91 426 06 04; Calle de José Ortega y Gasset 16;
☾ 10am-9pm; Ⓜ Núñez de Balboa
Although we love the intimacy of old-style Spanish wine shops, they can't match the selection of Spanish and international wines that are found at Lavinia, which has more than 4500 bottles to choose from. It also organises wine courses, wine tasting and excursions to nearby bodegas (wineries).

LOEWE Map p252　　Fashion, Clothes & Shoes
☎ 91 426 35 88; Calle de Serrano 34;
☾ 9.30am-8.30pm Mon-Sat; Ⓜ Serrano
One of the classiest (and most expensive) Spanish labels, Loewe is the place to go for fine leather handbags and shoes as well as elegant fashions that are never outrageous but always eye-catching.

MALLORCA Map p252　　Food & Drink
☎ 91 577 18 59; Calle de Serrano 6;
☾ 9.30am-9pm; Ⓜ Retiro
It may not have the old-world charm of many *pastelerías* (patisseries) across town (see boxed text p129), but this Madrid institution has magnificent cakes, pastries and cookies. You can also get takeaway gourmet dishes perfect for a picnic lunch or when surprise dinner guests come round. There are branches throughout the city.

MANOLO BLAHNIK Map p252　Fashion & Shoes
☎ 91 575 96 48; Calle de Serrano 58; ☾ 10am-2pm
& 4.30-8.30pm Mon-Sat; Ⓜ Serrano
If you're going to the Oscars, you must make a trip to this world-renowned designer from Spain's Canary Islands. He's a shoemaker to many Hollywood stars, and his Madrid showroom is exclusive – each shoe is displayed like a work of art. The shoes are bright and oh-so-classy.

THE LATEST DESIGNS IN SALAMANCA

The world's most exclusive international designers occupy what is known as *la milla del oro* (the golden mile) along **Calle de José Ortega y Gasset** (Map p252), especially close to the corner with Calle de Serrano.

In addition to the innovative and established Spanish designers covered in this chapter, other top and emerging names include the following.

Alma Aguilar (Map p252; ☎ 91 577 66 96; Callejón de Jorge Juan 12; ☽ 10am-2pm & 5-8pm Mon-Sat; Ⓜ Serrano) Classy Madrid designs; great for stylish formal wear.

Ángel Schlesser (Map p252; ☎ 91 575 55 74; Calle de Don Ramón de la Cruz 2; ☽ 10am-8pm Mon-Sat; Ⓜ Serrano) Latest catwalk fashions with subtler colours than most.

David Elfin (Map p252; ☎ 91 700 04 53; www.davidelfin.com; Calle de Jorge Juan 31; ☽ 10-am-2pm & 5-8pm Mon-Sat; Ⓜ Velázquez) Casual upmarket fashions with a rebellious spirit.

Farrutx (Map p252; ☎ 91 577 09 24; Calle de Serrano 7; ☽ 10am-2pm & 5-8pm Mon-Sat; Ⓜ Retiro or Serrano) Mallorca-based and one of Spain's top shoe brands.

Josep Font (Map pp246–7; ☎ 91 575 97 16; www.josepfont.com; Calle de Don Ramón de la Cruz 51; ☽ 10am-2pm & 5-8pm Mon-Sat; Ⓜ Núñez de Balboa) Artsy and refined women's fashion.

MO by María Roca (Map p252; ☎ 91 577 88 04; Calle del Conde de Aranda 10; ☽ 10.30am-8pm Mon-Sat; Ⓜ Retiro) Wonderful boutique with handbags, jewellery and other accessories.

Tous & Tous (Map p252; ☎ 91 575 51 71; Calle de Claudio Coello 65; Ⓜ Serrano) Trendy jewellery by Rosa Tous; no Spanish *pija* (a cross between a yuppie and a snob) could do without.

MANTEQUERÍA BRAVO
Map p252   Food & Drink
☎ 91 576 76 41; Calle de Ayala 24; ☽ 9.30am-2.30pm & 5.30-8.30pm Mon-Fri, 9.30am-2.30pm Sat; Ⓜ Serrano

Behind the attractive old façade lies a connoisseur's paradise, filled as it is with local cheeses, sausages, wines and coffees. The products here are great for a gift, but everything is so good that you won't want to share.

PURIFICACIÓN GARCÍA
Map p252   Fashion, Clothes & Shoes
☎ 91 576 72 76; Calle de Serrano 92; ☽ 10am-8.30pm Mon-Sat; Ⓜ Serrano

One of the most successful Spanish designers who always comes up with the goods, Puri offers elegant, mature designs for men and women with variety that is as at home in the workplace as at a wedding.

ROBERTO TORRETTA
Map p252   Fashion & Clothing
☎ 91 435 79 89; Callejón de Jorge Juan 14; ☽ 10.30am-2pm & 5-8.30pm Mon-Fri, 11am-2pm & 5-8.30pm Sat; Ⓜ Serrano

Romantic-yet-practical design is Roberto Torretta's trademark. His elegant evening op-tions are sophisticated in a flashy sort of way, while his broad selection of workwear has a more quietly classic style. In a country where people favour a combination of casual and formal wardrobes, it's a perfect mix.

ROBERTO VERINO
Map p252   Fashion, Clothes & Shoes
☎ 91 426 04 75; Calle Serrano 33; ☽ 10am-9pm Mon-Sat; Ⓜ Serrano

You'll find simple, classy designs for men and women in the shop of this Spanish de-signer whose popularity is shared equally between the critics and the ordinary fash-ion-seeker. There are great men's suits, and his casual wear is as clean-lined and sophis-ticated as you'll find anywhere.

SARA NAVARRO
Map p252   Fashion & Shoes
☎ 91 576 23 24; www.saranavarro.com; Calle de Jorge Juan 22; ☽ 10.30am-8.30pm Mon-Sat; Ⓜ Velázquez

Spanish women love their shoes and, per-haps above all, they love Sara Navarro. This designer seems to understand that you'll buy expensive shoes like these only rarely – so why not make each into a perfect work of art? The shop is a temple to good taste, with fine bags, belts and other accessories as well.

Shopping   SALAMANCA

SYBILLA Map p252 Fashion & Clothing

☎ 91 578 13 22; Callejón de Jorge Juan 12;
🕑 10.30am-8.30pm Mon-Sat; Ⓜ Serrano

One of the more original Spanish designers to combine local and international styles, Sybilla has the usual strong, Spanish colours, but they're rarely combined, making for deceptively simple pieces with stylish cuts that stand out in the crowd. She also does wedding dresses and some Japanese-inspired homeware.

MALASAÑA & CHUECA

Chueca is to funky-and-alternative what Salamanca is to designer exclusivity, as one look around Calle de Fuencarral or Calle de Hortaleza will quickly tell you. On the fringe of Madrid's flamboyant gay scene and the shopping area of choice for the cool clubbers of the capital, you'll find down-market designer clothes that will boost your street cred, all the while surrounded by a crowd that can be as entertaining as a night out. Staff in these designer shops won't look down their nose at you no matter what you wear – here, they've seen it all before.

As you fan out across Chueca and, to a lesser extent, Malasaña, you'll also come across leather of the kinky and refined variety, gay book shops and gourmet food stores, not to mention more designer wear in the east of Chueca around Calle de Piamonte. In short, there's something for everyone, which is Chueca in a nutshell.

CACAO SAMPAKA Map pp250-1 Food & Drink

☎ 91 521 56 55; Calle de Orellana 4; meal €9.50-12.50; 🕑 10am-9pm Mon-Thu, 11am-9pm Fri & Sat; Ⓜ Alonso Martínez

If you thought chocolate was about fruit 'n' nut, think again. This gourmet chocolate shop is a chocoholic's dream-come-true, with more combinations to go with humble cocoa than you ever imagined possible. The attached café serves breakfast and great coffee, light lunches and cakes.

CUSTO BARCELONA

Map pp250-1 Fashion, Clothes & Shoes

☎ 91 360 46 36; www.custo-barcelona.com; Calle de Fuencarral 29; 🕑 10am-9pm Mon-Sat; Ⓜ Gran Vía

The chic shop of Barcelona designer Custo Dalmau wears its Calle de Fuencarral address well, because the now-iconic T-shirts are at once edgy and awash in attitude, and artfully displayed. You'll find funky bags and shoes alongside the clothing for men and women. It's not to everyone's taste, but always worth a look. Other branches in Madrid include one on Calle Mayor 37 (☎ 91 354 00 99).

DIVINA PROVIDENCIA

Map pp250-1 Fashion, Clothes & Shoes

☎ 91 522 02 65; Calle de Fuencarral 45; 🕑 11am-9pm Mon-Sat; Ⓜ Gran Vía or Tribunal

Divina Providencia has moved seamlessly from offbeat new face on the Madrid fashion scene to almost mainstream stylish, creating fun clothes for women, with strong retro and Asian influences. The label is such a hit that its clothes are regularly seen in major Spanish TV series.

FUN & BASICS

Map pp250-1 Handbags & Accessories

☎ 91 523 36 91; Calle de Fuencarral 43;
🕑 10.30am-9pm Mon-Sat; Ⓜ Tribunal or Gran Vía

For a small but stylish selection of (mostly leather) handbags and other accessories, try Fun & Basics; it is frequented by Madrileñas who know quality when they see it. Despite the shop's name, it's fairly pricey but style is the key concept here.

HESPEN & SUÁREZ

Map pp250-1 Food & Drink

☎ 91 445 39 03; www.hespenysuarez.com; Calle de Barceló 15; 🕑 8.30am-10pm Mon-Fri, 10am-10pm Sat & Sun; Ⓜ Bilbao or Alonso Martínez

If you're spending any time in Madrid and plan to be cooking while here, this lovely little gourmet supermarket has Chinese noodles, coconut milk, curry powders, freshly made dips and other exotica that can be hard to find in Spanish supermarkets. It also does small-scale catering and bake up some mean cookies.

LA JUGUETERÍA Map pp250-1 Sex Shop

☎ 91 308 72 69; Travesía de San Mateo 12; 🕑 noon-3pm & 5-10pm Mon-Sat; Ⓜ Alonso Martínez

We don't normally include sex shops in our guides but this softly lit one tickled our fancy (so to speak). Home to sultry staff and carefully chosen feathers and erotic toys, there's nothing brown-paper-bag and men-in-anoraks about this place; you won't feel guilty entering. It's very Chueca.

CALLE DE PIAMONTE & AROUND

Salamanca may have the market cornered when it comes to designer fashion, but **Calle de Piamonte** (Map pp250–1; Ⓜ Chueca) is arguably the best street in Madrid for designer accessories. Start at **Piamonte** (Map pp250–1; ☎ 91 522 45 80; Calle de Piamonte 16; Ⓨ 10.30am-8.30pm Mon-Sat), one of the favourite shoe shops of Madrileñas looking for that special something. Next door, **Elsa** (Map pp250–1; ☎ 91 521 51 88; Calle de Piamonte 18; Ⓨ 11am-2pm & 5-8.30pm Mon-Sat) has beautiful, colourful jewellery, while the shoes at the small **Las Bailarinas** (Map pp250–1; ☎ 91 319 90 69; www.lasbailarinas.com; Calle de Piamonte 19; Ⓨ 11am-2pm & 5-8pm Mon-Sat) are popular with Spanish celebrities. French Connection and other stylishly casual lines are found at **Martel Kee** (Map pp250–1; ☎ 91 319 86 11; Calle de Piamonte 15; Ⓨ 11am-2pm & 5-8.30pm Mon-Sat), with more exclusive designer wear on sale at **Amore e Psique** (Map pp250–1; ☎ 91 319 46 29; Calle de Piamonte 17; Ⓨ 10.30am-2pm & 5-9pm Mon-Fri, 11am-2.30pm Sat). Hand-painted handbags and other accessories to die for are available just around the corner at **Iñaki Sampedro** (Map pp250–1; ☎ 91 319 45 65; Calle del Conde Xiquena 13; Ⓨ 10.30am-2pm & 5-8.30pm Mon-Sat), one of Spain's most innovative accessories designers.

MAISON BLANCHE

Map pp250-1   Food & Drink

☎ 91 522 82 17; Calle de Piamonte 10;
Ⓨ 10am-midnight Mon-Fri, 11am-1am Sat, noon-6pm Sun; Ⓜ Chueca
Just a few years ago, gourmet food shops like these were unheard of in Madrid, enabling too-cool-for-Madrid visitors from Barcelona to turn up their noses at the capital's more classic tastes. No more. A small but extremely tasteful selection of cookbooks, homemade pastas, wines and other delicacies are beautifully displayed, while the café is fast gaining a reputation among discerning food-lovers.

MERCADO FUENCARRAL

Map pp250-1   Shopping Centre

☎ 91 521 41 52; Calle de Fuencarral 45;
Ⓨ 11am-9pm Mon-Sat; Ⓜ Tribunal
Madrid's home of alternative club-cool is still going strong, with tightly-packed stores where what's on offer is so down-to-earth as to emerge stylish. This place revels in its reverse snobbery, and it's funky, grungy and filled to the rafters with torn T-shirts and more black leather and silver studs than you'll ever need.

PATRIMONIO COMUNAL OLIVERARO

Map pp250-1   Food & Drink

☎ 91 308 05 05; Calle de Mejía Lequerica 1;
Ⓨ 10am-2pm & 5-8pm Mon-Fri, 10am-2pm Sat;
Ⓜ Alonso Martínez
Spain is the world's largest producer of olive oils and some of the best available in the country are to be found here. Those from Andalucía have the best reputation,

but for a wide sample try the box of 10 mini bottles for just €8.

RESERVA & CATA Map pp250-1   Food & Drink

☎ 902 366 590; Calle del Conde de Xiquena 13;
Ⓨ 5-9pm Mon, 11am-3pm & 5-9pm Tue-Fri, 11am-3pm Sat; Ⓜ Colón or Chueca
In these days of one-stop megastores, it's comforting to know that an old way of doing things persists. This old-style wine shop stocks an excellent range of Spanish wines and the knowledgeable staff can help you pick out a great one for your next dinner party.

CHAMBERÍ & ARGÜELLES

One of Madrid's trendiest barrios, Chamberí is dotted with great shops – although for designer gear it's not a patch on Salamanca and it doesn't have the quirks of Malasaña and Chueca. Calle de Fuencarral and the surrounding streets offer the richest pickings.

ALTAÏR Map pp246-7   Books

☎ 91 543 53 00; Calle de Gaztambide 31;
Ⓨ 10am-2pm & 4.30-8.30pm Mon-Fri, 10.30am-2.30pm & 4.30-8pm Sat; Ⓜ Argüelles
One of the best travel bookshops in Madrid, Altaïr has an exceptional range of books, maps and magazines covering Spain and every region of the world. Most are in Spanish, but there are loads of English-language titles, calendars and world-music CDs: Altaïr is also the Spanish distributors for Moleskine notebooks, once beloved of Hemingway and Chatwin, and now enjoying a revival.

TOP SHOPS FOR CASUAL FASHION

- Inventive **Adolfo Domínguez** (p157) produces colourful designs and a few upmarket lines.
- Comfortable and down-to-earth women's clothes for work or play are on offer at **Mango** (Map pp250–1; ☎ 91 523 04 12; www.mango.es; Calle de Fuencarral 70; Ⓜ Bilbao or Tribunal).
- From the Zara stable, **Massimo Dutti** (Map pp250–1; ☎ 91 593 82 68; www.massimodutti .com; Calle de Fuencarral 139; Ⓜ Quevedo) is a step up in elegance.
- Stylish and casual gear for men and women at extremely reasonable prices can be found at **Often** (Map pp254–5; ☎ 91 521 05 44; www .often.com; Calle de Carretas 5; Ⓜ Sol).
- With popular men's, women's and children's wear **Zara** (Map pp254–5; ☎ 91 521 12 83; www.zara.es; Gran Vía 34; Ⓜ Gran Vía) now also has a sideline in homewares.

ANTIGÜEDADES HOM

Map pp246-7   Antiques & Crafts

☎ 91 594 20 17; Calle de Juan de Austria 31; Ⓨ 5-8pm Mon-Fri; Ⓜ Iglesia

Specialising in antique Spanish fans, this tiny shop is a wonderful place to browse or to find a special gift, especially delicately painted fans and fans made with bone. It's open afternoons only because the owner spends the morning restoring the fans you see for sale.

CASA CARRIL Map pp250-1   Photography

☎ 91 447 05 12; Calle de Luchana 27; Ⓨ 9am-8pm Mon-Fri; Ⓜ Bilbao

You could go to any photography shop in Madrid for your camera needs, but why not go where the professionals go? This place has a knowledgeable staff that is as savvy with older cameras as it is with digital ones. They also develop photos and sell a range of other accessories.

DMR MARÍA RIVOLTA

Map pp250-1   Jewellery

☎ 91 448 02 57; Calle de Fuencarral 146; Ⓨ 10am-8.30pm Mon-Fri, 10am-2pm & 5-8.30pm Sat; Ⓜ Quevedo

It's practically impossible to walk out of this tiny jewellery boutique without

buying something. The speciality of this Argentine designer is colourful glass and enamel rings, necklaces and bracelets; and each piece is a reasonably priced work of art.

HARLEY DAVIDSON MADRID

Map pp246-7   Specialist Store

☎ 91 447 17 59; Calle del General Álvarez de Castro 26; Ⓨ 10am-2pm & 5-8pm Mon-Fri, 10am-2pm Sat; Ⓜ Canal

For the Harley fans who long to connect with like-minded motorcyclists in Madrid, this is the place to go. You can ooh and ah over the bikes on show, and you'll also find Harley jackets, T-shirts, pins and other must-have paraphernalia.

NATURA SI Map pp250-1   Food & Drink

☎ 91 544 56 63; Calle de Guzmán El Bueno 28; Ⓨ 10am-8.30pm Mon-Sat; Ⓜ Argüelles

A supermarket dedicated only to healthy foods? Yes, they do exist and this is Madrid's biggest and best.

OCHO Y MEDIO

Map pp250-1   Books

☎ 91 559 06 28; Calle de Martín de los Heros 11; Ⓨ 10am-2pm & 5-8.30pm Mon-Sat; Ⓜ Plaza de España

Close to some of the best foreign-language cinemas in Madrid, this is a terrific resource for film buffs with a range of books, posters, magazines and other memorabilia. Most is in Spanish but there's a smattering of English-language titles and the friendly staff knows its films.

PASAJES LIBRERÍA INTERNACIONAL

Map pp250-1   Books

☎ 91 310 12 45; www.pasajeslibros.com; Calle de Génova 3; Ⓨ 10am-8pm Mon-Fri, 10am-2pm Sat; Ⓜ Alonso Martínez

Definitely one of the best English-language bookshops in Madrid, Pasajes has an extensive English section (downstairs) which includes high-quality fiction (if it's a new release, it'll be the first bookshop in town to have it), history, Spanish subject matter, travel as well as a few literary magazines. There are also French, German, Italian and Portuguese books, and a useful noticeboard.

Shopping

CHAMBERÍ & ARGÜELLES

Sleeping ▮

Sleeping

Madrid's accommodation used to be – how shall we put it? – unexciting, but not any more. A wave of chic minimalism and cutting-edge interpretations of traditional architecture is sweeping the city, with new hotels taking their place alongside the simple *hostales* (hostels) and grand old Madrid hotels that were once the city's trademark.

Travellers on a tight budget haven't been left out of the revolution with some fine new *hostales* as well as many old favourites, where a touch of character elevates them above the rest. Unusually, apart from the dorms, you'll often find private bathrooms and TVs in the rooms.

Midrange accommodation is similarly diverse with *hotels con encanto* (hotels with charm, often housed in historic buildings) sharing the market with supremely stylish monuments to 21st-century fashions. Entirely devoid of stuffiness, hotels and *hostales* in this category enable you to feel pampered without the price tag.

Madrid's five-star hotels represent the ultimate in luxury, whether in stately palaces or in places that represent the height of innovation.

Accommodation prices in Madrid vary with the not-always-discernible seasons. In general, most midrange and some top-end places have separate price structures for *temporada alta* (high season), *temporada media* (midseason) or *temporada baja* (low season), all usually displayed on a notice in reception or close by, but there's little agreement among hoteliers about when the seasons actually begin and end. As such, accommodation prices in this book are a guide only and you should always check room charges before putting down your bags; and remember that prices can and do change with time. In the better places, booking ahead is always a good idea.

Virtually all accommodation prices are subject to 7% IVA (the Spanish version of value-added tax). This is often included in the quoted price at cheaper places, but less often at more expensive ones. To check, ask: *'¿Está incluido el IVA?'* ('Is IVA included?'). In some cases you will be charged the IVA only if you ask for a receipt.

Choosing where to stay in Madrid is not just about price. Each barrio has its own distinctive identity and where you decide to stay will play an important role in your experience of Madrid. To get an idea of where you're most likely to feel at home, read the 'Best of the Barrio' boxed texts which correspond to each of Madrid's neighbourhoods throughout this chapter.

One final thing: in Spain a *habitación doble* (double room) usually indicates a room with two single beds. Cuddly couples should request a *cama de matrimonio* – literally a marriage bed – which is usually a queen-sized bed.

SLEEPING PRICE CATEGORIES

Throughout this chapter, accommodation is listed according to barrio, then by price range, followed by alphabetical order. Each place is accompanied by one of the following symbols:

€	€15-64 a night
€€	€65-150 a night
€€€	over €150 a night

The Hotel Ritz (p175) exudes class

BOOK ACCOMMODATION ONLINE

For more accommodation reviews and recommendations by Lonely Planet authors, check out the online booking service at www.lonelyplanet.com. You'll find the true, insider lowdown on the best places to stay. Reviews are thorough and independent. Best of all, you can book online.

LOS AUSTRIAS, SOL & CENTRO

With a wealth of historical sites, accommodation across a range of budgets, and traditional taverns, restaurants and shops, this the area is probably where you'll spend the most time while in Madrid; it is, therefore, a good place to be based. It's also where all the world congregates and where old Madrid meets the new, meaning that it can be at once exhilarating and slightly seedy (especially along Calle de la Montera). For more information on the barrio, see p59.

HOSTAL ACAPULCO

Map pp254-5   Hostel €

☎ 91 531 1945; www.hostalacapulco.com; Calle de la Salud 13, 4th fl; s/d/tr/q €42/52/71/87; Ⓜ Gran Vía

This immaculate little *hostal* is a cut above many other hostels in Madrid, with marble floors, recently renovated bathrooms (with bathtubs!), double-glazed windows and comfortable beds. Street-facing rooms have balconies overlooking a sunny plaza and are flooded with natural light. The staff are also friendly and always more than happy to help you plan your day in Madrid.

HOSTAL LUIS XV Map pp254-5   Hostel €

☎ 91 522 13 50; www.hrluisxv.net in Spanish; Calle de la Montera 47, 8th fl; s/d/tr €42/55/70; Ⓜ Gran Vía

All-new everything makes this family-run place feel pricier than it is, as do the balconies outside every exterior room from where the views are superb (especially from the triple in room 820). You're so high up that noise is rarely a problem.

HOSTAL MACARENA

Map pp254-5   Hostel €

☎ 91 365 92 21; www.silserranos.com in Spanish; Cava de San Miguel 8; s/d €53/59; Ⓜ Sol

On one of the old, cobblestone streets that runs past the Plaza Mayor, this charming *hostal* is at once homely and loaded with impeccable, old-style charm. The rooms are nicely spacious and decorated in warm colours, with the occasional antique writing desk.

TOP PLACES TO SLEEP
- Cat's Hostel (p171)
- Petit Palace Posada del Peine (p171)
- Quo (p174)
- Hotel Meninas (p170)
- Hotel Puerta América (p178)

HOSTAL ORLY Map pp254-5   Hostel €

☎ 91 531 30 12; www.hostalorly.com; Calle de la Montera 47, 7th fl; s/d/tr €32/45/56; Ⓜ Gran Vía

The street-facing rooms in this *hostal*, set in a grand old 19th-century building, have fabulous views; room 11 is the best, with a circular balcony stretching around the corner of the building high above central Madrid. One curious feature is the friendly owner's propensity to point out what she sees as deficiencies in her *hostal*; we found none.

HOSTEL METROPOL Map pp254-5   Hostel €

☎ 91 521 29 35; www.metropolhostel.com; Calle de la Montera 47, 1st fl; s/d/tr €30/44/54; Ⓜ Gran Vía; 🖳

It's not that the rooms here are great; in fact, they're simple and don't have a whole lot of character. But young travellers congregate here for that special something that few hostels have – an attitude, a young vibe, a chilled ambience. You'll also find art exhibitions, plenty of tourist information, young staff that merge seamlessly with the travellers, a few comfy chairs, picnic lunches, a laundry and a hint of alternative, street-wise advice.

LOS AMIGOS BACKPACKERS HOSTEL

Map pp254-5   Hostel €

☎ 915 47 17 07; www.losamigoshostel.com; Calle de Campomanes 6, 4th fl; dm €16-17, d €45; Ⓜ Ópera; 🖳

If you arrive in Madrid keen for company, this could be the place for you – lots of students stay here, the staff are savvy (and speak English) and there are bright dorm-style rooms (with free lockers) that sleep from four to 12 people. A steady stream of repeat visitors is the best recommendation we can give. Los Amigos also recently opened another hostel a couple of blocks away, the equally excellent Los Amigos Sol Backpackers Hostel (Map pp254–5; ☎ 91 559 24 72; Calle de Arenal 26, 4th fl; dm €16-19; Ⓜ Ópera).

Sleeping

LOS AUSTRIAS, SOL & CENTRO

BEST OF THE BARRIO – LOS AUSTRIAS, SOL & CENTRO

- Sleep at **Hotel Meninas** (below), chic minimalism is at its best, with clean lines and colour schemes or **Petit Palace Posada del Peine** (opposite), a stunningly renovated hotel which captures the spirit of Los Austrias alongside the best of modern, sophisticated Madrid.
- Munch a *bocadillo de calamares* (bread roll stuffed with calamari) at **Cervecería Compano** (p115), a long-standing Madrid ritual.
- Sip a late afternoon beer or coffee in **Plaza Mayor** (p65), one of the most beautiful city squares in Europe.
- Watch the sunset from Jardines Cabo Naval, next to **Plaza de Oriente** (p65), one of Madrid's most elegant plazas where people-in-the-know gather as the sun goes down.
- Eat roast suckling pig or lamb as Hemingway did at **Restaurante Sobrino de Botín** (p115), the world's oldest restaurant.
- Get a dose of high culture with a *zarzuela*, a home-grown and popular opera/theatre pastiche, at the **Teatro de la Zarzuela** (p147).
- Merge with the cool late-night crowd of **La Viuda Negra** (p133) before dancing the night away at **Teatro Joy Eslava** (p139).
- Gorge on a late-night or early morning *churros y chocolate* (a deep-fried stick of plain pastry immersed in thick hot chocolate) at the **Chocolatería San Ginés** (p129) – where else in the world could you enjoy such indulgence at dawn?

ATENEO HOTEL Map pp254-5   Hotel €€
☎ 91 521 20 12; www.ateneohotel.com; Calle de la Montera 22; s/d from €80/100; Ⓜ Sol; 🖳
Rooms here are quiet and come with attractive parquet floors as well as private balconies that look onto the busy street below and down to the Puerta del Sol. There's ample floor space, Internet access for those here on business, and the bathrooms have designer fittings.

HOTEL II CASTILLAS Map pp254-5   Hotel €€
☎ 91 524 97 50; www.hoteldoscastillas.com; Calle de la Abada 7; s/d €87/103; Ⓜ Sol
This is one place where a little bit of inside knowledge makes all the difference. Ask for a corner room and you'll be rewarded with a light-filled room with plenty of hardwood floor space and three windows – outstanding for the price in the centre of Madrid. We love the heated towel rails.

HOTEL ANACO Map pp254-5   Hotel €€
☎ 91 522 46 04; www.anacohotel.com; Calle de las Tres Cruces 3; s/d/tr €78/97/131; Ⓜ Gran Vía
We like a place that spends its renovation dollars on the rooms rather than the lobby – the latter is of a tired, 1970s vintage but the rooms are decorated in neutral tones with touches of red, and include modern fixtures such as stainless-steel basins. It doesn't quite reach the fashionable heights of chic minimalism but it's not far off.

HOTEL CARLOS V Map pp254-5   Hotel €€
☎ 91 531 41 00; www.bestwestern.es/carlosv; Calle del Maestro Vitoria; s/d €90/112; Ⓜ Callao
A loyal following is drawn to this family-run hotel which has been plushly renovated in an old-fashioned style, right down to the suit of armour in the lobby. The rooms are fine, though more functional than filled with charm; those on the top floors have large balconies.

HOTEL MENINAS Map pp254-5   Hotel €€
☎ 91 541 28 05; www.hotelmeninas.com; Calle de Campomanes; s €89-110, d €120-180; Ⓜ Ópera; 🖳
Opened in 2005, this is the sort of place where an interior designer licked their lips and created a master work of understated, minimalist luxury. The colour scheme is blacks, whites and greys, with dark-wood floors and splashes of fuchsia and lime-green. Flat-screen TVs in every room, modern bathroom fittings, Internet access points, and even a laptop in some rooms, round out the clean lines and latest innovations.

HOTEL PLAZA MAYOR
Map pp254-5   Hotel €€
☎ 91 360 06 06; www.h-plazamayor.com; Calle de Atocha 2; s €59, d €79-130; Ⓜ Sol or Tirso de Molina
Sitting just across from the Plaza Mayor, here you'll find stylish décor, charming original elements of this 150-year-old building and extremely helpful staff. The rooms

are attractive, some with a light colour scheme and wrought-iron furniture. The attic rooms boast minimalist dark wood and designer lamps, and have lovely little terraces with wonderful rooftop views of central Madrid.

HOTEL PRECIADOS Map pp254-5   Hotel €€
☎ 91 454 44 00; www.preciadoshotel.com; Calle de Preciados 37; s €90, d €116-174; Ⓜ Santo Domingo or Callao; 🖳
This hotel has a classier feel than many of the other business options around town and it gets rave reviews for its service. Soft lighting, light shades and plentiful glass personalise the rooms and provide an intimate feel.

HOTEL SENATOR Map pp254-5   Hotel €€
☎ 91 531 41 51; www.playasenator.com; Gran Vía 21; s €75-120, d €85-140; Ⓜ Gran Vía; 🖳 🏊
One of central Madrid's prettiest façades conceals some of the most attractive rooms in the city centre. Unusually, only one room on each floor doesn't face onto the street and the views down Gran Vía from the corner rooms are brilliant. Rooms are sophisticated and come with armchairs, wi-fi access, music sound systems and reclinable beds.

MARIO ROOM MATE Map pp254-5   Hotel €€
☎ 91 548 85 48; www.room-matehoteles.com; Calle de Campomanes 4; s €77-99, d €114-149; Ⓜ Ópera; 🖳
Entering this swanky boutique hotel is like crossing the threshold of Madrid's latest nightclub – staff dressed all in black, black walls and swirls of red lighting in the lobby. Rooms are spacious, with high ceilings and simple furniture, light tones contrasting smoothly with muted colours and dark surfaces.

PETIT PALACE POSADA DEL PEINE
Map pp254-5   Hotel €€
☎ 91 523 81 51; www.hthoteles.com; Calle de Postas 17; d €100-120; Ⓜ Sol; 🖳
One of the best hotels to open in central Madrid in recent years, this outstanding hotel combines a splendid historic building, brilliant location – just 50m from the Plaza Mayor – and modern hi-tech rooms that are supremely comfortable. The bathrooms sparkle and the rooms themselves are beautifully appointed and spacious. Friendly, attentive service is another highlight.

PETIT PALACE LONDRES
Map pp254-5   Hotel €€€
☎ 915 31 41 05; www.hthoteles.com; Calle Galdo 2; s/d €145/174; Ⓜ Sol; 🖳
This former palace is the ideal Madrid address – right in the centre, but surrounded by traffic-free shopping streets with few bars to keep you awake at night. Rooms vary, but there are a few mainstays: modern black-and-white photos adorning the walls; light colour schemes; supercomfortable beds; parquet floors; and hi-tech bathrooms with hydromassage showers and modern fittings.

LA LATINA & LAVAPIÉS

Staying in Lavapiés extracts you from the well-beaten tourist track, and while there are few sites to see, it's all about immersing yourself in an area that could only be found in Madrid. For more information on the barrio, see p75.

CAT'S HOSTEL Map pp254-5   Hostel €
☎ 902 889 192, 91 369 28 07; www.catshostel .com; Calle de Cañizares 6; dm €16, d €18-20; Ⓜ Antón Martín; 🖳
Now here's something special. The internal courtyard is Madrid's finest – lavish Andalucian tilework, a fountain, a spectacular glass ceiling and stunning Islamic decoration, all surrounded on four sides by an open balcony. There's a softly lit and supercool basement bar with free Internet connections;

The exquisite internal courtyard at Cat's Hostel (above)

there's occasional live flamenco. The dorms and bathrooms are new and very clean.

MAD HOSTEL Map pp254-5   Hostel €
☎ 915 06 48 40; www.madhostel.com; Calle de Cabeza 24; per bed €15-17; Ⓜ Antón Martín; ▣
From the people who brought you Cat's Hostel, Mad Hostel is similarly filled with a buzzing vibe. The 1st-floor courtyard – with retractable roof – is a wonderful place to chill, while the four- to eight-bed rooms are smallish but new and clean. There's a small, rooftop gym equipped with state-of-the-art equipment.

HOTEL REYES CATÓLICOS
Map pp254-5   Hotel €€
☎ 91 365 86 00; www.hreyescatolicos.com; Calle del Ángel 18; s €89-99, d €99-116; Ⓜ Puerta de Toledo or La Latina
If you like to be far removed from the bustle of downtown Madrid but on the cusp of fascinating La Latina, this place is a good choice. While the rooms are simple and not the most stylish in town, they do have bright décor and lots of natural light, and they look out onto a quiet street or the grand Basilica de San Francisco.

HUERTAS & ATOCHA
Huertas is Madrid's beating heart: the whole area is in uproar from Friday afternoon until Sunday morning as Huertas parties to the clamorous soundtrack of a city that knows how to have a good time (if you want to sleep, ask for an interior room). Being so central also adds to the Huertas appeal as a Madrid base…as long as you don't plan on sleeping on Saturday night. For more information on the barrio, see p79.

HOSTAL SARDINERO Map pp254-5   Hostel €
☎ 91 429 57 56; fax 91 429 41 12; Calle del Prado 16, 3rd fl; s/d from €45/60; Ⓜ Sol or Antón Martín
More than the cheerful rooms (which have high ceilings, air-conditioning, a safe, hairdryers and renovated bathrooms) it's the friendly old couple who run this place that gives it its charm. They love it if you take the time to sit down for a chat – preferably in Spanish or French as the owners speak both.

CATALONIA MORATÍN
Map pp254-5   Hotel €€
☎ 91 369 71 71; www.hoteles-catalonia.es; Calle de Atocha 23; s/d from €90/100; Ⓜ Antón Martín
If you like your hotels to be former palaces, this could be for you. The public areas are exquisite – a palm-filled, light-drenched patio and a sweeping staircase guarded by marble lions – and the rooms boast rustic chic, with a simple, warm colour scheme, hardwood floors and balconies.

HARD ROCK HOTEL Map pp254-5   Hotel
☎ 91 531 45 00; www.hardrock.com; Plaza de Santa Ana 14; Ⓜ Sol or Antón Martín
At the time of research, the western end of Plaza de Santa Ana was being transformed into a stylish new hotel run by the people who brought you the iconic Hard Rock Cafés of the world. Although prices and other information are currently unavailable, expect it to be one of Madrid's most exciting new hotels.

HOSTAL PERSAL Map pp254-5   Hostel €€
☎ 91 369 46 43; www.hostalpersal.com; Plaza del Ángel 12; s/d/tr from €60/75/105; Ⓜ Sol or Antón Martín
Combining hotel quality with *hostal* warmth, Hostal Persal is a fine choice at the

top end of Huertas; you're close to so much that is good (but also noisy) about Madrid. Rooms don't come with much character, but they're well appointed.

HOTEL EL PRADO Map pp254-5   Hotel €€
☎ 91 369 02 34; www.pradohotel.com; Calle del Prado 11; s €76-98, d €98-118, ste €155-185; Ⓜ Antón Martín or Sevilla; ▣

This newly renovated hotel is one of Madrid's most welcoming and offers style and service beyond its modest three-star rating. There's a wine theme running throughout the spacious rooms which have parquet floors, light tones, and places to sit and write. The double-glazed windows are also important, especially if you're here on a weekend.

HOTEL INGLÉS Map pp254-5   Hotel €€
☎ 91 429 65 51; fax 91 420 24 23; Calle de Echegaray 8; s €70-80, d €100-120; Ⓜ Sol

In this age of slick new boutique hotels, you have to admire a place that sticks to an old way of doing things. That's not necessarily a good thing – the smoking receptionist, the dark and somewhat depressing interior double rooms. The 'superior' rooms are, however, like small apartments with newly renovated bathrooms awash with marble.

HOTEL LOPE DE VEGA
Map pp254-5   Hotel €€
☎ 91 360 00 11; www.krishoteles.com; Calle de Lope de Vega 49; s €120-140, d €140-180; Ⓜ Antón Martín

This good hotel wears its setting in the middle of the *barrio de las letras* (literature district) on its sleeve; the overarching theme is the life and times of Spanish writer Lope de Vega (1562–1635) and his contemporaries. Most of the stylish rooms, which are decorated in warm colours, have private terraces. It's just a pity that the service is less warm.

HOTEL MEDIODIA Map p257   Hotel €€
☎ 91 527 30 60; www.mediodiahotel; Plaza del Emperador Carlos V 8; s/d/tr €63/74/94; Ⓜ Atocha

Handy for Atocha station, this old hotel with a grand façade is trading on its reputation a little because the rooms, though large and fine, aren't exactly luxurious (the pressed-wood furniture looks like it could have been bought at a garage sale) and the service is patchy. The best rooms look onto the tranquil plaza behind the hotel.

HOTEL MIAU Map pp254-5   Hotel €€
☎ 91 369 71 20; www.hotelmiau.com; Calle del Príncipe 26; s/d incl breakfast €88/98; Ⓜ Sol or Antón Martín

If you want to be close to the nightlife of Huertas or you can't tear yourself away from the beautiful Plaza de Santa Ana, then Hotel Miau is your place. Light tones, splashes of colour and elegant modern art adorn the walls of the rooms, which are large and well-equipped. Bring ear plugs if sleep is something you value.

HOTEL PARIS Map pp254-5   Hotel €€
☎ 91 521 64 91; fax 91 531 01 88; Calle de Alcalá 2; s/d incl breakfast €70/90; Ⓜ Sol

It's impossible to be more central than this classic 140-year-old hotel overlooking the Puerta del Sol. Noise can be a bit of a problem, so consider one of the interior rooms (which look onto a pleasant, plant-filled

Sleeping

HUERTAS & ATOCHA

BEST OF THE BARRIO – HUERTAS & ATOCHA

- Sleep overlooking Plaza de Santa Ana at **Hotel Miau** (above).
- Take an old-style Turkish bath in the evocative surrounds of **Hammam Medina Mayrit** (p154) in order to prepare for (or recover from) your night of Madrid revelry.
- Dine exceptionally well amid the soothing classiness (without the price tag) at **La Finca de Susana** (p120) or sample the best of Basque at **Zerain** (p120).
- Spend an afternoon at an outdoor table in **Plaza de Santa Ana** (p82) soaking up Madrid café culture at its best.
- Head down the hill for an infusion of extraordinary modern art at the **Centro de Arte Reina Sofía** (p80).
- Shout *¡Olé!* to your heart's content at **Cardamomo** (p145), where the smoky, bar feel is how flamenco ought to be experienced, or get into the groove of **Café Central** (p149).
- Catch the never-say-sleep buzz of the barrio along **Calle de las Huertas** (Map pp254–5), but preface it with vermouth on tap at **Casa Alberto** (p134) or a sherry straight from the barrel at **La Venencia** (p135).

courtyard). Rooms are elegantly kitsch, the owners exude an old-style grace and a reasonable buffet breakfast is included in the room price.

HOTEL VICTORIA 4 Map pp254-5   Hotel €€
☎ 91 523 84 30; www.hotelvictoria4.com; Calle de Victoria 4; d incl breakfast €74-129; Ⓜ Sol
We like a place where you can feel yourself to be in an oasis of calm even as vast crowds pass by the front door. Central location, handy for some of Madrid's best nightlife and attractive rooms add up to a package that is outstanding value for the centre of a major European capital.

HOTEL URBAN Map pp254-5   Hotel €€€
☎ 91 787 77 70; www.derbyhotels.com; Carrera de San Jerónimo 34; d €160-320; Ⓜ Sevilla; 🖥 🖵
The towering glass edifice of Hotel Urban is the epitome of art-inspired, superstylish designer cool. With its clean lines and modern art, it's a wonderful antidote to the more classic charm of Madrid's five-star hotels of longer standing. Dark-wood floors and dark walls are offset by plenty of light, while the dazzling bathrooms have wonderful designer fittings – the washbasins are sublime. The rooftop swimming pool is Madrid's best and the gorgeous terrace is heaven on a candle-lit summer's evening.

QUO Map pp254-5   Hotel €€€
☎ 91 532 90 49; www.hotelesquo.com; Calle de Sevilla 4; s €110-156, d €156-250; Ⓜ Sevilla; 🖥
Quo is Madrid's home of chic with black-clad staff, minimalist designer furniture, tall ceilings and huge windows that let light flood in. The colour scheme is black and red, with light surfaces providing perfect contrast. We're also big fans of the bathrooms, with glass doors, glass benches and stainless steel basins. All rooms have flat-screen TVs, black-and-white photos of Madrid, dark-wood floors, free ADSL Inter-

Artwork in the atrium, Hotel Urban (left)

net connection and comfy armchairs, while the rooms on the 7th floor have Jacuzzis and private terraces with terrific views over the rooftops of central Madrid.

PASEO DEL PRADO & EL RETIRO

The artistic splendour of the art galleries along the magnificent Paseo del Prado is a fine reason for choosing to stay in this former barrio of choice for Madrid's royalty; the sophisticated Parque del Buen Retiro is another of the joys of staying in this green and relatively tranquil area, and it's well connected by metro to the rest of Madrid. For more information on the barrio, see p82.

BEST OF THE BARRIO – PASEO DEL PRADO & EL RETIRO

- Sleep in style at **Hotel Ritz** (opposite) or the **Palace** (opposite), two of Europe's oldest and most exclusive hotels.
- Overdose on a feast of fine art in the peerless **Museo del Prado** (p83) and the **Museo Thyssen-Bornemisza** (p86).
- Amble through the glorious gardens of the **Parque del Buen Retiro** (p87), a luxuriant and animated park that has few rivals in Europe.
- Promenade under the shade like a Madrileño along the **Paseo del Prado** (Map p257), Spain's grandest boulevard.
- Sample the best in creative Madrileño cooking at **Balzac** (p120) where innovation meets hearty Madrid cuisine.

HOTEL MORA Map p257   Hotel €€

☎ 91 420 15 69; www.hotelmora.com; Paseo del Prado 32; s €62, d €65/75; Ⓜ Atocha

Near the main museums and a short walk from the centre, this simple, friendly hotel offers great value, although when we visited it was surrounded by building works that clatter on throughout the day. Rooms are a bit sparse and the furnishings a little tired, but they're spacious and clean, and some overlook the Real Jardín Botánico (Royal Botanical Gardens).

NH NACIONAL Map p257   Hotel €€

☎ 91 429 66 29; www.nh-hotels.com; Paseo del Prado 48; d Fri-Sun €99-128, Mon-Thu €169; Ⓜ Atocha; ▢

The excellent NH chain of hotels doesn't get any better than this place, where the stylish rooms are beautifully decorated in warm colours, and combine luxury comfort with all the necessary technology (including satellite TV and Internet connection in every room). Close to both Atocha station and Madrid's three big art galleries, this could just be Paseo del Prado's best place to stay.

HOTEL RITZ Map p257   Hotel €€€

☎ 91 701 67 67; www.ritzmadrid.com; Plaza de la Lealtad 5; d €480-580, ste €550-4500; Ⓜ Banco de España; ▢

The grand old lady of Madrid, the Hotel Ritz is the height of exclusivity. One of the most lavish buildings in Madrid, the classic style and impeccable service is second-to-none. Not surprisingly it's the hotel of choice for presidents, kings and celebrities. The public areas are palatial and awash with antiques, while the rooms are extravagantly large, opulent and supremely comfortable. In the Royal Suite, the walls are covered with raw silk and there's a personal butler to wait upon you. We challenge you to find a more indulgent hotel experience anywhere in Europe.

THE PALACE Map pp254-5   Hotel €€€

☎ 91 360 80 00; www.westinpalace.com; Plaza de las Cortes 7; d €369-470, ste €659-1265; Ⓜ Banco de España or Antón Martín; ▢

An old Madrid classic, this former palace of the Duque de Lerma opened as a hotel in 1911, and was Spain's second luxury hotel. Ever since, it has looked out across Plaza de Neptuno at its rival, the Ritz, like a lover unjustly scorned. Its name may not have the world-famous cachet of the Ritz, but it's not called the Palace for nothing and is extravagant in all the right places.

SALAMANCA

Salamanca is Madrid's most exclusive address, home to a wealth of suitably grand sights, not to mention some of the best shopping that Madrid has to offer. It's generally a quieter choice than anywhere else in the capital and good restaurants abound. For more information on the barrio, see p89.

HESPERIA HERMOSILLA Map p252   Hotel €€

☎ 91 246 88 00; www.hesperia.com; Calle de Hermosilla; s/d €125/135; Ⓜ Serrano; ▢

If you're here on a mission to shop or you otherwise value quiet, exclusive streets away from the noise of central Madrid, this modern and subtly stylish hotel is a terrific choice. The furnishings are vaguely minimalist, especially in the public areas, and LCD flat-screen TVs and other creature comforts are rare luxuries in this price range.

NH LAGASCA Map p252   Hotel €€

☎ 91 575 46 06; www.nh-hotels.com; Calle de Lagasca; d Fri-Sun €124, d Mon-Thu €174; Ⓜ Serrano; ▢

With the clean lines and vaguely minimalist look of the excellent NH chain, NH Lagasca is a sophisticated choice in a sophisticated

BEST OF THE BARRIO – SALAMANCA

- Sleep at **Bauzá** (p176), a stylish boutique hotel that's all about Salamanca's upmarket chic.
- Mingle with the beautiful people and the international designer names along **Calle José Ortega y Gasset** (Map p252) or seek out the latest Spanish fashions in the boutiques all the way along **Calle de Serrano** and in the surrounding streets.
- Dine with the celebrities amid the flowery sophistication at **Thai Gardens** (p123), pick at the designer Basque *pintxos* (tapas) in **Biotza** (p121), or sample the cosy, classy atmosphere and exceptional food at **La Galette** (p121).
- Put on your hair gel and the latest in Salamanca designer wear to be seen amid the curves of **Colette Café** (p136) or in the oh-so-Salamanca wine bar, **El Lateral** (p136).

barrio. The price structure suggests that this is a business hotel, which is true in the sense that the service is good and the facilities and fittings top-notch.

BAUZÁ Map pp246-7 · Hotel €€€

☎ 91 435 75 45; www.hotelbauza.com; Calle de Goya 79; s €138-174, d €190-275, ste €326-350; Ⓜ Goya; 🖳

Minimalist and modern, the new Bauzá would be right at home in Soho. The generous rooms boast dark-wood floors, soothing greys and blues, and flashes of originality like Indian textile prints. Computers, sound systems, designer lamps and even plants add appeal without crowding the rooms.

MALASAÑA & CHUECA

There's an unmistakeable sense that by staying in Malasaña or Chueca you're a discerning traveller keen to live like a Madrileño; these are some of Madrid's oldest inner-city barrios and they are being transformed by a process of subtle, urban regeneration, making them addresses of choice for upwardly mobile Madrileños. You're close to everything, reasonably well served by transport and sure to have a good time once you step out the door of your hotel. For more information on the barrio, see p93.

HOSTAL AMÉRICA Map pp250-1 · Hostel €

☎ 91 522 64 48; www.hostalamerica.net; Calle de Hortaleza 19, 5th fl; s/d/tr €36/48/67; Ⓜ Gran Vía

This place is run by a lovely mother–son–dog team who preside over superclean, spa-

cious and IKEA-dominated rooms. As most rooms face onto the usual interior 'patio' of the building, you should get a good night's sleep despite the busy area. For the rest of the time, there's an expansive terrace with tables, chairs and a coffee machine.

HOSTAL DON JUAN Map pp250-1 · Hostel €

☎ 91 522 31 01; Plaza de Vazquez de Mella 1, 2nd fl; s/d €33/46; Ⓜ Gran Vía

Paying cheap rates for your room doesn't mean you can't be treated like a king. This elegant two-storey *hostal* is filled with art (each room has original works) and antique furniture that could grace a royal palace. Rooms are large, and simple but luminous; most have a street-facing balcony.

HOSTAL LA ZONA Map pp250-1 · Hostel €

☎ 91 521 99 04; www.hostallazona.com; Calle de Valverde 7, 1st fl; d €50-65; Ⓜ Gran Vía; 🖳

Catering primarily to a gay clientele, the stylish Hostal La Zona has exposed brickwork, subtle colour shades and wooden pillars. We like a place where a sleep-in is encouraged – breakfast is from 9am to noon, which is exactly the understanding Madrid's nightlife merits. Other highlights include free Internet, helpful staff and air-conditioning/heating in every room.

HOSTAL SAN LORENZO

Map pp250-1 · Hostel €€

☎ 91 521 30 57; www.hostal-lorenzo.com; Calle de Clavel 8; s/d from €60/80; Ⓜ Gran Vía

Hostal San Lorenzo is a terrific deal: original stone walls and occasional dark-wood

BEST OF THE BARRIO – MALASAÑA & CHUECA

- Sleep in **Hostal San Lorenzo** (above), with its hostel name and hotel quality, or the **Hostal La Zona** (above), offering the best of gay Madrid hospitality.
- Spend a day shopping at the **Mercado Fuencarral** (p165) for that essential down-and-dirty Malasaña look and find the perfect shoes to go with it on **Calle de Agusto Figueroa** (Map pp250–1).
- Choose any of the exceptional restaurants for lunch along **Calle de Manuela Malasaña** (Map pp250–1), pause for a coffee at the old-world institution that is **Café Comercial** (p123) and then look no further than **Calle de Libertad** (Map pp250–1) for a great evening meal and cool company.
- Dive into the life of the barrio in **Conde Duque** (Map pp250–1), but make a special detour for drinks at the intimate **El Jardín Secreto** (p137) or the live music of **Café La Palma** (p141).
- Carouse in **Plaza de Chueca** (Map pp250–1), Madrid's liveliest and most exuberantly gay corner, slide into place at the funky and downtempo **Café Belen** (p137) or mix it with the celebrities at **Museo Chicote** (p138).
- Lose all decorum and return to Madrid's *la movida* (the sociocultural movement set off by the explosion of liberties after the death of Franco) of the '80s at **La Vaca Austera** (p137) or **Penta Bar** (p142), long-standing favourites on Malasaña's buzzing rock bar-and-club scene.

beams from the 19th-century in the public areas and modern, comfortable and bright rooms that you'll be more than happy to return to at the end of the day. It's just a pity some of the rooms aren't larger.

SIETE ISLAS HOTEL Map pp250-1   Hotel €€
☎ 91 523 46 88; www.hotelsieteislas.com; Calle de Valverde 14-16; s/d €138/148; Ⓜ Gran Vía
Rooms here are comfortable and stylish, with generous, marble-lined bathrooms and cool beige-and-navy blue tones throughout. The owners hail from the Canary Islands – they have a marine theme running throughout the public areas.

PETIT PALACE HOTEL DUCAL
Map pp254-5   Hotel €€€
☎ 91 521 10 43; www.hthoteles.com; Calle de Hortaleza 3; s/d €145/174; Ⓜ Gran Vía; 🖳
The idea of fusing elegant old buildings with state-of-the-art rooms and hi-tech facilities is fast catching on in Madrid. The rooms here boast strong, contrasting colours, polished floorboards, clean lines, comfy beds and armchairs, and plenty of light and mirrors. Each room also has its own computer with free ADSL Internet connection. The hi-tech theme continues in the bathrooms.

CHAMBERÍ & ARGÜELLES

Chamberí has bars, shops, cinemas and restaurants in just the right measure and you'll quickly feel less like a tourist and more like a local by staying here. There aren't many places to stay, but those that are here are excellent, and you're only a short metro ride from the main sites of interest. For more information on the barrio, see p95.

HOTEL TRAFALGAR
Map pp246-7   Hotel €€
☎ 91 445 62 00; www.hotel-trafalgar.com; Calle de Trafalgar 35; s/d €81/112; Ⓜ Quevedo; 🖳
If you asked Madrileños where they would most like to live, the chances are it would be within a 1km radius of this hotel. The hotel itself is modern and comfortable with good-sized rooms with all the mod-cons (in-room movies, Internet and good bathrooms).

BEST OF THE BARRIO – CHAMBERÍ & ARGÜELLES

- Sleep at **Hotel AC Santo Mauro** (below) where you can spend it like Beckham.
- Take up residence on a summer's evening at the outdoor tables of **Plaza de Olavide** (Map pp250–1), an essential Madrid experience with scarcely a tourist in sight.
- Stroll down **Calle de Fuencarral** (Map pp250–1), between the Glorieta de Quevedo and Bilbao, on a Sunday morning when it's traffic-free and see the barrio come alive with families.
- Partake in old Madrid traditions by eating *churros y chocolate* at **El Brillante** (p119) or *patatas bravas* (potato chunks bathed in a slightly hot red sauce) at the atmospheric **Bodega de la Ardosa** (p127) and then continue the tapas theme at **Sagarretxe** (p129).
- Put on your best to rub shoulders with Madrid's beautiful people at **Moma 56** (p142), then return to earth with some great live music at **Clamores** (p149).

TRYP ALONDRAS Map p245   Hotel €€
☎ 91 447 40 00; www.solmelia.com; Calle de José Abascal 8; s/d €130/150; Ⓜ Alonso Cano; 🖳
Although primarily aimed at a business clientele, Tryp Alondras is a good choice at the northern end of Chamberí. Some rooms are small but all are well-appointed, with wooden furniture crowded in and deep colour tones throughout. Request a room on an upper floor if you need quiet.

HOTEL AC SANTO MAURO
Map pp250-1   Hotel €€€
☎ 91 319 69 00; www.ac-hoteles.com; Calle de Zurbano 36; s €250, d €250-365, ste €423-467; Ⓜ Alonso Martínez; 🖳 📶
Everything about this recently renovated place oozes exclusivity and class, from the address – one of the elite patches of Madrid real estate – to the mansion that is the finest in a barrio of many. This is a place of discreet elegance and warm service, and rooms are suitably lavish; the Arabian-styled indoor pool isn't bad either. David Beckham may well be derided for many things, but the fact that he chose to make this his home for six months certainly suggests he has a high degree of taste.

MOVING TO MADRID

If you're moving to Madrid and are looking for a place to live, there are several services that can be useful. **Room Madrid** (Map pp254–5; ☎ 91 548 03 35; www.roomeurope.com; Calle de Conde Duque 7) organises rental apartments, flat-share and student accommodation. They can be a bit slow to answer so contact them well in advance of arriving in Madrid, but they're generally reliable. International web agencies such as **www.easyroommate.com** and **www.easyexpat.com** pair up people (often foreigners or students) looking for rooms with those who have rooms to rent; they usually have options in Madrid. There are also real estate and relocation companies specialising in helping foreign clients; try **Solution Relocation Services** (☎ 91 550 03 97; www.solucionmad.com) or **Immo Madrid** (☎ 91 766 06 61; www.immomadrid.com). Once you're living here, pick up a copy of *The Notebook Madrid – Settling & Living in Madrid* for €20, a locally produced publication with loads of useful tips and contacts; it's in English and French and can usually be found at **Petra's International Bookshop** (p158). Another good resource is the **Expat Survival Guide** which is available at www.expatica.com.

LONG-TERM STAYS & APARTHOTELS

APARTASOL
Long-term Stays

☎ 91 512 81 16; www.apartasol.com; apt per night per person for 1/5 persons €50/20
This traveller-friendly agency has well-equipped modern apartments scattered around the vicinity of the Puerta del Sol and Gran Vía. Prices are first-rate and there are discounts available for longer stays.

APARTHOTEL TRIBUNAL
Map pp250-1   Apartments

☎ 91 522 14 55; www.aparthotel-tribunal.com in panish; Calle de San Vicente Ferrer 1; apt per night €60-90; Ⓜ Tribunal
Simple but spacious and functional apartments with kitchenettes and satellite TV

WORTH A TRIP

Hotel Puerta América (Map p244; ☎ 917 44 54 00; www.hotelpuertamerica.com; Avenida de América 41; d €225-300; Ⓜ Cartagena; 🖳) When the owners of this hotel saw their location – halfway between the city and the airport – they knew they had to do something special. Their idea? Give some of world architecture's most innovative names a floor each to design. The result? An extravagant pastiche of styles, from curvy minimalism or zany montages of 1980s chic to bright red bathrooms that feel like a movie star's dressing room. Even the bar ('a temple to the liturgy of pleasure'), restaurant, façade, gardens, public lighting and car park had their own architects.

are on offer here. Sizes range from 25 sq metres to 50 sq metres, which means many are more like studios than apartments, but they are well-maintained. Unfortunately there are no longer weekly rates available, which makes them a less appealing option should you be visiting Madrid for a while.

HOSTAL MADRID
Map pp254-5   Long-term Stays

☎ 91 522 00 60; www.hostal-madrid.info; Calle de Esparteros 6, 2nd fl; apt per night/month from €100/1200; Ⓜ Sol
The excellent apartments here range in size from 33 sq metres to 130 sq metres and each has a fully-equipped kitchen, its own sitting area, bathroom and, in the case of the larger ones (room 51 on the 5th floor is one of the best), an expansive terrace with views over central Madrid. Tastefully modern wrought-iron furniture and attractive colour schemes mix with period pieces throughout.

SUITE PRADO HOTEL
Map pp254-5   Apartments

☎ 91 420 23 18; www.suiteprado.com; Calle de Manuel Fernández y González; s/d/tr €124/156/179; Ⓜ Sevilla
The spacious modern suites at this centrally located hotel have plenty of room and are semiluxurious, although they don't have a whole lot of character. All have sitting rooms and good bathrooms, and some even have kitchenettes. The location is also a great base for your Madrid explorations.

Excursions

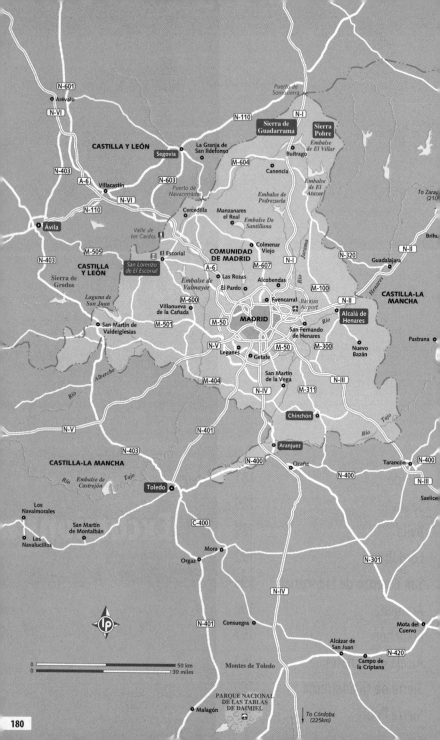

N-601
Arévalo
N-VI
N-403
A-6
Villacastín
N-VI
N-110
Ávila
M-505
N-403
CASTILLA Y LEÓN
Sierra de Gredos
Laguna de San Juan
San Martín de Valdeiglesias
M-501
N-V
CASTILLA-LA MANCHA
N-403
Río
Alberche
Embalse de Castrejón
Tajo
Los Navalmorales
San Martín de Montalbán
Los Navalucillos

CASTILLA Y LEÓN
Segovia
La Granja de San Ildefonso
N-603
Puerto de Navacerrada
Cercedilla
Valle de los Caídos
El Escorial
San Lorenzo de El Escorial
A-6
Embalse de Valmayor
Villanueva de la Cañada
M-600
M-50
N-V
Leganés
M-404
N-IV
N-401
N-403
Toledo
C-400
Mora
Orgaz
N-401
Consuegra
Montes de Toledo
PARQUE NACIONAL DE LAS TABLAS DE DAIMIEL
Malagón

Puerto de Somosierra
N-110
N-I
Sierra de Guadarrama
Sierra Pobre
Embalse de El Villar
M-604
Buitrago
Canencia
Embalse de El Atazar
Embalse de Pedrezuela
Manzanares el Real
Embalse De Santillana
COMUNIDAD DE MADRID
Colmenar Viejo
M-607
N-I
Las Rozas
Alcobendas
El Pardo
Fuencarral
Barajas Airport
M-100
N-II
MADRID
Getafe
San Fernando de Henares
M-50
M-300
San Martín de la Vega
M-311
Chinchón
Aranjuez
N-400
Ocaña
N-400
N-400

To Zarag (210
Brihu
N-II
Guadalajara
N-320
CASTILLA-LA MANCHA
Alcalá de Henares
Pastrana
Nuevo Bazán
Río Tajo
Tarancón
N-400
N-III
Saelice
N-301
Mota del Cuervo
Alcázar de San Juan
N-420
Campo de la Criptana
To Córdoba (225km)

0 50 km
0 30 miles

Excursions

Madrid has the advantage of being smack bang in the centre of Spain with excellent transport connections to the rest of the country, and there are a wealth of beautiful historical towns and other extraordinary sights which can easily be visited as a day trip from the capital.

The choices are endless, but you haven't really been to Spain unless you've been to **Toledo** (below), a grandly austere and imperious city that once rivalled Madrid for the role of capital. Coming here is like stepping back into the Middle Ages, into a history when Christians, Muslims and Jews turned this into one of Spain's most polyglot cities. **Ávila** (p189), too, resonates with history, most notably in its imposing cathedral and its encircling medieval walls.

The Unesco World Heritage–listed town of **Segovia** (p185) has an entirely different, light-filled charm as it surveys the surrounding mountains from its hill-top perch. The exceptional *alcázar* (Muslim-era fortress) and Roman-era aqueduct are its signature sights, but this is also a place where eating is an art form, with plenty of restaurants to warm the heart and fill the stomach.

Away to the south, sun-drenched **Córdoba** (p192), one of the great cities in European and world history, boasts the astonishing Mezquita, which is surrounded by white-washed homes of tiles and terracotta that are so evocative of its Andalucian location.

Within the Comunidad de Madrid, the splendid 16th-century monastery and palace complex of **San Lorenzo de El Escorial** (El Escorial; p195) guards the gateway to Madrid from the northwest. To the south, graceful **Aranjuez** (p196) is home to a magnificent palace and expansive gardens and it now serves as a fine retreat from the noise and bustle of Madrid just as it did for Spanish royalty down through the ages. Nearby **Chinchón** (p197) has a stunning, but far more ramshackle charm, its sloping and porticoed Plaza Mayor being one of Spain's most enchanting plazas; Chinchón is also a fine place for eating.

Alcalá de Henares (p198), east of Madrid, is also worth as much time as you can give it, for it is the birthplace of Miguel de Cervantes, home to one of Spain's oldest universities and rich in architectural elegance. Protecting Madrid from the north, are the mountains; the Sierra de Guadarrama and Sierra de Pobre shelter charming old villages, and skiing is possible in winter. **Manzanares El Real** (p199) has an enchanting storybook castle, while **Buitrago** (p200) is another especially beautiful village to explore.

TOLEDO

Toledo is one of Spain's stand-out cities for medieval grandeur and for centuries it was considered Spain's capital-in-waiting. It's an easy day trip from the capital.

'Toletum', as the Romans called it, was always a strategically important city. In the 6th century it was the capital of the Visigoth empire and after 711 it became an important

FIESTAS & FESTIVALS

It's worth planning a trip to coincide with some of the extravagant fiestas going on in towns around Madrid. Here's our pick of the most interesting:

- Semana Santa, Córdoba (Easter week) – Elaborate, otherworldly and sombre processions with flowers and pointy-headed penitents fill the Andalucian city for one of the year's holiest festivals. Other important processions take place in Chinchón, Toledo and Ávila.
- Corpus Christi, Toledo (June) – Several days of festivities culminate in a procession featuring the massive **Custodia de Arfe** (p184).
- Fiesta Mayor, Chinchón (12–18 August) – The town's main plaza is turned into a bullring and bullfights are held each morning. Cheer from the surrounding balconies over breakfast and coffee.
- Santa Teresa, Ávila (around 15 October) – In honour of Saint Teresa, who was born in Ávila, this festival sees the town indulge in days of celebrations and processions.

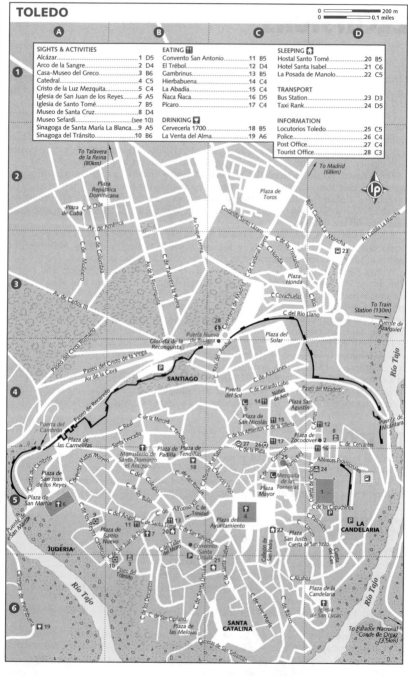

TOLEDO

0 —————— 200 m
0 —————— 0.1 miles

SIGHTS & ACTIVITIES		EATING 🍴		SLEEPING 🏠	
Alcázar.............................1 D5		Convento San Antonio............11 B5		Hostal Santo Tomé...............20 B5	
Arco de la Sangre.................2 D4		El Trébol...........................12 D4		Hotel Santa Isabel................21 C6	
Casa-Museo del Greco............3 B6		Gambrinus........................13 B5		La Posada de Manolo.............22 C5	
Catedral............................4 C5		Hierbabuena.....................14 C4			
Cristo de la Luz Mezquita.........5 C4		La Abadía.........................15 C4		TRANSPORT	
Iglesia de San Juan de los Reyes...6 A5		Ñaca Ñaca........................16 D5		Bus Station........................23 D3	
Iglesia de Santo Tomé.............7 B5		Pícaro.............................17 C4		Taxi Rank..........................24 D5	
Museo de Santa Cruz.............8 D4					
Museo Sefardí...................(see 10)		DRINKING 🍷		INFORMATION	
Sinagoga de Santa María La Blanca...9 A5		Cervecería 1700...................18 B5		Locutorios Toledo.................25 C5	
Sinagoga del Tránsito............10 B6		La Venta del Alma................19 A6		Police.............................26 C4	
				Post Office........................27 C4	
				Tourist Office.....................28 C3	

To Talavera
de la Reina
(80km)

To Madrid
(68km)

Plaza
República
Dominicana

Plaza de
Toros

Plaza
de Cuba

C de Chile

Av. de América

C de Colombia

C de Molinero

Av de la Reconquista

Costanilla Santo Lázaro

C de Cardenal Tavera

C de los Trinitarios

Bajada Cuesta La Mancha

Av Capilla La Mancha

Av de Carlos III

C Covachuelas

Plaza
Honda

C del Río Llano

To Train
Station (130m)

Paseo del Circo Romano

Paseo del Cristo de la Vega

Puerta Nueva
de Bisagra

Plaza del
Solar

Puente de
Azarquiel

Río Tajo

Glorieta de la
Reconquista

Av de la Cava

SANTIAGO

Puerta
del Sol

C de Azacanes

C de Gerardo Lobo

Paseo del Miradero

Puerta del
Cambrón

C de la Merced

Santa Leocadia

Plaza de
San Nicolás

Núñez
de Arce

Plaza San
Agustín

Puente de
Alcántara

Plaza de
las Carmelitas

C Real

Monasterio de
Santo Domingo
el Antiguo

Plaza de
Padilla

Plaza de
Tendillas

C de los Alféizes

C de la Sillería

Plaza de
Zocodover

C de Cervantes

Plaza de
San Juan
de los Reyes

C de Santo Ángel

C del Colegio

C de las Bulas

C de Alfonso X
de Trinidad

C de la Plata

Comercio

Alféreces Provisionales

JUDERÍA

Plaza de
San Martín

Plaza de
Barrio
Nuevo

C del Ángel

C de Santo Tomé

C de San Román

C de San Salvador

Plaza del
Ayuntamiento

Mezquita
de las
Tornerías

Plaza
Mayor

Cuesta de Carlos V

LA
CANDELARIA

Puente
de San Martín

C de los Reyes Católicos

C de San Juan de Dios

Convento
Santa
Úrsula

C del Taller
del Moro

Callejón de
San Pedro

Plaza
San Justo

Cuesta de San Justo

C de los Capuchinos

Paseo del
Tránsito

C de Santa Isabel

C Alcahoz

Plaza de la
Candelaria

Río Tajo

C de los Descalzos

C de San Cipriano

Plaza de
las Melojas

SANTA
CATALINA

C de Santa Úrsula

C de Ave María

C de Barco

Iglesia
de San Lucas

To Parador Nacional
Conde de Orgaz
(3.5km)

Carretera de Pedrezuela

Río Tajo

Carreteras de San Sebastián

EL GRECO IN TOLEDO

Few artists are as closely associated with a city as El Greco is with Toledo – many of you may want to come here for his paintings alone as a complement to your artistic tour of Madrid.

Born in Crete in 1541, Domenikos Theotokopoulos (El Greco; the Greek) moved to Venice in 1567 to be schooled as a Renaissance artist. Under the tutelage of masters such as Tintoretto, he learned to express dramatic scenes with few colours, concentrating the observer's interest in the faces of his portraits and leaving the rest in relative obscurity, a characteristic that remained one of his hallmarks. From 1572 he learned from the Mannerists of Rome and the work left behind by Michelangelo.

El Greco came to Toledo in 1577 hoping to get a job decorating El Escorial, although Felipe II rejected him as a court artist. In Toledo, the painter began painting in a style different from anything local artists were producing. He even managed to cultivate a healthy clientele and command good prices.

His rather high opinion of himself and his work, however, did not endear him to all. He had to do without the patronage of the cathedral administrators, who were the first of many clients to haul him to court for his obscenely high fees.

El Greco liked the high life and took rooms in a mansion on the Paseo del Tránsito, where he often hired musicians to accompany his meals.

As Toledo's fortunes declined, so did El Greco's personal finances, and, although the works of his final years are among his best, he often found himself unable to pay the rent. He died in 1614, leaving his works scattered about the city, where many have remained to this day.

Muslim centre of power. Under the Muslims, Toledo was a flourishing centre of art, culture and religion, a multifaith city which was home to peacefully co-existing Jews, Christians and Muslims. Alfonso VI wrestled the city back into Christian hands in 1085, and shortly after it was declared 'the seat of the Church' in Spain. This marked the beginning of a golden age where Toledo's power knew few limits, a state of affairs that lasted through the Inquisition and into the 16th century.

But therein lay Toledo's problem. Too powerful for its own good, Toledo was bypassed when it came time to choose a capital as nervous kings favoured the more compliant and then-less-grand Madrid as their seat of power. Ever since, this imperious city has glowered out across the plains from its hill-top perch above the Río Tajo.

Modern Toledo sprawls away to the north, but the old city and the most important sights are stacked stone upon stone in a crook of the Río Tajo. The hills here make for steep strolls through the centre, so for a more relaxing view of the old town, hop on the **Zoco Tren** (adult/child €4/2.50), a small train that does a 45-minute loop up the hill and through Toledo. The train leaves hourly and tickets are available in the tourist office.

Toledo lacks a true centre – its rich concentration of monuments is scattered throughout the old city – but the **Plaza de Zocodover**, at the northeastern end of the old town, is a good place to start. This oddly-shaped plaza was once an Arab livestock market and later became the main city market, but is now lined with terrace cafés and filled with day-trippers. Pass through the **Arco de la Sangre** (Gate of Blood) which once marked the city's walls on the eastern side of the square and down to the rewarding **Museo de Santa Cruz**, a splendid early 16th-century pastiche of Gothic and Spanish Renaissance styles, fine cloisters and a number of El Greco paintings.

Up the hill to the south is Toledo's signature fortress, the **alcázar**, which began life as a Roman military base, later became an Arab fortress, and then a Christian one rebuilt by Alfonso VI in the 11th century. Later, Carlos V converted the harsh square block of a building into a royal palace and used it to house his visitors until it was damaged by fire in 1710. The palace burned again in 1810 (thanks to Napoleon) and was nearly destroyed yet again during the Civil War. It remains closed while restoration works prepare it for its new role as the Museo del Ejército (Army Museum). Meantime, this is the highest point in Toledo and just beyond the *alcázar* are some fine views out over the Río Tajo.

Follow the spires down the hill to Toledo's **Catedral**, the spiritual home of Catholic Spain and one of the largest and most opulent cathedrals in the world. An essentially Gothic

Excursions

TOLEDO

creation with a few *mudéjar* (a Moorish architectural style) afterthoughts, it was built in the 13th century atop an earlier mosque. All the chapels and side rooms are worth peeking into, but the **Capilla de la Torre** (Tower Chapel) in the northwestern corner and the **Sacristía** (Sacristy) are well worth your time. The latter boasts a lovely vaulted ceiling and a small gallery of El Greco's works (see boxed text, p183), while the Tower Chapel has one of the most extraordinary monstrances in existence, the 16th-century **Custodia de Arfe**. With 18kg of gold and 183kg of silver, this shimmering mass of metal has a whopping 260 statuettes. Other important sights are the imposing high altar, the Transparente window and the choir stalls.

Down the hill are a cluster of must-sees for El Greco fans, among them the wonderful **Iglesia de Santo Tomé**, which houses one of El Greco's greatest works, *El Entierro del Conde de Orgaz* (The Burial of the Count

Toledo's Muslim-inspired Sinagoga del Transito (below)

of Orgaz). The painting tells the legend of the pious count's funeral in 1323, when St Augustine and St Steven appeared to lay the body in the tomb. Among the onlookers are El Greco himself and Cervantes. The **Casa-Museo del Greco** is nearby with around two dozen of the master's minor works.

You're now in the heart of the **Judería** (Toledo's old Jewish Quarter). Here, the **Sinagoga del Tránsito** should on no account be missed. Built in 1355 by special permission of Pedro I (construction of synagogues was by then prohibited in Christian Spain), the rich *mudéjar* decoration in the main prayer hall has been expertly restored. It's now the **Museo Sefardí** which provides an insight into the history of Jewish culture in Spain.

A short way north, **Sinagoga de Santa María La Blanca** is less grand but definitely worthwhile, while further along Calle de los Reyes Católicos is the imposing **Iglesia San Juan de los Reyes**, a fine Franciscan monastery and church with tranquil cloisters and the chains of Christian prisoners liberated in Granada dangling from the walls.

For a glimpse of Muslim Toledo, head to the **Cristo de la Luz Mezquita**. During Muslim rule, there were 10 mosques in the city; this one, quite beautiful, is typical of their style and is the only one that remains.

Information

Locutorios Toledo (☎ 92 528 30 43; Plaza de la Magdalena 7; Internet per hr €2.50; ☽ 11am-2.30pm & 5-11pm Mon-Wed, Fri & Sat, 4-11pm Thu, 11am-3pm Sun)

Police (☎ 091, 092; Calle de las Cadenas; ☽ 24hr)

Post Office (☎ 92 549 04 21; www.correos.es in Spanish; Calle de la Plata 1; ☽ 8.30am-8.30pm Mon-Fri, 9.30am-2pm Sat)

Tourist Office (☎ 92 522 08 43; www.toledoweb.org; Carretera de Madrid; ☽ 9am-6pm Mon-Fri, 9am-7pm Sat, 9am-3pm Sun)

Sights & Activities

Catedral (☎ 92 522 22 41; admission € 5.50, free after 4pm; ☽ 10.30am-6.30pm Mon-Sat, 2pm-6pm Sun)

Casa-Museo del Greco (☎ 92 522 40 46; www.mcu.es/museos/index in Spanish; Calle Samuel Leví; admission €2.40; ☽ 10am-2pm & 4-9pm Tue-Sat, 10am-2pm Sun)

Cristo de la Luz Mezquita (☎ 92 525 41 91; Cuesta de los Carmelitas Descalzos 10; admission €1.50; ☽ 10am-6pm, until 7pm in summer)

Iglesia de Santo Tomé (☎ 92 525 60 98; www.santotome.org; Plaza del Conde; admission €1.50; ☽ 10am-6pm)

Museo de Santa Cruz (☎ 92 522 10 36; Calle de Cervantes 3; admission free; ☽ 10am-2pm & 4-6.30pm Mon, 10am-6.30pm Tue-Sat, 10am-2pm Sun)

Iglesia San Juan de los Reyes (☎ 92 522 38 02; Plaza de San Juan de los Reyes; admission €1.50; ☽ 10am-6pm)

Sinagoga de Santa María La Blanca (☎ 92 522 72 57; Calle de los Reyes Católicos 4; adult/child €1.50/free; ☽ 10am-5.45pm)

Sinagoga del Tránsito & Museo Sefardí (☎ 92 522 36 65; www.museosefardi.net in Spanish; Calle Samuel Leví; admission €4.50; ☺ 10am-2pm & 4-9pm Tue-Sat Mar-Nov, 10am-2pm & 4-6pm Tue-Sat Dec-Feb)

Zoco Tren (☎ 92 522 03 00; Plaza de Zocodover; adult/child €3.75/2.30)

Eating & Drinking

Of Toledo's specialities, *cuchifritos*, a potpourri of lamb, tomato and egg cooked in white wine with saffron, is especially good.

Cervecería 1700 (☎ 92 522 25 60; Plaza de Tendillas 1; ☺ 10am-11pm Mon-Sat) The tables of this relaxed beer bar spill out onto the cobblestones; and it serves decent tapas.

Convento San Antonio (☎ 92 522 00 47; Plaza San Antonio 1; ☺ 11.15am-1.30pm & 4-6pm) The Franciscan nuns here sell their sweet speciality, *corazones de San Antonio* (San Antonio hearts) for €7.50 a box.

El Trébol (Calle de Santa Fe 1; raciones €4; ☺ 1-4pm & 8.30pm-midnight) El Trébol gets a great rap from locals for its *bomba* (crumbed potato stuffed with minced meat).

Gambrinus (☎ 92 521 44 40; Calle de Santo Tomé; raciones €5-14, menú del día €9.50) As good for a meal as for beer and tapas, this place has pleasant outdoor tables.

Hierbabuena (☎ 92 522 39 24; Calle de Navalpino 45; meals €35-40; ☺ 1.30-4pm & 9.30pm-midnight Mon-Sat, 1.30-4pm Sun) Expensive but imaginatively classy, Hierbabuena is a cut above the usual traditional fare.

La Abadía (☎ 92 525 11 40; Plaza de San Nicolás 3; menú del día €10; meals €15-25; ☺ 8am-midnight Sun-Thu, 8am-2.30am Fri & Sat) The downstairs restaurant serves excellent and typical Toledano dishes and offers a great wine list.

La Venta del Alma (☎ 92 525 42 45; Carretera de Piedrabuena 35; ☺ 3.30pm-2am Sun-Thu, 3.30pm-6am Fri & Sat) Mild-mannered during the day, La Venta del Alma really gets going on Friday and Saturday.

Ñaca Ñaca (Plaza de Zocodover; ☺ 9am-11pm Mon-Thu, 9am-4am Fri, 9am Sat-11pm Sun) This place is good for chunky *bocadillos* (filled rolls; from €2) deep into the night.

Pícaro (☎ 92 522 13 01; Calle de las Cadenas 6; ☺ 4pm-2.30am Sun-Wed, 4pm-6.30am Thu-Sat) Pícaro is a popular café-*teatro* (theatre) serving an eclectic range of *copas* (drinks) and there's live music every Friday night.

Sleeping

Hostal Santo Tomé (☎ 92 322 17 12; www.hostalsanto tome.com; Calle de Santo Tomé 13; s/d/tr €40/49/62) In this friendly hostel on one of the old town's busiest streets you'll find spacious, superclean rooms with satellite TV.

Hotel Santa Isabel (☎ 92 525 31 20; www.santa-isabel .com; Calle de Santa Isabel 24; s/d €32/48) The 19 rooms in the annexe are stylish and help to make the Santa Isabel one of the best in the old town.

La Posada de Manolo (☎ 92 528 22 50; www.laposadade manolo.com; Calle de Sixto Ramón Parro 8; s €50, d €66-72) You can't get much closer to the cathedral than this thoughtfully designed, well-run hotel with each floor reflecting one of the 'three cultures' of Toledo. The views of the old town and cathedral from the rooftop terrace are stunning.

Parador Nacional Conde de Orgaz (☎ 92 522 18 50; www .parador.es; d €140-150) High above the southern bank of the Río Tajo, Toledo's Parador boasts a classy interior and breathtaking views of the city.

SEGOVIA

Recognised by Unesco for its unique mix of Roman aqueduct, fine medieval monuments and spectacular setting amid the rolling hills of Castile, Segovia is one of the must-see cities in Spain.

It may not have been founded by Hercules or the son of Noah, as some city historians have claimed, but the area has undoubtedly been inhabited since ancient times. The Romans used Segovia as a military stronghold from which to govern the surrounding territory. The city would later come under the sway of the Visigoths and the Moors, but after the Christian reconquest Segovia began to come into its own, and beautiful Romanesque churches and splendid palaces sprung up across the compact city centre. In the 1500s the Comuneros Revolt, a fight against King Carlos I led by Juan Bravo, brought on economic and social decline, and the city didn't recover until tourists began arriving in large numbers in the 1960s.

SEGOVIA

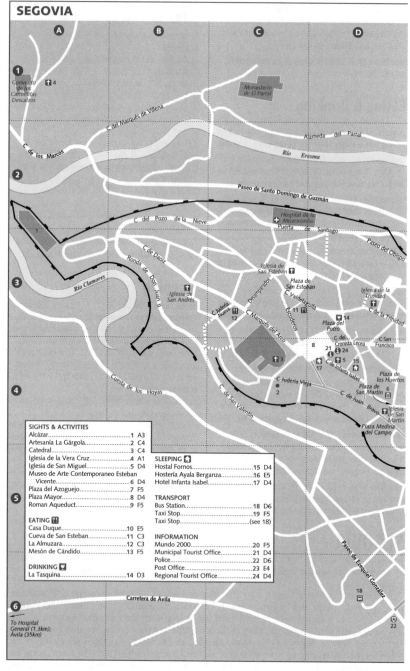

SIGHTS & ACTIVITIES

Alcázar	1 A3
Artesanía La Gárgola	2 C4
Catedral	3 C4
Iglesia de la Vera Cruz	4 A1
Iglesia de San Miguel	5 D4
Museo de Arte Contemporaneo Esteban Vicente	6 D4
Plaza del Azoguejo	7 F5
Plaza Mayor	8 D4
Roman Aqueduct	9 F5

EATING

Casa Duque	10 E5
Cueva de San Esteban	11 C3
La Almuzara	12 C3
Mesón de Cándido	13 F5

DRINKING

La Tasquina	14 D3

SLEEPING

Hostal Fornos	15 D4
Hostería Ayala Berganza	16 E5
Hotel Infanta Isabel	17 D4

TRANSPORT

Bus Station	18 D6
Taxi Stop	19 F5
Taxi Stop	(see 18)

INFORMATION

Mundo 2000	20 F5
Municipal Tourist Office	21 D4
Police	22 D6
Post Office	23 E4
Regional Tourist Office	24 D4

Excursions

SEGOVIA

186

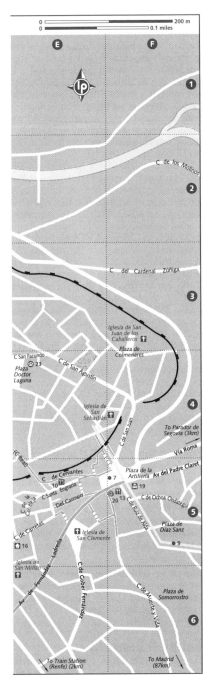

The medieval walled city is in the far western corner of modern Segovia. The **11th-century walls** stretch from the Roman aqueduct to the *alcázar* on the edge of town, encompassing just about everything worth seeing in a short visit. Two major plazas, the **Plaza del Azoguejo** near the aqueduct and the **Plaza Mayor** by the cathedral, are the nerve centres of the city. The lively commercial streets of **Calle de Cervantes** and **Calle de Juan Bravo** (together referred to as 'Calle Real') serve as the main artery connecting the two plazas. There are many shops worth browsing here, but make sure you check out the unusual handmade crafts and souvenirs at **Artesanía La Gárgola**.

Start your visit at the **Roman aqueduct**, an 894m-long engineering wonder that looks like an enormous comb plunged into Segovia. It's 28m high, has 163 arches and was built without a drop of mortar, just good old Roman know-how. Although no-one really doubts that the Romans built the aqueduct, a local legend asserts that a young girl tired of carrying water from the well voiced a willingness to sell her soul to the devil if an easier solution could be found. No sooner said than done. The devil worked through the night, during which the girl recanted and prayed to God for forgiveness. Hearing her prayer, God sent the sun into the sky earlier than normal, catching the devil unawares and with only a single stone lacking to complete the structure. The aqueduct's pristine condition is attributable to a major restoration project in the 1990s.

From the Plaza del Azoguejo, climb Calle Real into the ancient heart of Segovia, passing the sunny **Plaza de San Martín**, crowned with the lovely 13th-century Romanesque **Iglesia de San Martín**, with the Segovian touch of a *mudéjar* tower and arched gallery. The interior boasts a Flemish Gothic chapel. Well worth a brief detour is the **Museo de Arte Contemporaneo Esteban Vicente**, which showcases modern artworks in a 15th-century palace of Enrique IV, complete with Renaissance chapel and *mudéjar* ceiling.

Take a right turn on the Calle de Isabel Católica to come to the shady, elongated **Plaza Mayor** which is adorned by a fine pavilion. At the western end of the plaza the **Catedral** towers over the plaza. Completed in 1577, 50 years after its Romanesque predecessor had been destroyed in the revolt of the Comuneros, the cathedral is one of the most

Excursions

SEGOVIA

Segovia's late-Gothic 16th-century cathedral (p187)

homogenous Gothic churches in Spain. The austere, three-naved interior is delicate and refined, with a handful of side chapels, a fine choir stall and stained-glass windows from the 1600s. You can visit the cloister and museum, with its fantastic collection of sacred art and 17th-century Belgian tapestries. The smaller **Iglesia de San Miguel** recedes humbly into the shadows by comparison to the cathedral, despite its historical significance – Isabel was crowned Queen of Castile in this small church.

From the Plaza Mayor head down Calle del Marqués del Arco to reach the fortified **alcázar**, a fairytale castle perched dramatically on the edge of Segovia. If it looks familiar don't be surprised; Walt Disney reputedly copied Segovia's *alcázar* for Sleeping Beauty's Castle in California's Disneyland. Fortified since Roman days, the site takes its name from the Arabic *al-qasr* (castle), but what you see today is a reconstruction of a 13th-century structure that burned down in 1862. Inside is an interesting collection of armour and military gear, but even better are the 360-degree views from the *alcázar's* rooftop, which is a balcony overlooking the hills and pastures of Castile. From here you can make out one of Segovia's most interesting churches, the 12-sided **Iglesia de la Vera Cruz** (Church of the True Cross), built in the 13th century following the floor plan of the Church of the Holy Sepulchre in Jerusalem. A relic of what was said to be the 'true cross' was once housed in the church. For great views of the town and countryside, hike uphill behind the church.

By night, head for **Calle de la Infanta Isabel** which is known locally as the 'Calle de los Bares' (Street of the Bars). This is the destination for serious drinking, cheap eating and merriment all around. Just northeast of the Plaza Mayor, **La Tasquina** is a wine bar that spills out onto the footpath and here you'll get good wines, *cavas* (sparkling wines) and cheeses.

Information

Mundo 2000 (Plaza de Azoguejo; per hr €2.40; ☼ 11am-11pm)

Municipal Tourist Office (☎ 92 146 60 70; www.segoviaturismo.es in Spanish; Plaza Mayor 6; ☼ 10am-8pm)

Police (☎ 091; Paseo de Ezequiel González 22; ☼ 24hr)

Post Office (☎ 92 146 16 16; www.correo.es in Spanish; Plaza Doctor Laguna 5; ☼ 8.30am-8.30pm Mon-Fri, 9am-2pm Sat)

Regional Tourist Office (☎ 92 146 03 34, 90 220 30 30; www.turismocastillayleon.com; Plaza Mayor 10; ☼ 9am-2pm & 5-8pm)

Sights & Activities

Alcázar (☎ 92 146 07 59; www.alcazardesegovia.com; Plaza de la Reina Victoria Eugenia; admission €3.50, tower €1.50, admission free on Wed for EU citizens; ☼ 10am-6pm Oct-Mar, 10am-7pm Apr-Sep)

Artesanía La Gárgola (☎ 67 074 70 80; www.gargolart.com; Calle Judería Vieja 4; ☼ 11am-2pm & 5-8pm)

Catedral (☎ 92 146 22 05; Plaza Mayor; admission €2, admission free after 1.30pm Sun; ☼ 9.30am-5.30pm, until 6.30pm in summer)

Iglesia de la Vera Cruz (☎ 92 143 14 75; Carretera de Zamarramala; admission € 1.75; ☼ 10.30am-1.30pm & 3.30-7pm Tue-Sun Mar-Aug; 10.30am-1.30pm & 3.30-6pm Tue-Sun Sep-Feb)

Museo de Arte Contemporaneo Esteban Vicente (☎ 92 146 20 10; www.museoestebanvicente.es; Plazuela de las Bellas Artes; admission €2.40; ☼ 11am-2pm & 4-7pm Tue-Fri, 11am-7pm Sat, 11am-2pm Sun)

Eating & Drinking

If you love your meat, you'll love Segovia. Almost every restaurant in town serves delicious *cochinillo asado* (roasted suckling pig) and *asado de cordero* (roasted lamb).

Casa Duque (☎ 92 146 24 87; www.restauranteduque.es; Calle Cervantes 12; mains €6-23, menú del día €21) The speciality is suckling pig in this rustic place of old-world charm, while downstairs is the informal *cueva* (cave), where you can get tapas and yummy *cazuelas* (stews).

Cueva de San Esteban (☎ 92 146 09 82; Calle Valdelaguila 15; menú del día €7.50-12; ☻ 1-11pm) One of the only restaurants in Segovia not pushing suckling pig, this popular spot focuses on seasonal dishes and has an excellent wine list.

La Almuzara (☎ 92 146 06 22; Calle Marqués del Arco 3; dishes under €8; closed Sun lunch & Mon) If you're a vegetarian, La Almuzara offers respite in this carnivorous city with lots of pastas and salads, and the ambience is warm and artsy.

La Tasquina (☎ 92 146 19 54; Calle de Valdeláguila 3; ☻ 9pm-late)

Mesón de Cándido (☎ 92 142 81 03; Plaza del Azoguejo 5; mains €10-16, meals €30) At the foot of the aqueduct, this is another one of Segovia's most popular places for suckling pig.

Sleeping

Hostal Fornos (☎ 92 146 01 98; Calle de Infanta Isabel 13; s €32-38, d €45-51) This tidy little hostel has a cheerful air thanks to its spacious rooms which have that fresh white-linen-and-wicker-chair look.

Hostería Ayala Berganza (☎ 92 146 04 48; www.partner-hotels.com; Calle de Carretas 5; r incl breakfast €110-133) Each of the 17 rooms in this boutique hotel (housed in a restored 15th-century palace) is different, though all have tiled floors, beautiful bathrooms and rustic accents.

TRANSPORT

Distance from Madrid 90km

Direction Northwest

Car From Madrid, take the A-6 motorway to the N-603 national highway, which will take you to the city centre. Driving time is 1¼ hours.

Bus La Sepulvedana buses (☎ 92 142 77 07; Paseo de Ezequiel González) leave every half-hour from Madrid's Paseo de la Florida bus stop and arrive in Segovia's central bus station one hour and 30 minutes later. Tickets cost €5.87.

Train Renfe (☎ 90 224 02 02; www.renfe.es; one-way €5.45) has up to nine trains between Segovia and Madrid each day. The trip takes about two hours.

Hotel Infanta Isabel (☎ 92 146 13 00; www.hotelinfantaisabel.com; Plaza Mayor 12; s €60-77, d €78-114) Sitting right on Plaza Mayor, this utterly charming hotel is one of the best in town. The colonnaded building provides some hint to the hotel's interior, where the rooms have period furnishings and plenty of character. Rooms are large and those with balconies overlooking the Plaza Mayor are the best.

Parador de Segovia (☎ 92 144 37 37; www.parador.es; Carretera de Valladolid; r from €120) On a hill-top perch about five minutes' drive from the centre, this is one of the more modern Paradors in Spain. It's nonetheless deluxe and offers great views of Segovia. Breakfasting in their glass-walled dining room as the sun glitters on the *alcázar* and the cathedral must be one of Segovia's greatest pleasures.

ÁVILA

Medieval kingdoms battled over Ávila for centuries and it remains huddled behind stone walls with eight monumental gates, 88 watchtowers and more than 2500 turrets (to protect archers), which seem to spring from a child's imagination. A relative backwater under the Romans and Muslims, Ávila's population didn't begin to rise until Alfonso VI tried to repopulate the territory after his victory in Toledo in 1085. By the 1500s, Ávila was an economic powerhouse, with an important wool industry, illustrious palaces and new churches popping up all over town – many of these remain as the landmarks of this distinguished old city.

It was also during this golden age that the city's most important figure, Santa Teresa (see boxed text, p191), was born. Shortly after her death in 1582, the city's fortunes began a downward spiral that ended in its economic ruin; Ávila has only recently shaken off its slumber.

One word of warning: before setting out for Ávila, prepare for the fact that this is one of the highest and windiest cities in Spain and it can get bitterly cold in winter.

The **Catedral** is embedded in the eastern wall of the old city. Although the main façade hints at the cathedral's 12th-century, Romanesque origins, the church was finished 400 years later in a predominantly Gothic style, making it the first Gothic church in Spain. The grey, sombre façade betrays some unhappy 18th-century meddling in the main portal, but within are rich walnut choir stalls, a dazzling altar painting begun by Pedro de Berruguete showing the life of Jesus in 24 scenes and a long, narrow central nave that makes the soaring ceilings seem all the more majestic. The cloisters, sacristy and small museum are superb; the latter includes a painting by El Greco.

Excursions

ÁVILA

ÁVILA

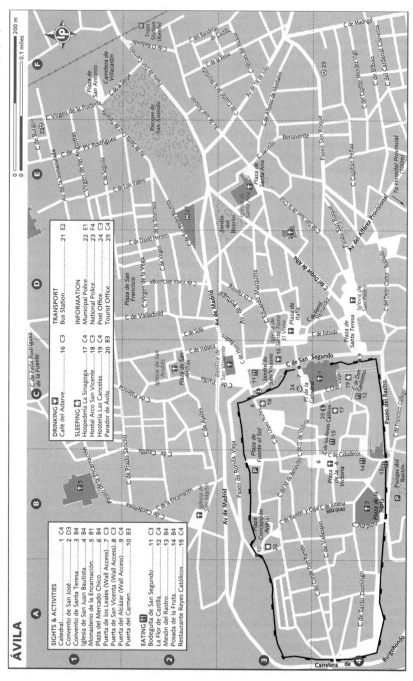

SIGHTS & ACTIVITIES
Catedral	1 C4
Convento de San José	2 D3
Convento de Santa Teresa	3 B4
Iglesia de San Juan Bautista	4 B4
Monasterio de la Encarnación	5 B1
Plaza del Mercado Chico	6 B4
Puerta de los Leales (Wall Access)	7 C3
Puerta de San Vicenta (Wall Access)	8 C3
Puerta del Alcázar (Wall Access)	9 C4
Puerta del Carmen	10 B3

EATING
Bodeguita de San Segundo	11 C3
La Flor de Castilla	12 C4
Mesón del Rastro	13 B4
Posada de la Fruta	14 B4
Restaurante Reyes Católicos	15 C4

DRINKING
Café del Adarve	16 C3

SLEEPING
Hospedería La Sinagoga	17 C4
Hostal Arco San Vicente	18 C3
Hostería Las Cancelas	19 C4
Parador de Ávila	20 B3

TRANSPORT
Bus Station	21 E2

INFORMATION
Municipal Police	22 E1
National Police	23 F4
Post Office	24 C3
Tourist Office	25 C4

IN THE FOOTSTEPS OF SANTA TERESA

Probably the most important woman in the history of the Catholic church in Spain, Santa Teresa spent most of her life in Ávila, and you don't have to be here long to feel her enduring presence. From the convent, plaza, and gate that bears her name to the sweet *yemas de Santa Teresa* (yummy cookies made with egg yolk and supposedly invented by the saint) her trail seems to cover every inch of the city.

Teresa de Cepeda y Ahumada – a Catholic mystic and reformer – was born in Ávila on 28 March 1515, one of 10 children of a merchant family. Raised by Augustinian nuns after her mother's death, she joined the Carmelite Order at age 20. Shortly thereafter, Teresa nearly succumbed to a mysterious illness that paralysed her legs for three years. After her early, undistinguished years as a nun, she was shaken by a vision of Hell in 1560 which crystallised her true vocation: she would reform her order.

With the help of many supporters Teresa founded convents of the Carmelitas Descalzas (Shoeless Carmelites) all over Spain. She also co-opted San Juan de la Cruz (St John of the Cross) to begin a similar reform in the masculine order, a task that earned him several stints of incarceration by the mainstream Carmelites. Santa Teresa's writings were first published in 1588 and proved enormously popular, perhaps partly for their earthy style. She died in 1582 in Alba de Tormes, where she is buried. She was canonised by Pope Gregory XV in 1622.

After a visit to the **Convento de Santa Teresa**, you can pop into the nearby **Iglesia de San Juan Bautista,** where she was baptised. The first convent she founded, **Convento de San José**, is here too, and you can visit its small museum packed with Teresa artefacts and memorabilia. To see a replica of her monastic cell, head to the **Monasterio de la Encarnación** outside the city walls where she lived and worked for 27 years.

Before diving into the city, climb up to the top of Ávila's splendid **12th-century walls** *(murallas)* which rank among the world's best-preserved medieval defensive perimeters. Access points include **Puerta de los Leales** and **Puerta del Carmen**, while the most impressive gates, the **Puerta de San Vicente** and **Puerta del Alcázar**, are flanked by towers more than 20m high and stand on either side of the cathedral's apse. You can walk atop more than 1km of the 2.5km wall and the views are fabulous. The last tickets are sold 45 minutes before closing time.

From here the important commercial **Calle de los Reyes Católicos**, which is lined with shops and bars, snakes its way into the busy **Plaza del Mercado Chico**. Southwest of the plaza, the **Convento de Santa Teresa** is even more beloved by locals and pilgrims than the cathedral because it was built on the sight where Teresa de Cepeda y Ahumada (Santa Teresa) was born. This church was built in 1636 and today you can see its simple interior and the gold-smothered chapel that sits atop Teresa's former bedroom, though more interesting are the relics (including a piece of the saint's ring finger!) and the small museum about her life.

After the churches and museums have closed, check out Ávila's cheerful bar scene. There are several good nightlife options just outside the Puerta del Peso de la Harina, along Calle de San Segundo.

Information

Municipal Police (☎ 092; Avenida Inmaculada 11; 🕒 24hr)

National Police (☎ 091; Paseo San Roque 34; 🕒 24hr)

Post Office (☎ 92 031 35 06; Plaza de la Catedral 2; 🕒 8.30am-8.30pm Mon-Fri, 9.30am-2pm Sat)

Tourist Office (☎ 92 021 13 87; www.avilaturismo.com; Plaza de la Catedral 4; 🕒 9am-2pm & 5-8pm Sep 15-Jun, 9am-8pm Sun-Thu, 9am-9pm Fri & Sat Jul-Sep 14)

Sights & Activities

Catedral (☎ 92 021 16 41; Plaza de la Catedral; admission €3; 🕒 10am-5pm Mon-Fri, noon-5pm Sat & Sun Nov-Mar, until 7pm Mar-Oct)

Convento de San José (☎ 92 022 21 27; Calle del Duque de Alba; admission €1; 🕒 10am-1.30pm & 3-6pm)

Convento de Santa Teresa (☎ 92 021 10 30; Plaza de la Santa; museum admission €2; 🕒 museum 10am-2pm & 4-7pm, relic room 9.30am-1.30pm & 3.30-7pm, church 8.30am-1.30pm & 3.30-8.30pm)

Iglesia de San Juan Bautista (☎ 92 021 11 27; Plaza de la Victoria; admission free; 🕒 before & after mass)

Monasterio de la Encarnación (☎ 92 021 12 12; Paseo de la Encarnación; admission €1.30; 🕒 9.30am-1.30pm & 3.30-6pm Mon-Fri, 10am-1pm & 4-6pm Sat & Sun)

Walls (☎ 92 021 13 87; admission €3.50; 🕒 11am-6pm Tue-Sun Oct-Apr, 11am-8pm Tue-Sun May-Sep)

TRANSPORT

Distance from Madrid 101km
Direction West

Car From Madrid, take the A-6 motorway northwest, then take the N-110 west. Driving time is one hour.
Bus At least four buses connect Madrid's Estación Sur and Ávila daily. The trip takes 1½ hours and costs €6.50. Contact the bus station (☎ 92 022 01 54; Avenida de Madrid 2) for more information.
Train Renfe (☎ 90 224 02 02; www.renfe.es; one-way from €6.05) has up to 30 trains to Ávila daily. The trip takes up to two hours, although the occasional train goes express, takes 1¼ hours and costs €7.35.

Eating & Drinking

Ávila is famous for its *chuleton de avileño* (T-bone-steak) and *judias del barco de Ávila* (white beans, often with chorizo, in a thick sauce).

Bodeguito de San Segundo (☎ 92 021 42 47; Calle de San Segundo 19; ⏰ 11am-1am) This place has a great selection of Spanish wines; and delicious tapas.

Café del Adarve (Calle de San Segundo 40; ⏰ 3pm-late) To soak up a youthful vibe, drop in at this hip spot which has coffee during the day, drinks at night and live music during winter.

La Flor de Castilla (☎ 92 025 28 66; Calle de San Gerónimo) This is best place to buy the *yema de Santa Teresa,* an ultra-sweet, sticky biscuit made of egg yolk and sugar, and said to have been invented by the saint.

Mesón del Rastro (☎ 92 021 12 18; Plaza del Rastro 4; dinner/lunch menú del día €13/14.50) The dining room, with its dark-wood beams, exudes Castilian charm and the *cochinillo* is particularly good.

Posada de la Fruta (☎ 92 022 09 84; Plaza de Pedro Dávila 8; meals €8-15) Simple, informal meals can be had at the café-bar in a light-filled courtyard, while the traditional *comedor* (dining room) serves *menús* (fixed-price meals) and à la carte dishes.

Restaurante Reyes Católicos (☎ 92 025 56 27; Calle de los Reyes Católicos 6; meals €25-35) A refreshing surprise for those sick of *asado*, this stylish bistro offers a mix of traditional and more imaginative dishes.

Sleeping

Hospedería La Sinagoga (☎ 92 035 23 21; lasingoga@airtel.net; Calle de los Reyes Católicos 22; s/d €54/75) Central and quiet, this delightful hotel, built on the site of a synagogue, has bright, good-sized rooms.
Hostal Arco San Vicente (☎ 92 022 24 98; fax 92 022 95 32; Calle de López Núñez 6; s/d €39/58) For it's combination of comfort, character-filled rooms, friendly owners and value for money, this place is outstanding.

Hostería Las Cancelas (☎ 92 021 22 49, www.lascancelas.com; Calle de la Cruz Vieja 6; s/d/tr €45/65/95) Another top choice, the rooms here are spacious and the traditional furniture adds a touch of character.

Parador de Ávila (☎ 92 021 13 40; avila@parador.es; Marques de Canales y Chozas 2; s/d €110/120) Occupying a 16th-century palace, the Parador has all the essential elements of this chain: elegant public areas, helpful staff and stylish bedrooms.

CÓRDOBA

The allure of Andalucía is nowhere better experienced than in Córdoba, a beautiful town of whitewashed patios, twisting old streets and an epic history of Moorish, Christian, Jewish and Roman occupation. Although it lies 400km south of Madrid, with the high-speed (AVE) train you can be there in under two hours.

The Romans founded the colony of 'Corduba' here in the 2nd century BC, and due to its strategic location on the Río Guadalquivir quickly made it the provincial capital. When Moorish invaders took the city in AD 711, they agreed to let locals keep their customs and religious beliefs, and the city flourished with the peaceful coexistence of Christians, Jews and Muslims. Córdoba lay at the heart of Al-Andalus and was home to vast libraries, buildings of extraordinary splendour and astronomers, mathematicians and philosophers whose works far surpassed anything that Christian Europe could muster. The emirs (princes) of Córdoba founded Europe's first universities and paper-making factories, while street-lighting illuminated the city's streets as the rest of Europe stumbled around in darkness. When Ferdinand reclaimed the city in the early Middle Ages, its splendour began to fade and it never regained the powerful status it once enjoyed.

Nowhere better illustrates the mixture of Muslim and Christian tradition in Spain than the grand and hybrid **Mezquita de Córdoba**, at one time the largest temple in the world. Construction

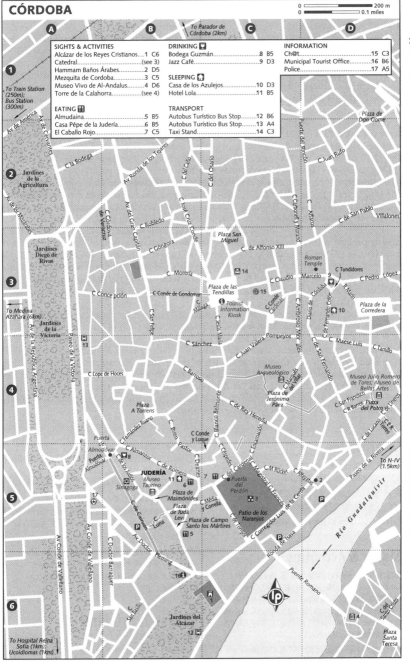

CÓRDOBA

0 — 200 m
0 — 0.1 miles

SIGHTS & ACTIVITIES
Alcázar de los Reyes Cristianos....1 C6
Catedral................................(see 3)
Hammam Baños Árabes.............2 D5
Mezquita de Cordoba.................3 C5
Museo Vivo de Al-Andalus...........4 D6
Torre de la Calahorra................(see 4)

EATING 🍴
Almudaina.................................5 B5
Casa Pépe de la Judería.............6 B5
El Caballo Rojo..........................7 C5

DRINKING 🍷
Bodega Guzmán.........................8 B5
Jazz Café..................................9 D3

SLEEPING 🛏
Casa de los Azulejos..................10 D3
Hotel Lola.................................11 B5

TRANSPORT
Autobus Turístico Bus Stop........12 B6
Autobus Turístico Bus Stop........13 A4
Taxi Stand................................14 C3

INFORMATION
Ch@t.......................................15 C3
Municipal Tourist Office..............16 B6
Police.......................................17 A5

Excursions

CÓRDOBA

on the mosque began in AD 784 on the site of an old Visigoth basilica, though the mammoth masterpiece took another 200 years to complete. Its graceful double arches and pillars (850 are still standing out of the original 1300) were as splendid then as today.

When Christians took control of the city in 1236, King Ferdinand immediately consecrated the mosque as a church, although he left the structure intact out of appreciation for its beauty. For centuries the original architecture was respected, even while Christians used it as a cathedral, but in the 16th century a few overzealous church leaders committed architectural sacrilege when they built a Gothic **catedral** in the centre of the mosque. King Carlos I approved the work, but supposedly he deeply regretted giving his support when he saw the irrevocable damage that had been done.

In addition to plonking their church in here, the Christians closed off the arches that were intended to let light in from the **Patio de los Naranjos** (Courtyard of the Orange Trees) outside, and the result is decidedly more gloomy than the original. Still, there's no masking the glorious beauty of this place. Pay special attention to the many ornate domes in the ceiling and to the **Sagrarium**, a small room smothered in elaborate paintings.

Southwest of the Mezquita is the **Alcázar de los Reyes Cristianos**, the Castle of the Christian Monarchs. Built in the 13th century as a military base, the Alcázar was remodelled by the Catholic King Ferdinand and Queen Isabella to use as a residence. Although its interior has little to catch your attention, the lush gardens are fine places to stroll.

From here you can cross the **Río Guadalquivir** on the **Puente Romano**, a bridge that has a barely distinguishable Roman base, to reach the **Torre de la Calahorra**, a former defence tower that now houses the **Museo Vivo de Al-Andalus**. There's a fascinating exhibit on Córdoba's cultural history and the unique mixture of Christian, Jewish and Islamic culture here. But Córdoba is a place where history lives and breathes, and a walk around the enchanting **Judería** (Jewish Quarter), west of the Mezquita, may be the only history lesson you need to imagine the city's polyglot past.

If you feel like pampering yourself and want to learn a little about Arab culture at the same time, visit the **Hammam Baños Árabes** where you can take a dip in luxurious baths built to look like those used by Córdoba's Muslim community. If you have a little more time, head 6km outside town to **Medina Azahara**, the ruins of a 10th-century Muslim palace complex. A guided tour leads you through what's left of the mosque, the ornate gardens and other buildings. This splendid creation burned down just 70 years after being built, and it has been in ruins ever since. You can get there on the Autobus Turístico, which makes trips from Tuesday to Saturday (inclusive) at 11am leaving from the Avenida Alcázar. Get tickets and information from the tourist office or at hotels.

Information

Ch@t (Calle Claudio Marcelo 15; per hr €2; ☾ 10am-1pm & 5-9.30pm Mon-Fri, 10am-2pm Sat)

Municipal Tourist Office (☎ 90 220 17 74; Plaza de Judá Leví 1; www.turismodecordoba.org; ☾ 9.30am-7pm)

Police (Avenida Doctor Fleming 2; ☎ 091, 092)

Sights & Activities

Alcázar de los Reyes Cristianos (☎ 95 742 01 51; Campo Santo de los Mártires; admission €2, free Fri; ☾ 10am-2pm & 4.30-6.30pm Tue-Sat mid-Oct–Apr, 10am-2pm & 5.30-7.30pm Tue-Sat May-Jun & Sep–mid-Oct, 8.30am-2.30pm Tue-Sat Jul-Aug, 9.30am-2.30pm Sun year-round)

Hammam Baños Árabes (☎ 95 748 47 46; www.gru poalandalus.com; Calle del Corrigedor Luis de la Cerda; bath/bath & massage €12/16; ☾ 10am-midnight)

Medina Azahara (Madinat al-Zahra; ☎ 95 732 91 30; Carretera Palma del Río; admission €1.50, EU citizens free; ☾ 10am-6.30pm Tue-Sat, until 8.30pm May–mid-Sep, 10am-2pm Sun year-round)

Mezquita de Córdoba & Catedral (☎ 95 747 05 12; Calle de Torrijos; admission €6.50; ☾ 10am-7pm Mon-Sat Apr-Sep, 10am-5.30pm Mon-Sat Oct-May, 1.30-6.30pm Sun year-round)

Torre de la Calahorra & Museo Vivo de Al-Andalus (☎ 95 729 39 29; Puente Romano; admission €4; ☾ 10am-6pm Oct-Apr, 10am-2pm & 4.30-8.30pm May-Sep)

Eating & Drinking

Almudaina (☎ 95 747 43 42; Plaza de Campo Santo los Mártires 1; meals €20-30; ☾ daily) You'll eat well (and with atmosphere) in this exquisite 16th-century mansion with an ivy-clad patio.

Bodega Guzmán (Calle de los Judíos 7; ⏰ 1pm-late) *Montilla* (a sherrylike tipple from the surrounding area) is served straight from the barrel in this traditional bodega (wine cellar).

Casa Pepe de la Judería (☎ 95 720 07 44; Calle de Romero 1; meals €20-25; ⏰ daily) This cosy tavern has some of the best tapas in Córdoba and you get to eat on one of the city's most intimate patios.

El Caballo Rojo (☎ 95 747 53 75; Calle del Cardenal 28; meals €20-30; ⏰ daily) A classic Córdoban restaurant, here the speciality is 'Arabic-Andalus' cuisine, a fusion of Moorish and Spanish cooking that grew out of the cultural mix here.

Jazz Café (☎ 95 747 19 28; Calle Espartería; ⏰ 8am-late) This is a casual and decidedly hip place to hear fine jazz, often live.

Sleeping

Casa de los Azulejos (☎ 95 747 00 00; www.casadelosazulejos.com; Calle de Fernando Colón 5; s €75-90, d €85-115) Original wooden ceilings, colourful tile accents and a beautiful, light-filled interior patio make this one of Córdoba's most original hotels.

Hotel Lola (☎ 95 720 03 05; www.hotelconencantolola.com in Spanish; Calle Romero 3; s €28-51, d €44-73) In

TRANSPORT

Distance from Madrid 400km
Direction South
Car From Madrid, take the N-IV South, the so-called Andalucía highway, all the way to Córdoba. Driving time is four hours.
Bus Five buses make the 4¾-hour trip daily from Madrid's Estación Sur. The trip costs €11.35.
Train Renfe (☎ 90 224 02 02; www.renfe.es) operates the AVE (high-speed) train running 20 times per day between Madrid and Córdoba. The trip lasts about one hour and 40 minutes and costs from €52.10, one way.

the heart of the *Judería*, this place is a work of art with Art-Deco touches, antiques and individually designed rooms. The views of the Mezquita from the terrace are wonderful.

Parador de Córdoba (☎ 95 727 59 00; www.parador.es; Avenida de la Arruzafa; r €125-135; 🏊) On a hill to the north of town, the Parador offers lovely city views (especially at night) and is a quiet, elegant place to stay. The pool hits the spot in summer and it was here that Europe's first palm trees were planted.

SAN LORENZO DE EL ESCORIAL

Home to the majestic monastery and palace complex of San Lorenzo de El Escorial, this one-time royal getaway rises up from the foothills of the mountains that shelter Madrid from the north and west. Although it attracts its fair share of foreign tourists, this prim little town is overflowing with quaint shops, restaurants and hotels (many of which close when things are quiet) that cater primarily to Madrileños who are intent on escaping the city on weekends: the fresh, cool air, among other things, has been drawing city dwellers here since the complex was first built on the orders of King Felipe II in the 16th century.

Several villages were razed to make way for the massive project, which included a monastic centre, a decadent royal palace and a mausoleum for Felipe's parents, Carlos I and Isabel. Architect Juan de Herrera oversaw the project.

The **monastery's** main entrance is on the west. Above the gateway a statue of St Lawrence stands watch, holding a symbolic gridiron, the instrument of his martyrdom (he was roasted alive on one). From here you'll first enter the **Patio de los Reyes** (Patio of the Kings) which houses the statues of the six kings of Judah.

Directly ahead lies the sombre **basilica**. As you enter, look up at the unusual flat vaulting by the choir stalls. Once inside the church proper, turn left to view Benvenuto Cellini's white Carrara marble statue of Christ crucified (1576).

You'll be led through rooms containing tapestries and an El Greco painting – impressive as it is, it's a far cry from the artist's dream of decorating the whole complex – and then downstairs to the northeastern corner of the complex. You pass through the **Museo de Arquitectura** and the **Museo de Pinturaf**. The former tells (in Spanish) the story of how the complex was built, the latter contains a range of 16th- and 17th-century Italian, Spanish and Flemish art.

Head upstairs into a gallery around the eastern part of the complex known as the **Palacio de Felipe II** or **Palacio de los Austrias**. You'll then descend to the 17th-century **Panteón de los Reyes** (the

Crypt of Kings), where almost all Spain's monarchs since Carlos I are interred. Backtracking a little, you'll find yourself in the **Panteón de los Infantes** (Crypt of the Princesses).

Stairs lead up from the **Patio de los Evangelistas** (Patio of the Gospels) to the **Salas Capitulares** (chapterhouses) in the southeastern corner of the monastery. These bright, airy rooms, whose ceilings are richly frescoed, contain a minor treasure chest of works by El Greco, Titian, Tintoretto, José de Ribera and Hieronymus Bosch (known as El Bosco to Spaniards).

Just south of the monastery is the **Huerta de los Frailes** (Friars Garden) which merits a stroll, while the **Jardín del Príncipe**, which leads down to the town of El Escorial (and the train station), contains the **Casita del Príncipe**, a little neo-Classical gem built under Carlos III for his heir, Carlos IV. The road to Ávila boasts another neo-Classical gem, the Casita de Arriba (Casa del Infant).

Information

Tourist Office (☎ 91 890 53 13; Calle de Grimaldi 2; ☽ 10am-6pm Mon-Fri, 10am-7pm Sat & Sun)

Sights & Activities

Casita de Arriba (☎ 91 890 59 03; admission €3.40; ☽ daily Jul-Sep, Sat & Sun only Oct-May)

Real Monasterio de San Lorenzo (☎ 91 890 59 02; www.patrimonionacional.es in Spanish; admission €8, free Wed for EU citizens; ☽ 10am-6pm Apr-Sep, 10am-5pm Oct-Mar, closed Mon year-round) Admission to the basilica is free, and for a small fee you can join a guided tour of the pantheons.

Eating & Sleeping

Hotel Parrilla Príncipe (☎ 91 890 16 11; www .parillaprincipe.com; Calle de la Floridablanca 6; s €42-44, d €53-59) Rooms are bare and could do with a style overhaul but they're clean, and some have views of the monastery. The restaurant here – great grilled

meats abound – is one of the best in town. Meals cost around €30.

La Cueva (☎ 91 890 15 16; Calle de San Antón 4; meals €20-25; ☽ Tue-Sun) A dark place founded in 1768, this is one of the town's classic eateries.

ARANJUEZ

Aranjuez was founded as a royal pleasure retreat, away from the riff-raff of Madrid, and it remains a place to escape the rigours of city life. The palace is opulent, but the fresh air and ample gardens are what really stand out.

The **Palacio Real** started as one of Felipe II's modest summer palaces but took on a life of its own as a succession of royals, inspired by the palace at Versailles in France, lavished money upon it. By the 18th century, its 300-plus rooms had turned the palace into a sprawling complex filled with a cornucopia of ornamentation. Of all the rulers who spent time here, Carlos III and Isabel II left the greatest mark.

Taking the obligatory guided tour (which is in Spanish) provides a real insight into the palace history and the art that fills it. Afterwards, a stroll in the lush **gardens** takes you through a mix of local and exotic species, the product of seeds brought back by Spanish botanists and explorers from Spanish colonies all over the world. Within their shady perimeter, which stretches a few kilometres from the palace, you'll find the **Casa de Marinos** which contains the **Museo de Faláas**, a museum of royal pleasure boats from days gone by. Further away, towards Chinchón, is the **Jardín del Príncipe**, an extension of the massive gardens. The **Chiquitren**, a small tourist train, loops through town and stops at all the major sites.

Information

Tourist Office (☎ 91 891 04 27; www.aranjuez.net in Spanish; Plaza de San Antonio 9; ☑ 10am-6.30pm Nov-Apr, 10am-8.30pm May-Oct)

Sights & Activities

Casa de Marinos & Museo de Falúas (☎ 91 891 03 05; admission €3.50, bookings essential; ☑ 10am-5.15pm Oct-Mar, 10am-6.15pm Apr-Sep)

Casa del Labrador (☎ 91 891 03 05; admission €5, bookings essential; ☑ 10am-5.15pm Oct-Mar, 10am-6.15pm Apr-Sep)

Chiquitren (☎ 90 208 80 89; train stop near palace entrance; adult/child €5/3; ☑ 11am-5.30pm Tue-Sun Oct-Feb, 10am-8pm Mar-Sep)

Palacio Real (☎ 91 891 07 40; admission to palace €4.50, EU citizens free Wed, gardens free; ☑ palace 10am-5.15pm Tue-Sun Oct-Mar, 10am-6.15pm Tue-Sun Apr-Sep; gardens 8am-6.30pm Tue-Sun Oct-Mar, 8am-8.30pm Tue-Sun Apr-Sep)

Eating & Sleeping

Casa José (☎ 91 891 14 88; Calle de Abastos 32; meals €25-35; ☑ 9am-midnight Tue-Sat, 9am-4pm Sun) An elegant spot, Casa José is packed on weekends with

TRANSPORT

Distance from Madrid 50km
Direction South
Car From Madrid take the N-IV south to the M-305, which leads to the city centre.
Bus The AISA bus company (☎ 90 219 87 88; www.aisa-grupo.com in Spanish) sends buses to Aranjuez from Madrid's Estación Sur every 15 minutes. The 30-minute trip costs €3.15.
Train C3 *cercanía* trains leave every 15 or 20 minutes from Madrid's Atocha station. The 45-minute trip costs €2.17.

Madrileños who revere it as one of the best in town for meats and local dishes.

El Rana Verde (☎ 91 801 15 71; Plaza Santiago Rusiñol; meals €25-35; ☑ 9am-midnight) The 'Green Frog' is a classic riverside restaurant whose speciality is frogs legs.

Hostal Castilla (☎ 91 891 26 27; www.hostalesaranjuez.com in Spanish; Carretera Andalucía 98; s/d €37/48) Impeccable little rooms with their own bathrooms.

NH Príncipe de la Paz hotel (☎ 91 809 92 22; www.nh-hoteles.com; Calle de San Antonio 22; r €89-121) Sleek, modern design and attentive service make this the best hotel in town.

CHINCHÓN

Chinchón is just 45km from Madrid yet worlds apart. Although it has grown beyond its village confines, visiting its antique heart is like stepping back into another era to a charming, ramshackle world. The heart of town is its unique, almost circular **Plaza Mayor**, which is lined with sagging, tiered balconies – it gets our vote as one of the most evocative plazas mayor in Spain. In summer, the plaza is converted into a bullring (see boxed text, p181). It's also the stage for a popular passion play shown at Easter. Chinchón's other main attraction is made up of the traditional **meson-style restaurants** scattered in and around the plaza, some with wonderful balcony tables.

There are a few other sights worth seeking out, particularly the 16th-century **Iglesia de la Asunción** that rises above the Plaza Mayor and the late-16th-century Renaissance **Castillo de los Condes** which is out of Chinchón about 1km to the south and which was abandoned in the 1700s. Chinchón's main sights are usually closed to public visits, but the local tourist office has details of their irregular opening hours (usually on weekends). But these sights are only a diversion from Chinchón's real charm and you'll find yourself wanting to spend as much time as you possibly can in the plaza or eating fine *cordero asado* (roast lamb).

Information

Tourist Office (☎ 91 893 53 23; www.ciudad-chinchon.com; Plaza Mayor 6; ☑ 10am-8pm Mon-Fri, 11.30am-8pm Sat & Sun Mar-Jun & Sep-Oct, until 9pm Jul & Aug, until 7pm Nov-Feb) Small office but staff are extremely helpful.

Eating

Café de la Iberia (☎ 91 894 08 47; Plaza Mayor 17; meals €30; ☑ Tue-Sun) This is definitely our favourite of the mesons on the Plaza Mayor perimeter; it offers wonderful food, attentive staff and an atmospheric dining area.

Mesón Cuevas de a Comendadora (☎ 91 894 09 47; Calle Teniente Ortíz de Zárate; meals €25-30; ☒ Thu-Tue) The maze of caves that extends underneath the restaurant is worth seeing even if you don't eat here.

Meson Cuevas del Vino (☎ 91 894 02 06; www.cuevasdelvino.com; Calle Benito Hortelano 13; meals €30-35, ☒ Wed-Mon) From the huge goatskins filled with wine and the barrels covered in famous signatures, to the atmospheric caves underground, this is sure to be a memorable eating experience.

Sleeping

Hostal Chinchón (☎ 91 893 53 98; www.hostalchinchon.com; Calle de José Antonio 12; s/d €35/42; ☒) The public areas are nicer than the smallish rooms, which are clean but worn around the edges. The highlight is the surprise rooftop pool which overlooks the Plaza Mayor.

Parador de Chinchón (☎ 91 894 08 36; www.parador.es; Avenida Generalísimo 1; r €130-140) The Parador, once the Convento de Agustinos (Augustine Convent), is one of the town's most important historical buildings and is a suitably luxurious place to stay.

ALCALÁ DE HENARES

So close to Madrid and just off an unappealing motorway, Alcalá de Henares is full of surprises and like a smaller Salamanca, with historical sandstone buildings seemingly at every turn. Throw in some sunny plazas and the legendary university, and Alcalá de Henares is a terrific place to go to escape the city.

The **university**, founded in 1486 by Cardinal Cisneros, is one of the country's principal seats of learning. A guided tour gives a peek into the *mudéjar* **chapel** and the magnificent **Paraninfo** auditorium, where the King and Queen of Spain give out the prestigious Premio Cervantes literary award every year. The town is also dear to Spaniards because it is the birthplace of the country's literary figurehead, Miguel de Cervantes Saavedra (see p28). The site believed by many to be Cervantes' birthplace is recreated in the illuminating **Museo Casa Natal de Miguel de Cervantes**, which lies along the beautiful, colonnaded Calle de Mayor.

Information

Tourist Office (☎ 91 881 06 34; Plaza de los Santos Niños; ☒ 10am-2pm & 5-7.30pm Jun–mid-Sep, 10am-2pm & 4-6.30pm Sep–mid-May)

Sights & Activities

Museo Natal de Miguel de Cervantes (☎ 91 889 96 54; Calle de la Imagen 2; admission free; ☒ 10am-6pm Tue-Sun Jun-Sep, 10am-1.30pm & 4-6.30pm Oct-May)

University (☎ 91 883 43 84; 6 free guided tours per day Mon-Fri, 11 per day Sat & Sun; ☒ 9am-9pm)

Eating & Sleeping

El Ruedo (☎ 91 880 69 19; Calle de los Libreros 38; meals €20-25; ☒ 9am-11pm Thu-Tue) With a quiet patio for outdoor eating, this is a great place to get informal fare such as salads and mixed plates.

Hostería del Estudiante (☎ 91 888 03 30; Calle de los Colegios 3; meals €25-35) A charming restaurant in the main university building.

Husa El Bedel (☎ 91 889 37 00; www.husa.es; Plaza San Diego 6; s/d €90/105) Perfect location and elegant, spacious rooms.

Castillo de los Mendoza, Manzanares el Real (below)

SIERRA DE GUADARRAMA

To the north of Madrid lies the Sierra de Guadarrama, a popular skiing destination and the home of several charming towns. In **Manzanares El Real** you can explore the small 15th-century **Castillo de los Mendoza**, a perfectly preserved storybook castle with round towers at its corners and a Gothic interior patio.

Cercedilla is a popular base for hikers and mountain bikers. There are several marked trails through the sierra, the main one known as the **Cuerda Larga** or **Cuerda Castellana**. This is a forest track that takes in 55 peaks between the **Puerto de Somosierra** in the north and **Puerto de la Cruz Verde** in the southwest. Get more information at the **Centro de Información Valle de la Fuenfría.** Small ski resorts such as **Valdesqui** welcome weekend skiers from the city.

Information

Centro de Información Valle de la Fuenfría (☎ 91 852 22 13; Carretera de las Dehesas; ◔ 10am-6pm) You'll find this place 2km outside Cercedilla on the M-614.

Navacerrada Tourist Information (☎ 91 852 22 02; www.puertonavacerrada.com in Spanish)

Sights & Activities

Castillo de los Mendoza (☎ 91 853 00 08; Manzanares El Real; admission incl guided tour €2; ◔ 10am-2pm & 3-6pm Tue-Sun Apr-Sep, 10am-5pm Tue-Sun Oct-Mar)

Valdesqui Ski Resort (☎ 91 570 12 24; Puerto de Cotos; lift tickets €25-34)

TRANSPORT

Distance 50-70km

Direction North

Car Take the A-6 motorway to Cercedilla.

Bus The 724 runs to Manzanares from Plaza de Castilla in Madrid (€2.67, 40 minutes). Bus 691 from Madrid runs regularly to Navacerrada (Intercambiador de Autobuses de Moncloa; platform 14; €2.67, one hour) and bus 684 heads to Cercedilla (platform 15; €2.98, one hour).

Train From Chamartín station you can get to Puerto de Navacerrada (C8B *cercanía* line; €1.51, two hours with train change in Cercedilla, four daily) and Cercedilla (C2 *cercanía* line; €1.28, one hour 20 minutes, 15 daily).

SIERRA POBRE

The 'Poor Sierra' is a toned-down version of its more refined western neighbour, the Sierra de Guadarrama. Popular with hikers and others looking for nature without quite so many creature comforts or crowds, the sleepy Sierra Pobre has yet to develop the tourism industry of its neighbours. And that's just why we like it.

Head first to **Buitrago**, the largest town in the area, where you can stroll along part of the old **city walls**. You can also take a peek into the 15th-century *mudéjar* and Romanesque **Iglesia de Santa María del Castillo** and into the small and unlikely **Picasso Museum**, which contains a few works that the artist gave to his barber, Eugenio Arias.

Hamlets are scattered throughout the rest of the sierra; some, like **Puebla de la Sierra** and **El Atazar**, are pretty walks and are the starting point for winding hill trails.

Sights & Activities

Picasso Museum (☎ 91 868 00 56; Plaza Picasso; admission free; ☾ 11am-1.30pm & 4-6pm Wed-Mon)

TRANSPORT

Distance 73km
Direction Northeast
Car Take the N-I highway to Buitrago.
Bus The Continental Auto Company (☎ 91 745 63 00; www.continental-auto.es) has a dozen daily buses connecting Madrid's Plaza de la Castilla with Buitrago (€4.37, 1½ hours).

Directory

Directory

The practical information in this chapter is divided into two parts, Transport and Practicalities. Within each section information is presented in strictly alphabetical order.

TRANSPORT

Flights, tours and rail tickets can be booked online at www.lonelyplanet.com/travel _services.

AIR

Although many European low-cost airlines bypass the capital and head for the beach, Madrid remains one of the busiest transport hubs in Europe and is easy to reach by air from anywhere within Spain, from elsewhere in Europe and from America.

Many airlines fly direct to Madrid from the rest of Europe. There are some direct intercontinental flights from North and South America too, although some flights from North America involve a change of flight in another major European hub en route.

Of the burgeoning low-cost airlines now working out of the UK and, increasingly, other European hubs, easyJet is the main operator into Madrid. These airlines work on a first-come, first-serve basis: the earlier you book a flight the less you pay. These

---

INTERNET AIR FARES

Most airlines, especially budget ones, encourage you to book on their websites. Other useful general sites to search for competitive fares include the following.

- www.atrapalo.com (in Spanish)
- www.cheaptickets.com
- www.despegar.es (in Spanish)
- www.ebookers.com
- www.expedia.com
- www.lowestfare.com
- www.opodo.com
- www.orbitz.com
- www.planesimple.co.uk
- www.sta.com
- www.travel.com.au
- www.travelocity.com

---

no-frills airlines skip extras such as in-flight meals (although you can buy snacks).

Within Spain, air travel can be expensive. Iberia, Air Europa and Spanair all have dense networks across the country and, while at times costly, it may be worth booking with one of them if time is limited.

Airlines

Increasingly, airlines have abandoned their shopfront offices in Madrid so you'll have to go online, call the following numbers or try a travel agent (p218). At last count, there were 82 airlines that fly to Madrid. The following are among the more popular.

Aer Lingus (☎ in Ireland 0818 365000, in Spain 902 502 737; www.aerlingus.com)

Air Berlin (☎ in Germany 01805 7388880, in Spain 902 320 737; www.airberlin.com) German budget airline with flights to Madrid from cities all over Western Europe.

Air Europa (☎ in the UK 0870 777 7709, in Spain 902 401501; www.aireuropa.com) Flies to Madrid from London, Paris, Rome, Milan and New York, and from destinations all over Spain.

Air France (☎ in France 08 20 82 08 20, in Spain 902 207 090; www.airfrance.com)

Alitalia (☎ in Italy 06 2222, in Spain 902 100 323; www .alitalia.it)

American Airlines (☎ in the USA 1800 433 7300, in Spain 902 115 570; www.aa.com) Flies to Madrid from New York and other US cities.

Austrian Airlines (☎ in Austria 05 1789, in Spain 902 257 000; www.aua.com)

British Airways (☎ in the UK 0133 264 8181, in Spain 902 999 262; www.britishairways.com)

British Midlands (☎ in the UK 0870 850 9850, in Spain 902 111333; www.flybmi.com/bmi) Connects Madrid to the UK, Cologne, Copenhagen, Milan, Nice and Oslo.

Continental Airlines (☎ in the USA 1800 231 0856, in Spain 900 961 266; www.continental.com) Daily flights to New York with connections to other US cities.

EasyJet (www.easyjet.com) Flies to Madrid from London (Gatwick and Luton), Liverpool, Geneva, Milan, Berlin and Paris.

German Wings (☎ in Germany 0900 191 9100, in Spain 91 625 97 04; www.germanwings.com) Flies to Madrid from Cologne and Stuttgart.

CLIMATE CHANGE & TRAVEL

Climate change is a serious threat to the ecosystems that humans rely upon, and air travel is the fastest-growing contributor to the problem. Lonely Planet regards travel, overall, as a global benefit, but believes we all have a responsibility to limit our personal impact on global warming.

FLYING & CLIMATE CHANGE

Pretty much every form of motorised travel generates carbon dioxide (the main cause of human-induced climate change) but planes are far and away the worst offenders, not just because of the sheer distances they allow us to travel, but because they release greenhouse gases high into the atmosphere. The statistics are frightening: two people taking a return flight between Europe and the US will contribute as much to climate change as an average household's gas and electricity consumption over a whole year.

CARBON OFFSET SCHEMES

Climatecare.org and other websites use 'carbon calculators' that allow travellers to offset the level of greenhouse gases they are responsible for with financial contributions to sustainable travel schemes that reduce global warming – including projects in India, Honduras, Kazakhstan and Uganda.

Lonely Planet, together with Rough Guides and other concerned partners in the travel industry, support the carbon offset scheme run by climatecare.org. Lonely Planet offsets all of its staff and author travel.

For more information check out our website: www.lonelyplanet.com.

Iberia (☎ 902 400 500; www.iberia.es)

KLM (☎ in the Netherlands 0204 747 747, in Spain 902 010 321; www.klm.com)

Lufthansa (☎ in Germany 0180 583 8426, in Spain 902 220 101; www.lufthansa.com)

Scandinavian SAS (☎ 902 117 192; www.scandinavian.net)

Spanair (☎ 902 131 415; www.spanair.com) Flights from Barcelona and other destinations throughout Spain, as well as some European connections.

Swiss (☎ 061 582 0000 in Switzerland, 901 116 712 in Spain; www.swiss.com)

TAP Air Portugal (☎ in Portugal 707 205 700, in Spain 901 116 718; www.flytap.com)

Transavia (☎ in the Netherlands 0900 0737, in Spain 902 114 478; www.transavia.com) Low-cost flights from Amsterdam to Madrid.

Virgin Express (☎ in Belgium 070 353 637, in Spain 902 888 459; www.virgin-express.com) Regular flights from Brussels to Madrid.

Vueling (☎ 902 33 39 33; www.vueling.com) New Spanish company with flights between Madrid and Amsterdam, Brussels, Lisbon, Milan, Paris and Rome.

Airports

Madrid's **Barajas airport** (☎ 91 305 8343, flight information 902 353 570; www.aena .es) lies 15km northeast of the city. Although in 2005 it saw 25 million passengers pass through its doors, the February 2006 inauguration of the new and superstylish terminal 4 (T4) dramatically expanded the airport's annual capacity to 70 million.

The new T4 deals mainly with flights of Iberia and its partners (eg British Airways, American Airlines and Aer Lingus), while other intercontinental or non-Schengen European flights leave from T1 (eg Air France, Alitalia, Austrian Airlines, British Midlands, Continental Airlines, easyJet, German Wings, KLM, Lufthansa, Scandinavian SAS, Swiss and US Airways). Spanair and Air Europa operate from both T1 and T2, depending on the destination. Air Berlin and TAP Air Portugal also operate from T2. At the time of writing, only the tiny Lagun Air was operating out of T3. Iberia's Puente Aereo (air shuttle) between Madrid and Barcelona, which operates like a bus service with no advance booking necessary, operates from T4.

Although most airlines conduct check-in (*facturación*) in the airport's departure areas, some also allow check-in at the Nuevos Ministerios metro stop and transport interchange in Madrid itself – ask your airline. The service allows you to check your luggage in early, take the metro to the airport unburdened and avoid queues at the airport itself.

The **tourist office** (☎ 91 305 86 56; ☼ 8am-8pm Mon-Sat, 9am-2pm Sun) is on the

Directory

TRANSPORT

GETTING TO & FROM THE AIRPORT

The easiest way into town from T1, T2 or T3 is line 8 of the metro (www.metromadrid.es; entrance in T2) to the Nuevos Ministerios transport interchange, which connects with other metro lines and the local overground *cercanías* (local trains serving big cities, suburbs and nearby towns). It operates from 6.05am to 2am. A single ticket costs €1 (10-ride Metrobús ticket €6.15).

Alternatively, take **bus 200** (☎ 902 507 850; €1) to/from the transport interchange on Avenida de América (Map pp246–7). The first departure from the city and the airport is at 5.20am. The last scheduled service from the airport is 11.30pm; buses leave every 12 to 15 minutes.

Until the metro line is extended to T4 in 2007, bus 204 runs from platform 17 of the **Intercambiador de Avenida de América** (Avenida de América transport interchange; Map pp246–7). Alternatively, take metro line 8 from Nuevos Ministerios to the final station (Barajas station), from where Bus 201 runs to T4.

AeroCITY (☎ 91 747 75 70; www.aerocity.com; Calle de Marzo 34) is a private minibus service that takes you door-to-door between central Madrid and the airport. Depending on how many passengers (maximum of seven) there are, the fare ranges from €18 to €5.57 per person. It operates 24 hours and you can book by phone or on the Web.

A taxi to the centre will cost you around €19, depending on traffic and where you're going. There are cab ranks outside all four terminals.

ground floor in the T1 area. There's also an **information booth** (☼ 9.30am-8.30pm) in the new T4. There are **ATMs** and exchange booths in all terminals, and **post offices** (☼ 8.30am-8.30pm Mon-Fri, 9.30am-1pm Sat) in the arrivals lounges of T1 and T4. International car-rental companies have desks in the arrivals area of T1, T2 and T4.

There are three **consignas** (left-luggage offices; ☼ 24hr): one in T1 (near the bus stop and taxi stand), in T2 (near the metro entrance) and on the ground floor of T4. In either, you pay €2.75 for the first 24-hour period (or fraction thereof). Thereafter, it costs €4.87 per day (up to 15 days) in a big locker, or €3.48 in a small one. After 15 days the bag will be moved into storage (€1.39/0.70 for a large/small locker plus a €34.81 transfer fee). For lost property in the airport, call ☎ 91 393 61 19.

Parking is available outside T1, T2 and T4. Rates are €1.50 per hour and up to €15 for 24 hours. Further away from the terminals and linked by a free shuttle bus is the Parking de Largas Estancias (long-term carpark) if you plan to leave a vehicle for several days (€9.50 first day, €8.50 per day from the second to fifth day and €4.50 per day thereafter).

BICYCLE

Lots of people zip around town on *motos* (mopeds), but little has been done to encourage cyclists in Madrid and bike lanes are almost as unheard of as drivers who respect the rights of cyclists.

You can transport your bicycle on the metro only on weekends and holidays. You can also take your bike aboard *cercanías* (local trains serving big cities, suburbs and nearby towns) from 10am onwards Monday to Friday and all day on weekends.

Hire

If you've the nerve to brave Madrid's traffic, consider Bike Spain (p59). In addition to offering bike tours of the city, it should also be your first stop for practical information and finding bike-friendly accommodation.

Karacol Sports (Map pp246–7; ☎ 91 539 96 33; www.karakol.es; Calle de Tortosa 8; Ⓜ Atocha Renfe), rents out road bikes and mountain bikes for €15 per day. There's a refundable deposit of €50 and you need to leave an original document (passport, driving licence or the like).

BUS
Long Distance

Estación Sur de Autobuses (☎ 91 468 42 00; www.estaciondeautobuses.com; Calle de Méndez Álvaro 83; Ⓜ Méndez Álvaro), just south of the M-30 ring road, is the city's principal bus station. It serves most destinations to the south and many in other parts of the country. Most bus companies have a ticket office here, even if their buses depart from elsewhere.

The station operates a **consigna** (left-luggage office; ☼ 6.30am-midnight) near where the buses exit the station. There are cafés, shops, exchange booths, a bank, and a police post; there's also direct access to metro line 6.

Eurolines (www.eurolines.com), in conjunction with local carriers all over Europe, is the main international carrier connecting Spain to cities across Europe and to Morocco from the Estación Sur de Autobuses. For information and tickets, contact **Eurolines Peninsular** (☎ 902 405 040; www.eurolines.es). **ALSA Internacional** (☎ 902 422 242; www.alsa.es) is another international operator.

Several companies operate out of other terminals around the city. Of these, some useful ones include the following.

ALSA (Map pp246–7; ☎ 902 422 242; www.alsa.es; Intercambiador de Avenida de América; M Avenida de América) Buses to Barcelona via Zaragoza, and a host of services throughout Spain from Estación Sur.

AutoRes (Map pp246–7; ☎ 902 020 999; www.auto-res.net; Calle de Fernández Shaw 1; M Conde de Casal) Services to Extremadura (eg Cáceres), Castilla y León (eg Salamanca and Zamora) and Valencia via Cuenca. Also runs buses to Lisbon, Portugal.

Continental-Auto (Map pp246–7; ☎ 902 330 400; www.continental-auto.es; Intercambiador de Avenida de América; M Avenida de América) Extensive network includes services to Burgos, Bilbao, San Sebastián and Granada.

Herranz (Map pp246–7; ☎ 91 890 90 28; Moncloa Intercambiador de Autobuses; M Moncloa) Buses to San Lorenzo de El Escorial from platform 3 of the bus station below ground level at the Moncloa metro station.

La Sepulvedana (Map pp246–7; ☎ 91 559 8955; www.lasepulvedana.es; Paseo de la Florida 11; M Príncipe Pío) Buses to Segovia and La Granja de San Ildefonso.

La Veloz (Map pp246–7; ☎ 91 409 76 02; Avenida del Mediterráneo 49; M Conde de Casal) Buses to Chinchón.

Madrid

Buses operated by **Empresa Municipal de Transportes de Madrid** (EMT; ☎ 902 507 850; www.emtmadrid.es) travel along most city routes regularly between about 6.30am and 11.30pm. Twenty night-bus *búhos* (routes) operate from midnight to 6am. They run from Puerta del Sol and Plaza de la Cibeles, and the Ayuntamiento (town hall) has announced plans to significantly increase the number of buses running each night.

For details of the Madrid Visión sightseeing buses, see p59.

CAR & MOTORCYCLE
Driving to Madrid

Madrid is located 2622km from Berlin, 2245km from London, 1889km from Milan, 1836km from Paris, 1470km from Geneva, 690km from Barcelona and 610km from Lisbon.

It is the centre point in Spain from which most of the country's major highways radiate out to the coast. The A-1 heads north to Burgos and ultimately to Santander (for the UK ferry); the A-2 wends its way northeast to Barcelona and ultimately into France (as the AP-7). The A-4 takes you south to Andalucía, while the A-5 and A-6 respectively take you west towards Portugal via Cáceres and northwest to Galicia. The A-42 goes south to Toledo.

The city is surrounded by two main ring roads, the outermost M-40 and the inner M-30; there are also two additional partial ring roads, the M-45 and the more-distant M-50. The R-5 and R-3, opened in early 2004, are two of a series of planned new toll roads built to ease the epic traffic jams as Madrileños stream back from vacations and weekend getaways.

Coming from the UK you can put your car on a ferry from Portsmouth to Bilbao with **P&O Ferries** (☎ 0870 59 80 333; www.poportsmouth.com) or from Plymouth to Santander with **Brittany Ferries** (☎ 0870 36 65 333; www.brittany-ferries.com). From Bilbao or Santandar you barrel south to the capital. Otherwise, you can opt for a ferry to France or the Channel Tunnel car train, **Eurotunnel** (☎ 0870 53 53 535; www.eurotunnel.com).

Vehicles must be roadworthy, registered and insured (third party at least). Also ask your insurer for a European Accident Statement form, which can simplify matters in the event of an accident. A European breakdown-assistance policy (eg AA Five Star Service or RAC Eurocover Motoring Assistance in the UK) is a good investment.

If you're here on a tourist visa, you only need your national driving licence, although it's wise to also carry an International Driving Permit (available from the automobile association in your home country) as well; the same applies to drivers from EU countries regardless of how long you stay. If you're a resident in Spain and come from a non-EU country, it depends on whether your government has a reciprocal rights agreement with Spain allowing you to drive. If you're from Australia, for example, you'll need to go through the hassle of sitting your driving exams all over again. Check with your embassy.

Driving & Parking in Madrid

The Spanish drive on the right, it can be a little hair-raising. The grand roundabouts of the major thoroughfares sometimes require nerves of steel as people turn left from the right-hand lanes or right from the centre. The morning and evening rush hours frequently involve snarling traffic jams which are even possible in the wee hours of the morning, especially towards the end of the week when the whole city seems to be behind the wheel or in a bar. The streets are dead between about 2pm and 4pm, when people are either eating or snoozing.

Most of Madrid is now divided up into clearly marked blue or green street-parking zones. In both areas, parking meters apply from 9am to 8pm Monday to Friday and from 9am to 3pm on Saturday; the Saturday hours also apply for every day in August. In the green areas, you can park for a maximum of one hour (or keep putting money in the metre every hour) for €1.80. In the blue zones, you can park for two hours for €2.55. There are also private parking stations all over central Madrid.

You'll see local cars abandoned in the most unlikely of places, but following their example by parking in a designated no-parking area exposes you to the risk of being towed. Double-parking is similarly common and decidedly risky if you wander far from your vehicle. Should your car disappear, call the **Grúa Municipal** (city towing service; ☎ 91 345 06 66). Getting it back costs €120 plus whatever fine you've been given.

Hire

The big-name, car-hire agencies have offices all over Madrid. Avis, Europcar, Hertz and National/Atesa have booths at the airport. Some also operate branches at Atocha and Chamartín train stations. If prices at the bigger agencies seem too high, try www.auto-europe.com which operates as a clearing house for the best deals by the major companies. Smaller operators often have one reservation phone number and

an out-of-the-way office – ask if they can deliver the car to a convenient location. The rental agencies' most central offices include the following:

Avis (Map pp250–1; ☎ 902 180 854; www.avis.es; Gran Vía 60; Ⓜ Santo Domingo or Plaza de España)

Europcar (Map pp250–1; ☎ 902 105 055; www .europcar.es; Calle de San Leonardo de Dios 8; Ⓜ Plaza de España)

Hertz (Map pp250–1; ☎ 902 402 405; www.hertz.es; Edificio de España, Plaza de España; Ⓜ Plaza de España)

Moto Alquiler (Map pp250–1; ☎ 91 542 06 57; motoalquiler@telefonica.net; Calle del Conde Duque 13; Ⓜ San Bernardo) Motorbike rental. Something like a Honda CBF500 will cost you €335 for a Monday to Friday package and they'll take a credit card imprint as a deposit.

National/Atesa (Map pp250–1; ☎ 902 100 101; www .atesa.es; Gran Vía 80, 1st fl; Ⓜ Plaza de España)

Pepecar (Map pp250–1; ☎ 807 414 243; www.pepe car.com; underground parking area, Plaza de España; Ⓜ Plaza de España) Specialises in rentals for as low as €16 per day (with 100 free kilometres), plus a credit card handling fee and €14 cleaning charge. Bookings are best made over the Internet.

METRO & CERCANÍAS

Madrid's modern **metro** (☎ 902 444 403; www.metromadrid.es) is a fast, efficient and safe way to navigate Madrid, and generally easier than getting to grips with bus routes. It has 11 colour-coded lines, in addition to the modern southern suburban MetroSur system, and operates from about 6am to 1.30am.

This book contains a colour map of the main central Madrid metro system; the MetroSur is unlikely to be of interest to visitors.

The short-range *cercanías* regional trains operated by Renfe, the national railways, go as far afield as El Escorial, Alcalá de Henares, Aranjuez and other points in the Comunidad de Madrid. In Madrid itself, they're handy for making a quick, north–south hop between Chamartín and Atocha mainline train stations (with stops at Nuevos Ministerios and in front of the Biblioteca Nacional on Paseo de los Recoletos only). Another line links Chamartín, Atocha and Príncipe Pío stations.

Major infrastructure works are currently underway which, when completed, will connect Atocha station with Sol, Nuevos Ministerios (for connections to the airport), and Charmatín, making it a whole lot easier when arriving, passing through or leaving Madrid. Like most major works in Madrid, when they finish is anyone's guess.

Tickets

Unless you're only passing through en route elsewhere, it's worth your while to buy a Metrobús ticket valid for 10 rides (bus and metro) for €6.15; single-journey tickets cost €1. Tickets can be purchased at stations from manned booths or machines, as well as most *estancos* (tobacconists) and newspaper kiosks. Metrobús tickets are not valid on *cercanías* services.

Monthly or season passes (*abonos*) only make sense if you're staying long term and use local transport frequently. You'll need to get a *carnet* (ID card) from metro stations or tobacconists – take a passport-sized photo and your passport. A monthly ticket for central Madrid (Zona A) costs €39.

An **Abono Turístico** (Tourist Ticket; 1/2/7 days €3.50/6.30/18.40), is also available if you buy the Madrid Card (p211).

The fine for being caught without a ticket on public transport is €20 – in addition to the price of the ticket, of course.

TAXI

You can pick up a cab at ranks throughout town or simply flag one down. Flag fall is €1.75; make sure the driver turns the meter on. You pay €0.82 per kilometre (€0.95 between 10pm and 6am). Several supplementary charges, usually posted up inside the taxi, apply; these can include €4.50 to/from the airport, €2.40 from cab ranks at train and bus stations, €2.40 to/from the Parque Ferial Juan Carlos I. There's no charge for luggage.

Among the 24-hour taxi services are **Radio-Taxi** (☎ 91 405 55 00, 91 445 90 08, 91 447 51 80) and **Tele-Taxi** (☎ 91 371 21 31, 902 501 130).

Radio-Teléfono Taxi (☎ 91 547 82 00, 91 547 86 00) runs taxis for the disabled. Generally, if you call any taxi company and ask for a 'eurotaxi' you should be sent one adapted for wheelchair users.

A green light on the roof means the taxi is *libre* (available). Generally a sign to this effect is also placed in the lower passenger side of the windscreen.

TRAIN

Spain's rail network is modern and extensive with Madrid well-connected to cities and towns across Spain. A handful of international trains also serve the city. The latter can be a long haul and you may find flying cheaper as well as faster.

For information on travelling from the UK contact the **Rail Europe Travel Centre** (☎ 0870 83 71 371; www.raileurope.co.uk).

For travel within Spain, information (including timetables) is available from your nearest train station or travel agent or from the operator of the rail network, **Renfe** (☎ 902 240 202; www.renfe.es).

There are different types of service, but remember that saving a couple of hours on a faster train can mean a big hike in the fare. Most trains have *preferente* (1st class) and *turista* (2nd class).

High-speed Tren de Alta Velocidad Española (AVE) services connect Madrid with Seville via Córdoba in the south and Zaragoza, Huesca and Lleida (and one day Barcelona) in the northeast. There's also a shorter run to Toledo and a service planned to Valladolid. The AVE trains can reach speeds of 350km/h.

Train Stations

Two train stations serve the city. Note that many trains call in at either one or the other (but rarely both), so check when purchasing tickets. At **Atocha train station** (Map pp246–7; Metro Atocha Renfe), south of the old city centre, there's an information and ticket centre for long-distance services (including the high-speed AVE) in the old station (the part now serving as a tropical garden). In the same area are luggage lockers available from 6.30am to 10.20pm (€2.40/3/4.50 per day, depending on the size of the locker). Full timetables for long-distance trains are also posted outside the ticket office. Another **information office** (☽ 7am-11pm) near platforms 9 and 10 (look for the 'Atención al Cliente' sign) deals with regional and *cercanías* trains, and property lost on these trains. Tickets for regional trains can be bought at a separate counter.

In **Chamartín station** (Map p245; Metro Chamartín), information and tickets are available at the **Centro de Viajes** (☽ 7am-11pm), between platforms 7 and 10. Exchange booths and ATMs are scattered about the station. Lockers are located outside the main station building (take the exit opposite platform 18) and are available between 7am and 11pm (€2.40/3/4.50 per day, depending on the size of the locker).

PRACTICALITIES

ACCOMMODATION

Madrid once suffered by comparison to Barcelona when it came to cutting edge sleeping options. The capital still has its share of no-frills hostels and standard midrange digs, but these are now taking a back seat to modern, stylish choices across a range of budgets, not to mention a few grand old hotels. See the Sleeping chapter (p168) earlier in the guide for recommendations and prices.

The options are presented by district, in price and then alphabetical order. The emphasis is on midrange accommodation, but we have slipped in some of the city's best budget beds and some great top range hotels as well.

High season is most of the year for most hotels and many don't alter their rates significantly during the year. There are slow times, such as the depths of winter (late November to December, except Christmas, and mid-January to March) when hoteliers may be prepared to do deals, although this depends on whether or not trade fairs are being held. Many of the top, business-oriented hotels also cut good deals for weekend stays.

BOOK ACCOMMODATION ONLINE

For more accommodation reviews and recommendations by Lonely Planet authors, check out the online booking service at www.lonelyplanet.com. You'll find the true, insider lowdown on the best places to stay. Reviews are thorough and independent. Best of all, you can book online.

BUSINESS HOURS

Standard working hours are Monday to Friday from 8am or 9am to 2pm and then again from 3pm or 4pm for another three hours.

Banks open from 8.30am to 2pm Monday to Friday; some also open 4pm and 7pm on Thursday and/or 9am to 1pm on Saturday.

The Central Post Office opens from 8.30am to 9.30pm Monday to Saturday, while some post offices open from 8.30am to 8.30pm but most only open from 8am to 2pm Monday to Friday.

Restaurants usually open from 1pm to 4pm and again from 8.30pm to midnight (but later on Friday and Saturday)

Shops open from 10am to 2pm and 5pm to 8pm Monday to Friday; big stores (eg El Corte Inglés and Fnac) open between 10am and 10pm Monday to Saturday, while smaller shops open from 10am to 2pm on Saturday. Shops selling books and music, and some convenience stores, may open on Sunday and all shops are permitted to open on the first Sunday of each month and throughout December.

CHILDREN

For Madrileños (and Spaniards in general), going out to eat or sipping a beer on a late summer evening at a *terraza* (outdoor café or bar) rarely means leaving kids with minders. Locals take their kids out all the time and don't worry too much about keeping them up late.

Like any big city, Madrid has plenty of child-friendly sights and activities. Most churches and museums probably aren't among them but the interactive elements of the Museo del Libro (p90) should be fun once the interminable renovations are finished, and the Museo de Cera (Wax Museum; p93) usually works for young kids.

If your boy's a boy, he'll most likely love the Museo del Ferrocarril (p101) and the Museo Naval (p85), the railway and navy museums. Riding to the top of the Faro (p96) or high above Madrid in the Teleférico (p98) can also score points. Finally, the Parque del Buen Retiro (p87), has ample space to run around or you can rent a boat; on weekends and holidays you may catch some marionette theatre or see jugglers.

Not especially typical of Madrid, but fun nonetheless, are the amusement parks such as the more traditional Parque de Atracciones (p101) or Warner Brothers Movie World (p101), outside the city. For some animal fun, try Faunia (p100) or the Zoo Aquarium de Madrid (p102).

In the hot summer months you'll doubtless be rewarded by squeals of delight if you take the bairns to one of the city's municipal pools (p153). For something a little more exhilarating, try the Parque de Nieve (Ski Park) at Madrid Xanadú (p153) for year-round skiing.

For our choice of the top five for kids see boxed text, p58. For general advice on travelling with children, grab Lonely Planet's *Travel with Children*.

There's no real tradition in Spain of professional baby-sitting services, but most of the medium- and upper-range hotels in Madrid can organise baby-sitting. Alternatively, you can try to line something up through www.canguroencasa.com (*canguro* or 'kangaroo' also means baby-sitter in Spanish).

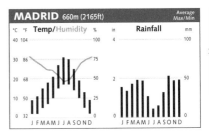

May, when the wet spells you missed earlier catch up with you! Never short of a saying, Spaniards say of April, *mes de abril, aguas mil* – it rains a lot in this spring month.

CLIMATE

Madrid is renowned for having a climate of extremes, as summed up by the phrase *nueve meses de invierno y tres de infierno* (nine months of winter and three of hell). The high inland plateau where Madrid is located indeed ensures scorching summers and bitterly cold winters.

July is the hottest month, with August running a close second. Average highs hover above 30°C, but the maximum is frequently in excess of 35°C and sometimes nudges 40°C. At 4am you can still be gasping for air. Air conditioning in your room is a godsend at this time of year. The only plus is that it's generally a dry heat with very little humidity, except when one of the capital's occasional apocalyptic summer storms approaches.

The coldest months are January and February, when daily average highs are below 10°C. At night it frequently drops below freezing, although it rarely snows in Madrid. Whatever the official temperature, you'll really notice the cold when an icy wind blows in off the snow-capped sierra. At any time during winter, you may, however, be lucky to get piercing blue skies and daytime temperatures do occasionally reach the mid-teens.

Spring and autumn are lovely times to be in Madrid, although it's also the period with the heaviest rainfall; more than 50mm are quite common in October, and March can be unpredictable. In Spain they say *cuando en marzo mayea, en mayo marzea*. In other words, if you get nice, warm dry days in March (weather more typical of May), you'll be wiping that grin off your face in

COURSES

Spanish Classes

Madrid is jammed with language schools of all possible categories, as eager to teach foreigners Spanish as locals other languages.

Non-EU citizens who want to study at a university or language school in Spain should have a study visa. These visas can be obtained from your nearest Spanish embassy or consulate. You'll normally require confirmation of your enrolment, payment of fees and proof of adequate funds to support yourself before a visa is issued. This type of visa is renewable within Spain but, again, only with confirmation of ongoing enrolment and proof that you're able to support yourself.

Some language schools worth investigating include the following.

Academia Inhispania (Map pp254–5; ☎ 91 521 22 31; www.inhispania.com; Calle de la Montera 10-12; Ⓜ Sol) Intensive, four-week courses start at €490.

Academia Madrid Plus (Map pp254–5; ☎ 91 548 11 16; www.madridplus.es; Calle del Arenal 21; Ⓜ Ópera) Four-week (30-hour) courses begin at €255.

Acento Español (Map pp254–5; ☎ 91 521 36 76; www.acentoespanol.com; Calle Mayor 4; Ⓜ Sol) Four-week courses start at €450.

Escuela Oficial de Idiomas (Map p244; ☎ 91 553 00 88; www.eoidiomas.com; Calle de Jesús Maestro; Ⓜ Canal) Here, you'll find courses in Spanish for foreigners *(español para extranjeros)* at most levels. A semester can cost from just €88.95 so demand is high.

International House (Map pp250–1; ☎ 91 319 72 24; www.ihmadrid.es; Calle de Zurbano 8; Ⓜ Alonso Martínez) Intensive courses start at around €369 for two weeks. Staff can organise accommodation with local families.

Universidad Complutense (Map p244; ☎ 91 394 53 36; www.ucm.es/info/cextran/Index.htm; Secretaria de los Cursos para Extranjeros, Facultadole Filologia [Edificio A] Universidad Complutense, Cuidad Universitaria, 28040 Madrid; Ⓜ Cuidad Universitaria) You can try a range of language and cultural courses throughout the year. An intensive semester course of 150 contact hours costs €400.

Wine & Cooking Courses

If you know where to look, there are plenty of places to learn Spanish cooking or wine appreciation. In most cases, you'd need at least passable Spanish, but some run special classes for English-speakers.

ACYRE (Map pp254–5; ☎ 91 420 19 26; elbc@elbuencomer.com; Calle de las Huertas 43; Ⓜ Antón Martín) This gastronomic school offers courses that last for months, but whether they're open to the public changes from season to season.

Alambique (Map pp254–5; ☎ 91 559 78 58; www .alambique.com; Plaza de la Encarnación 2; ☺ 10am-2pm & 5-8pm Mon-Fri, 10am-2pm Sat; Ⓜ Ópera or Santo Domingo) Cooking classes start from around €40 with English-speaking courses from €65.

Cooking Club (Map p245; ☎ 91 323 29 58; www.club -cooking.com in Spanish; Calle de Veza 33; Ⓜ Valdeacederas) The regular and respected programme of classes encompasses a range of cooking styles.

La Inquilina (☎ 627 511 804; Calle de Ave María 39; ☺ 7pm-2am Tue-Thu, 1-4pm & 8pm-3am Fri-Sun; Ⓜ Lavapiés) Wine appreciation classes are available for €75. See also p134.

La Maison (Map pp250–1; ☎ cooking 620 566 676, wine 649 803 283; www.lamaison.es in Spanish, yokocina@hotmail.com; Calle de San Mateo 26, 3rd fl; ☺ by appointment; Ⓜ Alonso Martínez or Tribunal) Try creative cooking and wine classes (€40 and €80 respectively) as part of this fascinating designer/decoration/artist space. Don't bother turning up without ringing or emailing first.

Lavinia (☎ 91 426 06 04; www.lavinia.es; Calle de José Ortega y Gasset 16; ☺ 10am-9pm; Ⓜ Núñez de Balboa) Wine courses (in Spanish) cost from €33 to €105.

Poncelet (☎ 91 308 02 21; www.poncelet.es; Calle de Argensola 27; ☺ 10.30am-8.30pm Mon-Sat; Ⓜ Alonso Martínez) Try the monthly primers on cheese and wine appreciation for €40.

Other Courses

Centro Cultural de Lavapiés (Map pp254–5; ☎ 91 506 07 12; Calle de Olivar 46; ☺ 8am-10pm Mon-Fri; Ⓜ Lavapiés) has a range of (mostly Spanish-language) courses as eclectic as the barrio itself, including ceramics, photography, t'ai-chi, guitar and reflexology.

If you've always wanted to learn how to play guitar like the flamenco greats, stop by **El Flamenco Vive** (p158; ☎ 91 547 39 17; www.elflamencovive.com in Spanish; Calle del Conde de Lemos 7; ☺ 10.30am-2pm & 5-9pm Mon-Sat; Ⓜ Ópera) and make an appointment for sessions (€20 per hour) with the resident teacher. You can also enquire about lessons at **Casa Patas** (p145). The best-known course for flamenco dancing (and probably the hardest to get into) is the **Academia Amor de Diós** (Map pp246–7; ☎ 91 530 16 61; Calle de Fray Luís de León 13; Ⓜ Palos de la Frontera), although it's more for budding professionals than the casual visitor.

CUSTOMS

People entering Spain from outside the EU are allowed to bring in duty-free one bottle of spirits, one bottle of wine, 50mL of perfume and 200 cigarettes. There are no duty-free allowances for travel between EU countries. For duty-paid items bought at normal shops in one EU country and taken into another, the allowances are 90L of wine, 10L of spirits, unlimited quantities of perfume and 800 cigarettes. For more information on obtaining VAT refunds, see p216.

DISABLED TRAVELLERS

Although things are changing slowly, Madrid remains something of an obstacle course for disabled travellers. Some hotels and public institutions have wheelchair access and metro lines built since the late 1990s generally have elevators for wheelchair access but the older lines are generally ill-equipped. The single-deck *piso bajo* (low flat) buses have no steps inside and in some cases have ramps that can be used by people in wheelchairs. In the long run, there are plans to make at least 50% of its buses on all routes accessible to the disabled. The Ayuntamiento de Madrid publishes a *Guía de Accesibilidad* which contains information on disabled access to everything from the city's cinemas through to its public service buildings; it's designed mostly for residents. One sight which is wheelchair-friendly is the Museo del Prado (p83). For information on taxis for disabled travellers, see p207.

Directory PRACTICALITIES

Organisations

Access-able Travel Source (☎ 303-232 2979; fax 303-239 8486; www.access-able.com; PO Box 1796, Wheatridge, CO, USA) Has a forum and links to travel agents and other travel-related topics.

Accessible Travel & Leisure (☎ 0145 272 9739; www.accessibletravel.co.uk; Avionics House, Naas Lane, Gloucester GL2 4SN) Claims to be the biggest UK travel agent dealing with travel for the disabled. The company encourages the disabled to travel independently.

Holiday Care (☎ 0845 124 9971; www.holidaycare.org.uk; 2nd fl, Imperial Buildings, Victoria Rd, Horley, Surrey RH6 7PZ) Information on hotels with disabled access, where to hire equipment and tour operators dealing with the disabled.

ONCE (Organización Nacional de Ciegos Españoles; Map p252; ☎ 91 436 53 00; www.once.es; Calle de José Ortega y Gasset 22-24; Ⓜ Núñez de Balboa) The Spanish association for the blind. You may be able to get hold of a Madrid guide in Braille, although it is not published every year.

Royal Association for Disability & Rehabilitation – RADAR (☎ 0207 250 3222; www.radar.org.uk; Unit 12, City Forum, 250 City Rd, London EC1V 8AS) Publishes *European Holidays & Travel Abroad: A Guide for Disabled People,* which provides a good overview of facilities available to disabled travellers throughout Europe.

DISCOUNT CARDS

The International Student Identity Card (ISIC; see www.isic.org) and the Euro<26 card (www.euro26.org), for youth under 26, are available from most national student organisations and can gain you discounted access to sights.

If you intend to do some intensive sightseeing and travelling on public transport, it might be worth looking at the **Madrid Card** (☎ 902 877 996; www.madridcard.com). It includes free entry to 43 museums in and around Madrid and free Descubre Madrid (p59) walking tours, as well as discounts on public transport, the Madrid Visión tourist bus and in certain shops and restaurants. The ticket is available for one/two/three days (€36/46/56). There's also a cheaper version (€22/26/30) which just covers cultural sights. You save €4/5 off the two- and three-day cards respectively by purchasing online. Otherwise, purchase it at the tourist offices on Plaza Mayor and in Calle del Duque de Medinaceli (see Tourist Information, p218), on the Madrid Visión bus and in some tobacconists and hotels.

ELECTRICITY

The electric current in Madrid is 220V, 50Hz, as in the rest of continental Europe. Several countries outside Europe (such as the USA and Canada) use 110V, 60Hz, which means that it's safest to use a transformer. Plugs have two round pins, as in the rest of continental Europe.

EMBASSIES & CONSULATES

Most countries have an embassy or consulate in Madrid; there's a full list at www.esmadrid.com.

Australia (Map p245; ☎ 91 353 66 00; www.spain.embassy.gov.au; Plaza del Descubridor Diego de Ordás 3; Ⓜ Ríos Rosas)

Canada (Map p252; ☎ 91 423 32 50; www.canada-es.org; Calle de Núñez de Balboa 35; Ⓜ Velázquez)

France (Map p257; ☎ 91 423 89 00; www.ambafrance-es.org; Calle de Salustiano Olózaga 9; Ⓜ Retiro)

Germany (Map p252; ☎ 91 557 90 00; www.embajada-alemania.es; Calle de Fortuny 8; Ⓜ Rubén Dario)

Ireland (Map p252; ☎ 91 436 40 93; embajada@irlanda.es; Paseo de la Castellana 46; Ⓜ Rubén Dario)

New Zealand (Map p257; ☎ 91 523 02 26; www.nzembassy.com/home.cfm?c=27; Plaza de la Lealtad 2; Ⓜ Banco de España)

UK consulate-general (Map p257; ☎ 91 524 97 00; Paseo de Recoletos 7/9; Ⓜ Colón); embassy (Map p252; ☎ 91 700 82 00; www.ukinspain.com; Calle de Fernando el Santo 16; Ⓜ Colón)

USA (Map pp246–7; ☎ 91 587 22 00; www.embusa.es; Calle de Serrano 75; Ⓜ Núñez de Balboa)

EMERGENCY

For practical information on keeping your wits about you in Madrid, see p216. To report thefts go to the national police. There's a handy central **police station** (Comisaría; Map pp254–5; ☎ 91 322 10 07; Calle de las Huertas 76; Ⓜ Antón Martín), where they may have an officer who speaks English.

Ambulance ☎ 061

EU standard emergency number ☎ 112

Fire brigade (Bomberos) ☎ 080

Local police (Policía Municipal) ☎ 092

Military police (Guardia Civil) ☎ 062

National police (Policía Nacional) ☎ 091

GAY & LESBIAN TRAVELLERS

It's a great time to be gay in Madrid. Under laws passed by the Spanish Congress in June 2005, same-sex marriages now enjoy the same legal protection as those between heterosexual partners, even extending into the realm of full adoption and inheritance rights. At the time there was something of a conservative backlash, but opinion polls showed that the reforms were supported by more than two-thirds of Spaniards.

Madrid has always been one of Europe's most gay-friendly cities and the gay community is credited with reinvigorating the once down-at-heel inner-city barrio of Chueca. Today, Chueca is one of Madrid's most vibrant barrios and is very much the heart and soul of gay Madrid. Restaurants, cafés and bars clearly oriented to a gay clientele abound, and new book, video and adult-toy shops aimed at gay people continue to spring up in and around Chueca. Several gay-friendly hotels operate around this barrio too. All of which means that gay travellers will quickly feel at home in this vibrant community.

A couple of informative free magazines are in circulation in gay bookshops and gay-friendly bars. One is the bi-weekly *Shanguide* which is jammed with listings and contact ads. A companion publication is *Shangay Express*, better for articles and a handful of listings and ads. The *Mapa Gaya de Madrid* lists gay bars, discos, saunas and other places of specific gay and lesbian interest in the city. You can pick up a copy in the **Berkana bookstore** (Map pp250–1; ☎ 91 522 55 99; Calle de Hortaleza 64; Ⓜ Chueca). There you'll also find the useful *Punto Guía de España para Gays y Lesbianas*, a countrywide guide for gay and gay-friendly bars, restaurants, hotels and shops around the country. The monthly *MENsual* costs €2 at newsstands, but is free at Berkana; there's a web version at www.mensual.com.

Madrid's gay and lesbian pride march (p10) is held on the last Saturday in June.

You can also check out the following sites on the Web:

Chueca.com (www.chueca.com) Its Guía Nocturna (Night Guide; for bars and clubs) is only available to subscribers to Chueca XL (the members-only section of the website; €20 per year).

Guía Gay (www.guiagay.com) Forums, news and public events.

Nación Gay (www.naciongay.com) News on the gay community across Spain.

Orgullo Gay (www.orgullogay.org) Website for the gay and lesbian pride march and links to gay organisations across the country.

Voz Gay (www.vozgay.com) Plenty of listings for the capital.

Organisations

Colectivo de Gais y Lesbianas de Madrid (Cogam; Map pp254–5; ☎ 91 522 45 17; www.cogam.org; Calle de las Infantas 40; Ⓜ Chueca) Offers an information office and social centre and runs an information line (☎ 91 523 00 70) from 5pm to 9pm on Fridays. The Comunidad de Madrid also has a toll-free information line (☎ 900 720569) from 10am to 2pm and 5pm to 9pm, Monday to Friday.

Federación Estatal de Lesbianas, Gays, Transexuales & Bisexuales (Felgt; Map pp254–5; ☎ 91 360 46 05; www.felgt.org; Calle de Infantas 40; Ⓜ Chueca) A national advocacy group that played a leading role in lobbying for the legalisation of gay marriages.

Fundación Triángulo (Map pp246–7; ☎ 91 593 05 40; www.fundaciontriangulo.es; Calle de Eloy Gonzalo 25; Ⓜ Iglesia) Another source of information on gay issues.

HOLIDAYS

When a holiday falls close to a weekend, Madrileños like to make a *puente* (bridge) and take the intervening day off. On the odd occasion when a couple of holidays fall close, they make an *acueducto* (aqueduct)! For Madrileños, however, the main holiday periods are during summer (July and especially August), Christmas–New Year and Easter. August can be a peculiar time as locals make their annual migration to the beach and the city they left behind grinds to a halt – this is a bad time to be trying to do business. Madrid's 14 public holidays are as follows:

Año Nuevo (New Year's Day) 1 January – see p9.

Reyes (Epiphany or Three Kings' Day) 6 January – see p9.

Jueves Santo (Good Thursday) March/April – see p10.

Viernes Santo (Good Friday) March/April – see p10.

Labour Day (Fiesta del Trabajo) 1 May.

Fiesta de la Comunidad de Madrid 2 May – see p10.

Fiestas de San Isidro Labrador 15 May – see p10.

La Asunción (Feast of the Assumption) 15 August.

Día de la Hispanidad (Spanish National Day) 12 October – a fairly sober occasion with a military parade.

Todos los Santos (All Saints' Day) 1 November.

Día de la Virgen de la Almudena 9 November – see p11.

Día de la Constitución (Constitution Day) 6 December.

La Inmaculada Concepción (Feast of the Immaculate Conception) 8 December.

Navidad (Christmas) 25 December – see p11.

For more information on the city's colourful festivals and other events, see the City Calendar section, p9.

INTERNET ACCESS

Travelling with a portable computer is a great way to stay in touch with home, but make sure you have a universal AC adapter, a two-pin European plug adapter and a reputable 'global' modem. Spanish telephone sockets are the US RJ-11 type. Some of the better hotels have Internet connections and sometimes just plugging into the room's phone socket will be sufficient (unless you have to go through a switchboard).

Major Internet service providers (ISPs) such as **CompuServe** (http://webcenters.com puserve.netscape.com) have dial-in nodes in Spain; download a list of the dial-in numbers before you leave home.

Some Spanish Internet servers can provide short-term accounts. Try **Tiscali** (☎ 902 765 902; www.tiscali.es) or **Terra** (☎ 902 152 025; www.terra.es). It's also worth checking out http://spain.dialer.net/and www.on spanishtime.com/web.

If you intend to rely on cybercafés for your email you'll need to carry three pieces of information: your incoming (POP or IMAP) mail server name, your account name and your password.

When it comes to wireless (wi-fi) access, the number of wi-fi hotspots is growing and short-term accounts (monthly subscriptions and prepaid accounts) are possible through **Telefonica** (www.telefonica.es). Otherwise, check out www.totalhotspots.com/direc tory/es for an updated list of places (eg airports, hotels and some cafés, such as Starbucks) where wi-fi access is available.

Internet Cafés

Madrid is full of Internet centres. Some offer student rates, while others have deals on cards for several hours' use at reduced rates. In addition to the following handful of options, the Ayuntamiento's Centro de Turismo de Madrid (p218) on the Plaza Mayor offers free Internet for up to 15 minutes.

Cyber Total (Map pp254–5; ☎ 91 532 26 22; Calle de Espoz y Mina 17; per hr €2; ☉ 10am-10pm; Ⓜ Sol) High-speed Internet connections, fax, printing, scanning and CD burning are all possible at this modern, savvy place.

Drop & Drag (Map pp250–1; ☎ 91 532 93 72; Calle de Augusto Figueroa 7; per hr €2.20; ☉ noon-1am Mon-Fri, 3pm-midnight Sat & Sun; Ⓜ Tribunal or Chueca) Handy if you're in Chueca.

La Casa de Internet (Map pp250–1; ☎ 91 594 42 00; Calle de Luchana 20, 1st fl; per hr €2.10; ☉ 9am-12.30am Mon-Fri, 10am-12.30am Sat, 5pm-12.30pm Sun; Ⓜ Bilbao) Terrific Internet café with 60 fast computers and where prices drop as low as €1.25 the more time you use. There are smoking and nonsmoking areas, computer courses, and free tea and coffee.

Nevada 2000 (Map pp250–1; ☎ 91 521 20 94; Calle de los Reyes 7; per hr €1.80; ☉ 8am-1am daily; Ⓜ Noviciado) Get past the smoky old café with one-armed bandits and you'll find that this place has fast connections out the back.

Navega Web (Telefonica; Map pp254–5; Gran Vía 30; per hr €2; ☉ 10am-2pm & 5-9pm Mon-Sat; Ⓜ Gran Vía) This Internet café is housed within the national telephone company's phone centre.

LOST PROPERTY

The **Negociado de Objetos Perdidos** (☎ 91 588 43 48, 91 527 95 90; Plaza de Legazpi 7; ☉ 9am-2pm; Ⓜ Legazpi) holds lost property handed in around the city (including things found on the metro and buses). If you leave something in a taxi, call the taxi company concerned. If you lose something on a *cercanías* train, check at the information desk at Atocha train station.

MAPS

Long-termers seeking comprehensive map books and atlases are spoiled for choice. A good one is Almax's *Callejero de Madrid*, scaled at 1:12,000. The same publisher produces *Atlas de Madrid*, that covers Madrid and the surrounding municipalities. You could also try the superdetailed *Guía Urbana*. If you're looking for a specific address, check out www.qdq.com and click on *Callejeros Fotográficos* and you'll get a photo of the building you're looking for.

MEDICAL SERVICES

All foreigners have the same right as Spaniards to free emergency medical treatment in a public hospital. European Union citizens are entitled to the full range of health-care services in public hospitals free of charge, but you'll need to present your E111 form (enquire at your national health service before leaving home). Even if you have no insurance, you'll be treated in an emergency.

Non-EU citizens have to pay for anything other than emergency treatment – a good reason to have a travel insurance policy.

For minor health problems, you can try your local *farmacia* (pharmacy; see opposite), where pharmaceuticals tend to be sold more freely without prescription than in other places such as the USA, Australia or the UK.

Your embassy should be able to refer you to doctors who speak your language. If you have a specific health complaint, obtain the necessary information and referrals for treatment before leaving home.

Some useful numbers and addresses for travellers:

Anglo-American Medical Unit (Map p252; ☎ 91 435 18 23; Calle del Conde de Aranda 1; 🕙 9am-8pm Mon-Fri; Ⓜ Retiro) A private clinic where staff speak Spanish and English.

Hospital General Gregorio Marañón (Map pp246–7; ☎ 91 586 80 00; www.hggm.es in Spanish; Calle del Doctor Esquerdo 46; Ⓜ Sainz de Baranda) One of the city's main hospitals.

MONEY

As in 11 other EU nations (Austria, Belgium, Finland, France, Germany, Greece, Ireland, Italy, Luxembourg, the Netherlands and Portugal), the euro has been Spain's currency since 2002.

Changing Money

You can change cash or travellers cheques in currencies of the developed world without problems at virtually any bank or bureau de change (usually indicated by the word *cambio*). Central Madrid also abounds with banks – most have ATMs.

Exchange offices are open for longer hours than banks but generally offer poorer rates. Also, keep a sharp eye open for commissions at bureaus de change.

American Express (Amex; Map pp254–5; ☎ 91 369 7202; Plaza de las Cortes 2; 🕙 9am-7.30pm Mon-Fri, 9am-2pm Sat; Ⓜ Sevilla) It also has a branch (☎ 91 393 82 26) at Barajas airport.

Credit/Debit Cards

Major cards, such as Visa, MasterCard, Maestro, Cirrus and, to a lesser extent, Amex, are accepted throughout Spain. They can be used in many hotels, restaurants and shops; in doing so you'll need to show some form of photo ID (eg passport). Credit cards can also be used in ATMs displaying the appropriate sign, or (if you have no PIN) you can obtain cash advances over the counter in many banks. Check charges with your bank.

If your card is lost, stolen or swallowed by an ATM, you can call the following numbers toll-free to have an immediate stop put on its use.

Amex ☎ 900 994 426

Diners Club ☎ 902 401 112

MasterCard ☎ 900 971 231

Visa ☎ 900 974 445

Travellers Cheques

Most banks and exchange offices will cash travellers cheques. Get most of your cheques in fairly large denominations to save on per-cheque commission charges. Amex exchange offices do not charge commission to exchange travellers cheques (even other brands). It's vital to keep your initial receipt and a record of your cheque numbers and the ones you have used, separate from the cheques themselves. Take your passport when you go to cash travellers cheques. If you lose your cheques, call the following numbers.

Amex ☎ 900 994426

Diners Club ☎ 902 101 011

Thomas Cook ☎ 900 994 403

Visa ☎ 900 941 118

NEWSPAPERS & MAGAZINES

There's a wide selection of national newspapers from around Europe (including most of the UK dailies) available at newspaper stands all over central Madrid. The *International Herald Tribune (IHT)*, *Time*, the *Economist*, *Der Spiegel* and a host of other international magazines are also available. The *IHT* includes an eight-page supplement of articles from *El País* translated into English.

The free monthly English-language *In-Madrid* is a handy newspaper-format publication with articles on the local scene and classifieds. Pick it up in some bars and pubs, language schools, consulates and occasionally in tourist offices.

Spanish Press

The main Spanish dailies are divided roughly along political lines, with the old-fashioned *ABC* representing the conservative right, *El País* identified with the Partido Socialista Obrero Español (PSOE; Spanish Socialist Workers' Party) and *El Mundo* with the centre-right. For a good spread of national and international news, *El País* is the pick of the bunch. It also contains an informative central section devoted to the goings-on in Madrid itself. One of the best-selling dailies is *Marca*, devoted exclusively to sport. Free morning dailies that you're likely to find outside metro stations and busy intersections in the morning are *20 Minutos, Metro* (which has one English-language page devoted to international celebrity gossip) and the sensationalist *Que!*.

PHARMACIES

At least one pharmacy is open 24 hours per day in each district of Madrid. They mostly operate on a rota and details appear daily in *El País* and other papers. Otherwise you can call ☎ 010. Most pharmacies have a list in their window indicating the location of nearby after-hours pharmacies. Pharmacies that always remain open include the following:

Farmacia del Globo (Map pp254–5; ☎ 91 369 20 00; Calle de Atocha 46; Ⓜ Antón Martín)

Farmacia Velázquez 70 (Map p252; ☎ 91 575 60 28; Calle de Velázquez 70; Ⓜ Veláquez)

Real Farmacia de la Reina Madre (Map pp254–5; ☎ 91 548 00 14; Calle Mayor 59; Ⓜ Ópera)

POST

Correos (☎ 902 197 197; www.correos.es), the national postal service, has its **main office** (Map p257; ☎ 91 396 24 43; Plaza de la Cibeles; Ⓨ 8.30am-9.30pm Mon-Sat; Ⓜ Banco de España) in the ornate Palacio de Comunicaciones, although it's due to move in the not-too-distant future. To send big parcels, head for Puerta N on the southern side of the post office on Calle de Montalbán.

Sellos (stamps) are sold at most *estancos* (tobacconists' shops with *Tabacos* in yellow letters on a maroon background), as well as post offices.

Postal Rates

A postcard or letter weighing up to 20g costs €0.52 from Spain to other European countries, and €0.77 to the rest of the world. Sending such letters *urgente*, which means your mail may arrive two or three days quicker than normal, costs €2.35 and €2.65 respectively. The same letters would cost €2.71 and €2.96 respectively for *certificado* (registered) mail.

Receiving Mail

Delivery times are similar to those for outbound mail. All Spanish addresses have five-digit postcodes; using postcodes will help your mail arrive quicker.

Lista de correos (poste restante) mail can be addressed to you anywhere that has a post office. It will be delivered to the place's main post office unless another is specified in the address. Take your passport when you pick up mail. A typical *lista de correos* address looks like this:

Your name
Lista de Correos
28014 Madrid
Spain

Sending Mail

Delivery times are erratic but ordinary mail to other Western European countries can take up to a week; to North America up to 10 days; and to Australia or New Zealand anywhere between one and two weeks.

RADIO

The Spanish national network Radio Nacional de España (RNE) can be heard on RNE 1 (88.2 FM in Madrid) and has general interest and current affairs programmes. Spaniards also divide between those who listen to the left-leaning Cadena SER (105.4 FM or 810AM), or the conservative, right-wing COPE network (100.7 FM). Among the most listened-to music stations are 40 Principales (97.7 FM), Onda Cero (98 FM) and Kiss FM (102.7 FM).

You can pick up BBC World Service (www.bbc.co.uk) on, among others, 6195, 9410 and 15,485 kHz (short wave). Voice of America (VOA) can be found on a host of short-wave frequencies, including 6040, 9760 and 15,205 kHz.

SAFETY

There's no need to be paranoid while in Madrid but you should be on your guard as petty theft is a problem in the city centre, on some public transport and around most main sights.

Tourists are generally the prey of choice and the moment of most vulnerability is on arrival when visitors are lumbered with luggage and often disoriented. Always keep a close eye on all your belongings. This starts in the airport itself and continues on the transport into the city, although guards now patrol the trains and platforms of line 8 which connects central Madrid to the airport. Thieves operate on the metro and buses, and will be quick to whisk away that easily accessible wallet, or small backpack or briefcase left sitting in the aisle.

Tricks abound. They usually involve a team of two or more (sometimes one of them an attractive woman to distract male victims). While one attracts your attention, the other empties your pockets. If approached by strangers offering flowers, offering unsolicited help or simply getting too close to your personal space, move on fast. Be wary of jostling on crowded buses and the metro.

Where possible, only keep strictly necessary things on your person. Never put anything in your back pocket; small day bags are best worn across your chest. Money belts or pouches worn *under* your clothing are also a good idea. The less you have in your pockets or exposed bags the less you stand to lose if you're done.

You need to be especially careful in the most heavily touristed parts of town, notably the Plaza Mayor and surrounding streets, the Puerta del Sol and the Prado. Also keep an eye out in Malasaña, Huertas, Lavapiés and Plaza de Santa Ana areas when barhopping. Take particular care in the crush of bodies in El Rastro flea market.

The Casa de Campo swarms with ladies (and boys) of the night, pimps and junkies. In the city itself, a fairly sad collective of sex workers has traditionally worked Calle de Montera. The prostitutes present no real threat but their clients and pimps can be another story.

As a general rule, dark, empty streets are to be avoided. Luckily, Madrid's most lively nocturnal areas are generally busy with crowds having a good time – there's definitely safety in numbers. That said, certain bands of young delinquents are becoming more daring and ruthless and attacks in broad daylight on busy thoroughfares do occur. Frequently the attacks are made by minors who are well aware that, even if caught, they will be released within a few hours.

Never leave anything visible in your car and preferably leave nothing at all. Temptation usually leads at least to smashed windows and loss. It happens in broad daylight too, so take this seriously. Foreign and hire cars are especially vulnerable.

You can take a few precautions before you even arrive in Madrid. Take photocopies of the important pages of your passport, travel tickets and other important documents. Keep the copies separate from the originals and, ideally, leave one set of copies with someone at home. These steps will make things easier if you do suffer a loss or theft. Travel insurance against theft and loss is also highly recommended.

Don't expect the police to get too excited over your stories of theft and mishap. It's part of their daily diet. They will, however, take your statement, which you'll need for insurance purposes and to have new passports and other documents issued.

TAXES & REFUNDS

Value-added tax (VAT) is known as IVA (EE-ba; *impuesto sobre el valor añadido*). On accommodation and restaurant prices, IVA is 7% and is usually – but not always – included in quoted prices. On retail goods IVA is 16%.

Visitors are entitled to a refund of the 16% IVA on purchases costing more than €90.16, from any shop, if the goods are taken out of the EU within three months. Ask the shop for a Cashback refund form showing the price and IVA paid for each item, and identifying the vendor and purchaser; then present the form at the customs booth for IVA refunds when you depart from Spain (or elsewhere from the EU). At this point, you'll need your passport and a boarding card that shows you're leaving the EU. The officer will stamp the invoice and you hand it in at a bank at the departure point for the reimbursement. There are refund offices in terminals T1, T2 and T4 at Barajas airport.

TELEPHONE

The ubiquitous blue payphones are easy to use for international and domestic calls. They accept coins, *tarjetas telefónicas* (phonecards) issued by the national phone company Telefónica and, in some cases, credit cards. Phones in hotel rooms are more expensive than street payphones.

Codes & Dialling

To call Spain, dial the international access code (00 in most countries), followed by the code for Spain (34) and the full nine-digit number. The access code for international calls from Spain is 00. International reverse-charge (collect) calls are simple:

Australia ☎ 900 99 00 61

Canada ☎ 900 99 00 15

France ☎ 900 99 00 33

Germany ☎ 900 99 00 49

Ireland ☎ 900 99 03 53

New Zealand ☎ 900 99 00 64

UK ☎ 900 99 00 44 for BT, ☎ 900 99 09 44 for Mercury

USA ☎ 900 99 00 11 for AT&T ☎ 900 99 00 13 for Sprint and various others ☎ 900 99 00 14 for MCI

You'll get straight through to an operator in the country you're calling.

If for some reason the above information doesn't work for you, in most places you can get an English-speaking Spanish international operator on ☎ 1008 (for calls within Europe or for Morocco) or ☎ 1005 (for the rest of the world).

For international directory inquiries dial ☎ 11825. Be warned, a call to this number costs €2! Dial ☎ 1009 to speak to a domestic operator, including for a domestic reverse-charge (collect) call *(llamada por cobro revertido)*. For national directory inquiries dial ☎ 11818.

Mobile phone numbers start with 6. Numbers starting with 900 are national toll-free numbers, while those starting 901 to 905 come with varying conditions. A common one is 902, which is a national standard rate number. In a similar category are numbers starting with 803, 806 and 807.

Mobile Phones

You can buy SIM cards and prepaid time in Spain for your mobile phone (provided what you own is a GSM, dual- or tri-band cellular phone). This only works if your national phone hasn't been code blocked; check before leaving home. Only consider a full contract unless you plan to live in Spain for a good while.

All the Spanish mobile phone companies (Telefónica's MoviStar and Moviline, Vodaphone and Amena) offer *prepagado* (prepaid) accounts for GSM phones (frequency 900 mHz). The SIM card costs from €50, which includes some prepaid phone time. Phone outlets are scattered across the city. You can then top up in their shops or by buying cards in outlets such as tobacconists and newsstands.

You can rent a mobile phone by calling the Madrid-based **Cellphone Rental** (☎ 91 523 21 59; www.onspanishtime.com/web). In Madrid, delivery and pickup are done personally at a cost of US$25 (US$30 on weekends and holidays). The basic service costs US$30 a week for the phone plus postal costs (except in Madrid). You also pay a US$150 deposit. The whole operation is done on the Web.

Phonecards

Cut-rate phonecards *(tarjetas telefónicas)* can be good value for international calls. They can be bought from *estancos* (tobacco outlets) and newsstands in central Madrid. Most outlets display the call rates for each card. For calls to Australia or Western Europe, **Euro Hours** (☎ 90 181 00 91; www.lebara.es) offers more than 4000 minutes for €6. For calls within Spain, Telefónica's €6 cards are generally better.

TELEVISION

Most TVs receive six or seven channels: two from Spain's state-run Televisión Española (TVE1 and La 2), four independent (Antena 3, El Cuatro, Tele 5 and Canal Plus) and the regional Telemadrid station.

News programmes are generally decent and you can often catch an interesting documentary or film (especially on La 2). Otherwise, the main fare is a rather nauseating diet of soaps (many from Latin America), endless talk shows and almost vaudevillian variety shows (with plenty of glitz and tits). Canal Plus is a pay channel dedicated mainly to movies: you need a decoder and subscription to see the movies, but anyone can watch the other programmes.

Many private homes and better hotels have satellite TV. Foreign channels include BBC World, CNN, Eurosport, Sky News and the German SAT 1.

TIME

Like most of Western Europe, Spain (and hence Madrid) is one hour ahead of Greenwich Mean Time/Coordinated Universal Time (GMT/UTC) during winter, two hours during the daylight-saving period from the last Sunday in March to the last Sunday in October. Spaniards use the 24-hour clock for official business (timetables etc), but often in daily conversation switch to the 12-hour version.

TIPPING

In restaurants, most Spaniards leave small change or around €1 per person. If there's no service charge included in the bill, you could leave a 5% tip, but it's rarely expected. In bars, Spaniards often leave any small change as a tip, often as little as €0.10. Tipping taxi drivers is not common practice, but you should tip the porter at higher-class hotels.

TOILETS

Public toilets are almost nonexistent in Madrid and it's not the done thing to go into a bar or café solely to use the toilet; ordering a quick coffee is a small price to pay for relieving the problem.

TOURIST INFORMATION

The Ayuntamiento's **Centro de Turismo de Madrid** (Map pp254–5; www.esmadrid.com; Plaza Mayor 27; ☉ 9.30am-8.30pm; Ⓜ Sol), housed in the delightful Casa de Panadería on the north side of the Plaza Mayor, is slick and allows free access to its outstanding website and city database, free downloads of the metro map to your mobile; staff are helpful. It also runs a useful general information line (☎ 010; Spanish only) dealing with anything from transport to shows in Madrid (call ☎ 91 540 40 10

from outside Madrid). The Ayuntamiento's other website, www.munimadrid.es, is also handy. For advice on the Comunidad de Madrid region call ☎ 012.

The Ayuntamiento also runs bright orange **information points** (☉ 9.30am-8.30pm) which can be found at Plaza de Cibeles, Plaza de Callao and the new T4 terminal building at the airport.

The Comunidad de Madrid runs the helpful **Comunidad de Madrid Tourist Office** (Map pp254–5; ☎ 902 100007, 91 429 49 51; Calle del Duque de Medinaceli 2; ☉ 8am-8pm Mon-Sat, 8am-2pm Sun; Ⓜ Banco de España) covering the city and surrounding region. There are also branches at the following places:

Atocha station (☎ 91 528 46 30; ☉ 8am-8pm Mon-Sat, 8am-2pm Sun; Ⓜ Atocha Renfe)

Barajas airport (Aeropuerto de Barajas; ☎ 91 305 86 56; Terminal T1, ground fl; ☉ 9am-9pm daily)

Centro Comercial de la Puerta de Toledo (Map pp246–7; ☎ 91 364 18 76; Ronda de Toledo 1; ☉ 9am-5pm Mon-Fri, 9am-2.30pm Sat; Ⓜ Puerta de Toledo)

Chamartín train station (☎ 91 315 99 76; ☉ 8am-8pm Mon-Sat, 9am-3pm Sun; Ⓜ Chamartín)

TRAVEL AGENTS

Some travel agents worth consulting include the following.

CTS Viajes (www.ctsviajes.es) Lists independent travel agencies across Madrid.

Halcón Viajes (Map pp254–5; ☎ 807 227 222; www.halconviajes.com; Gran Vía 39; Ⓜ Callao) A reliable chain with branches all over Madrid, including one at Calle de la Princesa 27 (get off at Ventura Rodríguez metro station).

Viajes Marsans (Map pp250–1; ☎ 902 306 090; www.marsans.es; Calle de Cardenal Cisneros 5; Ⓜ Bilbao) Another good chain with outlets across the capital.

Viajes Zeppelin (Map pp254–5; ☎ 91 542 51 54; www.v-zeppelin.es; Plaza de Santo Domingo 2; Ⓜ Santo Domingo) Good deals on flights; it has four other branches around town.

VISAS

Spain is one of 15 member countries of the Schengen Convention, under which all EU member countries (except the UK and Ireland) plus Iceland and Norway have abolished checks at common borders. The other EU countries are Austria, Belgium, Denmark, Finland, France, Germany, Greece,

Italy, Luxembourg, the Netherlands, Portugal and Sweden. Legal residents of one Schengen country do not require a visa for another Schengen country. Citizens of the UK, Ireland and Switzerland are also exempt. Nationals of the 10 countries that entered the EU in May 2004 (Cyprus, Czech Republic, Estonia, Hungary, Latvia, Lithuania, Malta, Poland, Slovak Republic and Slovenia) don't need visas for tourist visits or even to take up residence in Spain, but won't have the full work rights enjoyed by other EU citizens until 2011. Nationals of many other countries, including Australia, Canada, Israel, Japan, New Zealand and the USA do not require visas for tourist visits of up to 90 days. All non-EU nationals entering Spain for any reason other than tourism (such as study or work) should contact a Spanish consulate, as they may need a specific visa.

If you're a citizen of a country not mentioned in this section, check with a Spanish consulate about whether you need a visa. The standard tourist visa issued by Spanish consulates (and usually valid for all Schengen countries unless conditions are attached) is the Schengen visa (www.eurovisa.info), valid for up to 90 days. These visas are not renewable inside Spain.

WOMEN TRAVELLERS

Women travellers should prepare themselves to ignore stares, catcalls and unnecessary comments, although harassment is about on a par with most Western European countries. Think twice about walking alone down empty city streets at night. It's highly inadvisable for a woman to hitchhike.

Organisations

The **Asociación de Asistencia a Mujeres Violadas** (Association for Assistance to Raped Women; Map pp246–7; ☎91 574 01 10; Calle de O'Donnell 42; ☉10am-2pm & 4-7pm Mon-Thu, 10am-4pm Fri; Ⓜ O'Donnell) offers advice and help to rape victims. Staff speak only limited English.

WORK

Nationals of EU countries, Iceland, Norway and Switzerland are able to work in Spain without a visa, but for stays of more than three months they should apply for a *tarjeta de residencia* (residence card). If you're of-

fered a contract, your employer will usually steer you through the labyrinth.

Virtually everyone else is supposed to obtain, from a Spanish consulate in their country of residence, a work permit and, if they plan to stay more than 90 days, a residence visa. These procedures are well nigh impossible unless you have a job contract lined up before you begin them (or unless you're married to a Spaniard). Many people do, however, work without tangling with the bureaucracy.

Doing Business in Madrid

Madrid has imposed itself as the financial as well as political capital of Spain, much to the chagrin of eternal rival Barcelona, once considered the country's economic motor. The kind of comparison people used to draw between the two cities and Rome and Milan (respectively the political and financial capitals of Italy) now seems misplaced. Much of Madrid's business activity takes place in the northern half of the city centre, on and around the Paseo de la Castellana. The biggest trade fairs are held in the complex of the Feria de Madrid, east of the city near the airport.

People looking to expand their business into Spain should contact their own country's trade department (such as the DTI in the UK). The commercial department of the Spanish embassy in your own country should also have information – at least on negotiating the country's epic red tape. The trade office of your embassy may be able to help.

The **Cámara Oficial de Comercio e Industria de Madrid** (City Chamber of Commerce; ☎91 538 35 00; www.camaramadrid.es; Calle de Ribera del Loira 56-58; Ⓜ Campo des las Naciones) offers advisory services on most aspects of doing or setting up business in Madrid, as well as video-conferencing facilities and an accessible business database. The chamber has an **office** (☎91 305 88 07) in terminal T1 (arrivals hall) at Barajas airport with fax, phone and photocopy facilities and a small meeting area.

Employment Options

Perhaps the easiest source of work for foreigners is teaching English (or another foreign language), but, even with full qualifications, non-EU citizens will find permanent positions scarce. Most of the larger, more reputable schools will hire only non-EU citizens who already have work and/or residence permits, but their attitude can become more flexible if demand for teachers is high and you have particularly good qualifications. In the case of EU citizens, employers will generally help you through the bureaucratic minefield.

Madrid is loaded with 'cowboy outfits' that pay badly and often aren't overly concerned about quality. Still, the only way you'll find out is by hunting around. Schools are listed under *Academias de Idiomas* in the *Páginas Amarillas (Yellow Pages)*.

Sources of information on possible teaching work – school or private – include foreign cultural centres (the British Council, Alliance Française etc), foreign-language bookshops and university notice boards. Many language schools have notice boards where you may find work opportunities, or where you can advertise your own services. Cultural institutes you may want to try include the following.

Alliance Française (Map p252; ☎ 91 435 15 32; www.alliancefrancaisemadrid.net; Calle de Velázquez 94; Ⓜ Núñez de Balboa)

British Council (Map pp246–7; ☎ 91 337 35 00; www.britishcouncil.es; Paseo del General Martínez Campos 31; Ⓜ Iglesia)

Goethe Institut (Map p252; ☎ 91 391 39 44; www.goethe.de/madrid; Calle de Zurbarán 21; Ⓜ Colón)

Translating and interpreting could be an option if you are fluent in Spanish and have a language that's in demand.

Another option might be au pair work, organised before you come to Spain. A useful guide is *The Au Pair and Nanny's Guide to Working Abroad,* by Susan Griffith & Sharon Legg. Susan Griffith has also written *Work Your Way Around the World* and *Teaching English Abroad,* while Lonely Planet's *The Gap Year Book* is packed with useful information.

Exhibitions & Conferences

The **Oficina de Congresos de Madrid** (Madrid Convention Bureau; Map pp254–5; ☎ 91 588 29 00; www.munimadrid.es/congresos; Patronato de Turismo office, Calle Mayor 69; Ⓜ Ópera) publishes the *Guía de Congresos e Incentivos* (also in a CD-ROM version), in Spanish and English, which can be helpful for those interested in organising meetings or conventions.

Madrid's main trade-fair centre is the **Feria de Madrid** (IFEMA; ☎ 91 722 50 00; www.ifema.es; Parque Ferial Juan Carlos I; Ⓜ Campo de las Naciones) in Campo de las Naciones, one metro stop from the airport. It hosts events throughout the year, from the Fitur tourism fair through to the Arco arts show.

Another important trade-fair centre is the **Palacio de Congresos y Exposiciones** (Map p245; ☎ 91 337 81 00; www.pcm.tourspain.es; Paseo de la Castellana 99; Ⓜ Santiago Bernabéu). The auditorium can seat 2000 people and there are smaller meeting rooms, with technical support and secretarial services.

The **Palacio Municipal de Congresos** (☎ 91 722 04 00; www.campodelasnaciones.com; Ⓜ Campo de las Naciones), also in the Campo de las Naciones area, is yet another conference centre. It has various auditoriums equipped with all the technical facilities you're likely to need (videoconferencing, simultaneous translators and so on).

You can review the month's upcoming trade fairs in the free *En Madrid* booklet available at tourist offices.

The Oficina de Congresos can also help arrange events in such elegant settings as the **Círculo de Bellas Artes** (Map pp254–5; ☎ 91 532 44 37; Calle del Marqués de Casa Riera 2; Ⓜ Banco de España or Sevilla) and the Castillo de Manzanares El Real, north of Madrid.

Language

Language

It's true – anyone can speak another language. Don't worry if you haven't studied languages before or that you studied a language at school for years and can't remember any of it. It doesn't even matter if you failed English grammar. After all, that's never affected your ability to speak English! And this is the key to picking up a language in another country. You just need to start speaking.

Learn a few key phrases before you go. Write them on pieces of paper and stick them on the fridge, by the bed or even on the computer – anywhere that you'll see them often. You'll find that locals appreciate travellers trying their language, no matter how muddled you may think you sound. So don't just stand there, say something! If you want to learn more Spanish than we've included here, pick up a copy of Lonely Planet's comprehensive but user-friendly *Spanish Phrasebook*.

SOCIAL
Meeting People

Hello.
¡Hola!
Goodbye.
¡Adiós!
Please.
Por favor.
Thank you.
(Muchas) Gracias.
Yes.
Sí.
No.
No.
Excuse me.
Perdón.
Sorry.
¡Perdón!/¡Perdóneme!
Do you speak English?
¿Hablas ingles?
Does anyone speak English?
¿Hay alguien que hable ingles?
Do you understand?
¿Me entiende?
Yes, I understand.
Sí, entiendo.
No, I don't understand.
No, no entiendo.
Pardon?; What?
¿Cómo?

Could you please ...?
¿Puedes ... por favor?

speak more slowly	hablar más despacio
repeat that	repetir
write it down	escribirlo

Going Out

What's there to do in the evenings?
¿Qué se puede hacer por las noches?

Is there a local entertainment guide?
¿Hay una guía del ocio de la zona?

What's on ...?
¿Qué hay…?

locally	en la zona
this weekend	este fin de semana
today	hoy
tonight	esta noche

Where are the ...?
¿Dónde hay ...?

places to eat	lugares para comer
nightclubs	discotecas
pubs	pubs
gay venues	lugares gay

PRACTICAL
Question Words

Who?	¿Quién? (sg)
	¿Quiénes? (pl)
What?	¿Qué?
Which?	¿Cuál? (sg)
Which?	¿Cuáles? (pl)
When?	¿Cuándo?
Where?	¿Dónde?
How?	¿Cómo?
How much?	¿Cuantos?
How many?	¿Cuánto?
How much is it?	¿Cuánto cuesta?
Why?	¿Por qué?

Numbers & Amounts

0	cero
1	una/uno
2	dos
3	tres
4	cuatro
5	cinco
6	seis
7	siete
8	ocho
9	nueve
10	diez
11	once
12	doce
13	trece
14	catorce
15	quince
16	dieciséis
17	diecisiete
18	dieciocho
19	diecinueve
20	veinte
21	veintiuno
22	veintidós
30	treinta
31	treinta y uno
32	treinta y dos
40	cuarenta
50	cincuenta
60	sesenta
70	setenta
80	ochenta
90	noventa
100	cien
1000	mil
2000	dos mil

Days

Monday	lunes
Tuesday	martes
Wednesday	miércoles
Thursday	jueves
Friday	viernes
Saturday	sábado
Sunday	domingo

Banking

I'd like to change some money.
Me gustaría cambiar dinero.
I'd like to change a travellers cheque.
Me gustaría cobrar un cheque de viajero.

Where's the nearest ...?
¿Dónde está ... más cercano?

ATM	el cajero automático
foreign exchange office	la oficina de cambio

Do you accept ...?
¿Aceptan ...?

credit cards	tarjetas de crédito
debit cards	tarjetas de débito
travellers cheques	cheques de viajero

Post

Where's the post office?
¿Dónde está correos?

I want to send a/an ...
Quisiera enviar ...

fax	un fax
parcel	un paquete
postcard	una postal

I want to buy a/an ...
Quisiera comprar ...

aerogramme	un aerograma
envelope	un sobre
stamp/stamps	un sello/sellos

Phones & Mobiles

I want to buy a phone card.
Quiero comprar una tarjeta.

I want to make a ...
Quiero hacer ...

call (to ...)	una llamada a ...
reverse-charge/ collect call	una llamada a cobro revertido

Where can I find a/an ...?
¿Dónde se puede encontrar un ...?
I'd like a/an ...
Quisiera un ...

adaptor plug	adaptador
charger for my phone	cargador para mi teléfono
mobile/cell phone for hire	móvil para alquilar
prepaid mobile/ cell phone	móvil pagado por adelantado
SIM card for your network	tarjeta SIM para su red

Internet

Where's the local Internet cafe?
¿Dónde hay un cibercafé cercano?

I'd like to ...
Quisiera ...

get Internet access	usar el Internet
check my email	revisar mi correo electrónico

Language

223

Transport

What time does the ... leave?
¿A qué hora sale el ...?

boat	barco
bus	autobús
bus (intercity)	autocar
plane	avión
train	tren

What time's the ... bus?
¿A qué hora es el ... autocar/autobús?

first	primer
last	último
next	próximo

Is this taxi free?
¿Está libre este taxi?
Please put the meter on.
Por favor, ponga el taxímetro.
How much is it to ...?
¿Cuánto cuesta ir a ...?
Please take me (to this address).
Por favor, lléveme (a esta dirección).

FOOD

breakfast	desayuno
lunch	comida
dinner	cena
snack	tentempié

Can you recommend a ...?
¿Puede recomendar un ...?

bar	bar
cafe	café
coffee bar	cafetería
restaurant	restaurante

Is service/cover charge included in the bill?
¿Il servicio está incluido en la cuenta?

For more detailed information on food and dining out, see 'Eating' on p112.

EMERGENCIES

Help!
¡Socorro!
It's an emergency!
Es una emergencia!
Could you help me please?
¿Me puede ayudar, por favor?
Where's the police station?
¿Dónde está la comisaría?

Call ...!
¡Llame a ...!

the police	la policía
a doctor	un médico
an ambulance	una ambulancia

HEALTH

Where's the nearest ...?
¿Dónde está ... más cercano?

(night) chemist	la farmacia (de guardia)
dentist	el dentista
doctor	el médico
hospital	el hospital

I need a doctor (who speaks English).
Necesito un doctor (que hable inglés).

Symptoms

I have (a/an) ...
Tengo ...

diarrhoea	diarrea
fever	fiebre
headache	dolor de cabeza
pain	dolor

I'm allergic to ...
Soy alérgico ...

antibiotics	a los antibióticos
nuts	las nueces
peanuts	los cacahuetes
penicillin	a la penicilina

GLOSSARY

abierto – open
abono – season pass
acueducto – aqueduct
aduana – customs
albergue juvenil – youth hostel; not to be confused with hostal
alcade – mayor
alcázar – Muslim-era fortress

Almoravid – member of a fanatical people of Berber origin and Islamic faith who founded an empire in North Africa that spread over much of Spain in the 11th century
apartado de correos – post-office box
auto de fe – elaborate execution ceremony staged by the Inquisition
autonomia – autonomous community or region; Spain's 50 provincias are grouped into 17 of these
autopista – motorway (with tolls)
AVE – Tren de Alta Velocidad Española; high-speed train

ayuntamiento – city or town hall; city or town council

asador – restaurant specialising in roasted meats

bailaores – flamenco dancers

baño completo – full bathroom, with a toilet, shower and/or bath, and washbasin

barrio – district, quarter (or a town or city)

biblioteca – library

billete – ticket (see also *entrada*)

bodega – literally a cellar (especially a wine cellar); also means a winery or a traditional wine bar likely to serve wine from the barrel

bomberos – fire brigade

bota – leather wine or sherry bottle

botellón – literally 'big bottle'; young adolescents partying outdoors

buzón – postbox

cajero automático – automatic teller machine (ATM)

calle – street

callejón – lane

cama – bed

cambio – change; currency exchange

cantadora(a) – flamenco singer (female)

capilla – chapel

Carnaval – carnival; a period of fancy-dress parades and merrymaking, usually ending on the Tuesday 47 days before Easter Sunday

carnet – identity card or driving licence

carretera – highway

casco – literally, helmet; often used to refer to the old part of a city

castillo – castle

castizo – literally 'pure', refers to people and things distinctly from Madrid

catedral – cathedral

centro de salud – health centre

cercanías – local trains serving big cities, suburbs and nearby towns; local train network

cerrado – closed

certificado – registered mail

cervecería – beer bar

chato – glass

churrigueresque – ornate style of Baroque architecture named after the brothers Alberto and José Churriguera

comedor – dining room

comunidad – fixed charge for maintenance of rental accommodation

Comunidad de Madrid – Madrid province

condones – condoms, also preservativos

consejo – council

consigna – a left-luggage office or lockers

coro – choirstall

correos – post office

corrida (de toros) – bullfight

Cortes – national parliament

cuesta – lane (usually on a hill)

cutre – basic or rough-and-ready

día del espectador – cut-price ticket day at cinemas

diapositiva – slide film

discoteca – nightclub

documento nacional de identidad (DNI) – national identity card

ducha – shower

duende – an indefinable word that captures the passionate essence of flamenco

embajada – embassy

entrada – entrance; ticket for a performance

estación de autobuses – bus station

estanco – tobacconist shop

farmacia – pharmacy

faro – lighthouse

feria – fair; can refer to trade fairs as well as city, town or village fairs, bullfights or festivals lasting days or weeks

ferrocarril – railway

fiesta – festival, public holiday or party

fin de semana – weekend

flamenco – flamingo; Flemish; flamenco music and dance

fútbol – football (soccer)

gasólea – diesel

gasolinera – service station

gatos – literally 'cats'; colloquial name for Madrileños

gitanos – the Roma people (formerly known as the Gypsies)

glorieta – big roundabout

guiri – foreigner

habitaciones libres – rooms available

hostal – commercial premises providing accommdation in the one- to three-star category; not to be confused with albergue juvenil

iglesia – church

infanta – princess

infante – prince

interprovincial – national (call)

IVA – impuesto sobre el valor añadido (value-added tax)

judería – Jewish quarter

largo recorrido – long-distance train

lavabo – washbasin; a polite term for toilet

lavandería – laundrette

librería – bookshop

lista de correos – poste restante

locutorio – telephone centre

luz – electricity

macarras – Madrid's rough but usually likeable lads

Madrileño – a person from Madrid

marcha – action, life, 'the scene'

marisquería – seafood eatery

media-raciones – a serving of tapas, somewhere between the size of tapas and raciones

menú del día – fixed-price meal available at lunchtime, sometimes evening too; often just called a menú

mercado – market

meseta – the high tableland of central Spain

metropolitana – local (call)

mezquita – mosque

mihrab – prayer niche in a mosque

monasterio – monastery

morería – former Islamic quarter in town

moro – 'Moor' or Muslim, usually in medieval context

moto – moped

movida – a zona de movida is an area of town here lively bars and maybe discos are clustered (in Madrid the movida refers to the halcyon days of the post-Franco years when the city plunged into an excess of nightlife)

mozarab – Christians who lived in Muslim-ruled Spain; also style of architecture

mudéjar – Muslim living under Christian rule in medieval Spain, also refers to their style of architecture

muralla – city wall

museo – museum

objetos perdidos – lost-and-found office

oficina de turismo – tourist office

Páginas Amarillas – Yellow Pages phone directory

panteón – pantheon (monument to a famous dead person)

parador – state-owned hotel in an historic building or beauty spot

pensión – guesthouse

peques – children, little ones

piscina – swimming pool

plateresco – plateresque, ornate architectural style popular in Spain during the 16th century

plaza mayor – main plaza, square

preservativos – condoms, also condones

provincial – (call) within the same province

pueblo – village

puente – bridge

puerta – door or gate

RACE – Real Automóvil Club de Españ; Royal Automobile Club of Spain

ración – meal-sized serve of tapas

rastro – flea market, car-boot (trunk) sale

ronda – ring road

salid – exit or departure

Semana Santa – Holy Week, the week leading up to Eastern Sunday

servicios – toilets

sierra – mountain range

sinagoga – synagogue

sin plomo – lead-free petrol

sol – sun

sombra – shade

tabernas – taverns

taifa – small Muslim kingdom in medieval Spain

tapas – bar snacks traditionally served on a saucer or lid

taquilla – ticket window/office

tarde – afternoon

tarjeta de crédito – credit card

tarjeta de residencia – residence card

tarjeta telefónica – phonecard

tasco – tapas bar

temporada alta/media/baja – high, mid or low season

terraza – terrace; often means outdoor tables at a cafe or bar

tetería – teahouse, usually in Middle Eastern style with low seats round low tables

tienda – shop or tent

torero – bullfighter or matador

toro – bull

torreón – tower

turismo – means both tourism and saloon car

urgencia – first-aid station

villa – town

Behind the Scenes

THIS BOOK

The 1st and 2nd editions of Madrid were written by Damien Simonis. For the 3rd edition he was joined by Sarah Andrews. The 4th edition of *Madrid* was written by Anthony Ham. This guidebook was commissioned in Lonely Planet's London office and produced by the following:

Commissioning Editors Stefanie Di Trocchio, Sally Schafer
Coordinating Editor Cahal McGroarty
Coordinating Cartographer Barbara Benson
Coordinating Layout Designer Jacqueline McLeod
Managing Editor Imogen Bannister
Managing Cartographers Mark Griffiths, Adrian Persoglia
Assisting Editors Kate Evans, Evan Jones
Cover Designer James Hardy
Project Manager Fabrice Rocher, Sarah Sloane
Language Content Coordinator Quentin Frayne

Thanks to Sally Darmody, Barbara Delissen, Jennifer Garrett, Emma Gilmour, Michala Green, Helen Koehne, Kate MacDonald, Trent Paton, Julie Sheridan, Meagan Williams, Celia Wood, Meg Worby, Wendy Wright

Cover photographs: street party to promote Madrid's 2012 Olympic bid, Denis Doyle/Getty (top); Spain, Aranjuez, Royal Palace, colonnade, Anna Lee/Getty (bottom); flamenco show at Casa Patas, Sol, Richard Nebesky/Lonely Planet Images (back).

Internal photographs
Internal photographs by Lonely Planet Images and Krzysztof Dydyński except for the following: p74(#2) Conor Caffrey; p67(#3), p67(#4), p71(#3) Juliet Coombe; p72(#3) Elliot Daniel; p67(#2) Jeff Greenberg; p2(#4), p12 p19 p33, p40, p48, p70(#3), p70(#4), p71(#1), p74(#1), p74(#3), p76, p81, p86, p89, p115, p127, p138, p148, p151, p156, p168 Guy Moberly; p2(#2), p2(#5), p24, p30, p37, p63, p67(#1), p68(#2), p69(#2), p70(#2), p71(#2), p72(#1), p73(#1), p118, p132, p141 Richard Nebesky; p199 David Tomlinson; p69(#3) Bill Wassman; p73(#3) Christopher Wood. All images are the copyright of the photographers unless otherwise indicated. Many of the images in this guide are available for licensing from Lonely Planet Images: www.lonely planetimages.com.

Acknowledgments
Many thanks to the following for the use of their content:
Madrid Metro Map © 2004 Metro de Madrid SA

THANKS
ANTHONY HAM

My greatest debt of gratitude is to the people of Madrid who have welcomed me into their city as one of their own, especially Alejandro, Dulce, Leo, Verónica, Javier, Noelia, Yolanda, Nacho, Eva, Pedro, James and all my Spanish family. My family in Australia has been tremendously supportive of my long absences and I am immensely grateful for their visits, and to Ron and Jan for understanding why I choose to live here. And to Marina – you are Madrid's greatest gift of all. Huge thanks to the outstanding editing team of Cahal McGroarty, Evan Jones, Sally Schafer, Mark Griffiths and Barbara Benson, who have helped make this a dream project from start to finish. This book is dedicated to the memory of those Madrileños and others who died on their way to work on that terrible day in March 2004.

OUR READERS

Many thanks to the travellers who used the last edition and wrote to us with helpful hints, useful advice and interesting anecdotes:

Leo Alvarado, Elisa Åström, Kathy Buenger, Eduardo Ca, Juan Manuel Perez Campo-Cossio, Patrick Cavanagh, Dan Convey, Bronwyn Cousins, Rachel Cowood, David Crowley, Elissa Davies-Colley, Dirk de Wilde, Josie Dean, Annemieke Dekker, Andrew Dier, Nicola Escario, Linda Finch, Russ Fretwell, Peter Gebert, Muriel Goldberg, Paul Henchliffe, Karsten Klint Jensen, Chris Jones, Kosta Karapas, Hannah King, Dave Klassen, Rosolind Lowson, Eliane Martinez, Kev McCready, Thomas McGuire, Carol Murphy, Paul Roberts, Emma Ródenas Picardat, Juan Carlos Sanchez, Clare Staines, Donald Toney, Keren Tuch, Sandra van Maasakkers, Barbara Watt

Index

See also separate indexes for Eating (p239), Drinking & Nightlife (p240), Entertainment (p240), Shopping (p241) and Sleeping (p241).

000 map pages
000 photographs

Index

Index

Index

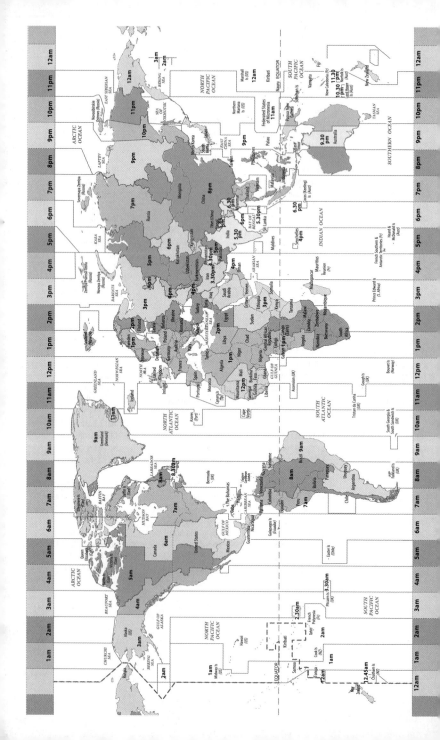

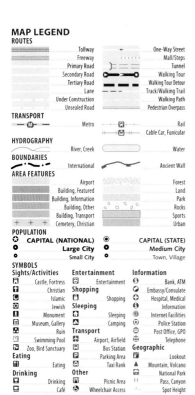

MAP LEGEND
ROUTES

	Tollway	→	One-Way Street
	Freeway	......	Mall/Steps
	Primary Road	)===(	Tunnel
	Secondary Road	●━━●━	Walking Tour
	Tertiary Road		Walking Tour Detour
	Lane	– – –	Track/Walking Trail
	Under Construction		Walking Path
	Unsealed Road		Pedestrian Overpass

TRANSPORT

——Ⓜ——	Metro	＋—▣—＋	Rail
		┼—▥—┼	Cable Car, Funicular

HYDROGRAPHY

〰	River, Creek	⬭	Water

BOUNDARIES

–·–·–	International	⌇	Ancient Wall

AREA FEATURES

	Airport		Forest
	Building, Featured		Land
	Building, Information		Park
	Building, Other	◦◦◦	Rocks
	Building, Transport		Sports
+ + +	Cemetery, Christian		Urban

POPULATION

✪	CAPITAL (NATIONAL)	◉	CAPITAL (STATE)
●	Large City	●	Medium City
●	Small City	●	Town, Village

SYMBOLS

Sights/Activities		Entertainment		Information	
🏰	Castle, Fortress	🎭	Entertainment	⊖	Bank, ATM
✝	Christian	**Shopping**		✪	Embassy/Consulate
☪	Islamic	🛍	Shopping	✚	Hospital, Medical
✡	Jewish	**Sleeping**		❸	Information
🗿	Monument	🏠	Sleeping	@	Internet Facilities
🏛	Museum, Gallery	⛺	Camping	☺	Police Station
🏚	Ruin	**Transport**		✉	Post Office, GPO
🏊	Swimming Pool	✈	Airport, Airfield	☎	Telephone
🦜	Zoo, Bird Sanctuary	🚌	Bus Station	**Geographic**	
Eating		🅿	Parking Area	◪	Lookout
🍴	Eating	🚕	Taxi Rank	▲	Mountain, Volcano
Drinking		**Other**		⌂	National Park
🍺	Drinking	⛱	Picnic Area	)(	Pass, Canyon
☕	Café	♿	Wheelchair Access	⸫	Spot Height

Maps ▮

GREATER MADRID

0 -------- 2 km
0 -------- 1 mile

See Northern Madrid Map (p245)

To Alcobendas (8km)

TETUÁN

CHAMARTÍN

Chamartín

See Central Madrid Map (pp246-7)

Dehesa de la Villa

ARAVACA

COMPLEJO AZCA

CIUDAD UNIVERSITARIA

VALLEHERMOSO

ARAPILES

CHAMBERÍ

TRAFALGAR

See Malasaña & Chueca Map (pp250-1)

See Salamanca Map (p252)

ARGÜELLES

SALAMANCA

MALASAÑA

CHUECA

RECOLETOS

Parque de la Montaña

Príncipe Pío

To Casa de Campo (800m);
Parque de Atracciones (3km);
Zoo Aquarium de Madrid (3km)

See Centro & Huertas Map (pp254-5)

See Paseo del Prado & El Retiro Map (p257)

CENTRO

RETIRO MEDIODÍA

HUERTAS

Parque del Retiro

LA LATINA

LAVARIÉS

EL RASTRO

To Museo del Ferrocarril
(800m); Negociado de
Objetos Perdidos (1.5km)

To Cine Imax
(500m); Estación
de Autobuses (7km)

To Warner Brothers
Movie World (25km)

To Parque
Capricho (5k
Barajas Airp
(8k
Parque J
Carlos I (8k

To Estadio d
Comuni
de Madrid (11

To Faun
(4.5km

To Estadio Vallecas
Teresa Rivero (4.5km)

NORTHERN MADRID

0 ——————— 500 m
0 ——————— 0.3 miles

TETUÁN

CHAMARTÍN

Duque de
Pastrana

COPLEJO AZCA

EL VISO

VALLEHERMOSO

RÍOS ROSAS

CENTRAL MADRID

ARAPILES

TRAFALGAR

CHAMBERÍ

ARGÜELLES

See Malasaña & Chueca Map (pp250-1)

MALASAÑA

CHUECA

Parque del Oeste

Plaza de la Moncloa

La Rosaleda

Parque de la Montaña

Plaza de España

Gran Vía

See Centro & Huertas Map (pp254-5)

CASA DE CAMPO

Glorieta San Vicente

Cuesta de San Vicente

Príncipe Pío

Campo del Moro

Catedral de Nuestra Señora de la Almudena

Plaza de Oriente

Plaza de la Armería

Plaza de Isabel II

Santo Domingo

Callao

Gran Vía

Plaza de España

CENTRO

Ópera

Plaza Mayor

LOS AUSTRIAS

Sol

SOL

Sevilla

HUERTAS

Glorieta de Boccherini

Parque de Atenas

LA LATINA

Plaza de Gabriel Miró

Jardines de las Vistillas

Plaza de la Cebada

La Latina

Tirso de Molina

Antón Martín

EL RASTRO

Lavapiés

Plaza Campillo del Mundo Nuevo

Puerta de Toledo

Glorieta de Puerta de Toledo

Jardín del Rastro

Ronda de Toledo

Glorieta de Embajadores

Embajadores

Estadio Vicente Calderón

Puente de San Isidro

Plaza de Ortega y Munilla

246

A C de Melendez Valdés 108

B C de Baltasar Gracián

C Plaza del Conde del Valle de Suchil

D Quevedo M

C de Arapiles

C de Jord

106

1

Calle de Guzmán El Bueno

C de Rodríguez San Pedro

ARGÜELLES

C de Vallehermoso

C de Rodríguez San Pedro

C de San Bernardo

C de Jerónima de la Quintana

Calle de Blasco de Garay

C de Alberto Aguilera

2

C de Alberto Aguilera 26

Glorieta de Ruiz Jiménez

San Bernardo M

San Bernardo

C de Monteleón

C de Carra

C de los Mártires de Alcalá

C de Santa Cruz de Marcenado

C de Baltasar Gracián

C del Acuerdo

126

C de Manuela Malasaña

31

32

C de San Bernardo

C de la Galería Robles

C de Ruiz

C de la Princesa

3

8

1

C del Conde Duque

C de Amaniel

C de Montserrat

C de San Dimas

C del Divino Pastor

C de Daoiz

Plaza del Dos de Mayo

Plaza Guardias de Corps

C del Cristo

García

C de Bernardo López

Plaza de las Comendadoras

C Quiñones

53

65

C del Norte

C de la Palma

5

45

C de San Andrés

Ventura Rodríguez M

C de Tutor

Duque de los Negras

C Manuel

Travesía del Conde

121 59

C del Limón

Duque

C de Juan de Dios

C del Acuerdo

C de San Vicente

C de Santa Lucía

19

C del Dos de Mayo

San Andrés

4

C de la Princesa

C de Ventura Rodríguez

C Santa María Micaela

60

C de San Bernardino

62

C del Duque de Osuna

23

124

C del Ponciano

Plaza de Cristino Martos

Noviciado

C del Noviciado

C de San Bernardo

C de las Minas

39

46

Plaza de Juan Pujol

Plaza de Emilio Jiménez Millas

78

55

Plaza del Conde de Toreno

Travesía de Pozas

C del Tesoro

C de la Estrella

C de la Marqués de Santa Ana

C de Jesús del Valle

MALASAÑA

84

10

125

C de San Leonardo

C de Maestro Guerrero

C de los Reyes

134

C de Manzana

Noviciado M

C de la Cruz Verde

C de Andrés Borrego

C de la Madera

C del Pez

86

C del Molino de Vi

5

5

109

85

128

3

Plaza de España P

Plaza de España M

127

87

Mitre

C del General

C del Ricardo

C de Antonio Grilo

C García Molinas

33

Parada

Beatas

C de San Bernardo

C de la Luna

C de San Roque

C de la Madera

Baja d

C de Ferraz

Cuesta de San Vicente

C del Doctor Casado

C del Río

C del Reloj

C del Fomento

C de la Flor Baja

114

Gran Vía

C de Isabel la Católica

C del Marqués de Leganés

123

C de la Flor Alta

C de Silva

Plaza de Santa María Soledad

C del Loreto y Chico

C de la Ballest

83

6

Palacio del Senado

C de Ballén

Plaza de la Marina Española

C de Torija

79

57

11

90

Santo Domingo M

C de San Bernardo

Santo Domingo

C de Silva

91

Gran Vía

C de Tudescos

70

Callao M

C del Desengañ

C Horno la Mata

C del Arnial

C Gonzalo Queso

Jardines de Sabatini

C de Torija

C de Jacometrezo

C Miguel Moya

250

Plaza de Santo Domingo M

C de la Princesa

C de Martín de los Heros

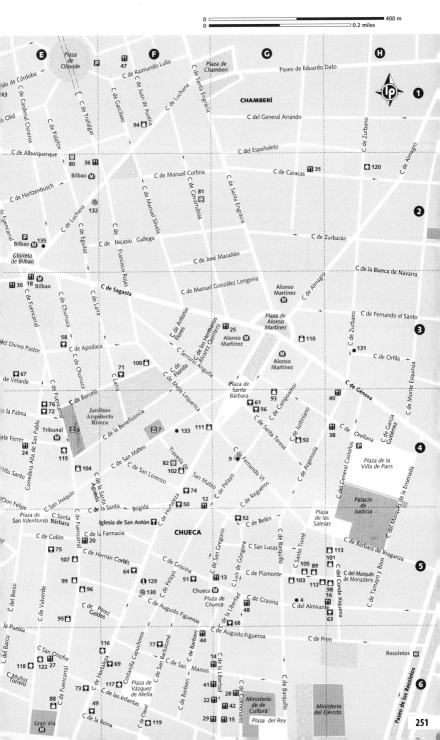

SALAMANCA

SALAMANCA

A   **B**   **C**   **D**

Jardines de Sabatini

C de Torija
C de Guillermo Rolland
C del Fomento
C de la Bola
Plaza de Santo Domingo
M Callao
213
Plaza del Callao
Tourist Information Kiosk

C de Bailén
C del Encarnación
87
204
14
Plaza de la Encarnación
217
185
C de Preciados
79
C de las Navas Tolosa
153

Jardines Cabo Noval
C de San Quintín
C de San Quintín
163
181
Cuesta de Santo Domingo
C de Veneras
C de Trujillos
Travesia de Trujillos
Plaza de San Martín
15
176

C de Pavía
33
86
Felipe V
69
190
193
C de Carlos III
C de Carlos del Peral
Costanilla los Angeles
C del la Priora Flora
Plaza de las Descalzas
191
Plaza de los Descalzas
148

Plaza de Oriente
137
Plaza de Isabel II
Donados
C de Francisco Piquer
@3w.com
Plaza de Celenque

Plaza de la Armería
Jardines de Lepanto
C de Carlos III
C de Vergara
Amnistia
41
Opera
201
C de las Hileras
39
21
C de San Martín
111
Travesia del Arenal
C del Arenal
202
Sol M

C de Requena
C de Nobejas
Plaza de Ramales
C de la Unión
105
C de Lazo
C del Espejo
C de la Escalinata
Plaza Santiago
Plaza de los Bordadores
C de San Ginés
48
C Mayor

31
P
Plaza de Lemos
149
C de Santiago
Costanilla Santiago
Plaza Herradores
46
152
196
172
Espartero
207
35
Plaza Mayor
C de Postas
C de San Cristóbal
C del Marqués de Pontejos

11
C de Biombo
22
Juan de Herrera
158
C de Nicolás Lepanto
Señores de Luzón
C Mayor
216
C Ciudad Rodrigo
C de Zaragoza
Plaza de Santa Cruz
C de la Bo

36
C Mayor
56
215
2
Plaza de la Villa
10
16
Plaza de San Miguel
San Miguel
78
Cava de
171
147
Plaza de la Provincia
47
C de Atocha
184

30
C del Sacramento
C de Duque de Nájera
Plaza del Conde de Miranda
LOS AUSTRIAS
72
C de Ccw
26
C de Toledo

24
C de la Villa
C del Rollo
C del Cordón
128
6
Plaza del Conde de Barajas
C del Maestro Villa
143
84
C de Lechuga
45

C de Segovia
Plaza de la Cruz Verde
C de San Justo
44
Jerónima
C de la Concepción

C de Segovia
Plaza del Alamillo
Costanilla de San Andrés
C del Príncipe Anglona
95
C de Segovia
Plaza de Puerta Cerrada
146
Plaza de Segovia Nueva
C Salvador
C del Conde de Romanones

124
52
C de Alfonso VI
54
115
155
82
3
C de la Colegiada

Costanilla de los Ciegos
Plaza de la Paja
50
C del Almendro
83
127
92
85
C de la Cava Baja
145
25
Tirso de Molina M
Plaza de T de Moli

LA LATINA
27
20
68
94
43
88
C de Toledo
Plaza del Duque de Alba
C del Duque de Alba

Plaza de Granado
C de Redondilla
C de Mancebos
Plaza de la Puerta de Moros
104
80
C de San Millán
Plaza de Cascorro
C de Juanelo

76
Plaza de la Cebada
77
32
La Latina M
La Latina M
C de Ruda
C de las Maldonadas
C de la Encomienda

Carrera de San Francisco
C de Oriente
C de la Cebada
75
EL RASTRO
136

186
59
C de Angel
C del Mediodia Grande
C de Sierpe
C de López Silva
C de Santa Anna
C de las dos Hermanas
C de Abades

Gran Vía de San Francisco
C de Calatrava
C de la Paloma
C de Mediodia Chica
Plaza Genral Vara del Rey
150
C de San Cayetano
C de Cabest

C de la Ventosa
C de Aguila
C de Toledo
C Argazuela
Mira el Rio Alta
C del Carnero
Mira el Rio Baja
C de Carlos Amiches

Ronda de Segovia
Cjon Mellizo
de Rodas
C de Rodas

254

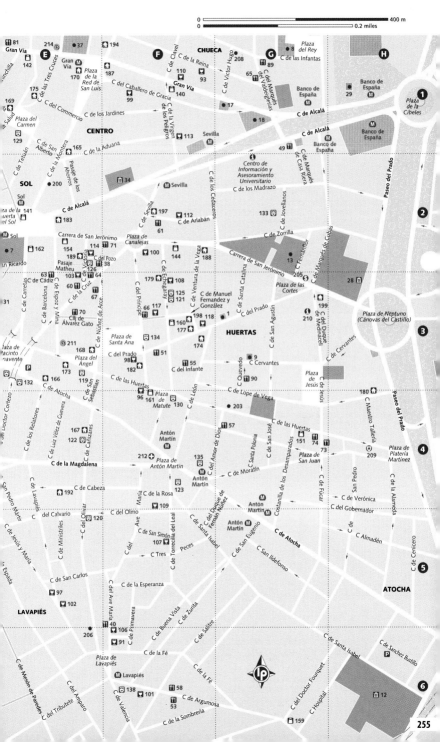

CENTRO & HUERTAS (pp254–5)

PASEO DEL PRADO & EL RETIRO

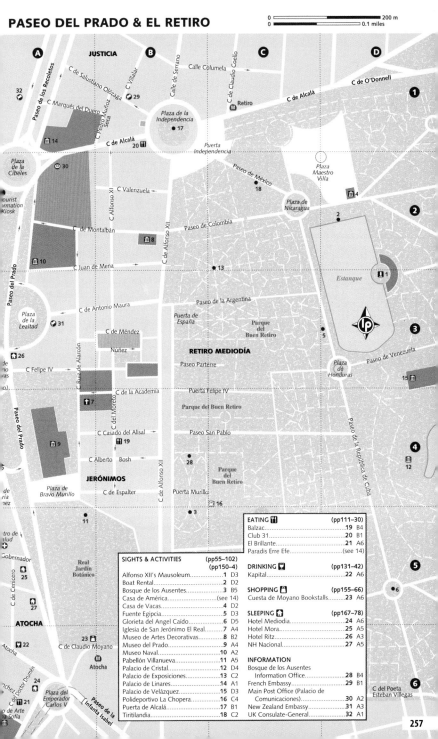

JUSTICIA		
Calle Columela		
C de O'Donnell		
C de Salustiano Olózaga	C de Alcalá	
C Villalar	Retiro	
29		
32	Plaza de la Independencia	
C Marqués del Duero	17	
Plaza de la Cibeles	20	
C de Alcalá	Puerta Independencia	
30	Paseo de México	Plaza Maestro Villa
C Valenzuela	18	4
C de Montalbán	Paseo de Colombia	Plaza de Nicaragua
8		2
10		
C Juan de Mena	13	Estanque
C de Antonio Maura	Paseo de la Argentina	1
Plaza de la Lealtad	Puerta de España	Parque del Buen Retiro
31		5
C de Méndez	**RETIRO MEDIODÍA**	Paseo de Venezuela
26	Núñez	Plaza de Honduras
C Felipe IV	Paseo Parterre	15
7	Puerta Felipe IV	
C de la Academia	Parque del Buen Retiro	
19	Paseo San Pablo	
C Casado del Alisal		
9	28	12
C Alberto Bosch	Parque del Buen Retiro	
JERÓNIMOS		
Plaza de Bravo Murillo	C de Espalter	Puerta Murillo
11	16	
3		

EATING (pp111–30)
- Balzac..................................**19** B4
- Club 31................................**20** B1
- El Brillante...........................**21** A6
- Paradis Erre Efe..................(see 14)

SIGHTS & ACTIVITIES (pp55–102)
(pp150–4)
- Alfonso XII's Mausoleum.................**1** D3
- Boat Rental...**2** D2
- Bosque de los Ausentes...................**3** B5
- Casa de América.........................(see 14)
- Casa de Vacas...................................**4** D2
- Fuente Egipcia...................................**5** D3
- Glorieta del Angel Caído..................**6** D5
- Iglesia de San Jerónimo El Real.......**7** A4
- Museo de Artes Decorativas............**8** B2
- Museo del Prado................................**9** A4
- Museo Naval.....................................**10** A2
- Pabellón Villanueva.........................**11** A5
- Palacio de Cristal.............................**12** D4
- Palacio de Exposiciones..................**13** C2
- Palacio de Linares............................**14** A1
- Palacio de Velázquez.......................**15** C3
- Polideportivo La Chopera...............**16** C4
- Puerta de Alcalá..............................**17** B1
- Tiritilandia...**18** C2

DRINKING (pp131–42)
- Kapital.................................**22** A6

SHOPPING (pp155–66)
- Cuesta de Moyano Bookstalls.......**23** A6

SLEEPING (pp167–78)
- Hotel Mediodia..................**24** A6
- Hotel Mora.........................**25** A5
- Hotel Ritz............................**26** A3
- NH Nacional.......................**27** A5

INFORMATION
- Bosque de los Ausentes
  Information Office...........................**28** B4
- French Embassy................................**29** B1
- Main Post Office (Palacio de
  Comunicaciones).............................**30** A2
- New Zealand Embassy.....................**31** A3
- UK Consulate-General......................**32** A1

257

METRO MAP

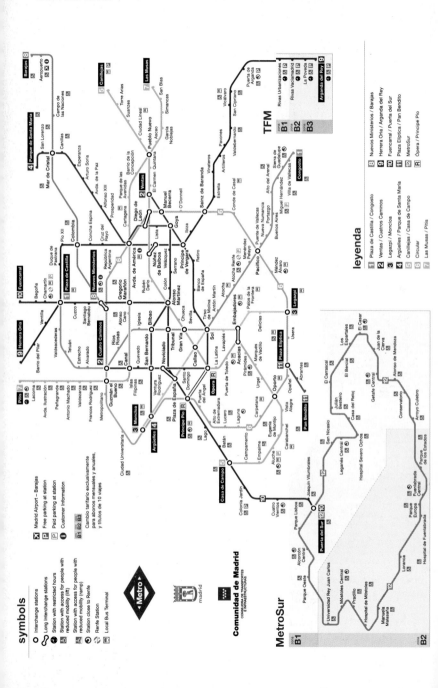